55-56
59
61
93-96

NATIONS OF THE MODERN WORLD

NIGERIA	Sir Rex Niven, C.M.G., M.C.
	Administrative Service of Nigeria, 1921–54 *Member, President and Speaker of Northern House of Assembly, 1947–59*
PAKISTAN	Ian Stephens, C.I.E.
	Formerly Editor of The Statesman, *Calcutta and Delhi, 1942–51* *Fellow, King's College, Cambridge, 1952–58*
PERU	Sir Robert Marett, K.C.M.G., O.B.E.
	H.M. Ambassador in Lima, 1963–67
POLAND	Václav L. Beneš
	Professor of Political Science, Indiana University
	Norman J. G. Pounds
	Professor of History and Geography, Indiana University
PORTUGAL	J. B. Trend
	Late Fellow, Christ's College, and Emeritus Professor of Spanish, Cambridge
SOUTH AFRICA	John Cope
	Formerly Editor-in-Chief of The Forum *and South Africa Correspondent of* The Guardian
THE SOVIET UNION	Elisabeth Koutaissoff
	Professor of Russian, Victoria University, Wellington
SPAIN	George Hills
	Formerly Correspondent and Spanish Programme Organizer, British Broadcasting Corporation
SUDAN REPUBLIC	K. D D. Henderson, C.M.G.
	Formerly of the Sudan Political Service and Governor of Darfur Province, 1949–53
TURKEY	Geoffrey Lewis
	Senior Lecturer in Islamic Studies, Oxford
YUGOSLAVIA	Stevan K. Pavlowitch
	Lecturer in Balkan History, University of Southampton

NATIONS OF THE MODERN WORLD

HUNGARY

HUNGARY

By
PAUL IGNOTUS

LONDON
ERNEST BENN LIMITED

First published *1972* by Ernest Benn Limited
Bouverie House · Fleet Street · London · EC4A 2DL

Distributed in Canada by
The General Publishing Company Limited, Toronto

© *Paul Ignotus 1972*

Printed in Great Britain

SBN 0 510–38604–0

Preface

THIS BOOK HAS BEEN WRITTEN with the initial intention of giving
an idea of what Hungary is like. *Is*, I repeat, for I meant to concentrate on her present. But no sooner had I started jotting down my
notes on the dominant features of that present as I saw them than I
had to recognize that I could only approach my subject, if I were
intellectually honest, in a completely indirect way, that is, discussing
mainly the past. There are of course other ways of looking at present-
day Hungary. To present a cross-section of actual life is possible about
the Hungary of the 1970s as it is about any country of any epoch. But
the outcome would be, at best, an objective and comprehensive text-
book – useful but not what I had in mind. Another legitimate method
of treating the subject would be to make first an assessment of what
conditions in the Soviet-controlled part of the world are like and then
to trace these international features, as well as their local variations,
on Hungarian soil. This would be a Kremlinologist's task – valuable, but, again, unlikely to result in pointing to the essentials which
made Hungary an integral and yet clearly distinguishable part of
Central and south-eastern Europe, whether under Soviet guidance
or locked in any other sphere of interest. I, for my part, have made
use of recent text-book material as well as of studies of communist
affairs, in and outside the Soviet sphere, and hope my work will not
be found lacking the indispensable references to these. But I was more
interested in what could only be explained in the Hungary of the
passing moment by dissecting her heritage from yesterday and from
the day before yesterday. How far has one to go to trace the seeds of
the present? Further, certainly, than any writer on social affairs can
go. But when writing of a European country, one should go, at any
rate, as far as the recorded beginnings of that European country. And
proceed from that moment to the most recent.

My book thus took the shape of a history of Hungary, though a
very unusual history, unusual mainly in its proportions. I started as it
were at the beginning; but then permitted myself now to skip a
century, now to dwell at some length on a detail comparatively
insignificant in itself, according to what I felt necessary to explain the
developments of the last few decades. My narrative subsequently

fanned out more and more as I approached the events which are still in living memory. And the events in living memory were to grow into the bulk of what I had to say, with the distant past merely as their introduction, and with the report on the present mainly to cap them. I should perhaps apologize for such a seemingly arrogant degree of disproportion but, in honesty, it is due to my search for truth.

Another, even more blatant, disproportion of my narrative consists in the comparatively large space I devote to men of letters as they could be seen in political action. Were then these activities, the reader may ask, decisive in shaping Hungarian life? Only on exceptional occasions, as can be seen from my text; and even then, as I point out several times, the heroes of such activities might have been practically unknown both to the masses of the common people and to their leaders or masters. Yet neither the aspirations of those masses, nor the attitudes of those leaders or masters, are understandable without setting them against the visions of those poets, fiction-writers, and literary essayists who at some exceptional moments sprang out of darkness as over-refined advocates of inarticulate mass instincts. The poet Attila József, to mention just one person to make my point clear, was certainly not among the most famous, let alone influential, Hungarians of his time; most of the politicians of his day are unlikely to have known even his name. After his death, controversy about some of his verses hit the headlines, and today, anybody inquiring into the problems of young Hungarian intellectuals will find them brooding over the meanings of his metaphors. And the average bricklayer or shop assistant turns out to be very similar to that young intellectual at the moment when he feels like adding his genuine voice to the concert of public life. Academic though such a concern with verses may sound, they offer an indispensable key to the puzzles of national life from the elegies and martial dithyrambs of the sixteenth century right to our time.

After the world upheavals of the late 1700s, there were two moments when Hungary, in the focus of international attention, appeared to be acting for the human race: in 1848–49; and in October–November 1956. Whether it was right or wrong to see a miracle in what Hungarians performed at those moments, it certainly struck observers as such; a miracle manifested, no doubt, in acts of warfare but prompted by literary circles, some of them esoteric. Surely it is not irrelevant, when searching for the sources of the 'miracle', to have a close look at the state of mind of the prompters? This, in fact, has already been done by several observers; no historian of the 1848 War for Freedom would have overlooked the Hungarian Ides of March when the young poet Petőfi headed a café-full of

scribblers in overthrowing a feudalistic Empire; and long accounts
have been printed and publicized about the turmoil in the Hungarian
Writers' Union which preceded the Revolution of October 1956.

These were volcanic events, no less than the armed battles in their
wake, and therefore well-known; but the decades of intellectual
heart-searching that led up to them were really more significant,
though less noticed. All that was heroic in the Hungary of 1848–49,
and all that matured in economic, scientific, and social advancement
in the Hungary of the last fifty years of the Habsburg Empire, was
created by that Reform Generation of poets and thinkers that entered
the scene in the mid-1820s. Few would deny this in Hungary–
although opinions may differ as to which particular step taken by one
or another eminent ancestor should in retrospect be approved or
deplored.

The interdependence of happenings of similar nature has been less
obvious and less indirect in our century. The Second Reform Generation that emerged in the early 1900s was in breadth of vision and in
creative power, artistic and scientific, equal or even superior to the
First; but the social eruptions and the acts of external and internal
violence which intersected and numbed its activities in 1918–20,
struck a blow even more fatal to what it stood for than had been the
tragedy of 1848–49 for liberal reformers and patriots. 'The Hungarian 1848' was a glorious failure, with its pathos reverberating all
over the world; 'The Revolution of Chrysanthemums' of 31 October
1918 went down in memory as a pathetic show, one that inspired
apologies rather than eulogies even amongst its–very few–dedicated
defenders. The main reason for this difference was that March 1848
came on the wave of international risings, and October 1918 as a
result of military defeat; and to turn the wreckage of a military
defeat into an ideological triumph is a skill in which the otherwise
very meritorious Revolutionaries of Chrysanthemums were conspicuously lacking. In the nausea that permeated the intellectual life
of Hungary after 1919, the heritage of the Second Reform Generation was obscured and distorted: the continuity of its driving force
was not so evident as that of the First after 1849; but its delayed-
action effects were even more powerful. The mid-1930s witnessed an
upsurge of interwoven intellectual and social currents, feverish and
chaotic, often appearing as a revival of the pre-1918 reform era and
often as its perversion or reaction, often as the echo of the totalitarian
claim to create a New Order in Europe and often as the determination to repulse it. This set the pattern that prevails even today (with
an amount of 'Marxism-Leninism' added) in the discussions on
public life–or, for that matter, private life–whether in the shape of
newspaper reportage or psychological novel or even a film script.

The turmoil in the Writers' Union from 1953 to 1957 was also part of that development, hardly understandable without having in sight the ferment of the 1930s; even its strikingly novel feature–communist men of letters initiating the fight against communist practice–can be traced back to those years when communism in Hungary was both outlawed and on the defensive. In a word, without seeing what writers were after in the Hungary of 1830, 1910, 1936, and September 1956, there is no way of seeing what either the masters or the masses of town and country people are after in the Hungary of 1971.

*   *   *

As to the words 'Magyar' and 'Hungarian'; there was originally no difference between their meanings. In Hungarian, *magyar* (pronounced approximately like 'mawdiawr') stood for what was *hungaricus* or *ungherus* like in the Late Latin *lingua franca* and in most European languages. The habit spread later to refer to the 'Magyars' in international use, particularly when their uniqueness was thus to be stressed, either with admiration or with contempt; and again later–in the twentieth century–the distinction has been adopted in political literature that the ethnic or language group is 'Magyar' whereas the political nation or the state is 'Hungarian'. According to this definition, it is right to say that, in 1914, there were slightly more than twice as many Hungarians as Magyars; whereas today, Magyars outnumber Hungarians by some 50 per cent–as will be seen from what follows.

In principle, I would accept this distinction as, indeed, ethnic Magyardom and political adherence to the Hungarian nation have never been congruent; but I felt in the course of writing that to keep to it rigidly would be misleading. The two notions have been inseparably mingled–first, until some two hundred years ago, because nobody thought that the mother-tongue should be made the main criterion of nationhood; secondly, once the language renaissance had come about, because it has been natural for any Magyar to 'feel Hungarian'. I used the two adjectives, therefore, according to what I felt their shades of meaning warranted in a given context, adding from time to time a word of explanation. Similar explanatory remarks were required for the use of the geographical term 'Hungary' which has shifted considerably through the centuries.

About the use of Hungarian first names, I have decided for eclecticism. The two strictly consistent methods, that is, either to stick to the Magyar original or always to print what corresponds to it in English usage, struck me, after trying, as equally artificial; it would be rather affected to refer to the first King of Hungary,

St Stephen, as Saint (or rather Szent) István in the Magyar way; but I could understand my English and American friends who had some knowledge of Hungarian and who found ridiculous in my draft references to the poet John Arany whom they had only heard about as János Arany, or rather Arany János . . . So I permitted myself the inconsistency of keeping to János when writing about Arany but calling his contemporary, Jókai Mór (as he was in Magyar), Maurus Jókai, as his name figured on the title-page of the English translations of his novels. And Latin, French, and German versions of Christian names will also figure in my text–since Matthias Corvinus, Louis Kossuth, Franz Joseph, and Franz Molnár were mostly known under these names in the Western world. The habit of keeping foreign Christian names as they are in the original is a fairly recent one, and correspondingly I shall 'translate' Christian names of contemporaries less frequently than those occurring in past histories. (It should be noted that in the English-speaking world Molnár used his Magyar first name, Ferenc.)

Another problem was that of titles, particularly of the lesser nobility. My readers will see the reason why, until recently, a very high percentage of the *dramatis personae* belonged to the nobility, or were supposed to belong to it. Below the rank of Baron the most usual way of signifying nobility was to use one's 'predicate', of which most noblemen had one (sometimes two or three), for instance: 'nagybányai Horthy Miklós'–literally translated 'Nicolas Horthy of Nagybánya'. This *of* is *de* in Late Latin, or French, or *von* in German; and it has been a habit to alter its position so that–if I may dwell on the same name–it should sound 'Nicolas de Horthy' or 'Nikolaus von Horthy'. When should I denote the nobility of the men figuring in my narrative? There was no way of doing it consistently. It would have been too tedious to refer to L. de Kossuth, F. de Deák, Endre (or Andrew) de Ady all the time when they themselves did not do likewise. On some occasions, however, the context warranted the use of that *de* or *von* or both. (Incidentally, the English reader may be amused by a survey of the British-naturalized Hungarians who did, and of those who did not, style themselves as *de* when they chose their English name. I know of some who *did*–there is no law to prevent them from doing so in the United Kingdom–although, as far as previous Hungarian law was concerned, they were not entitled to do so.)

* * *

I am indebted to many friends who in the course of my work helped me with information and advice, some even by reading my typescript or part of it and making their critical remarks. Of their long list, I recall these names: Miss Eleanor Breuning; Mme Anna Kéthly; The Hon. Margaret Lambert; Mrs Mary Sur; Miss Elizabeth Wiskemann; my sister Charlotte Ignotus; Mr and Mrs John Gordon; General Béla Aggteleky; Dr János Baracs; Mr Robert Conquest; Mr P. S. Falla; M. François Fejtő; Dr Peter Gosztony; Dr Bertalan Hatvany; Dr János Marton; Mr Neville Masterman; M. Imre Máté; Dr. George Schöpflin; Mr Frederick A. Spragg; Mr John Weissman–and I apologize to them for not saying more about their kind contributions as I also apologize to those whose names may at this moment escape me. But my gratitude is due in particular to my friend Mrs Rose Elton who went through my script with invaluable patience and understanding as she helped me in overcoming the difficulties of style which I ran into; and to Miss Jenny Mackilligin who displayed the ingenuity of a code-breaker, combined with the competence of a devoted typist, as she deciphered the alarmingly scribbled pages and produced her tidy copies in their stead.

London   P.I.
September 1971

Contents

List of Illustrations

Maps

Acknowledgements

ACKNOWLEDGEMENT for kind permission to reproduce illustrations is made to the following, to whom the copyright of the illustrations belongs:

Bibliothek für Zeitgeschichte, Stuttgart: 12
Camera Press Ltd: 8, 10, 11, 13, 15, 17, 19, 20, 21, 22, 23, 24, 25, 26
Imre Lukinich, *A History of Hungary:* 3
Keystone Press Agency Ltd: 18
National Museum, Budapest (Historical Section): 1, 2, 4, 7
Paul Popper Ltd: 14
Sándor Petőfi Literary Museum, Budapest: 5, 9
United Press International (UK) Ltd: 16
No. 6 is from the author's own collection

Chapter 1

The Foundation of European Hungary

Race and Language

THE HUNGARIAN NATION IN THE MID-DANUBIAN BASIN is supposed to be distinguished by its Asiatic race and language. All that has been said about its race is rubbish; language alone is the distinctive reality.

Europe consists of racially impure nations, but Hungary tops the list for racial impurities. If the various Slav national groups to her north and south, the Austro-Germans to her west, and the Romanians to her east are all mixtures, Hungary is simply a mixture of those mixtures. Of the blood and features of her Mongol-like forefathers she has retained as much as all her neighbours combined. Those neighbours, however, for all their differences, have in common that their tongues are classified as European.

The Hungarian language is classified as Ural-Altaic. Its nearest relations among living languages are those spoken by Vogul and Ostiak tribes in Siberia; more distant relations are the Estonians and Finns on the Baltic Sea; and far more distant still, though geographically nearer, the Turks. How much, then, I was often asked by Englishmen, could a Hungarian and a Vogul understand of each other's speech? About as much as an Englishman and a Russian— or possibly less.

This should be borne in mind about the psychology of an 'Asian' mother-tongue. It does not imply the feeling of having relatives at a geographical or historical distance—except, perhaps, in romantic mood—but rather that of having no relatives at all; that, or being related to everybody. Hungarian evokes the poetry of loneliness and humanism. Its syntax as we know it today is the outcome of a long and involved process of mainly European history. Its rudiments, however, were brought by savage hordes from somewhere in or near the Urals at times not precisely known or ascertainable.

Flight and Conquest

The first Hungarians who set foot on European soil were nomad warriors on the run from fellow-warriors stronger than themselves and on the look-out for towns and villages to plunder, for pastureland to graze their horses and cattle, and for princes rich enough to employ them as mercenaries. They were highly accomplished archers and horsemen; their stirrups were so carved as to enable them to stand upright in full gallop and shoot their arrows in any direction.

From the middle of the sixth until the beginning of the ninth centuries A.D., the Hungarians seem to have been roaming over the vast territory of the Khazar empire, centred round the shores of the Caspian Sea, accepting the overlordship of its Divine Kaghan, but living in a society of autonomous tribes. Their familiarity with agriculture seems to have started in those centuries, though it broadly lapsed into oblivion later when that empire disintegrated and the Hungarians, as nomads in search of booty and homeland, were both enabled and compelled to become independent.

Their appearance in the ninth century A.D. on the shores of the Don, the Volga, the Black Sea, and finally the Danube represented one wave in the influx of Turanian peoples from Asia into Europe which continued from the early fourth century down to the thirteenth or fourteenth. Its most spectacular and memorable chapters were, at the outset, the empire of the Huns and, at the end, the Mongol raids. The Turkish invasion centuries later, along a more southerly path and under very different religious and technical conditions, may or may not be counted as a post-influx; the definition of Turanians is hazy enough to have included the Turks.

'On-ogur', from which the word Hungarian, or Ungar (in German) or Hongrois (in French) derives, meant 'Ten arrows', and probably stood for a loose federation of archer tribes in which the ancient Hungarians were organized. When, in the 870s, they started invading the mid-Danubian valley, seven tribes were represented, plus the Kabars (three splinter tribes of the Khazars). They had all, by then, associated and mingled with a great variety of peoples, not only Turks and the like, but Aryan (or Indo-European) nations as well; of the latter, the Persians had made the greatest impact, notably on their taste in clothing and ornaments. They were a 'heathen' community; they observed a motley of totem beliefs inherited from different regions and epochs; their Kabar fellow-nomads tended to the Jewish or Moslem faiths, but nobody cared. Their attitude to religion seems to have been unco-ordinated, and therefore tolerant.

On the eve of the mid-Danubian invasion, the Seven Chiefs elected a prince to lead them. The strongest tribe being the Megyer (whose name, transformed into Magyar, was given later to the whole nation), the choice fell on its chief, Álmos. The Seven ceremoniously cut their veins, mixed their blood in a vessel, and drank it. Álmos was then lifted on a shield by his six peers—which stood for coronation. So the national saga has it, though there is good reason for doubt.

Under the rule of Álmos's son Árpád the conquest of the territory known in later centuries as Hungary was accomplished by–according to the officially accepted date–896 A.D.

The defeated and subsequently enslaved population seems to have been overwhelmingly Slav, particularly in the north where the Moravian kingdom had a wide hold. But nobody at the time conceived this as a 'racial' triumph ('Turanian versus Slav') in the manner of later interpreters; Árpád himself had in his army Slav auxiliaries. A large minority of the defeated seem to have been Avar–an extinct race. The territory conquered stretched from the Carpathians in the north, the Transylvanian range of mountains in the east, and the river Leitha in the west, to the end of the Plainland dominated by the rivers Danube and Tisza in the south–a borderline rather flexible, as at times it did embrace, and at others did not, Croatia-Slavonia and Dalmatia, or both.

That part of the country first occupied by the Megyer tribe and other privileged conquerors was its west, the hilly country of Transdanubia, known formerly as the Roman colony of Pannonia. Another early Hungarian settlement, whose origin has been often and passionately disputed, and which would play its own special role in later history, was in the mountainous eastern province of Transylvania–once Dacia under the Romans, and today part of Romania.

Least inhabitable was the great plain bordered by hills to the east and west; it was mostly forest and marshland, not unrewarding for hunters and fishermen, but most uncomfortable to settle in. The Kabar helpers were allowed to make it their habitat. In later centuries, as it dried out–too much so in many districts–it became known as the Hungarian steppe, the *puszta*–a byword for what is most typical in the Hungarian countryside.

Once established on that fertile moorland which was probably the basic feature of their new country, the Seven Tribes felt encouraged–and maybe also driven by want–to raid further afield. Hungarian hordes appeared in the provinces of present-day Central Europe, even now and then in western Europe, and pillaged wherever they could. They became involved as mercenaries in battles mainly between German member states of the Roman Empire; for they were not considered too barbarous to be made use of by one Christian prince against another. Thanks to the surprise value of their attacks, and to Christian disunity, they did quite well for some sixty years. But surprise wore off, and impatience with the professional raider brought Christian princes together for a while. In 955 the Hungarian expeditionaries were struck a fatal blow by the Emperor Otto I and his associates. Pannonia was invaded from the West. The time came for Hungarians to see reason. This meant settling for agriculture and

Christianity. It was right in the mid-Middle Ages, or at the end of the Dark Ages and on the threshold of the Middle Ages, as others would term it, with chivalry and fanaticism rampant and feudalism in full bloom all over the civilized world.

The first Prince of Hungary to adopt Christianity was Géza, in the last decade of the tenth century. Under his rule, Jesus and the saints coexisted happily with the totems of pagandom. Géza himself, just to be on the safe side, went on sacrificing to heathen gods; but his son Vajk, baptized István (Hungarian for Stephen), meant business. Under him, Christianity in the Roman version was declared to be the state religion, and the devout ruler pitilessly destroyed those reluctant to subscribe to the Gospel of Love. He was crowned at Christmas in 1000 A.D., and Hungary thus became (as she was to style herself in later centuries) an 'Apostolic Kingdom'.

It was the unique achievement of the Hungarian nation, then and in subsequent agitated centuries, to preserve a Ural-Altaic language. Unique, at any rate, in that part of Europe; all other really or supposedly kindred peoples who at that time or earlier had turned up in these provinces either withdrew to Asia (the bulk of the Huns and Mongols), or disintegrated (Avars, Khazars) to the extent of losing their national identity, or survived as a nation but with a Slavified language (Bulgarians), or else were absorbed (Comans, Pechenegs) by the one remaining Ural-Altaic community of the district, the Hungarians. There was of course no plan to this effect; the word 'nation' when used at all meant something substantially different from what it was to mean in the centuries of nationalism; and the very idea that a national vernacular should be taken care of and polished could not have entered the mind of anyone either there or anywhere else. The man mainly responsible for this achievement seems to have been St Stephen (he was canonized after his death), a ruler of apparently dedicated and broadminded cruelty. He crammed his country with foreigners, German, Italian, Slav, French, Byzantine, even English, ranging from royal advisers and courtiers to missionaries, mercenaries, and artisans; and had no scruples in using them to keep down his own refractory countrymen and granting them privileges when expedient. The one authentic *leitmotiv* that survived of his teachings may be epitomized as: 'Be kind to foreigners'.

In his Admonitions to his son and heir-apparent, Prince Imre, he explained that 'a unilingual country is one without strength'. It sounds a surprising statement; one would think that a ruler in his place would have preferred unilingualism (not counting, of course, the Latin of the Church and the Law as a 'foreign' vernacular), simply because it facilitates administration. Stephen may just have wished to rationalize his Christian conviction that what educated and skilled people brought to the country was to her advantage, no matter where they came from. But whatever he had in mind, his formula proved very useful, in centuries to come, for countering jingo intolerance and snobbish parochialism. He preserved his nation, in short, by being boldly un-national, as un-national as any ruler coming of ancient, indigenous, tribal stock (the Megyer-Magyar) could be.

The Seeds of a Constitution

He substituted for the tribal system a more centralized one, the key unit of which was the *megye*. This is a Magyarized Slav word, which in later centuries was quite accurately rendered in English as 'county'; but under Stephen its main function was to administer the royal estates, that is, all land the king thought worth laying his hands on. After Stephen's death, however, the counties were gradually converted from executives of the royal power into bulwarks of their own landowning gentry against it. In 1222, only seven years after Magna Carta, the lesser nobility of Hungary compelled their king to sign a Golden Bull which guaranteed on the one hand their rights against himself and his barons (i.e., great magnates), and on the other their established prerogatives (which it further enlarged) against immigrants, non-Christians, traders, and the serfs who formed the mass of the people.

The main difference between the two—Magna Carta and the Bull—is that in England it was the barons who first, and irrevocably, broke through royal absolutism, whereas in Hungary it was the common 'freemen' or 'king's servants' (as they were generally called), in defiance of the barons. How can this difference be explained? I have come across the suggestion that in Hungary the hold of the Megyer-Magyar tribe on the counties was too strong to be overruled either by the monarch or by the barons. This does not sound to me convincing; all that one knows of Stephen's outlook and methods makes it most unlikely that he should have allowed the counties, the instruments of his own power, to be run as a tribal privilege. It seems more likely that Stephen's bureaucracy, adulterated with his foreign protégé elements, had by the thirteenth century struck root and transformed itself into a class of privileged (though, on the whole, far from prosperous) landowners. With some hindsight, one might even conclude that this was how Hungary's so-called 'gentry' first emerged as her ruling class (though not yet with the *megye* as its stronghold).

Similarities or analogies between the two documents, and the use made of them, hold good nonetheless. The present writer, being concerned with the past only to the extent that it throws light on recent history and on the present, is naturally more interested in the analogies than the similarities–and/or differences–between paragraphs whose implications cannot be appreciated without examining the struggles for power that had prompted them. The unpleasant use made of the two documents in later centuries amounted to a mythologizing of the national past, with feudal privileges represented as human and civic rights. In Hungary particularly, this analogy between them served to inflate national vainglory: it was to inspire many a sentence beginning with 'We and the English' at a time when Britain stood at the forefront of world power as well as of democratic progress. 'We and the English' could do without a written constitution; we as well as they had one built into our history; pride and love of freedom were in our blood.

But there is seldom a myth without a spark of truth in it. Those county squires in Hungary, like the barons in England, did introduce a new notion into medieval public life. The Golden Bull did lay the foundation stone, however rough, for constitutional development. If, when later the dividing-line between the more developed Western and the less developed Eastern halves of Europe had become clearly apparent, Hungary–surprisingly for an East European country– excelled in legalism and often in fights for freedom and the poetry they inspired, this could well have been due indirectly to the championship of narrow landowners' privileges in 1222.

Not quite twenty years after the Bull, in 1241, the Mongol armies of Khan Batu invaded, sacked, and devastated Hungary. The king, Béla IV, though no incapable leader or coward, fled his country; and when, shortly after the Khan's withdrawal to Asia (a godsend never perfectly explained by historians), he returned, he found a shambles, a wasteland of misery. He proved efficient in restoring, improving, and repopulating; which meant a huge influx of foreign settlers, Italian, German, Russian, Slavonic, Polish as well as Coman. In 1301, the Árpád dynasty died out. By then, the descendants of the Seven Tribes had mingled with all sorts of foreigners so many times as to make them perfectly unidentifiable. But the Hungarian language survived, even if only here and there in some few districts.

Feudalism Streamlined

In the late Middle Ages, while a constant tug-of-war went on between various East, West, and Central European dynasties for possession of 'St Stephen's crown', Hungary flourished and reached the peak of her power. It is difficult to gauge whether, and to what extent, her growth in size and fortune affected her common people; but it helped them, at any rate, to survive. The character of Hungary's wealth was entirely different from what it had been before and what it has since become. Hungarians had been huntsmen, fishermen, herdsmen, gradually turning into agriculturalists; and later, again, particularly until the collapse of the Habsburg monarchy in 1918, Hungary was known as a country of stud-farms and cattle farms, as the 'granary' and 'vineyard' of any empire that included her. But in the 1300s her economic appeal was different. It consisted in the situation of her trade-routes and, especially, in her mining resources. She lay on the highroad from Central Europe to the Balkan Peninsula and thus to Asia Minor. More important still, her mines provided one-third of Europe's gold.

Under the rule of Louis I, the Great (1342–82), of the Naples house of Anjou, Hungary grew into a world power. Louis's realm at its zenith extended from the Atlantic shores to the Black Sea and the Mediterranean, from Poland to Romania and Naples. Or should one rather say that the Apostolic Kingdom of Hungary was just one province in the multitude of Louis's provinces? A matter of definition. The Anjou dynasty had, no doubt, more to do with France and Italy than with Hungary; but the permanent centre of Louis's realm was nevertheless Buda, the Hungarian capital.

Within Hungary, Anjou rule was marked by the perfection of centralized feudalism. The barons who, whenever a scramble for the throne gave them a chance, took it to assert their independence from the central power, had been the real masters of the country (and generally known as 'the little kings') when Louis's father became king. The Anjous smashed their little kingdoms; the national oligarchy was only allowed to carry on as a strictly integrated part of the royal army and administration, with special powers and symbols of power meted out to each according to his wealth and services, but all so as to accentuate his subordination to the sovereign. In one way, and for a time only, this arrangement did help some strata of the 'plebs' or rabble (the ordinary masses outside the privileged 'freemen') to acquire rights and opportunities withheld from them before, inasmuch as the ranks of the noblemen's *banderia* (trained levies), initiated under the Anjous, were open to serfs. But more important and lasting in its effect was a move in the opposite direction. It was under Louis the Great that the population of the kingdom was strictly divided into two basic categories: the privileged, comparatively few, and the non-privileged, overwhelming majority. The privileged few, again, were subdivided, with the oligarchs on top and a mass of glorified peasants and servitors below; but they were all noblemen, beneficiaries of the so-called *una et eadem libertas*, all owners of some land, which meant status as well as property. They owned it without soccage or *corvée*, or any other ignoble duties or burdens; they owned it inalienably, and therefore free of mortgage;

and the ownership was transferable to their legal heirs, however remote, and irrespective of the owner's wishes. This principle, referred to as *aviticitas* in Hungarian law, had had some rudiments in the Golden Bull, but reached its full legal expression under the Anjous, with the clear aim of wedding the noblemen's community, rich and poor, in privileges as well as duties, to the cause of the crown. Considered against a background in which the idea of extending freedom to everybody would have been unthinkable, the Anjous' reform may well be called relatively democratic; the 'little king' was compelled to recognize even the meanest of the privileged as his near-equal. But the long-term results of *aviticitas* were disastrous: partly because it blocked the development of agricultural resources, but mainly because by establishing a caste-like barrier between free and non-free, it condemned the masses of the rural proletariat to absolute serfdom.

Another historic feature of Louis's legislation was to abolish any distinction that had hitherto existed between land acquired by invasion and conquest and land subsequently bestowed by royalty. 'Foreigners' among the nobility were thereby irrevocably naturalized. Intellectually, Louis strengthened Hungary's links with a Papacy oscillating between humanist extravagance and authoritarian obscurantism. Latin scholarship of the day found patronage in Buda, though Petrarch judged Louis's literary culture inadequate.

Feudalism Loosened

From the late 1300s to the early 1500s Hungary, like most of Christian Europe, moved away from what we see today as a stream-lined version of feudalism towards an Estates system with the early rudiments of a less caste-ridden, 'capitalist' society, that of the Renaissance. Philosophy no longer contented itself with serving the cause of theology; arts, letters, inquiries into the laws of nature began making their own rules; and so did the trades and professions, gradually freeing themselves from ducal protection and control. The advancement followed an erratic course, and its heroes were–even more than the bankers, explorers, or painters of giant canvases–the *condottieri*. Hungary took her historic steps in this direction under the two Hunyadis, father and son, who, though strikingly different in character, were both enormously enterprising and imaginative warlords.

The father, János (in English, John), was a self-made man, uneducated but receptive, strong in physique and will-power, an inventive organizer and money-maker, devout and ambitious. He came of a Romanian (more specifically, Vlach) family, his father having been allowed to settle as a member of the Hungarian lesser nobility in Transylvania, where he was granted the estate of Vajda-hunyad (hence their Hungarian name). Young János started as a page and became a mercenary officer, serving for years far away from Hungary. In a comparatively short time, he became the most powerful of Hungary's captains and the richest of her barons, indeed rich enough to lend money to his king (Sigismund, who was then, incidentally, also Holy Roman Emperor). The barons regarded him with envy and hatred but were powerless against his tactical wizardry; the battles in which he halted, and partly reversed, the Turkish thrust into Europe enhanced his prestige both at home and abroad. It was to commemorate his victory over the Moslems at Belgrade in 1456 that Pope Calixtus III first ordered Christian churches to toll their bells at midday–as they have done ever since.[1]

From 1446 to 1452, János Hunyadi ruled Hungary as her regent, wielding royal powers *de facto*; his career eclipsed that of any other 'commoner' in Hungary, from the foundation of the kingdom down to the Republic of 1849. The key to Hunyadi's career may be found, apart from favouring circumstances of the time, in two main factors– one psychological and the other (if one may apply such modern jargon) ideological. The first was his exceptionally well-integrated abilities, capped by an unshakeable belief that the God of the Christians had chosen him, János Hunyadi, to excel in wealth and power and to defeat the pagan Turks. The second was his disbelief in feudal levies. Instead of noble warriors he wanted well-trained mercenaries and masses of fanatical volunteers. He was one of the first to realize the supreme value of regular military forces in war, but at the same time did not underestimate appeals to idealism; one of his chief propagandists was the Italian Franciscan friar, Giovanni de Capistrano, promoter of religious fervour among the overwhelmingly plebeian troops whom Hunyadi led against the Moslems when most of the Hungarian noblemen had deserted.

János Hunyadi's son, Matthias Corvinus as he styled himself (referring to the *corvo*, or raven, on his crest), was elected king when only eighteen, and in his absence, by the Diet at Buda on New Year's Day 1458, and acclaimed by crowds gathered on the icefloes of the Danube–a most spectacular triumph of the Hungarian *una eademque nobilitas* over foreign dynasties claiming the Hungarian throne and the Hungarian barons who supported them. But his rule (lasting until his death in 1490) evolved quite differently from what was expected of it–at any rate, by the electors. The kingmaker, and for a while the king's guardian, was his maternal uncle Michael

---

[1] More precisely, he ordered a midday prayer for victory while the fight was still on, of which the sound of bells remained as a memorial, later merging with the *Angelus.*

Szilágyi, himself an ambitious politician and soldier, who hoped to make a puppet of his nephew. Instead, Matthias had him thrown into gaol and only released him when Szilágyi not only reaffirmed his loyalty to the king but undertook to lead a campaign against the Turks to liberate Serbia, which in turn was promised to him as his own principality. The Sultan, however, captured and beheaded Szilágyi–to Matthias's relief perhaps even more than to his own satisfaction.

Matthias, unlike his father, was a highly educated man, an enlightened amateur of scholarship and the fine arts. His European outlook made him less interested in saving Europe from the Turks than in extending his control to regions westward of his own country. His great ambition, for which he made various preliminary manoeuvres, was to become Holy Roman Emperor. He did not get so far as to attempt it. Would it have been a good or bad thing if he had tried and succeeded? A shrug is the only possible answer today. But the good and bad things that sprang from his manoeuvres are clearly discernible. His fiscal policy was ruthless and exacting: the sweat of millions for the artistic luxury of the few, and especially for military expeditions and keeping armed forces in readiness for them. This was the debit side of his rule. But the credit side heavily outweighed it. To get those 'golden eggs' he had to favour the goose that laid them: in other words, fiscal interests compelled him to act in a socially liberal way, to further trade, to do away with feudal restrictions, to protect the peasants, to extend plebeian liberties. Under Matthias's rule, the noblemen's exemption from taxation was eroded and serfdom almost eliminated. His rationalization of the legal system and his frequent championship of the oppressed earned him the epithet 'the Just'.

What it meant for him to be 'Hungarian' is hardly explicable in the terms of later, nationalist centuries. His Court was riddled with foreigners, and so even more were his armed forces. His famous Black Army–estimated at 30,000 men–consisted of Czech and German mercenaries (whom he used as much for controlling his own countrymen as for expeditions abroad), for he was very much his father's son in preferring professional to feudally raised soldiers. The Italian historians and Hungarian men of letters under his patronage wrote in Latin; and the *Corvina* books produced for his library were among the finest specimens of Renaissance craftsmanship. Under the most national of Hungarian kings, Hungary became utterly cosmopolitan. Meanwhile, he prided himself on being Attila's heir.

After Matthias's death the usual tug-of-war for St Stephen's crown was renewed, with its usual features: the central power getting weaker, the barons stronger, and the potential conquerors keener. In the circumstances, the greatest losers inside the country seemed to be the peasants, now pushed back into serfdom by the nobility who, on this one issue, were united; and the external power to which the most glamorous prospects of expansion offered themselves was the Ottoman Empire.

Two Tragedies: 1514 and 1526

Two series of events thereafter swept Hungary away from the midstream of European development; and each can be dated from one year, 1514 and 1526 respectively. In 1514, a Crusade army was recruited among the serfs; subsequently, as the landowners resented their serfs' prolonged absence from the fields, it was ordered to demobilize. The soldiers resisted this order, first by robbing the estates and then in open revolt under the leadership of a petty nobleman, György (George) Dózsa. The rising was defeated, and bloody retribution followed: 70,000 peasants were killed; Dózsa was burnt alive on a white-hot throne as 'the king of the peasants', and his followers were compelled to pick the flesh from his bones and eat it. The panic and then triumph of the Hungarian nobility resulted in cruel and retrograde legislation, in which the leading spirit was the famous Hungarian lawyer István Werbőczi; he promoted the identification of the Hungarian nation with the community of noblemen, with the one and indivisible nobility, *una eademque nobilitas*, which comprised every free man, rich or poor, and made him a master in the country of the Hungarians, whatever his mother-tongue might be. The great majority of the population, on the other hand, Magyar and non-Magyar alike, was dissociated from the nation; it was not even accepted as *populus*, it was merely *plebs*, the 'wretched tax-paying mass'. The two Latin words 'populus' and 'plebs' were used to denote different, almost contrasting things. 'Populus hungaricus' (occasionally 'populus werbőczianus') was the community of noblemen, 'freemen', many of them poor and peasant-like but still privileged; whereas 'plebs', the ignoble taxpayers, 'misera plebs contribuens', was used to describe the community of serfs. The serfs were tied to the soil and, although this bond was officially abolished forty years later, it remained actually valid for centuries, because justice and administration were controlled by the nobility.

The second sequence of events which decisively shaped Hungary was the invasion of Europe by the Turks. On 29 August 1526 at the battle of Mohács—a market town on the Danube commanding the southern approaches to both Transdanubia and the Hungarian Plain —the Sultan's army struck the Hungarian forces a shattering blow. The king himself was killed in flight (allegedly by one of his outraged subjects); whereupon the country fell a prey to both inter-dynastic competition and military invasion. Turkish conquests in the Danubian region were just reaching their climax when Hungary had re-petrified the division of her society between noblemen and serfs.

Between Ottomans and Habsburgs

The Turkish conquest was responsible for the distinction which has existed ever since between Central Europe and the Balkans. Wherever the Turks set foot, European civilization disappeared; they expelled or exterminated landowners, except for those they used as their own agents, and they pillaged and destroyed cities. The Balkan peoples have to thank them for one inheritance from this devastating rule: their freedom from aristocratic landlords. But they paid for it with the destruction of their national wealth, with long years of foreign tyranny that barred the way to industrialization and progress, and, far from making them really free, degraded their countries to the level of pawns of foreign powers and buccaneering chieftains. That is why the Balkans are so backward, even today, compared with the flourishing areas to their west.

As for Hungary, the crucial factor in her development was that, lying just where the wave of Turkish invasion broke, she was half-occupied and torn into three or more fragments. (It must be remembered that when we speak of the Hungary of those days, we have to include the whole of 'historical Hungary', roughly identifiable with St Stephen's kingdom and about three times the size of Hungary today. Besides Transdanubia and the Great Hungarian Plain, which is practically all that now remains of that historical Hungary, there were the Carpathians to the north, Transylvania to the east, and districts of what today is western Yugoslavia.) The Plain and about half of Transdanubia, being most exposed to the Turks, were overrun and ruled by them for a hundred and fifty years; the rest of Transdanubia, being geographically linked with Austria, accepted the protection of the Habsburgs 'against the heathen', and became their kingdom and thus dependent on the Holy Roman Empire; Transylvania, defended by her huge mountains, but jutting deep into the Turkish provinces, succeeded in maintaining a relative independence under the rule of Hungarian princes who relied now on the Sultan and now on the Emperor; while the northern country of the Carpathians, owing to its geographical position, lived in a state of civil war, alternately ruled by the Emperor and revolting against him.

Turkish rule was savagely pragmatic. The Turks wished to squeeze as much money or valuables as possible out of the territories they conquered and cared about nothing else. Racialism was unknown to them, and converted sons of the subject Christian peoples often outnumbered the Turks themselves among their high officials.

They were not even keen proselytizers: anyone outside the Moslem faith was a 'dog', but there was no harm in employing obedient dogs. Hungarians were sent by the tens of thousands to the slave-markets in Asia Minor, others were bled white by extortions; many, unable to bear the burden, left all their belongings behind and fled to the Transdanubian 'kingdom' under the Emperor or to semi-independent Transylvania. Such impartial cruelty implied a sort of tolerance. The 'dogs' enjoyed religious freedom; the differences between Greek Orthodox and Roman Catholic and various Protestant and Jewish rituals were of no greater consequence than different ways of barking and tail-wagging. Nor did political attitudes count with the Turks for more than a moment. They were easy-going in making and breaking agreements, in awarding high offices to their enemies of the day before and imprisoning or beheading them the day after, as the Turkish interest or whim demanded. The Hungarian distinction between noblemen and serfs was ignored by them, but this did not mean any opposition in principle to the Estates system; whenever Hungarian noblemen who had taken refuge under the King-Emperor managed – as, strangely enough, they often did – to collect dues from their unfortunate serfs left under Turkish occupation, the Turkish administrators made no objection, and the codifier of the One and Indivisible Nobility of Hungary, Werbőczi, rose with Turkish patronage to the dignity of Chief Justice in the conquered fortress city of Buda. As a matter of fact, the Hungarian 'National' party, as distinct from that of the dynastic Loyalists, preferred the Turks to the Austrians, at any rate as a centre of power to manoeuvre round; and at times even the presence of barbarous Asiatic troops seemed more tolerable to many Hungarians than that of the Western mercenaries, whose no less brutal greed and lawlessness heralded the bloodthirsty religious zealots and restorers of Imperial order. One need not be a nationalist to recognize both Hungary's foreign overlordships as inhuman.

Thus industry and urban life, as well as feudal landowning, vanished from the Plain, while the nobility succeeded in stabilizing their own position in the west, north, and east. In the west, the Catholic magnates were protected as the representatives of dynastic interests; in Transylvania, the large national communities of warrior freemen preserved into later ages their claim to privileges over the mass of the population; and both types of noblemen flourished in the northern part of the country where, from time to time, whole villages were 'knighted' as a reward for their activities in civil wars, and where huge estates were allocated by the Emperor to magnates who supported him. When, therefore, the Turks withdrew from the Central Danubian basin, and when both the Plain and the moun-

tainous districts in the east and north came under Habsburg rule
(about 1690–1700), there existed in historical Hungary a vastly
inflated nobility, estimated at some five per cent of the total population; while the cities had been either destroyed or paralysed in their
development. The Turkish occupation of Hungary went deep
enough to destroy industry, but not to liquidate 'feudalism'–or,
more precisely, the Estates system. (Analogous events led to similar
results in Poland, equally notorious for her large masses of proletarian gentry. The opposite happened in Bohemia-Moravia:
there, while the nobility were exterminated or absorbed by the
Austro-Germans, the bourgeois middle classes survived, expanded,
and prospered.)

Hungary was depopulated by the end of this period, particularly
in the Plainland from which so many had fled or been deported by
Moslem slave-traders (Protestants in smaller numbers being also sent
to the galleys by foreign Catholic rulers), while throughout the
country warfare, civil strife, and starvation followed by the Black
Death and other epidemics, had taken their toll. Under King
Matthias, two hundred years before, the population of Hungary had
been estimated at four million and a half: there were no more than
two million and a half when the Turks left. The Plainland, bereft of
its forests and much of its husbandry, had degenerated into great
poisonous swamps or dried into shifting sand–the *puszta* which, as
an adjective, means 'bare, deserted'. The change in the ethnic, or
linguistic, pattern of the population was no less remarkable, though
the migrations that brought it about cannot be reconstructed with
even approximate accuracy. Before the Turkish invasion, the majority
of the people (85 per cent, according to some sources) had been
Hungarian, Magyar, by mother-tongue; as other nationalities moved
in, the proportion of Magyars sank to 45 per cent or less. Who moved
where, and why, remains a source of controversy between East
European historians, and of conflicting national claims which are all
equally unprovable. But this much can be asserted without national
self-pity: while the Sultan and the Emperor wrestled for possession
of Hungary, Hungarians died.

While Hungary, mutilated, writhed under the heel of Moslem and
Christian conquerors, Hungarian patriotism imbued with love of
liberty was born, or reborn; a long series of struggles *pro patria et
libertate* began. This noble passion issued from class-consciousness–
or Estate-consciousness, to put it less anachronistically–and from the
reactions of the courageous outcast who chose banditry rather than
respectable servitude.

Patrician pride and trigger-happiness were the initial motives of
the poet, essayist, statesman, and general Count Miklós Zrínyi

(1620–64), who did more than any of his contemporaries to unite Hungarians and broaden patriotism into something greater than its components. His background was cosmopolitan: he came from a Croat family, was brought up in Austro-Germany, completed his education in Italy, and expressed his thoughts naturally in Latin. He was known to speak six languages fluently, but his preference was for Hungarian, in poetry as well as war. When he emerged, the kingdom of Hungary was but a strip of what it once had been. Zrínyi took it into his head that Hungarians of all lands must unite and liberate themselves from Turkish rule, and thereby liberate Europe and Christendom as well. He appealed to the King-Emperor for support, but followed his own–not wholly impracticable–intuitions. An obsessed, competent, and reckless warrior, he became notorious for harrying the Turks and often embarrassing the Austrians at a time when co-existential quietness in the Hungarian bufferland would have suited them better. He was proud of 'writing his name with his sword in the book of history', but used the pen as a noble accessory; he pamphleteered in Hungarian against the Turks and wrote an epic in Tasso's vein but in traditional Magyar verse (it was about his great-grandfather and namesake, who had valiantly fought the Turks). In his fury against the barbarous invader, he conceived a vision of Hungarian unity which turned him into a humanist as well as a warmonger. Although a haughty nobleman, he urged conciliation towards rebellious serfs; although a Roman Catholic, he went so far in making common cause with Protestants as to be mistaken for a Protestant himself; although a royalist, he plotted with France against the Court when he saw Hungary's cause betrayed by Vienna. He died a martyr of anti-Habsburg as well as anti-Ottoman resistance–at any rate in the public mind. He was killed, when forty-four, by a wild boar which patriotic legend insists was set upon him by Habsburg lackeys.

Among the serfs, some occupational groups found it easier than others to rise to the status of freemen. The cattle-drivers, or *hajtók*, for instance, needed only toughness and temerity to form themselves into independent gangs, appropriate the cattle entrusted to them, and then act as highwaymen and/or freedom-fighters and/or mercenaries who, led by their own elected captains, offered their services to the highest bidder among rival princes. Unlike other peasant gangs whose activities turned into a struggle against the nobility–Dózsa's in 1514 remains the most memorable–these 'drivers' or *hajtók* or (as they were known later) *hajduk* concerned themselves only with money and their own ultimate freedom. This latter they actually obtained: one of the warlords of the early 1600s, István Bocskai, Prince of Transylvania and for a while of Hungary, ennobled them – that is, he allowed them to settle as peasant farmers free of feudal obligations. Their case was to some extent exceptional in Hungary. Most of the ennobled peasants, the 'mocassined squire-archy' (i.e., unable even to afford boots), insisted on the pride and privileges of their Estate; whereas the *hajdu* valued only what it brought him in acres and cash. East of the river Tisza, around the large market town of Debrecen, the 'Calvinist Rome' as Hungarians called it, the peasants of the *hajdu* villages developed a style of life somewhat akin to that of the Calvinist farmers in Switzerland and Holland: thrifty, sober and narrow, defiant of overlordship, averse to flamboyance of any kind, suspicious of the unusual. For Hungary it was, on balance, a blessing.

The firmest bastion in the struggle *pro patria et libertate* appeared, throughout the seventeenth century, to be the principality of Transylvania. She remained a token of Hungarian independence and a guardian of the Hungarian culture inherited from the years before the Turkish and Austro-German invasions. Her independence was limited, and her liberalism ambiguous. Independence meant elbow-room for manoeuvring between the two liege lords, Sultan and Emperor, and enlisting at times the support of other powerful rulers such as the King of France or the King of Sweden, the Pope or the Russian Tsar, all of whom used the bloodshed on Hungarian soil for their own ends. Yet the wisest and most patriotic thing a Prince of Transylvania could do was to avail himself of such opportunities; and the one who did it with most diplomatic skill and success was Gábor (Gabriel) Bethlen (ruled 1613–29), an energetic, albeit cautious, Calvinist who leaned far more towards Constantinople than towards Vienna.

Transylvania did have a constitution, and sometimes was even able to abide by it. Her Estates were almost free to elect their prince. And she displayed an equity almost unparalleled in those times by enacting equal rights (though 'some more equal than others') for various 'nations' and religions. The source of that generosity towards 'nations' was a will to oppress the peasantry. In 1437, a rising of the serfs flared up in Transylvania, which by then (thanks probably to geographical conditions) had already become an autonomous province of the Hungarian kingdom. The rising was quelled, and to seal its defeat the three communities of freemen of the province formed what they called an *unio trium nationum Transylvaniae*. The 'three nations', pledged to guarantee each other's privileges and exclude from them the bulk of the population, were: the Hungarian nobility; the Székelys, a purely Magyar community which for some obscure reason had since time immemorial considered itself, and been considered by others, a self-contained clan; and the Saxons, or burghers of the guilds. This union survived in independent Transylvania and, far from degenerating, developed into an almost genuinely liberal arrangement when, from the 1570s onward, total freedom was secured for the four recognized religions: Catholic, Lutheran, Calvinist, and Unitarian. Along with the spirit of tolerance, humanist traditions of learning flourished in Transylvania as much as was possible in a parochial rump of a country, exposed to the ravages of warfare. Just one example: in 1650 the Prince of Transylvania, György Rákóczi II, invited the famous Moravian humanist and educational reformer Comenius (Jan A. Komensky) to take over a college and put his theories into practice. The idea foundered on petty intrigues and jealousies, as brave and noble ideas so often do; but the fact that, with religious intolerance rampant under the Habsburgs and barbarism under the Turks, such a plan could be tried at all shows that the humanism of independent Transylvania was not altogether a façade.

Yet there was more than one snag to it. Broadened though the classes of the privileged were in that province, they were still a minority; and to make the cleavage between privileged and underprivileged still more objectionable, the largest national entity in Transylvania, that of the Romanians, was not recognized as a 'nation' at all. The Romanians were just *plebs*. Nor was the faith of most Romanians, the Greek Orthodox, 'recognized' as a religion; at best it was 'tolerated'. This was not meant as a slight upon the Romanian-speaking population. A member of the Hungarian nobility was 'Hungarian' whatever his mother-tongue, while the majority of Magyars were *plebs* as much as the majority of non-Magyars; but still the effect of the whole arrangement was to embitter the Romanians *as* Romanians. Down to the late eighteenth century, however, conflicts between 'nations' as identified by language were but sporadic, and Hungarian, Romanian, Ruthenian, and other Slav serfs fought side by side on the few occasions when they dared to take up arms against their masters–who, for their part, also forgot about national feuds when it was a question of bringing the serfs to heel.

I referred to the Romanians as the majority nation of Transylvania, which for the last two centuries they have undoubtedly been; whatever the discrepancies between census results as organized and rigged by different authorities, Romanians held a clear overall majority in that province. Whether this had always been so is one of the questions disputed *ad nauseam* between partisan historians of the nations concerned, especially the Romanians and Hungarians, but including also the Germans (on account of the Saxons) and the Ruthenians and Yugoslavs in border territories. According to the

Romanian ultra-nationalist, the Romanians of Transylvania were Roman settlers from the days of Trajan: according to his Hungarian counterpart, they just 'infiltrated', particularly from Moldavia and Wallachia, begging to be 'tolerated' as they subsequently were–and anyway, had never been real Romans but a mixed rabble of Slavs, Gypsies, and Levantines who adopted the idiom of the erstwhile Legionaries. Whatever the facts, it should be conceded to the Romanians that large numbers of them were living in Transylvania at the time of the Three Nations Union which ignored *their* national existence. Nevertheless, to the benefit of her whole population–not excluding the Romanians–Transylvania did manifest a degree of liberalism very rare in the century of religious wars when she introduced the settling of disputes by discussion between bodies of citizens of different creeds, tongues, and social standing.

The Kuruc Rising and its Heritage

The ambiguity of the Hungarian love of freedom–genuine, but caste-ridden–was tragi-comically exposed in the *Kuruc* rising against the Habsburgs in the early 1700s, when the Turks had already been driven out of all parts of Hungary. The name Kuruc, pronounced 'cooroots', originally referred to the crucifix worn by Dózsa's Crusade army, and implied a sneer at the guerrillas and marauders who roamed their disorganized country in the vacuum left by the Turks. The Kuruc who subverted the royal and Imperial order was put down by armies of similar characters, hired as a rule by the dynastic power and nicknamed *Labanc* (pronounced something like 'law-bawnts'); and the Labanc-Kuruc battles might have seemed to some observers like a parody of those fought by Cavaliers and Roundheads in the England of half a century before. But having risked this analogy, I invite the reader to forget it.

It was a combination of social unrest and court intrigues that fanned the random skirmishing of the Kuruc into a general conflagration. Ferenc (Francis) Rákóczi, the heir of lordly Hungarian *frondeurs* and Transylvanian princes, himself brought up under Imperial supervision not unlike any high-born Austrian, was called on by rebellious serfs to accept the leadership of their insurrection. Rákóczi was an emotional and sensitive personality, already involved in quarrels with the dynasty; he was often motivated by hurt personal and family pride, but just as genuinely by sympathy for the destitute –whether they were penniless nobles or *plebs*. On the advice of his friend, the intelligent and hotheaded landowner Miklós Bercsényi, he accepted the invitation, and with an army of Ruthenian, Slovak, and Romanian as well as Hungarian peasants (and noblemen also) he set out to liberate Hungary from Habsburg absolutism. He conquered the northern part of the country where most of his estates lay, and Transylvania, which he ruled as Ferenc Rákóczi II. From early 1703 to early 1704, with the combined support of the freedom-loving people of Hungary and the power-loving Sun King of France, he advanced at a speed which seemed to bring victory within sight. But from the moment that Louis XIV agreed to make it up with the Emperor, Kuruc enthusiasm flagged. Rákóczi was defeated, and from 1711 until his death in 1735 he lived in exile.

A movement so powerful and nationwide as the Kuruc insurrection can never blow over without leaving some trace in men's souls; the longing for freedom, as Rákóczi and his followers understood it, survived. What sort of freedom did they mean? Did it imply a less caste-ridden, less authoritarian order than that offered by the Habsburgs? In one respect it undoubtedly did: in the treatment of men's religion. Rákóczi, though a devout Catholic–and in moments of despair perhaps not free from bigotry and superstition–wholeheartedly championed his Protestant countrymen against the Habsburg policy of Catholicizing by force. As an exile, he tried to get nations of all creeds, from Spain to Russia and Turkey, to unite against Habsburg tyranny; at the same time, even while a guest of the Sultan, he risked his displeasure by submitting a plea for protection of the religious freedom of Roman Catholics under Ottoman rule. The Sultan did not take his advice amiss: he gracefully ignored it. Rákóczi, when his political plans went awry, took refuge in Jansenist meditation. Though far from ascetic–especially about sex–he took his own faith seriously, and with equal sincerity respected the faith of others. At a less devout level, this could be said of the whole Kuruc camp: in matters of faith they were truly liberal.

Hungary Crippled by her Privileges

But in matters of social status, wealth, and power they were, to say the least, inconsistent. Rákóczi himself, with his leanings towards universal charity, had some ideas that seem to break through the conventional barriers of his time; yet even he took for granted that, while the Habsburg ruler who assumed absolute power was usurping the people's rights, the Bourbon ruler was entirely justified in doing so; for power over France had been delegated by God to the king, whereas in Hungary, and particularly in Transylvania, divine wisdom had put the people themselves in charge–'the people', that is, as embodied in the Estates. Few, if any, of his followers were more broadminded than he; and it would be hard indeed to distinguish when they were fighting primarily against tyranny itself, and when against an authority that insisted on their responsibilities towards, among other things, their serfs. Some churchmen and magnates in

the Austrian and Labanc camps showed, indeed, more understanding for the economic needs of the underprivileged than did most of
the freedom-fighters. A striking example was Cardinal Leopold
Kollonich, chief adviser to the Emperor on Hungarian affairs on the
eve of the rising. Few people were more unpopular with the Hungarians than he, particularly among the Calvinist gentry who attributed
to him the saying: 'I shall make of the Hungarian first a slave, then a
beggar, and finally a Roman Catholic.' He had no use for political,
let alone for religious, dissenters, and certainly felt little sympathy
for the Hungarians, whom he saw as rebels incarnate. But the great
wave of hatred against him was inspired by his plans to make the
administration more rational and improve the lot of the *plebs*,
ignoring some of the noblemen's privileges. The tyrant in him could
have been condoned, but not the social reformer.

One explanation put forward for the conflicting tendencies in the
Hungarian independence camp is that the aspirations of two classes,
two ideologies, mingled in it: those of the nobility and those of the
common people. This is at best only a half-truth. Class and factional
differences did exist within the Kuruc camp; and, to give the distinction between lordly opportunists and heroic plebeian guerrillas
some poignancy, it is a fact that the Kuruc general who ultimately
came to terms with the dynasty and the Labanc, Sándor Károlyi by
name, had previously excelled in putting down peasants' revolts. He
was rewarded for his compliance with large estates confiscated from
the refugee Rákóczi's properties, and was created a count, with
appropriate ribald comment from the Kuruc who had wanted to
fight on. His was an unsavoury career, even though when he
capitulated there was clearly little choice left. But to assume that the
plebeian Kuruc fighters were any less caste-conditioned would be a
false analogy with later revolts. For all of them freedom meant
privileges; and they were only too willing, as soon as they had taken
up arms, to consider themselves a special caste whose freedom was to
be secured at the expense of the population as a whole and not
shared with it.

From their years of battle and dereliction, spent sleeping in mud
and snow, starving, hunted, and still fighting on, there remained a
beautiful poetic legacy: slow, virile melodies and fiery marches. They
utter heartrending cries about the devastation of the country, the
misery of the people, the tears of the widows and orphans, the
wickedness of the oppressor—socialist poetry in its most enchanting
infancy. And in the same breath they sang: 'Kuruc comrades, if you
see a peasant, pull his beard, drive away his cattle, box his ears',
because this was their noble privilege. The wretched Labanc, they
sang, mercenary of the Germans, has nothing on him worth a silver

florin; he has 'no cattle but the lice that feed on his chest', while 'the
Kuruc is smart', he has silk and silver and pearls on his clothes and a
shako of marten's fur with a glittering plume. A leading Dutch
merchant, who negotiated about help for the Hungarian fight for
liberty with a Kuruc leader, suggested that, in view of their financial
difficulties, the Kuruc warriors should dispense with their silver
buttons. 'I'm sorry, sir', the fighter for freedom replied, 'we can't do
that, we are not a nation of tramps'. Life without silver buttons was
not worth living. They meant it and they perished for it. From 1711
until 1848, the Habsburgs ruled without a break over Hungary and
Transylvania.

The defeat of the Hungarians was bad, but that defeat was not
total made it worse. Just enough freedom had been left for the
Hungarian nobles to block any move towards social and economic
improvement which the Habsburg administrators might have been
willing to encourage. Not all promises made to the Hungarian
Estates were scrupulously kept. They had been promised religious
freedom (notably for the Protestants) – a promise which the Habsburgs alternately observed and disregarded, according to the ruler's
inclinations and the trends prevailing among his advisers. Roman
Catholics were in the great majority among Hungarians, but for
historical reasons a Calvinism less puritanical than its Western
counterpart had come to be regarded as the 'Magyar religion'; and
though discrimination against Calvinists and other non-Catholics
displeased the Hungarians, it did not outrage them. Reformation
and Counter-Reformation had blown over, and they showed no
desire to get involved once again in theological arguments.

The Diets were more or less regularly convoked, with an Upper
House consisting of magnates and high church dignitaries, and a
Lower House dominated by the deputies of the counties (that is, the
common nobles), beside whom the free cities (that is, the burghers)
had merely symbolic representation. The Diets, and particularly
their Lower Houses, supported by the County Council meetings,
carried on a Kuruc-type campaign, though rather perverted in form
and spirit: it was waged mainly to preserve what 'freedom' remained
to them, and that consisted of freedom to bully and exploit the serfs
and freedom from taxation. The idea had originally been that the
nobleman served his sovereign with the sword, while the duty of the
plebs contribuens was to pay expenses. This freedom of the nobleman
was later enlarged by exemption from the most tiresome military
duties through recruitment of serfs to the Imperial army, while his
freedom from taxation remained intact. Hungarian nobles had in
some ways never had it so good as under the repressive authoritarianism of the Empire. Their hearts bled for the Kuruc martyrs and

exiles; tears flowed in torrents, but so did the wine, and laments were
followed in the *lingua franca* of the Hungarian nobles by the exhilarat-
ing cry: '*Extra Hungariam non est vita! Si est vita, non est ita!*'–there is no
life outside Hungary, certainly none worth living.

In truth it was a dismal state of affairs for the whole country,
including her nobles, whenever they awoke from their self-induced
euphoria. The poverty and squalor were appalling; conditions in
agriculture and all industries, in transport, public health measures,
and education lagged centuries behind those prevailing in the Western countries with which Hungary could easily have borne com-
parison before the Turkish invasion. The Turks had pushed Hungary
back into the Middle Ages, the Austro-Christian liberators had
pushed her back further still, but most fatal in keeping her backward
was the attitude of the Hungarian nobles themselves. The Habsburg
rulers and their multinational advisers had some sensible ideas about
modernization for Hungary, which ran, broadly speaking, on the
lines of economic progress in countries to their west and also in some
of their own *Länder*, mainly Austria and Bohemia. Their motives were
both fiscal and philanthropic; one need not idealize them to be sure
they were shocked to see the *misera plebs contribuens* crippled in soul
and emaciated in body under the heel of a privileged and parasitical
populus; and they knew that without a more equitable distribution of
rights and burdens there was no hope of increasing production, consumption, or revenues. But the resistance offered by the nobles to any
reform affecting their prerogatives was enormous: the more tenuous
the prerogative, and the poorer the people it distinguished, the more
passionately they clung to it. And the privileged guild bourgeoisie of
the cities, small in numbers and fearful of competition, were no
progressive force either. The masses of serfs were, as a political force,
non-existent; their élite in courage, imagination, and dash had,
during the Labanc-Kuruc struggle, either been massacred or
graduated into the category of freemen, and the rest were like a vast
herd of cowed, resentful animals.

Hungary insisted on sticking in the mud, and the Habsburgs
decided they must make the best of it. If it was not practicable to
develop Hungary into a prosperous and exploitable country, it was
all the easier to exploit her as she was; the central Imperial agencies
of banking, customs, and trade regulations, out of reach of the
Hungarian Diet and counties, had the means to discriminate against
her. While the industries of the Austro-German and Czech-Moravian
provinces reaped the benefits of cautious progress, the penurious
kingdom of Hungary and principality of Transylvania found comfort
in the idea that–though under foreign rule–their sacred, ancient
constitution could be saved. The Golden Bull of 1222, protecting the

nobles against both the despotic impulses of the sovereign and the egalitarian effrontery of the serfs, still counted as a Charter of National Freedom in the middle of the eighteenth century.

Hungary, in a word, was a glorified colony. And she had another useful function in the Empire, that of providing soldiers, which she did efficaciously; indeed, on some occasions the nobility's traditional call-to-arms saved the throne. Solemn moments evoked dramatic gestures: in 1741, responding to the appeal of Queen Maria Theresa, the Hungarian nobles are said to have offered her *vitam et sanguinem* — their 'lives and blood'. They are said, too, to have added, only half in jest, *sed avenam non*—'. . . but no fodder for her horses'; and the bargain was gratefully honoured by the queen for decades until one day she again discovered the oppressed condition of the serfs and tried to do something about it. Then the Kuruc passion which had slumbered through all the country's poverty and exploitation flared up and vented itself in, among other things, a stream of obscene anecdotes about the ageing woman ruler. 'Nation' had never included the non-nobles; but by the second half of the eighteenth century, when feudal privileges were grossly outdated, all that survived of 'national' fighting spirit concentrated itself so single-mindedly on the defence of Estate prerogatives as to do more harm to the community than a spirit of submission.

There were people carrying in their genes the heritage of the Seven Tribes plus one which, late in the ninth century, had conquered the territory called Hungary. There were Hungarian nobles, the *populus hungaricus*. And there were people, both among the privileged *populus* and the underprivileged *plebs*, who spoke Hungarian as their mother-tongue. And the three had little in common.

Chapter 2

The Foundation of Liberal Hungary

The Inventing of the Hungarian Nation

A NATION IS BORN when a few people decide that it should be. This applies to India with her innumerable languages as much as to Eire with her one and only national language, the one she has not yet been able to learn, and it most signally applies to Hungary. It would be difficult to ascertain when Hungary as a nation was first invented; almost as difficult as to find out when the concept of a 'nation' was invented at all. But we know of several solemn moments when the Hungarian nation seems to have been re-invented, after a long period during which her moral and intellectual fibres had been numbed. Such solemn moments appear to have been those of Matthias the Just, or of Zrinyi the poet: very different moments, incidentally, since the former marked the peak of a country's grandeur, the latter the despair of her dismemberment and protest against it. Neither of them lasted long, and by the middle of the eighteenth century the adjective 'Hungarian' only denoted an assembly of legalistic and ethnic curiosities in the Habsburg Empire. Then, once again, the Hungarian nation was invented. This was an event recent enough to be dated: 1772, the year of publication of some unreadable works by the versatile Hungarian author György Bessenyei, then a resident in Vienna and serving in Maria Theresa's bodyguard. Bessenyei–coming from a family of the landed but miserably impoverished Calvinist gentry in north-eastern Hungary– was one of those prolific creative spirits, plentiful in the literary history of every country, whose *magna opera* might as well have remained unwritten, but whose pamphleteering, letters, or philosophical fragments could still, with the right kind of editing, be readable today. Bessenyei's *magna opera* were meant to prove that the Hungarian language was suitable for the very highest literary genre. He did prove it, but his polemic drive was more convincing than the aesthetic value of the examples he produced.

National Renewal – Turning against Liberalism or Making Use of it?

This brings us to what definitely distinguished this national rebirth from previous, comparable moments: it was centred on the national

44

language. So close a link between the political nation and its dominating language was a comparatively recent idea, in Europe as well as Hungary, though one can see indications of it much further back in Hungarian history. When Zrinyi, the polyglot, tuned himself to using the Hungarian language as his main means of expression, this certainly implied a gesture of allegiance to his nation. Yet it was on more than a gesture, however deeply felt; whereas from Bessenyei's time onwards it counted as a test of patriotism.

Was it a change for the better? This seems an alarming question, though some may think it irrelevant. 'It was in line with history'. Horrors as well as blessings have been in line with history. The rise of nationalism which, not in all but in most countries, at any rate in Europe, was marked by the acceptance of language as the acid test of nationhood, generated cross-currents more democratic and more aggressive, more humanitarian and more murderous, than anything seen before. Its blessings have since vanished, but not its horrors. Today, nationalism, degenerated into racial hatred, is a mass obsession that cripples the mind more than anything else, irrespective of whether it does call itself Nationalism, as in the Arab countries, or parades as Cultural Revolution, as in China. This I confess rather inhibits me in pointing out the progress mankind owes to the development of vernaculars into the main vehicles of thought and poetic vision. There is reason to recall with nostalgia the time when Latin was the *lingua franca* of all learned men, at any rate throughout the world of Western civilization. But if ever it really was so, it had certainly ceased to be so by the end of the Middle Ages; Latin had then degenerated into the glorified slang of a mandarinism whose learning defeated its own ends. The alternative to stagnation was to explore the potentialities of 'the sweet new language', first in Tuscany and then gradually everywhere; and the poets and thinkers who did most to further this process came, not unnaturally, from the élite most deeply inspired by classical Latin (and Greek and Hebrew) examples, from Dante to Erasmus. Humanism, at that time, thrived on the search of each nation for its own identity.

The 'Two Fatherlands', as Hungary and Transylvania used to be referred to by Hungarian writers of those days, were a motley mixture of languages, varying not only from district to district, but also between social strata. The high aristocracy, acclimatized to the Court in Vienna, spoke alternately French and German, diluted with some Spanish or Italian and, later, English. The lesser nobility or, precisely, the men of the middle-nobility, the office-holders in the counties and the like, conversed in a dog-Latin strewn with Magyar but also with Slovak, Serb, and Romanian expressions, and vernacular German, such as the 'Swabian' in the west and south or the

'Saxon' dialects in Transylvania and the north, according to the district. Their wives used slightly more Austro-German and local vernacular, naturally. The lowest stratum of the nobility, particularly the 'armalists' (who had only a crest to distinguish them from the *plebs* but no land, no title, and whose privileges were often ignored), did their best to keep up with gentlemanly Latinism but, being short of schooling, rarely managed it; so in this respect they did not strikingly differ from the serfs.

The city bourgeoisie were small in numbers and, with very few exceptions, non-Magyar and overwhelmingly German-speaking. The Jews in the outskirts of the cities added the 'Yiddish' shade of German to the Viennese, 'Saxon', and 'Swabian' dialects current among lower-middle-class gentiles and farmers.

As for the serf population of the Two Fatherlands, about one-third of it might have been Hungarian by speech, or, to use this discriminatory term, Magyar. And the Magyars were not, in general, better off than the non-Magyars; most of them had a somewhat higher standard of living than the Slovaks in the north, the Ruthenians in the north-east, and the Romanians in Transylvania, all mountainous and largely barren districts; but the various southern Slav tribes (Serbs, etc.) settled on the fertile southern part of the Plain, and the Swabian farmers scattered over both the southern Plain and Transdanubia, and endowed with some special liberties, were, on account of their social and economic standing, definitely nearer to the privileged 'Hungarian nation' than were the Magyar serfs. Whether this detachment of the ruling castes from their original ethnic background was a good thing or not, whether it would have been better to maintain the preponderance of Latin in public affairs in some form as a token of national tolerance in a multilingual country, may be open to argument; but as things stood in the 1770s, a nation that in public affairs stuck to Latin rather than to its own vernacular seemed, quite understandably, one that had not yet come of age.

The question, then, whether Magyar was or was not fitted for literature, legal discussion, and 'educated conversation' became suddenly a national issue. The impetus came from two directions. One was the tide of contemporary thought and feeling. Scholars and amateurs, Hungarian bodyguards at the Habsburg Court and Hungarian priests in Jesuit Seminaries, wondered why the language of their mothers and nurses should not be able to express the thoughts of a Voltaire or a Horace. As they had learned, in their cosmopolitan environments, to appreciate the infiltration of popular idioms into the feudal and clerical circles of European capitals, they naturally tried to develop a similar trend in their own fatherland; to refine and urbanize the special characteristics of their own language and bring them nearer to the common Hungarian. Their examples were later taken up and developed by some little *bel esprit* county squires, farmers, and lawyers, and by turbulent students in the Calvinist colleges. These were, as a rule, black sheep in the society of the middle or petty nobility to which they belonged: mostly ignored, sometimes distinctly persecuted, and only very rarely followed.

A more conclusive impetus was given to the Magyar Renaissance by the leaders and rank-and-file of the nobility themselves, who originally accepted this attitude as a protest *against* the tide of contemporary thought. In the 1780s, in the years foreshadowing the Revolution which was to come in France, the kingdom of Hungary as well as the Holy Roman Empire was ruled by Joseph II Habsburg (1765–90), a monarch who stood for 'enlightened absolutism' and who had refused to take the Hungarian coronation oath because it would have bound him to respect the constitutional rights of the *populus werbőczianus*. He undertook to rationalize and to secularize his provinces, notably Hungary. He took steps towards the abolition of serfdom and of noblemen's privileges; he granted legal support to the peasants; he had the population registered as a preliminary to general taxation; he restricted censorship to the minimum; he issued an Act of Toleration securing full rights to the Protestants; he banned religious orders; and as a matter of expediency, with a view to strengthening the ties between his countries, he ordered German to be the language of officialdom, instead of Latin. The Josephine rule meant for many the ascendancy of Free Thought; but it meant exactly the opposite of the kind of freedom defended by the Hungarian nobility. Save for the Toleration Act, which corresponded with the ideas of a largely Protestant nobility, all products of the Josephine legislation struck the *populus werbőczianus* as despotic denials of their traditional demands; while the traditional Habsburgists had also reason to be shocked. Upper and lower nobility had previously been willing to barter away a part of each other's privileges to successive monarchs: a part, but not the whole, as that would have endangered the position of *all* privileged classes. Joseph's radicalism gave the impression that such danger was imminent, and most of the magnates, whose role had been to act as the agents of the Habsburg dynasty against the lesser nobility, now turned against the monarch. So, of course, and even more vigorously, did the second traditional pillar of Habsburg rule, the Catholic Church. All these feudal and quasi-feudal powers, rich and poor, ecclesiastical and worldly, court-ridden and soil-bound, were driven together in unparalleled 'national unity' against the enlightened tyrant.

Yet among the big landowners there was comparatively more

willingness to comply with Joseph's orders than among the penniless
gentry. For one thing, they could more easily afford it. Another
reason was the magnates' adherence, in spite of the disquieting wave
of reform, to the Habsburg power. And some of them at least showed
understanding for the needs of economic expansion. The county
squirearchy, on the other hand, were totally outraged, feeling their
very existence threatened. The attacks on the Josephine reform movement were so phrased as to be directed, as was natural in such circumstances, against those regulations most likely to offend the
national feelings of the masses. They protested against Germanization, which under Joseph implied a trend towards the abolition of
privileges; and since, in the long run, a Magyar administration
seemed to be the only workable alternative to a German one, they
accepted the cause of the Magyar language as their own.

But even then they did not entirely accept it. The attitude
towards Magyar as a language did not necessarily determine one's
attitude for or against the reforms. Among the few 'traitors' of the
lesser nobility who served the unconstitutional Emperor and advocated his reforms was the leader of the Magyar literary and linguistic
renaissance, Ferenc Kazinczy, while the vast majority of the nobility
still insisted on Latin as their official language for another forty years.
Hungarian was not declared the official language until 1844, but the
wave of Magyarization, once unleashed, was bound to spread. The
Hungarian *populus* came round, although reluctantly, to recognizing
the use of the language of the Hungarian *plebs* as one part of the
freedom for which it was fighting.

These details may perhaps give an idea of the liberty which the
Hungarian noblemen never ceased to take seriously while interpret-
ing it in a way that some foreigners thought nothing but hypocrisy.
It was certainly not that. It really contained elements of parliamentarianism and local self-government, and enabled Hungarians
to be the forerunners of constitutionalism in eastern Europe. Once it
is appreciated why, as a result of their historical development during
the two centuries after 1514, they identified 'the rights of the people'
as their own privileges, as against those of the other 90 to 95 per cent
of the people, it is not difficult to understand the revolutionary zeal
with which they protested against the despotic conception of general
taxpaying. It would be just as difficult today to appreciate the
Jacobin fervour coming from the other side, that of the Germanizing
Habsburg dynasty. There were moments when the spokesmen of both
the Court and the Hungarian nobility disputed in terms of French
revolutionary rhetoric.

True, this did not last long; Joseph had to revoke most of his
orders, and he did not live long anyway. His brother and successor,

Leopold II (1790–92), tried to make a success of the Josephine reforms, but with methods less provocative, more elastic, and more conspiratorial. A kind of dynastic Jacobinism seethed during the short spell of his rule–Catholic monks engaged in Freemasonry, philosophers linked with the secret police. His son Franz I (1792–1835), a narrow-minded weakling, naturally accessible to illiberal advice, ascended the throne just at the time when fear of, and resentment against, everything akin to the French Revolution was most widespread. Court and aristocracy and *populus werböczianus* concluded a sort of internal Holy Alliance, prior to the international one, re-establishing Hungarian national feudalism at the expense of the peasantry and of the country as a whole. At the end of the eighteenth century, a group of Josephine and Leopoldine intellectuals, led by the Abbot Martinovics and comprising some of the finest Hungarian thinkers and writers, decided to launch a movement in secret on behalf of the common people and the hoped-for Hungarian Third Estate. This conspiracy was the first attempt to combine a Hungarian national fight for freedom with the elements of social progress. It failed, before it had done more than distribute a few leaflets. Seven of its leaders were beheaded in 1795 in Buda; others died in Austrian prisons; and those who survived (Kazinczy, for instance) thought it wiser to concentrate on poetry and philology.

The tendencies of those striving for national liberty were once again separated from and turned against the forces fighting for human liberty, for economic and social progress. The Hungarian version of love of freedom did not cease to be genuine, but it did cease to make sense. Yet this period–which may be said to have lasted from 1795 to 1825 or 1830–had one great achievement to its credit: the exploration of the Hungarian language and its adjustment to both the emotional and the rational needs of modern man in Europe. And there were still a few among the cultivators of language and style–such as Ferenc Kölcsey (1770–1838), poet, philosopher, lawyer, and orator, author of the beautiful poem *Hymnus*, which was to become the text of the Hungarian national anthem–who did not lose sight of the social aspects of their literary efforts and thus grew into the forerunners of the liberal Reform Era dawning on them.

The Reform Era

The 1830s are recorded in Hungarian history as the Era of Reform. In a broader sense, the era started as early as 1825 when, on the insistence of the nobles, a Diet was convoked, and continued into the following decades until the outbreak of the Revolution on 15 March 1848; but its intellectual pattern was set in the 1830s. It was an epoch in which the currents towards national and human liberty united, at least for a while. It was an idealistic epoch. Its idealism, as effective idealism always is, was the outcome of fairly selfish considerations, controlled and co-ordinated by wisdom. Neither the aristocracy nor the lesser nobility stopped asserting their claims to as many privileges as they could reasonably hope to retain. But more and more of them recognized that nothing short of sacrifices by all privileged classes could save them. The economic backwardness of the country was too conspicuous to be ignored. Hungary lacked industry, workable lines of communication; she was the prisoner of her own landowners, and her landowners were the prisoners of their own privileges. Immobilized by the feudal land-tenure system, they were unable to obtain credit and compete with less privileged farmers abroad.

While the benefits from their privileges dwindled to a sullen comfort and to such moral attributes as a right to terrorize the non-privileged, they had increasingly to bear the hatred of the peasantry, Magyar and non-Magyar alike, who held them responsible for all sorts of evils such as cholera and starvation. The peasants' riots had been violent but non-political, since the whole peasantry was politically uneducated, unaware, and disorganized. The probability, however, seemed to be that sooner or later everybody would demand his own share of rights. And in one respect the peasants grew incessantly shrewder: in the go-slow technique with which they sabotaged the services they owed to their masters under feudalist legislation. An increasing number of landowners felt that hiring free labour would be more profitable; yet, to give up prerogatives does mean a plunge into the unknown.

'Bourgeois' liberalism had by then been victorious for a second time in France. Unlike its republican and despotic excesses during and after the Great Revolution, which had shocked the Hungarian magnates and *populus*, its second edition in 1830, combining personal with constitutional liberties, and with both a royalist and gentlemanly hierarchy, provided a pattern of human progress in general which they thought exemplary. They were still more attracted by English examples. 'Something', it was decided, must be done.

The panaceas proposed were different. The generosity of both the high aristocracy and the county squirearchy showed itself first at each other's expense.

The Pragmatic Approach of a Romantic—Széchenyi

The most decisive impetus was given by a most romantic figure of the re-Magyarized high aristocracy, Count István Széchenyi (1791–1860). As a hussar officer in his youth, as a world-travelling *grand seigneur* later, as an eruptive though in some ways inhibited reformer,

Benthamite, Roman Catholic, and Anglo-maniac, devoted to horses, women, and occasionally to God, torn and tossed between his loyalty to the dynasty which he despised and his solidarity with the Magyars whom he despised even more, he set out to turn Hungary into a free and civilized country. His style was a mixture of visionary zeal and obsession with practical details. In Britain he was as much fascinated by perforated soapholders and the water-closet as by more spiritual tokens of the dignity of man. He liked to indulge in dramatic gestures, but was seized with panic when he encountered them in others. Throughout most of his life he wrote a diary in the polyglot staccato phrases of a tortured mind, referring with the same passion to public affairs as to his amorous exploits. In its pages, in September 1825, he blamed his fellow-nobles for their caste-ridden attitudes. 'To defend this anti-liberal Constitution [the Hungarian] is no noble undertaking. We see 400,000 souls who try to make their exclusive privileges and prerogatives prevail against ten million.' This was the moment of the epoch-making Diet: there he staggered his fellow-magnates by addressing them in Magyar, though the official language of discussion was still Latin. In the same year, he surprised the Estates by offering his whole income for one year for the establishment of a Hungarian Academy of Arts, Letters, and Science, with a view mainly to developing the Hungarian language. With his own incomplete knowledge of that language he undertook to make it fit for urban consumption, and coined words that are used to this day.

He undertook to make the Danube navigable; the Iron Gate and steam shipping in that part of Europe were really his creation. He tried to improve the quality of animal husbandry and of social life by establishing horse-racing and an aristocratic club in Pest, both of which soon after became famous institutions of gentlemanly gambling; but it would be too puritanical to deny on that account their contribution to the development of metropolitan colour and elegance. His greatest single work, however, was the first bridge erected between Buda and Pest, the Chain Bridge built, on his initiative, by the Scottish engineer Adam Clark. That bridge was, and is, a fine monument of city architecture (demolished by the retreating Nazis at the end of their war, it has been rebuilt in its original style still identifiable today); but its social implications were even more important. By uniting the city of Buda, erstwhile residence of powerful Hungarian kings, with the city of Pest, centre of commerce and of the intelligentsia, it gave the Hungarian nation a *capital* at the centre of the country, destined to replace the official capital, Pozsony, which, situated in the north-western borderland, was felt to be an agent of the sovereign and of the Estates rather than a platform of public opinion. And, most important in Széchenyi's plan, the bridge toll was to be the first fiscal contribution levied on noblemen and *plebs* alike. That tuppence, the 'zwei Groschen', was meant to be the thin end of the wedge for overturning the feudal system. Once the exemption from taxpaying was demolished, Széchenyi hoped that everything else would look after itself.

The bulk of the nobility were shocked by his suggestions. When his seminal book, *Credit*, appeared in 1830, one county after another burned it in protest. Most infuriated of all were the 'moccasin-wearers', the privileged beggars who felt that, deprived of that privilege, they would sink into beggary pure and simple. The spokesmen of the high aristocracy also warned him that the game he was playing with liberty was dangerous. In the palace of the Chancellor, Prince Metternich, where, as a dandy and a sensitive if rather erratic intellect, he enjoyed considerable popularity (not least with the princess), teasing and paternal reprimands were the most frequent response to his ideas. The Chancellor did not turn them down off-hand: he even experimented with economic reforms, if only to take the wind out of the radical sails, and it was his elasticity which enabled Széchenyi to put many of his economic and technological ideas into practice. But Széchenyi's liberal sympathies, however qualified, roused suspicions against him, often in more hostile spirit than was meted out to the radicals proper. All right, it was argued, *he* wanted to carry out liberal reforms without rebellion against the dynasty, but where was the guarantee that his disciples would not go further? And was not Széchenyi the most dangerous of all reformers, because he shielded subversion with respectability? And Széchenyi was indeed quickly outstripped in reforms, if not by the majority, yet by the liveliest section of the noble *populus*.

Liberalism and Nationalism Competing and Combined: Eötvös, Kossuth, Wesselényi

Between the two reactionary extremes of silk-wearing courtiers and moccasin-wearing gentry, it was mainly the educated middle-nobility and the thin upper-crust of the plebeians admitted to the Civil Service and the professions who showed most understanding for the needs of the common people. While on the one hand a group of 'doctrinaires' led by the son of a Habsburgist high official, the poet and philosopher Baron József Eötvös (1811–71), demanded the abolition of county autonomies, considering them to be strongholds of feudal oppression, on the other the new leader of the advanced lesser nobility, the lawyer Lajos (Louis) Kossuth (1802–94), urged the extension of the rights of the counties, considering them to be guarantees of national independence and constitutionalism. In economic policy, unlike Széchenyi who had been influenced by

British Free Trade, Kossuth, mainly under the influence of the German economist Friedrich List, envisaged industrial development as a result of protection. Kossuth was an impulsive and magnetic personality, an orator above all, a vain but sincere enthusiast who carried himself as well as his audience in the belief that fast progress was compatible with the preservation of what is dearest to the nobleman's heart. If only Imperial tutelage could be done away with!

Among the Hungarian nobles of Transylvania it was Baron Miklós Wesselényi (1796–1850) who combined with most vigour the struggle for economic improvements as demanded by Széchenyi with that for national and constitutional liberties as demanded by Kossuth, and to a large extent also with the efforts towards social emancipation urged by Eötvös. He was an ebullient and outstandingly courageous man, quixotic in spite of his clearsightedness, popular with his contemporaries and yet ultimately let down by them—and by fate—as such very good men often are; while Széchenyi was absorbed in building his Bridge, and Kossuth in clamouring for Liberty, and Eötvös in writing novels and essays, Wesselényi was kept in prison, to which the Imperial judges confined him for his outspokenness. When released he was half-blind, and the political climate was that of gathering storm: he was revered but no longer needed, and certainly not heeded. He passionately defended Széchenyi against Kossuth's radical young men who pooh-poohed his achievements; but when somebody accused Kossuth of opportunism he challenged the 'calumniator' to a duel. It seems he was dissuaded from it.

The general feeling that the world was in ferment accounted for the fact that such controversial movements were able, although with bitter personal and doctrinal clashes, to unite at decisive moments on the same path. The problem of priority between economic and political reforms (the original difference between the conceptions of Széchenyi and Kossuth) faded away as everybody in the reformers' camp agreed that both were required; the differences between the reformers boiled down, by the late forties, to the question of how radically the reforms should be urged. Kossuth, the most radical among them as far as rhetoric was concerned, though originally the most conservative because of his county-bound outlook, accepted and outbid Széchenyi's demands for the abolition of privileges, and now concentrated his attacks on the aristocracy which, he asserted, stood in the way of reform. After a term of imprisonment for illicitly publishing parliamentary reports, he returned to public life as the champion of national democracy, agitating for the abolition of the prevailing feudal system and the establishment of parliamentary government, for general taxation, for industrialization, for economic expansion through overseas trade, and above all for what was called 'admission of the people to the strongholds of the constitution'. *People* now no longer meant only those recognized by Werbőczi as such; the division between noblemen and plebeians was declared to be out of date although, as Kossuth insisted, it could only be of benefit to all if the lower nobility, as the natural counterweight between the classes above and below it, kept and even increased its influence in shaping the fate of the country. Whether he said so because he meant it, or because he wanted his fellow-noblemen to mean it, is something which perhaps even he did not know.

In spite of his insistence, however, the lesser nobility represented in the Diet were in as little hurry to open the 'strongholds of the constitution' as were the high dignitaries in the Upper House and the officials of the Austrian dynasty. Even the most obvious national demand, the substitution of Magyar for Latin in public affairs, was not achieved before the forties. Still greater was their reluctance to carry out social and economic reforms: after some alleviations had been granted to the serfs, the proposals for abolition of serfdom were vetoed either by the Imperial administration and the magnates, or by the counties.

The Hungarian Quatorze Juillet: *15 March 1848; Petőfi and the Radicals*

It was eventually the wind of the third French revolution which swept away the Hungarian 'Bastille' in 1848. The news of the barricades in Paris and of the subsequent riots in Vienna – where, by the way, Kossuth had been fêted as a freedom hero of all Habsburg-ruled peoples – strengthened the will of the hesitating liberals and broke the willpower of the conservatives. The Austro-Imperial magistrates in Hungarian cities were paralysed, the Magyar nobility panic-stricken by rumours of an approaching peasants' rising. The Hungarian *Quatorze juillet* took place on 15 March. A handful of unfledged barristers, assistant teachers, intellectual shop-assistants, and journalists, led by the 'Jacobin' poet Sándor (Alexander) Petőfi (1823–49) in Pest, occupied a printing office in order to issue the first uncensored Hungarian leaflets. They stormed the historic fortress of Buda to free all the political prisoners gaoled there; unfortunately, since national leaders such as Kossuth and Wesselényi had already been released earlier under the pressure of public opinion, they found only a single prisoner, the one and only socialist in the whole country at that time: an old weaver-writer called Mihály Táncsics. He was a loquacious and tiresome apostle, unpopular even with the March Youth, but he had an impressive long beard and made a striking symbol when carried about on their shoulders. Liberty, Equality, Fraternity were declared at once; the abolition of the privileges of the landlords and the guilds, the liberation of serfs, and the establishment of parliamentary rule. Kossuth, absent from the scene when it happened, was at first shocked by the uncalled-for plebeian aid given to the struggle for universal freedom and considered having Petőfi and his friends arrested, but then decided that he had better use the Pest rising as a lever to impose his own idea of a change to liberalism on the frightened nobility, and through them on the still more frightened magnates, high magistrates, and the King-Emperor himself. Anything short of a revolutionary gesture of generosity by the Estates was doomed to failure by then. Consequently, as was to be taught for decades to come in Hungarian schools, 'the event unparalleled in world history occurred, and the nobility of Hungary, of their own free will, renounced their privileges for the benefit of the whole people.'

This was the period that changed Hungary into a technically liberal, parliamentary, and independent country. The Imperial governors had gone, and so had the Diet consisting of Deputies of the Noble Counties; they were replaced by a government appointed by the king but responsible to a directly elected Parliament. Entailment of land was more or less abolished, and so were exemption from tax-paying and other privileges, particularly those of the nobility and of the guilds. Freedom of religion, Press, occupation, enterprise, and competition was declared. A Magyar people's nation was substituted for the Hungarian noblemen's nation; the 'strongholds of the constitution' were opened, at least theoretically, to all subjects of the Hungarian crown.

From then onwards, it was decided, everybody speaking Hungarian should be Hungarian (in the same way as only the privileged had been before), and every Hungarian should speak Hungarian (in the same way as only the 'Magyars'[1] had done before). Since everybody would be glad to do so, it would mean freedom for all.

Needless to say, the reality proved less rosy than the theory. Both the Imperial ruling circles and the nobility, after recovering from the shock of March, started to revoke their generous offers—the former by sabotaging the liberation of Hungary from Austrian tutelage, the latter by delaying the measures to emancipate the serfs. Kossuth, the leading spirit of the government, was infuriated against the Court. Széchenyi, the moderating spirit in the government, was resentful of Kossuth. The aristocrats cursed Kossuth for inciting the people, and reproached Széchenyi for sowing the seed that had been reaped in whirlwind. The March Youth, grouped in the Radical Club, threatened the aristocrats with the rope, and attacked the govern-

---

[1] About the use of the word 'Magyar', see above, p. 12.

ment as a whole. The new Press Law, the radicals asserted, was even more oppressive than the old. Indeed, 'everybody was free to propagate his ideas in print' against a deposit which only few could afford to pay. Likewise, 'everybody' had the right to vote—that is, besides the noblemen who had always had it, all male adult citizens, provided only that they belonged to a high taxpaying category which, in fact, comprised very few. Furthermore, even if the liberation of ideas, of land, and of the nation had been more complete than it was, even then the striking inequality between rich and poor would not have automatically diminished; freedom of property means little to him who has none.

But not all these shortcomings were peculiar to the Hungarian revolution and the liberal order initiated by it. Neither English nor French parliamentarianism started either with a wider suffrage or with more socially-minded legislation than did Hungarian. They, too, established freedom and tolerance in many fields, but certainly not in all; it did not automatically free the whole nation from want or neighbouring nations from fear. Liberal societies were established originally on the assumption that each person has only to look after his own interests, within the framework of a law securing the rights of property, to make the whole nation happy, and that each nation has only to look after her own interests, with no restriction whatever, to make the world happy.

The leaders of Hungary at the time of the changeover from a feudal to a parliamentary constitution were on the whole neither more nor less farsighted than their forerunners or opposite numbers in those countries which have since become known as the most advanced democracies. Some of them, especially among the 'doctrinaires', foresaw the consequences of the problems left open by a one-sided and far too restricted interpretation of the Rights of Man; but their number was small, and their tone hesitant. The 'nation' was, by the standard of that time (which viewed the rise of the twin stars of Liberalism and Nationalism with boundless optimism), justified in feeling itself extremely generous when it 'admitted' the Magyar peasant with no discrimination save for that relating to property; and the non-Magyar Christians on condition they became Magyar; and eventually, with some reluctance and a delay of twenty years, the Jews.

Chapter 3

The War for Freedom and its Aftermath

THE HUNGARIAN WAR FOR FREEDOM against Habsburg absolutism in 1848–49 was a unique feat of valour which mesmerized liberal world opinion and resounded for decades to come in the poems of Swinburne and W. S. Landor and Matthew Arnold, of François Coppée and Heinrich Heine. A closer look at the miracle shows its noble passions to have been not so noble and, above all, not so united after all; but the fact that common squabbles and intrigues could add up to what it appeared to be, and to some extent really was, makes the spectacle even more miraculous.

The Batthyány Government

The formation on 7 April 1848 of the first parliamentary government, seated at Pest, united the best political brains of the country in a symbolic spectrum of talents and ideals: Széchenyi in charge of Transport and Public Works, Kossuth of Finance, Eötvös of Education, and Bertalan Szemere, a cosmopolitan radical of the most ancient county squirearchy, in charge of the Ministry of the Interior. The premiership was allotted to a man of unoriginal intellect but impressive personality, handsome in physique and generous in manners, Count Lajos Batthyány (1806–49), who, on account of his popularity both with the Hungarophobe archduchesses in Schönbrunn and with the Jacobin patriots in the Hungarian cafés, was trusted to act as bridge and balance between all the forces concerned. He was assisted by his Minister of Justice, the Transdanubian gentleman farmer and lawyer Ferenc Deák (1803–76), who had a genius for compromise; so long as there was a chance to reconcile divergent interests without sacrificing the principles of patriotism and humanism, he would not fail to take it, and whenever times became hopeless for a liberal evolutionist like himself he withdrew into offended but dignified silence. Did this attitude show modesty and wisdom or a convenient defeatism? In any case, it seemed to pay high dividends from 1847 onwards when he undertook to work out the formulas on which all liberal reformers could agree; and his presence in the Batthyány government was looked upon as a guarantee of moderation and realism among personalities so excitable in their own different

ways as Széchenyi and Kossuth, or Eötvös and Szemere. With so
many elements working together, with the plebeian masses jubilant
about the extension of their rights, and a nobility relieved of the fear
of bloody upheavals, prospects for the moment seemed bright.

But it only lasted for a moment. The Court and central administration in Vienna, having pulled themselves together after the first
panic, gradually went back on their concessions and brought pressure
to bear upon the rulers in Pest, setting the national minorities of
Hungary against them. It was the old game of 'Divide and rule':
among Hungarians they supported the retrogrades, but the Ban of
Croatia, Baron Jellačić, was encouraged by them to promise the
peasants a redistribution of land more 'Jacobin' than anything
offered from Pest. Croatia had some home rule, and direct links with
the King-Emperor, and offered the most suitable proving-ground for
a manoeuvre to combine the re-establishment of hereditary powers
with prospects of social reform. The authority of the Habsburg King-
Emperor over both Hungary and Croatia was still unchallenged in
principle when these two countries, or provinces, were practically at
war, each accusing the other of (a) violating the legality of the realm
as guaranteed by the decrees of the hereditary ruler, and (b) serving
sectional interests, feudalist oppressors, by obstructing popular progress. Croats, with their strong dynastic and Roman Catholic traditions, seemed a safe people to manoeuvre with. But the Habsburgs
went further, and took the riskier course of inciting the Serbs in
southern Hungary, the Slovaks in the north, and (riskiest of all,
because poorest and most numerous of all) the Romanians in Transylvania to seize every chance of massacring the Hungarians and the
'gentlemen'. The manoeuvre had some prospects of success because,
for these masses of non-Hungarian paupers, the words 'Hungarian'
and 'gentleman' were practically interchangeable. The only Christian national minority to sympathize with the Hungarian national upsurge was the 'Swabians', who might have been expected to resent it
most; and the only non-Magyar group to welcome its egalitarianism
were the Jews, who were excluded from its benefits. The rest of the
poverty-stricken non-Magyars only knew that they had not ceased
to be poverty-stricken and felt, if anything, irritated by the triumphant mood of the Hungarians.

Hungarians, on the other hand, were simply unaware of this;
particularly those Hungarians who set the pace of public opinion in
the National Assembly, the cafés, and the streets of Pest. Kossuth's
negotiations with the various non-Hungarian national leaders came
to nothing. With Jellačić a rupture was unavoidable, since he was
determined to thwart Hungarian aspirations. But for the rest, the
main question was whether they were to be recognized as 'nations' or

not. Kossuth insisted that it could not be done. Towards the Slovaks, particularly, he professed personal goodwill–he came from partly Slovak stock–but insisted that they had no 'historical personality' and therefore no choice but to join the Hungarians. In later years, once Kossuth's nationalist myopia had been realized, the left-wing interpretation ran that it was part of his county squire's heritage: had he advanced more boldly along the democratic road, he could not have been so shortsighted. Nothing could be further from the truth. Kossuth did indeed have his 'county' background, and many of its superstitions, which it took him a long time to get rid of; but even his most democratic supporters, and indeed his radical and socialist opponents such as the poet Petőfi and the deputy Táncsics, were as fanatically chauvinist as he. Incidentally, both were of Slovak origin, like Kossuth; but, unlike Kossuth, outside the 'historical nation', i.e. the Hungarian nobility: in fact, plebeians and paupers. Táncsics, in Parliament, urged the most radical legislation towards liquidating the feudal system and introducing some economic equality; but that equality should also be established between national groups did not enter his head. Petőfi was enthusiastic about World Freedom, and had broad humanitarian views, stronger even than his patriotism; he was willing to risk his nation's prosperity for the sake of mankind; but the sake of mankind, for him, had nothing to do with the restive non-Magyars of Hungary, whom he dismissed as 'ulcers on the body of the motherland'. It was not the limitations of revolutionary zeal but rather its excesses that blinded Hungarians to the desires of non-Hungarians; and it took some time for the nationalism born in revolutionary spirit to betray its retrograde and oppressive character.

Difference between Populus *and* Plebs *Lifted; but not between '*Nation*' and '*Nationalities*'*

It may be worthwhile at this point to mention a semantic sophistry which enabled Hungarians to deny to other national groups the rights they claimed for themselves, without feeling guilty of discrimination. The reader may remember the distinction between *populus* and *plebs* which had dominated Hungarian legal argument almost down to 1848: it enabled a system to pride itself on democratic as well as aristocratic merit because the 'people' who enjoyed liberties were the privileged 'populus' as distinct from the underprivileged 'plebs'. The era of liberal nationalism, though it abolished this distinction, substituted for it another one, namely the distinction between a 'nation' and a 'nation*ality*'. In Hungary, according to the Hungarians, they alone were a 'nation', the others at best 'nationalities'. A 'nation', with not only a language of her own but a historical personality as well, was by divine or natural law the mother of her 'nationalities'. They, protected by her, were entitled to their own religions, private languages, and other ethnic peculiarities; but any 'nationality' that tried to back out of the organic unity created by the 'nation' was a traitor not only to their common cause but to the cause of humanity.

Hair-raising though this sophistry may sound today, there was more to it than at first appears. It was hypocritical, or at least self-deceiving, insofar as it ignored the fact that Hungary owed the 'historical personality' which distinguished her from simple 'nationalities' precisely to those noblemen's privileges which had just been given up in principle; it meant that the Hungarian nobleman tried to save through the back door of nationalism what he had lost by opening the front door of constitutional rights to the plebeian masses. Yet the values in which Hungarian nationalists took such pride were real values, morally as well as intellectually, and much superior to anything that other national groups in their country had developed up to then; they were even superior in some ways to what any other nation in the whole Habsburg Empire had developed. No one in that area could match the Hungarians in parliamentary tradition, in love of liberty and eloquence of discussion, however Estate-ridden each of those cults had been. The Hungarians were a nation of lawyers and poets; their history, as already demonstrated, had conditioned them to be so. It was by no means an unmixed blessing, and lent itself to grotesque exaggerations. In the 1830s, in the University of Pest (at that time an overwhelmingly 'Swabian' city), masses of students pledged themselves to write 'three Hungarian poems daily' as a patriotic duty; with results as lamentable as might have been expected. And in the 1840s, when urban life, trades, and education in Hungary lagged far behind those of Bohemia (let alone of some Western countries), it was noted that the city of Pest alone housed more lawyers than Bohemia, Moravia, Styria, and Dalmatia put together. So great an emphasis on two intellectual disciplines in a largely uncivilized country reflected, no doubt, some instability even at its mandarin levels of scholarship. But the outcome was nonetheless impressive—not only in the skills of litigation and versification, but even more in fields where the two met, in oratory, in philosophic and historical treatises; or in novels and essays—sometimes (those by Eötvös, for example) not impeccable either as fiction or as political science, but yet extraordinarily highminded and forthright in their presentation of social problems past and present.

And now this Hungarian oratory was wedded to the cause of civic liberty. The spirit it expressed seemed the only alternative to that of feudal overlordship. Compared with the eloquence of Hungarian liberalism, the manifestos of the 'nationalities' seemed poor stuff, confused and banal, with intimations of mob violence and dynastic intrigue behind them. So at least the Hungarians, with their not quite unreasonable bias, felt. However highflown in expression, their Cause was the right one: and that was exactly what the diehard illiberals in and around the Habsburg dynasty–the 'Camarilla', as Hungarians called it–could not stomach. Mass emotionalism in Pest played into the hands of the retrogrades in Vienna. As a concession to pro-Hungarian and comparatively liberal circles in Vienna, a moderate high official, Count Lamberg, was in September 1848 appointed Commander-in-Chief of the Imperial forces in Hungary and sent to Pest to try to bring about a compromise. Mob violence, powerless to get at the long-distance intriguer, always takes it out on the man of goodwill on the spot: Lamberg, as he drove across the pontoon bridge over the Danube, was recognized by a crowd as 'the man from Vienna', dragged out of his coach, and stabbed to death. The anti-Hungarian *camarilla* exulted: now the reckoning could begin without further ado.

Kossuth Defeating the Habsburgs; the Romanovs Defeating Kossuth

Széchenyi, tormented by forebodings of catastrophe, had already escaped into madness and a sanatorium in Austria. Eötvös, unnerved by mob violence, fled to relatives in Munich; and Wesselényi, who was by now completely blind, in a gesture of despair settled in the same Austrian locality to which he had been forcibly restricted some years before. Of the cabinet ministers appointed by the king, only Kossuth and Szemere carried on in office, on a revolutionary basis which they had not sought. On the very last day of 1848, Count Batthyány, the ex-Prime Minister, and Deák, the genius of compromise, made a last attempt to re-establish peace and led a delegation to Marshal Prince Windisch-Graetz, the Habsburgs' plenipotentiary in Hungary; but they were not even received, the prince refusing to have any 'parley with rebels'. In 1849, a Hungary pushed into republicanism and isolated from her own hostile nationalities, faced the army of an empire alone.

From the outset the odds were against the Hungarians. No one had been surprised to see Windisch-Graetz occupy Pest and Buda in the first weeks of December 1848. The armed resistance organized by Kossuth from the east of the country–with Debrecen as temporary capital–seemed a gesture of valiant despair. The rebellions in the Austro-German and Italian provinces had been crushed. 'Europe is silenced', Petőfi lamented; and as a volunteer in the revolutionary army he urged his compatriots on to the last ditch, in frenzied verse that ran with resolution but no hope: 'Liberty, in this unfaithful time–We have been thy last and only faithful sons!' If a visionary poet saw no more reason for optimism, how could the administrators, the economists, and the strategists? But reality proved even stranger than the poet's apocalyptic vision. Matchless rhetoric actually produced efficiency in the field. The Hungarians beat the Habsburgs and by the end of May 1849 were back in Pest and the fortress (which had taken longer to reduce) of Buda.

And all this while they went on piling up mistakes. Kossuth had to waste most of his time in the displaced Parliament in arguing with right- and left-wingers about methods and degrees of compensation to the nobility for their loss of feudal services and dues; even while the very existence of the state was in jeopardy, heated debates continued about its dues. On 14 April, a declaration was passed dethroning the Habsburgs–a blunder, to say the least, since it made dynastic hostility more resolute and won no new supporters, while troubling the conscience of many an old supporter. Among the latter was the ablest military officer of the Hungarian forces, Major Arthur Görgey (1818–1916), who, in spite of his strained relations with Kossuth, swiftly rose to be one of the top-flight generals. He considered himself and his army as loyal to king and country, and obedient to the royal and parliamentary constitution; when the dethronement made such a combination of loyalties inconceivable, he still went on fighting for the national cause, but his relations with Kossuth grew even more precarious. Kossuth, meanwhile, was elected governor; Szemere was appointed his premier; and even these two were known to be on unfriendly terms. Yet Kossuth, under the avalanche of unavoidable crises, to which he added those of his own making, had enormous persuasive power and gifts of improvisation, in finance as well as politics; he conjured up an army of recruits, with supply-lines and the means to finance them. The tug-of-war between patriots behind the scenes did not prevent Görgey from advancing at the head of his army in the west; while in Transylvania the Polish refugee General Joseph Bem–with the poet Petőfi, by then a major and a war correspondent, at his side–defeated the Imperial forces.

The Imperial camp, humiliated, decided to throw overboard any pretence of either legality or dignity in order to crush the Hungarians. The ruler nominally responsible for the concessions to the Hungarians–a harmless man, meek and infantile–had been induced to abdicate; and the stalwart young man who followed him on the Imperial throne, eighteen-year-old Franz Joseph (1848–1916), was induced to apply to the Russian Tsar, Nicholas I, in frantic haste and humility for his armed intervention against the unruly Habsburg subjects. The Tsar granted his request and, in combination with the regrouped Imperial Austrians, launched an offensive against Hun-

gary; and against two great Powers united not even Kossuth's magic
and Görgey's skill united could avail. By August 1849 it was over.
Kossuth and Szemere had fled the country: the former, after handing
over full power to General Görgey; the latter, after failing in his last
attempt to engineer victory by granting practically equal rights at
last to all ethnic groups in Hungary, whether 'nation' or 'nationality'.
By now it was too late. On 13 August, at Világos, Görgey laid down
his arms to the Russians; his sole comfort being that he avoided doing
it to the Austrians. Ever since then, it has been a moot point in Hungary whether Görgey was a traitor (as the refugee Kossuth maintained) or a scapegoat. The military facts indicate that he was a
scapegoat; but it was certainly unsavoury to behold how, in the
subsequent era of bloody Austrian repression – with thirteen of his
generals hanged on 6 October alone – Görgey was allowed to retire
unharmed.

Two Memorable Martyrs: Petőfi and Batthyány

Of the toll in lives taken by the War for Freedom, two cases stand
out for their romantic appeal, but also for their political implications.
Petőfi died on the battlefield, possibly from a Russian bullet. He has
risen to be a legendary figure of the struggle for national liberty, and
as such can be found in pictures on the walls of country inns in company with angels, and Muses, and Kossuth (whom he hated). In
political debates, he was to be claimed as a predecessor by extreme
nationalists and left-radicals and socialists alike. His poetry, life, and
legend became part of Hungarian public life; it is largely due to him
that Hungarians thereafter could hardly conceive of a social reform
movement, let alone a war of independence, not inspired by a poet.

Count Lajos Batthyány is remembered in Hungary as the martyr
to scrupulous loyalty. Arrested after the Austrian reoccupation of
Pest in the palace of his sister-in-law Caroline who was rumoured to
be his mistress, he was sentenced to death by hanging, although he
had stood aside since the open breach with the dynasty. In prison, a
dagger hidden in a loaf of bread was smuggled to him by his sister-
in-law, to enable him to kill himself before the execution. Batthyány
cut his throat – which, at any rate, prevented hanging: he was shot.
Among aristocrats not guilty of active republicanism he was the only
one to be treated so harshly. The irony of his tragedy lay in the fact
that this exceptional harshness was due to the very thing which, in
March/April 1848, made him appear an ideal mediator and premier:
his virile charm. Archduchess Sophie, mother of the Emperor Franz
Joseph and known as the leading spirit of the *camarilla*, was in love
with him; she could have condoned his politics, but not his romance
with the Hungarian countess, and she insisted that he must die. This

is the way his story was remembered, *inter alia*, among the families of the high aristocracy concerned – Counts Batthyány, Károlyi, Zichy; and I see no reason to doubt its authenticity. It was just one of those cases where the shape of a woman's nose, whether Cleopatra's or Caroline's, determined the fate of millions; for if Batthyány, the ideal mediator, had been spared, it is at least conceivable that he might have reconciled the Habsburgs, to some extent, to the aspirations of his countrymen.

The Bach Period: Progress in Slavery

Hungary's defeat in the War for Freedom condemned her to despotic centralized control by Austria until 1860, and to seven or eight years in an administrative limbo until the Compromise of 1867.

The decade of absolutism, known as the 'Bach Period' after the then Austrian Minister of the Interior, Alexander Bach, has been characterized by practically all Hungarian historians and political writers, from diehard traditionalist to diehard communist, as an orgy of reaction, blood lust, vindictiveness, and hatred – hatred of everything Hungarian. Bach's way to power had indeed been paved by a military terror which, however trifling when measured against what Hitler or Stalin were to promote, revealed a savagery which understandably shocked the queasy nineteenth century; and the spying on, and hounding of, Hungarian patriots, particularly those guilty of sympathy for the common people and the poor, demonstrated the backwardness as well as the inhumanity of the policy pursued by the Habsburgs: namely, an all-out effort to revive the authoritarianism of decades or centuries ago.

But history proved as paradoxical in the 1850s as ever before or since, and a paradox-collector would have no difficulty in unearthing facts to demonstrate that the Bach Period was one of social and economic progress. It was then that the foundations of modern industrial Hungary were laid. It was then that the principle of general taxation, proclaimed earlier as the epoch-making reform of 1848, was really put into practice. Széchenyi had made the Danube navigable and launched the first Hungarian steamship; but steam transport on the Danube only grew into a commercial proposition – and a big one at that – when Széchenyi was already confined to the asylum for the insane at Döblin, and those whom he despised as Habsburg lackeys were standing at the helm. Petőfi had exultantly hailed the first stretch of Hungarian railway line, which amounted to barely more than a symbol: 'Break your chains', he urged his countrymen, 'and you will have enough iron to build more railways'. But the fifteen years after his death during which it developed into a national network were precisely those in which the chains were refastened most spectacularly upon his country. Even Széchenyi's Chain Bridge did not open to traffic before Bach's administration laid hands upon it. The victorious reactionaries began by castigating the citizens of Pest and imposing a severe penalty on the Jews of Buda for their unruly patriotism; but when matters of shipping, shipbuilding, trading, and banking had to be tackled, the administrators preferred to forget about minor sins of disloyalty to the Emperor, and chose businesslike partners where they could find them. The merging of the two (or, if we include suburban Old Buda, the three) cities into one trading community was the work of their oppressors. So was the abolition of serfdom in the villages.

The reason for these practical improvements was that they suited the interests of the Imperial exchequer. Liberalism may have been more repellent than feudalism, but in economic terms it paid higher dividends and in administration it helped to simplify problems. Besides, the specifically Hungarian brand of late feudalism, the rule of the county squirearchy from which the subversive Kossuth had sprung, was not particularly favoured by the Imperial administration; if the Magyar gentry were ready to lead the common people in a revolt against the Habsburgs, the Habsburg officials were ready to sacrifice the gentry in order to win over the peasants.

Bach himself was a fanatic for rational administration rather than for keeping up Imperial traditions; he accepted the devout assumptions of a good Habsburg loyalist with the same lukewarm pragmatism that made the Court accept him and his unaristocratic establishment. The aim was to restore order and get things going. The Hungarian landowners did get some compensation for the loss of their feudal prerogatives—probably neither more nor less than they would have got under Kossuth—but not enough to make most of them competitive in the market economy to which Hungarian agriculture and commerce had to readjust themselves, no matter whether it was through the tyranny of Imperial administrators or the liberalism of national republicans that the change had come about. Time was running out for those noblemen who could not carry the burden of taxation on their land and made a patriotic duty of dodging it. The Hungarian squire, if he could still afford the luxury of fancy tailoring, vented his bitterness by slipping into 'national dress'—a braided jacket and trousers, feathered hat, jackboots, and a sort of spontoon for walking-stick—as a protest against Austrian rule. He felt he was protesting against tyranny and reaction; but in fact what hurt him most was inevitable in the process of industrializing a society. The lesser nobility's estates were dwindling. The owners of the large *latifundia*, magnates and bishops alike, fared much better, partly because of their better start in getting the capital needed, and partly because they were more favoured by the Court. Besides, though the general inalienability of the noblemen's estates had been abolished, special provisions had been made in 1834 for establishing aristocratic and church-entailed properties, in the face of fierce opposition from such liberals as Deák and the poet and lawyer Kőlcsey. In the Bach Period and the subsequent years of transition, the dispossessed or desperately struggling lesser noblemen saw the social and financial gap between themselves on the one hand and the holders of large properties, old and new, on the other, widen into an unbridgeable gulf.

The experiences of the Bach Period fostered the development of a schizophrenic streak in the mind of the Hungarian lesser nobility, and it is one that has remained dominant in the Hungarian mind ever since: the attitude towards 'nationality'.

Nationalism: An Inescapable Schizophrenia

Almost until the end of the War for Freedom, it was taken for granted in the camp of Hungarian patriots and liberals that liberty for Hungary should and would lead to Magyarization. Conservative liberals, such as Széchenyi, warned against precipitancy in this as in other political matters. The radicals, with Kossuth as their most eloquent spokesman, and the 'Jacobins' who outstripped them, were on the whole as impatient to see Magyar introduced everywhere as to abolish the remnants of feudalism. Middle-of-the-roaders between Széchenyi and Kossuth–such as Batthyány, Deák, Eötvös–shared the same concept of the final aim; the differences between them were all differences of degree. There were a few exceptions, such as Wesselényi's vision of a Hungarian-Romanian fraternity to withstand the dangers of pan-Russian as well as pan-German pressure; a prophetic vision, as it foresaw (in 1843) the possibilities of a pan-German tyranny hostile to Austria and a savage pan-Russian or pan-Slav drive even if the Romanovs should no longer be there to head it. Yet, as is often the case with prophecies of genius, it made sense only in relation to what would emerge in a coming century and not to the realities of its own time; partly because, for all its supranational intuition, it was still imbued with that fervour for Magyarization which could not but estrange potential non-Magyar partners. The first man to grasp even the possibility of a nationally tolerant Hungarian radicalism was a sensitive, if unbalanced, amateur of letters, stagecraft, and politics: the Transylvanian magnate Count László Teleki (1810–61). Teleki was sent by the Batthyány-Kossuth government as their envoy (they hoped he would be accredited as ambassador) to Paris; and there he discovered the existence of opinion sympathetic to the liberal trends advocated by the Hungarian leaders but condemning them as oppressors for their discrimination against the non-Magyars in their country. In the light of such experiences, and reacting to the Habsburg army's determined move to crush Hungarian liberty, Teleki in early 1849 devised a plan for a federation of all ethnic groups, on the basis of perfect equality, as a means of defence against any tyrant from inside or out; he went even further and wondered whether a federation from the Baltic to the Black Sea could not be established to make the area safe against Romanov as well as Habsburg intrusion. Again, an idea which would have been worth considering, long after the exit of the Romanovs and Habsburgs, for instance, in 1935. Some Czech, Slovak, Serb, Croat, Polish, and Romanian emissaries whom he entertained in his house, as well as some of the Westerners, viewed his plans most sympathetically. He submitted them, of course, to the Hungarian government, and received a thoughtful and encouraging answer from Kossuth, but only in 1850 when they were already comrades in exile.

The Bach administration, unlike most of its Habsburg predecessors, was centralized, which implied Germanization at the expense of all non-German ethnic groups; the *mot* went round that 'the Croats got for reward what the Hungarians got for punishment'. This played into the hands of federation-planners and other spokesmen for a *rapprochement* with the non-Magyars. Inside Hungary, it was mainly the doctrinaires, such as Eötvös and his friend Baron Zsigmond Kemény (1814–75), the essayist, novelist, and editor, who spoke up for the idea that a patriotic and liberal Hungarian should view the cultural awakening and emancipation among Romanians and Slavs with as much enthusiasm as he expected for his own. Kemény was possibly the most profound thinker in the Hungary of his time; the one who as a journalist, in and before 1848–49, agitated most consistently for doing away with remnants of feudalism in the constitution while trying to find a *modus vivendi* with the Habsburg power, and who later made his permanent mark on Hungarian literature particularly as a historical novelist. He had a tragic vision of life which made him a realist in forecasting the future but not, unfortunately, in the handling of people, whose sensibilities he often offended. In spite of his aristocratic title, he came from the impoverished gentry of Transylvania and had to work hard for a living—which was not made easier by his involved style and high standards of journalism. His awkward manners, alternately shy and explosive, also tended to estrange people; and it says much for the exceptional generosity of spirit and respect for intellectual abilities at that time that during the War for Freedom he was entrusted with running a paper considered to be the government's mouthpiece. He was moderate by intention but extreme in expression, a combination which led him into regrettable outbursts against the refugee Kossuth after the defeat; and it took some time to allay the suspicion with which gloomy patriots have subsequently viewed him.

Baron Eötvös, the former Minister of Education–later President of the Academy of Sciences–returned to Budapest from his self-imposed exile in Bavaria with sensible proposals which, however, smacked of capitulation and were therefore doomed. He was pre-pared to see Hungary enter the Reichsrat, or Austrian Imperial Parliament, instead of retaining or reviving her own Parliament, whose existence had been regarded by all Hungarian liberals, moderates and revolutionaries alike, as the symbol and safeguard of everything achieved in 1848. Deák, who was gradually to become the rallying-point of 'passive resistance' that typified the Hungarian atti-tude until the Compromise, was adamant on this point: Hungary must have her own legislature, she must be treated as a kingdom out-side the Austrian Empire, and her differences must be settled directly with the ruler, the king, and not with any of the provinces that were ruled by him as Emperor. Eötvös's idea was in essence more radical; he hoped for an alliance between the Hungarian and Austro-German liberals in the Reichsrat to check the authoritarian trends which were likely to get support both from the Court and from the less developed nationalities. Hungarians, however, could only see in Eötvös that he was more moderate than the moderates; and his personal character, noble-minded but defeatist, gave some colour to this oversimplifica-tion. Gradually he himself came round to endorsing Deák's attitude on the constitutional issue; while Deák accepted Eötvös's social and cultural views.

The Refugee Kossuth

On the radical wing it was from 1850 onwards the refugee Kossuth himself who led the scheming for a Danubian Federation or some-thing like it–an association of Hungary and her neighbours with the prime object of liberating them all from Habsburg and Romanov tyranny. Kossuth's exile lasted from 1849, when he took uneasy refuge on Turkish territory, until his death as 'the Turin hermit' in united Italy; in the course of so many years, even a mind less elastic and a character less adventurous than his might have been induced to modify his conceptions more than once. Yet his overriding idea remained constant: in his own legalistic wording, this was the refusal to accept 'the cumulation of the dignities of the Emperor of Austria and of the King of Hungary in one and the same person.'

At the beginning of his exile, he was a fugitive in Bulgaria and then an internee in Asia Minor; the Sultan, under pressure from Vienna and St Petersburg to extradite him, and from London, Paris, and Washington to resist such demands, kept him imprisoned until an American boat, sent by the Federal Government, took him on board. Kossuth boarded the American frigate *Mississippi* (a particularly beautiful and comfortable ship of its kind, as noted by chroniclers) in September 1851. He landed at Spezia for a short stay, changed boat at Gibraltar, and on board the liner *Madrid* – joined by his family – sailed for England. He landed at Southampton on 23 October and received a hero's welcome. Meanwhile, Louis Napoleon, though known to share in the sympathy for him, forbade him to cross French territory, fearing diplomatic complications; and in England the Foreign Secretary, Lord Palmerston, did wish to see Kossuth, at least 'in private' in his country mansion, but was prevented from doing so by the horror of Queen Victoria and Prince Albert who put pressure on the cabinet to foil the plan. Non-officially, however, Whigs and Tories and opposition Liberals or Radicals (Cobden, for example) vied with each other and with the Chartist workers in celebrating the champion of Hungarian and world liberty; and Kossuth was at pains to wash his hands of Chartist or socialist bedfellowships as he neither agreed with them nor found public association with them useful, but would not, in the meantime, wish to offend them. Kossuth's popularity was tremendous. Over and above his 1848–49 record, his oratory wrought miracles. In prison he had learned English from the Bible and Shakespeare; and when he proceeded to address his audiences in their own language, his archaic solemnity, combined with the then modern belief in civic liberties and with a dazzling alacrity in grasping the significance of daily events, made people think that a modernized Messiah had arrived from eastern Europe.

His reception in the United States, which he toured through the first half of 1852, was even more thunderous than in England; and, from the point of view of internal politics, even more complicated. Here, his most enthusiastic supporters were the right wing, the Democrats; and Kossuth got into difficulties with the Abolitionists who resented his rhetorical beating about the bush when he was asked to pronounce on slavery. World Freedom for Whites only? He never said so, but professed non-interference with domestic politics. Was he always so discreet? Far from it: in the interests of his East European Liberation campaign he would conspire freely with one faction against another – in the United States as well as in Britain and continental Europe. He came up against insurmountable obstacles when he tried to persuade the Americans to bury every hatchet except the one destined to decapitate the double-headed Austrian eagle. Yet, with his tactical skill and oratory, he managed at any rate to make an impact such as no foreigner since La Fayette had made on American public life. In New York, he negotiated deliveries of arms and steamships for the insurgents who were to attack the Habsburg army, and in Washington the two Houses of Congress officially celebrated his visit. He issued special 'Kossuth dollars' to finance his revolution. His financial venture ended in scandal and failure, but at the same time in an aura of legend; it was splendid to see the poor homeless patriot given even a chance to set it up.

Back in England, he carried on, with intervals only for his excursions to the continent, for about eight years. Though he praised the British for their love of freedom, he chided them for their tendency to compromise, and made no bones about its penalties: 'You failed', he told them in October 1853, 'to aid Hungary when the Tsar struck down her new Republic, and now you have to pay for it with your blood in streams and your money in millions'. The British audience responded generously to appeals for the Hungarian cause when it was a question of rescuing refugees from starvation (an effort in which Cobden excelled) or commemorating Shakespeare's having taught Kossuth English. As to foreign affairs, however, everybody with a say agreed that Britain must keep out of trouble. Palmerston believed in the Balance of Power, and Cobden in Peace; for one reason or another, neither wished to see his country involved in an armed conflict with Imperial Austria. The Palace was definitely pro-Habsburg; and a small fraction of opinion markedly hostile to Kossuth – mainly *The Times*, which has never since got over its irritability towards crusaders for uncomfortable truths. He was accused of amassing arms for his subversive purposes. 'Never in England', he answered; though admitting that he did so in other countries 'where it is not illegal'. There was a moment when, despite his popularity, he feared arrest: when he was found to have been involved in manufacturing rocket arms – a rather unorthodox idea in the 1850s. In 1861 he migrated to Turin; and though Cavour, in whom he vested most of his hopes, died not long after, he stayed there for the rest of his life.

The statesmen with whom he negotiated and plotted during his long exile, and particularly in its first decade, ranged from Napoleon III to the refugee Ledru-Rollin and the socialist Louis Blanc; from the princes of Serbia and Romania to republicans of all nationalities; from Alexander Herzen to the Poles; from Cavour to Garibaldi. His most congenial fellow-conspirator seems to have been Mazzini, despite their mutual distrust; Mazzini referred to him as a 'necessary evil', with gifts indispensable for fomenting a European revolution but dangerous if he got hold of the leadership. His ideas indeed were constantly evolving; thanks partly to his extraordinary quickness and elasticity of mind but also to his emotionalism and intoxication with success. His many schemes even included one to placate and neutralize the Romanovs. But the Habsburg dynasty remained for Kossuth what Carthage had been for Cato. In 1867, when the Austro-Hungarian Compromise was concluded, making Austria and Hungary at least nominally equal, Kossuth could have taken his seat in the Hungarian Parliament, but he scorned to do so; and perhaps he was right. At home, he would have had to choose between the postures of quixotic obduracy and wise opportunism: in Turin, he could preserve his own legend.

There was above all one ambiguity which was difficult enough to gloss over in his absence but would have made his position impossible if challenged on the spot. This was his attitude to the nationalities question. The Kossuth figure waving his plumed hat, in his braided *redingote*, whom Hungarians continued to cherish in their hearts even after loyally accepting Franz Joseph as their constitutional ruler in 1867, was also the chauvinist leader of 1848, the ardent Magyar-izer; whereas the man who, from London or Turin, engineered one plot after another to free them from the Habsburgs, made more far-reaching concessions to the Slavs and Romanians than any Hungarian politician would have considered in 1848. Thanks to the inconsistency of political passions, this contradiction could for a while pass unnoticed even by the conspirators who on Kossuth's instructions were preparing Hungary for a showdown with the Habsburgs; a gesture of friendship for Serbs or Wallachs seemed just a tactical move to them. But when, in 1862, Kossuth's plan for a Danubian Confederation was published–one in which Magyars figured as equals among equals–it was first received in Hungary with consternation; and subsequently ignored. Most of the pan-Magyars drew the conclusion that they had better take a more adaptable attitude towards the Emperor–a change for which the exhaustion of rebellious passions on the one hand and the fall of Bach and a more conciliatory policy from Vienna on the other, had already conditioned them–while the minority who remained adamant for 'Father Kossuth' and "48' succeeded in pushing the whole 'Danube rigmarole' deep into their subconscious. In patriotic, *bien-pensant* circles, Kossuth could be quoted on everything but that.

Deák; the Ausgleich of 1867

The thaw of Austrian absolutism started in 1859 when, under the blows suffered from French and Italian forces, Imperial Austria gave up Lombardy and canvassed support from her subject Hungarians; and the Prussian victory over Austria in 1866 brought this process to a head. Besides, traditionalists in both the Austrian *Länder* and in Hungary disliked the bureaucratic despotism of Bach as much as the liberals and democrats did; it was all very well for 'restoring order' after 1848–49, but once this was achieved they made no objection to the pressure for a looser system. The result was the Compromise (*Ausgleich*) of 1867: a motley edifice of conservative and liberal features, of acquiescence in ancient prerogatives, and of insistence on personal and constitutional freedom. It established the Dual Monarchy which was to last until the end of the First World War. Hungary under that agreement re-emerged as a 'glorified colony', since her industry could not hope to compete with that of the Austro-Germans and Czechs; but in legislation and administration she emerged more independent of their common ruler than did her senior partner, Austria. And with this went a supremacy of the Magyar ruling classes over their own non-Magyar nationalities more blatant than was that of the Austro-Germans over theirs; because the non-German *Länder* such as Bohemia, Galicia, Dalmatia, etc., could run their local affairs in their own language and according to their own customs, but in Hungary the state was regarded as Magyar throughout, and so even more were the local governments in the cities and counties, except in Croatia which obtained a far-reaching autonomy. The schemes for transforming Hungary into a free association of nationalities, put forward simultaneously by moderates like Eötvös and radicals like Kossuth, were thus abandoned and practically buried for decades to come. They had contained sound ideas but were doomed to failure by the spirit that distorted them from the outset: the spirit of capitulation in Eötvös; and of an all-pervading hatred of the Habsburgs which grew into an obsession with Kossuth. And László Teleki had killed himself in 1861.

The man mainly responsible for putting forward the alternative of 'dualism', and getting Franz Joseph ultimately to accept it, was Ferenc Deák, known to history as The Wise Man of the Country. In spite of this label, it has since become fashionable to blame him for proceeding 'shortsightedly'; but really he did the best that could be done in the circumstances, and had his successors followed his example in manipulating the levers of the semi-independent Hungarian kingdom, they might well have averted the catastrophes which followed.

At that moment the Hungarian upper-middle nobility, for which the Compromise secured a key position in the Dual Monarchy, was still the most legally-minded and liberally-minded community among the peoples under Habsburg rule and general progress could have made a promising start under its guidance. The first administration in Hungary after the Compromise equalled in its intellectual range any Whig administration in Britain. Deák himself declined office, and the premiership fell to one who had been his right-hand man in the preliminary negotiations, Count Gyula Andrássy (1823–90). Andrássy was an ebullient and robust *grand seigneur*, a rebel in

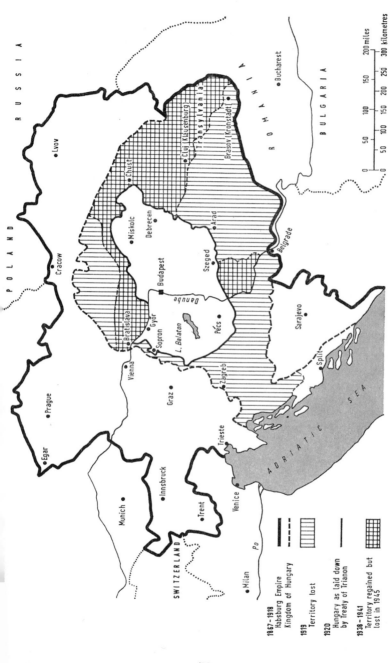

1. Hungary 1867–1945

1867–1918
Habsburg Empire
Kingdom of Hungary

1919
Territory lost

1920
Hungary as laid down
by Treaty of Trianon

1938–1941
Territory regained but
lost in 1945

his own aristocratic way since early youth. Kossuth had sent him on a diplomatic mission to Turkey; and for continuing to serve Kossuth after the dethronement, during the reaction, he was sentenced to be hanged *in absentia*; he became known in Paris, to which he managed to shift his base, as *le beau pendu*; but after the thaw, he was able to return unmolested to Hungary, where his diplomatic skill did much to win over the dynasty, and not least the beautiful Empress Elisabeth, for the Hungarian cause. He was no doctrinaire; not even a good speller; but his dislike of bigotry and servility was genuine, and in the cabinet he had an admirable foil in the highly erudite Baron Eötvös, who acted as his deputy, besides holding–as under Batthyány–the portfolio of Religion and Education.

As Andrássy himself had specialized in diplomacy (he was later to take over the Foreign Ministry of the Dual Monarchy in Vienna), the bill under his premiership which regulated the position of nationalities in Hungary, and was passed by Parliament in 1868, was the work of Deák and Eötvös. This was a perfectly liberal law; it granted to the national minorities every right they had ever claimed or could have claimed–short of turning Hungary into a federation. All nationalities, under this law, were entitled to the greatest freedom compatible with a unitary state. There were only two snags to it: one, that the minorities, once they became politically conscious, did not wish to live in a unitary state unless they themselves were the ruling nation within it; and the other, that the law was not implemented or not consistently. Deák trusted to the mellowing effects of time: if, on the basis of mutual tolerance, all nationalities got used to considering themselves equals within the state, it would be only natural for them to concede that the state itself should acquire the character of the largest nationality, the Magyars, whose number practically equalled the total of the rest. He went out of his way to make the Nationalities Law work properly; his intervention in favour of subsidizing a Serb National Theatre in the Voivodina district on the same basis as the Magyar National Theatre was typical of his attitude. Whether such a careful observance of cultural equality could in the end have won non-Magyar hearts for their common fatherland, Hungary, is anybody's guess. Nationalism was rampant, and the competing irredentist ideas were to absorb patriotic passions everywhere, with sordid and tragic consequences. These might or might not have been averted even if Deák's method had been consistently applied. But when he and his coevals–the rearguard of the 'Reform Generation' of the 1830s–faded into the background, the new vintage of noblemen in power made a patriotic virtue of getting round the Nationalities Law. The watershed year seems, in retrospect, to have been 1875, when the premiership was taken over–to be held for some fifteen years–by the leader of the Calvinist gentry of eastern Hungary Kálmán (Coloman) Tisza (1830–1902).

Tisza up till then had been known both as a more radical liberal and as a more aggressive defender of Hungarian independence than Deák and Deák's party; he had even shown some of the refugee Kossuth's federalist tendency. So the merger of the Deák and Tisza parties in a united Liberal Party appeared to be a leftward extension of the ruling policy; but, once in power, Tisza forgot his 'leftism' and proceeded more ruthlessly than anyone before him to streamline Hungary in the interests of the Magyar *junker*. Tisza was often and violently attacked as a turncoat during his premiership, and posterity has been no kinder to him either, but the thing which his countrymen at that time resented least was precisely his chauvinism. This was such a general feeling that until the emergence of a new Reform Generation hardly anybody opposed it; the government party, forgetful of the national tolerance urged by Deák and Eötvös, was even outdone in its pan-Magyarism by an opposition that paid lip-service to 'Father Kossuth' while suppressing any memory of his federalism. After a while it became a ministerial habit to admit quite freely that 'of course the 1868 Nationalities Law can't be observed'.

Thus after 1849 the Hungarians became aware of their interdependence with Romanians and all sorts of Slav nationalities–not to speak of German minorities–in the Danube basin; but at the same time developed a mechanism for ignoring their own awareness and the very fact of life which their eyes had been opened to. It was this double-thinking that inevitably pushed them towards a schizophrenic state of mind.

Chapter 4

From the *Ausgleich* to the
Millennium

Liberalism and its Limitations

HUNGARY IN THE DUAL MONARCHY was a Liberal country, very much with a capital L. The Liberal Party held power more often than not, and its opponents were even more vigorously committed to liberal policies. All factions were liberal in theory and accused one another of being so in theory only. And all were right. With a past and in a position such as Hungary's, both the worship of liberalism and its dilution seemed unavoidable. Parliamentary government, religious tolerance, free speech, free Press, freedom of trades and professions, freedom from arbitrary powers, equality before the law were the ideas for which Hungarians had taken up arms and earned the admiration of the world in 1848; and it was this moral capital which could have been converted into practical success in 1867. Hungary owed her renown to liberalism; any alternative to liberalism would have struck her as a gesture of national suicide. But to apply liberal principles honestly and in every field of activity would have seemed equally suicidal. How could non-Magyars be trusted to support a unitary Hungarian state unless paternally guided by Hungarian landlords, clergymen, bureaucrats? Moreover, how could even the illiterate Magyar paupers of the land be trusted to run their own affairs if suddenly given access to those levers of power which had always been the monopoly of the privileged? Liberalism, as we know it—and even more, as *they* knew it, in the nineteenth century, and not in Hungary alone—was the political projection of a large middle class; in the interplay of forces released by it, every social layer could have its own say, from the aristocracy to the labourers, but the catalyst of all their ideas was a class of people prosperous enough to have a stake in the existing order while not dependent on the prerogatives inherited from a feudal or absolutist past. This layer of society, the Third Estate in France, the 'middle class' in Britain, hardly existed in Hungary; that is why, ever since the mid-1820s, the liberal reformers felt it their main business to make good the deficiency by remoulding the masses of proletarian

76

gentry into well-to-do traders. Very little of this had been achieved by the 1870s when Liberalism was adopted as the guiding light in public affairs.

Feudal Power Re-emerges

Kálmán Tisza's remedy for social disorders was to maintain paternalistic, verging on feudal, rule over the rural areas whilst allowing the cities to glut themselves on *laissez-faire*. The machinery of control was provided jointly by the revived county administration and the Imperial forces; although there never was complete harmony between the Court of Vienna and the Magyar gentry–Tisza himself setting the tone for sulky complaints–they knew that at decisive moments they could count on each other. Severely limited suffrage and open voting were not peculiar to Hungary when the régime started; but as a preliminary to Tisza's taking control, the property qualifications for voters were raised still further to reduce the electorate (to less than 6 per cent of the population); and while 'rotten borough' constituencies were freely created, the pressure brought to bear on voters became so harsh that anyone opposed to the Establishment had less chance of getting a seat in Parliament than ever since the collapse of absolutism some fifteen years before. This was true of both local and national government. One may add, to underline the anti-democratic character of the system, that of the two Houses of Parliament, only the House of Deputies was technically elected, while the Upper House consisted mainly of hereditary magnates plus church and other dignitaries; and that in local councils the aldermen's seats were reserved for the highest taxpayers, i.e. the wealthiest citizens. But such openly aristocratic or plutocratic conditioning of the 'people's will' was really less tyrannical than its perversion by officers of the law. The symbol and safeguard of order and of the feudalistic hierarchy preserved in the counties was the pandoor, or gendarme (inherited from the autocratic Habsburg army, disbanded with the beginning of the Liberal era in 1867, but re-established under Kálmán Tisza in the 1880s), to whom the policing of rural areas was entrusted. The pandoor force, unlike the police proper established in cities, was a part of the army although put at the disposal of the county magistrates; in it the brutality of an alien Imperial power merged with the parochial despotism of the petty squire. The pandoors' very appearance was–or seemed to the common people–alarmingly strange. From 1867 onwards, government and local government agents were required to emphasize both in dress and behaviour their ties with the nostalgically romanticized Hungarian past. On festive occasions not only the magnates but high officials of the counties appeared in what was known as 'Hungarian gala dress'—glittering jackboots, braided and fur-lined dolman, and heavily ornamented, curved sword, recalling Turkish and Persian accoutrements; the coachmen, valets, doormen, commissionaires, etc., cash permitting, were liveried in the same style. Not so the pandoors. Their puritanical dark uniform, with a cock's feather on the shako as their sole ornament, was, when revived, taken over intact from the Imperial forces of the hated Bach Period; and their stern figures became as familiar features of the Hungarian countryside as the shadoof and the herds of curly-haired black pigs. They roamed the villages and fields, usually in pairs, the sergeant on foot ahead of the lance-corporal, but usually both on horseback, and always with bayoneted rifle on shoulder, ready to hit or stab or shoot as required. They put the fear of God into the peasants. The gendarmerie were more systematic and efficient at spreading fear than befitted the image either of a *gemütlich* Austria, with her authoritarianism humanized by easy-goingness and love of music, or of a liberal and legally-minded Hungary; but there they were, to symbolize the rule of the privileged over the rest. The privileged were by no means homogeneous, either socially or financially or in their ideas; but the pandoor's bayonet defended what they had in common.

The Aristocracy and its Entailed Land

Thanks to this power structure, the pattern of rural Hungary re-emerged as something very like what it had been before the abolition of the Estates system. Then, the privileged had been the magnates and the lesser nobility: now, they were the magnates and a more amorphous but no less privilege-bound layer of society, the offspring of the diluted lesser nobility, usually defined in Hungary by the English word 'gentry'. Basically the division of power between these two revitalized Estates consisted in this: that the magnates (together with a few princes of the Church) held the *latifundia* and went on increasing their landed properties right down to the end of the Dual Monarchy; while the gentry, through their monopoly of government and county offices and (in partnership with the Austrian officers' caste) of posts in the army, emerged during the 1870s as political masters of the country. Wealth, influence, and social distinction, though interlocked, were less integrated than might seem.

As the nature of these two privileged classes had a formative effect on Hungarians right up to the present day, it may be worth glancing at their anatomy. A 'magnate' or an 'aristocrat' was technically anyone holding the title of baron, count, or prince; which included all members of their families, as in Hungary the titles of both upper and lower nobility applied to all scions of the male holder (with the sole exception of the princes, altogether three in the

Hungarian aristocracy,[1] who each headed a family of counts and countesses). But the 'real' magnates, or 'aulic aristocracy', as they were often called, comprised only the upper crust of this conglomerate; they included the largest landowners, based mainly in western and northern Hungary, and were to a man Roman Catholics. The Transylvanian landowning aristocracy who were to a large extent Protestant (the Counts Teleki, for instance, had a Catholic and a Calvinist branch) ranked lower; the aristocracy rooted in the army and the state administration, though almost exclusively Catholic (for example, Eötvös), lower still; while a penniless baron belonged at best to the gentry. A special case was that of the Jewish or ex-Jewish barons who, though some of them were big landowners as well as big industrialists, counted (with the possible exception of the Wodianer family) as glorified bourgeois rather than 'magnates'.

In their efforts to retain and even extend their hold on the land, the magnates–the 'real' ones–were helped both by the vestiges of feudal tradition and by their own share in private enterprise. Entailed big estates went on existing, and in fact their number trebled from 1867 until 1918; so that, if one includes equally inalienable church properties, by the end of the Dual Monarchy more than one-third of the land was entailed. The landowning magnates, except when temporarily crippled by gambling debts, had money over for capital investment and their names were welcome on the managerial boards of limited companies. Through these channels, though no banking or merchant magnate was ever visible, free trade helped to reinforce their feudalistic monopoly of the land.

The way of life and social standing of the magnates developed accordingly. They were the absolute lords of their immense estates, residing, when not abroad, in huge *châteaux*; some could hardly remember how many manor houses they had, in addition to a palace in Buda or Pest. They lived not so much at the top of society as above it, more like maharajas than lords, though very much enamoured of Western ways–notably Schönbrunn, Ascot, or the Moulin Rouge– once they crossed the frontier. They were in process of becoming as estranged from their country as they had been in the eighteenth century, though for different reasons: with the cities developing their own bourgeois life, and political power slipping into the hands of the gentry, most of the magnates contented themselves with the pleasures

[1] Esterházy, Festetics, Pálffy; and a special near-princely status was granted to the Counts Károlyi who, in memory of their ancestor 'almost' created prince in the early eighteenth century, sported an eleven-pronged coronet over their crest instead of the nine-pronged one usual with counts' families. There were also a few Habsburg archdukes resident in Hungary (in precedence, of course, ahead of the Hungarians) and the offspring of expatriate foreign aristocrats (Prince Windisch-Graetz, Marquis (Őrgróf) Pallavicini, etc.; also, in lower ranks, 'knights') whose titles were subject to different rules.

of their lofty station, hunting, riding, giving balls, gambling, saluting the monarch, praying to God. The National Casino, Széchenyi's foundation, became their exclusive club, famous alike for its baccarat and its political intrigues; for, though most members took no interest in public life so long as the interests of their caste seemed secure, a few took to it all the more passionately and were to play most adventurous and decisive parts on the political scene. Their withdrawal from the intellectual life of the country, however, seemed total; at one time the chief patrons of Hungarian arts and letters, by the end of the nineteenth century they had lost absolutely all interest in them. The aristocracy, as everywhere in the world, included both empty-headed dandies and highly polished minds, but practically no readers of Hungarian literature. Some were well-versed in philosophical trends of German-speaking Central Europe and of the West but hardly noticed those in their own country; which did not prevent them from being, passionately and quite sincerely, Hungarian nationalists.

The Gentry and its Entailed Offices

The gentry had grown out of the landowning lesser nobility which was largely dispossessed as a direct result of the liberal reforms in land tenure and taxation promulgated by Kossuth and implemented by Bach. Owing to their lack of mental and capital equipment for competition in a free market economy, the process of their impoverishment continued after Bach's fall and throughout the period of the Dual Monarchy; by the 1910s, a well-off individual amongst the landed gentry could almost certainly be assumed to have had his family tree strengthened by rich upstarts. Nonetheless, the number of people qualifying as 'gentry' increased all the time. The attraction of a nobleman's standing did not diminish with his estate; and the blurring of the frontier between 'noble' and 'ignoble' made infiltration easier. The proletariat of the nobility, the 'moccasined' squireens and the 'armalists', either sank without trace into pauperdom or, if they managed to keep afloat, emerged as 'gentry', expecting to be compensated with social advantages for what they had lost in legal rights; a fraction managed thus to climb into the 'black-coated' ranks. More important, there were the Magyarized sons of the ancient guild burghers, mostly of 'Swabian' stock but including many also of Saxon, Romanian, Serb, Croat, Slovak, Ruthene, Greek, Armenian, Vend, and Italian origin. The liberal reformers had looked forward to their Magyarization as the basis for a Western-style Hungarian middle class; but it did not work out like that. Once they were Magyar, they felt like squires and outdid the original squires in their arrogance and mode of life. The same thing happened with the sons of the richest peasant farmers – 'pasha-peasants', as

they were called, the word 'kulak' not having been imported yet—
who were brought up as 'gentlemen'; there were quite a few of them
in Hungary, with their vast farms scattered about the Great Plain,
east and west of the river Tisza; but not enough to develop a farmer
middle class. In the large market town of Kecskemét, for instance,
they could be seen talking business and smoking their pipes on the
highway, in their braided grey suits with heavy silver buttons, and
their special kind of small bowler hats; they were the patriarchal
heads of their farmhands and small tenants rather than employers
and landlords so long as their 'pasha-peasant' status lasted; after
that, they became indistinguishable from the noblemen's families
into which they married so as to 'gild their coats-of-arms', i.e. to save
their in-laws' estates from the auctioneer's hammer.

The great problem, however, was how those whose land could not
be saved were to make a living. In trade they failed, partly from
inexperience and partly because, even though poor and used to
physical exertion, the ordinary artisan's or merchant's life involved
risks and services which they flinched from undertaking; one of the
gentry could not, after all, wait on customers in a haberdasher's
shop! The professions were not beneath their dignity, but, unless
attached to some official institution, required the competitive spirit
of a trader with more than a trader's learning; so these, too, were
unattainable for most of them. There remained only one refuge for
the dispossessed: the administrative network of national and local
government and the army. For these, Hungary needed a tremendous
staff; and if she did not she could at least pretend to. Half the country
consisted of 'nationalities' to be kept in check. To pay a host of
reliable, Magyar, gentlemanly county magistrates to control them,
so the argument ran, was a modest price for the national interest.
The problem of multi-nationalities was also a godsend: it excused the
proliferation of sinecures. In fact, the Magyar districts were often
more unruly and needed more administrative repression than the
nationalities districts. The period preceding Kálmán Tisza's coming
to power was a case in point. The frustration of dispossessed landowners and those struggling with debts was matched by the frustration of Magyar peasants who felt let down by the régime because
they had failed to obtain land or been left without the minimum of
capital they needed; in addition, a slump in agricultural products
upset all the calculations of peasant and gentleman farmers alike.
This caused a reaction in Magyar constituencies against the ruling
Deák party and towards either the refugee Kossuth or (which was the
lesser evil from the government's point of view) the 'Left-Centre' led
by Tisza. The Deák party were known as the "67-ers' and the opposition parties which were winning ground as the "48-ers'; and there

was no doubt that while the Magyar districts were mesmerized by "48', the nationalities, if only for lack of commitment, were ready to side with "67' in exchange for minor favours such as railway stations and roads through their boroughs. Kálmán Tisza, when transformed from a "48-er' opposition leader into a "67-er' premier, made ample use of the possibilities offered to him by these needs. He cajoled, bribed, and terrorized the gentry into his camp–and, together with the gentry, the rest of the 'black-coated' population and the rich peasants: in short, the voters.

Professor Parkinson would have watched with delight how he created jobs that created further jobs. Government and municipal administration was enormously inflated, officials in the administrative branch needed others in the clerical branch to assist them, and the whole set-up needed commissionaires, coachmen, charwomen. The administrative branch was reserved for the gentry. 'Armalists' and other strata on the threshold of gentlemanliness took their ease while plebeians toiled in the clerical jobs. For the farmhand's or petty farmer's son, it was a privilege to slip into the state or county commissionaire's uniform: it implied security, pension rights, favours, social standing, established links with authority and the squires. Charwomen were no officials, but in poverty-stricken districts the grant of even such a job could be used as a bribe. From the highest to the lowest, a solid pyramid of state and municipal employees was built up (cemented in rural districts by the gendarmerie and in larger towns and cities by the milder police force) which was powerful enough to see that feudal dues were in effect perpetuated under Liberalism. The magnates held their entailed properties: the gentry held their entailed jobs.

Through whatever changes came about in the social structure of Hungary, and irrespective of the party or parties in office, this arrangement continued until the end of the Dual Monarchy–and after. In the early twentieth century, the lesser nobility was already so adulterated that it took an expert genealogist to distinguish a 'genuine' nobleman from a parvenu or an impostor; but the social phenomenon known as the gentry held on to its official entrenched positions all the more firmly, and with an increasing number of caste rituals to distinguish it from the masses. As in every caste, there were sub-castes within the gentry, and differences in the degree of exclusiveness existed between one service and another; the county being more exclusive than the town hall, the Ministry of Agriculture more exclusive than that of Commerce, hussar regiments more exclusive than infantry; but everywhere the principle prevailed that the civil servant and the military officer were as much masters by virtue of their jobs as the landowner was by virtue of his estate. The salaries paid to the gentry were like the contribution previously owed by the serfs to their landlords, with the merely technical difference that the Exchequer now intervened to guarantee the payment. Even the *corvée* survived to some extent since it was rather risky for a labourer to refuse a county magistrate's request to clear his backyard or saw up some trunks in his spare time. The magistrate might then offer him a glass of wine and present him with a slightly worn pair of boots; just as his ancestor might have done a hundred years before, in the heyday of feudal domination.

The Intellectual Decadence of the Nobility

The rituals and pastimes of the gentry are difficult to record without a smile, although they had undeniably a tremendous fascination not only for the parvenus and the masses but also for many of the aulic magnates and quite sophisticated Western visitors to Hungary. Hungarians were supposed to be a 'nation of horsemen'; by the twentieth century, however, only the splendid national studs remained as evidence of Hungary's special relation with that noble animal, and, apart from village lads on their workaday mounts, only the rich could afford to ride—a smaller percentage than in England, for instance. Yet, in Hungarian minds the horseman persisted as a national type and the hussar as the most typical of Hungarian warriors. For the latter there was some historical justification: the very word *hussar* is one of the few international expressions of Magyar origin, and the light cavalry (overdressed, as in olden times proud soldiers always used to be) does seem to have been a genuine Hungarian contribution to Europe's military practice.

Another persistent gentry-symbol was the sword. Except with gala dress (which few could afford) hardly anybody wore it, but, though straightened and stripped of its heavy ornaments, it still had its uses in the fencing school, and for two purposes: sport and duelling. Neither of course was confined to Hungary; no one outdid the German *Burschenschaften* until the mid-1930s at collecting sabre scars on their faces, and even after the Second World War duels were occasionally fought in Europe (Italy, for instance). The 'code of honour' attached to duelling came from the West—yet Hungarian society, with its tone set by the gentry, went on duelling longer than any comparably civilized national community. To fight a duel was punishable under law—by short-term confinement to special places where the gaolers behaved like butlers—but to ignore the 'code' and fail to seek 'satisfaction' for an insult was to invite ostracism. Accordingly, 'affairs of honour' became an exacting social activity; and the quartet of 'seconds', solemnly preoccupied with drafting 'protocol' round a table at the inn, was a familiar scene. Hungarians excelled in sword-fencing as a sport–for instance, at the Olympic Games–and were convinced of an affinity between their prowess at the sport and their cultivation of 'affairs of honour'; although some of the Olympic fencing champions, far from being gentry, were Jews–as indeed were not a few of the most glamorous duellists. The gentry's concept of dashing behaviour had something very old-fashioned and parochial about it which did not, however, make it any less attractive; some Westerners loved it as an outlet for swashbuckling instincts suppressed or disguised in their own lives where middle-class respectability had supplanted the nobleman's panache.

Thus the more obsolete the pre-1867 forms of paternalism became, the more new distinguishing marks of 'gentlemanliness' were created. The gentry had a special way of shaking hands, with the forearm stretched parallel with the chest, and their ways of addressing one another degenerated into an orgy of involved formulae, capable of combining ceremoniousness with intimacy. No accurate chronicle of Hungarian society from the beginning of the nineteenth century to the present time can afford to overlook the intricacies of the use of the second person pronoun. There had never been a Magyar equivalent of *you*; one addressed one's neighbour either simply as *te*–'tu', 'thou', 'toi', 'du'–or in a variety of indirect ways, ranging from, say, 'thy excellency' (or in rustic parlance 'thi'xlency') to 'His Lordship' or 'Her Ladyship'. Széchenyi, wishing to establish the basis for civilized conversation, racked his brains to make up for this deficiency; and he devised as a substitute 'you' the word *ön*, derived from a root standing in Magyar for 'self'. This was a success inasmuch as it caught on; in business life it is still used even today; but it was the opposite of a success inasmuch as it only increased the number of second person pronouns, and complicated rather than simplified the problems involved. Who should *tutoyer* whom was a question that deeply affected the self-respect of plebeians just discovering their human dignity; among the demands put forward by shop and workshop assistants in the turmoil of 1848, 'the ending of *tutoiement*' was the most frequent, and by that they of course meant unilateral *tutoiement*. But, since Széchenyi's 'ön' seemed too stilted and official for general use, what should now be the Magyar *you*? In the heat of the War for Freedom, 1848–49, Hungarians found the time and energy to consider this. Táncsics, the socialist deputy, suggested that everyone should use the peasant-like *kend*–the form I was trying to evoke by 'thi'xlency'–but this idea was at once killed by ridicule. And the problem survived, though in modified forms. By the turn of the century, varieties of usage had developed according to which, for example, a cabinet minister was expected to *tutoyer* all his staff in the administrative (as distinct from the clerical) branch–an honour which was to be acknowledged by reciprocating half-way, for example with 'Thy Excellency', or 'Thou, Mr Excellency', according to the age and rank of the official. Social as well as office life was permeated by such problems. To the cry of workmen and labourers 'stop calling us thou!' was added the complaint of the cold-shouldered middle-class man: 'Why did he not call me thou?' An avalanche of 'affairs of honour' originated in humiliations like this; and a nightmare of social traumas and neuroses.

The Hungarian way of 'amusing oneself' or revelling – *mulatni* is the Magyar verb for it – did not originally differ very much from that of other comparable countries, mainly Russia and Poland perhaps, with landowners and officers excelling in uproarious practical jokes, and *muzhika* drowning themselves in the oblivion of whatever cheap alcohol they could get hold of. Yet the way that 'amusement' developed, especially among the gentry, deserves special attention for its importance in social and cultural history. The gypsy fiddler had become by the middle of the nineteenth century, if not earlier, an indispensable partner of the Hungarian bending over his wine and shouting, singing, and breaking the glass 'in joy and despair'. To have just one fiddler to 'play in your ear' was good enough but better still to have a band – at least five players, if complete: first fiddle, second fiddle, viola, double-bass, dulcimer – in which case the 'playing in the ear' was the privilege, and duty, of the first fiddler while the rest had to know how to accompany him. How much of those fiery rhythms and gloomy waves of sound were old Ugrian, how much came from or was modified by Slav and Romanian neighbours, and how much by gypsy influence? How much, moreover, came from even further afield – from Turkey and Persia? Whatever the present-day musicologist may think, it struck both Brahms and Liszt as *the* Hungarian song, and resounded as such in their compositions, to the applause of innumerable Western and Middle European concert halls. The most glamorous of the gypsy band-leaders, moreover, added to the glory of their native country by playing in Hungarian gala dress (which they had never worn in Hungary) in the smartest cafés and restaurants of Paris, Berlin, St Petersburg, and occasionally hit the headlines by eloping with a duchess. The Magyar shepherds and peasants whose 'joy and despair' figured as the emotional background of those songs, had little to gain from this triumph, and the songs themselves, particularly those which became most popular towards the turn of the century and after, were mostly composed in Budapest, by people who had hardly ever seen the *puszta* or the stud-farms of their fantasies. The whole art became more and more folksy, bogus, and sentimental; but the real shepherds and peasants who got that fancy picture of themselves through army life or by watching the 'amusements' of commercial salesmen and gentry were even more impressed than the educated or semi-educated townspeople who devised it. Gypsy music was universally adored in Hungary by rich and poor alike; only the tiny minorities of rigorous academic scholars and cosmopolitan modern artists denounced it as pseudo, but even they were swept into its mood after a bottle or two.

There was really nothing wrong with it except its negative aspect: by the turn of the century, the bogus folksong delivered in the coquettish and yearning style of a humble fiddler 'playing in the ear' was practically the only intellectual pleasure of the political ruling class of Hungary, the gentry. During the thirty or forty years that followed the Compromise, that layer of society had simply turned into a mass of bureaucratic parasites, with nothing more to say about the problems and sensations of changing times than could be expressed by a stiff upper lip, and occasional explosions of self-pity for which the gypsy fiddle provided an ideal accompaniment. It was a sad spectacle which can only be explained by the effects on character of the postures evolved in social conflict. In the 1830s, with hopes rising for a prosperous and educated, Liberal Hungary, the lesser or middle nobility developed a large intellectual élite, second to none in social and poetic sensibility. In 1848–49, this same class showed a moral fibre and imaginativeness that staggered the world. But once the fighting spirit was exhausted, and the sinecures accepted in compensation for the lost estates, the main concern of the gentry became to blind themselves both to their own situations and to the world outside their own caste and country. In politics, there were still some fields which offered the sensation of free opinion and party struggle. When one pillar of the Establishment was opposed to another – laity versus Church, or the county hall versus the aristocratic manor house, or the parochial chauvinism of county squires against the garrison housing officers of the Imperial and Royal Army, and so forth – even the common people had a chance of expressing their views; constituencies then seemed to be in a turmoil, and the traditional Hungarian art of legalistic rhetoric, though naturally debased by the needs of the soap-box, found many opportunities of proving its vitality. But there was an abhorrence of everything 'un-national'; and this included not only the bedevilled nationalities question but the facts of social and economic life as a whole. It also included, through a chain reaction of inhibitions, the new trends in arts, scholarship, science. To use one's brain became unworthy of a Hungarian gentleman.

Cultures often bloom most perfectly in their Indian summer. This happened to a circle of Hungarian writers known as 'the literary Deák party', who were allowed to run the Hungarian Academy of

Sciences, with the poet János Arany (1817–82) as its Secretary-General. Arany was a superb poet, whose magic it is impossible for anyone without a fair knowledge of the Hungarian language to appreciate, because of his subtle and complicated use of syntax, rhythm, and shades of meaning. He had something in common with Tennyson, but his style was denser and heavier than Tennyson's; and if Tennyson can be called a middle-class man risen to the peerage and the Laureateship, Arany came of a yeomanry with dubious claims to nobility and rose through assiduous study, thrift, and hard work into the professional classes. In the social setting of the 1860s and after, he represented the soundness and moderation of the Magyar peasant farmer. He was shy, diffident, industrious, and sufficiently afraid of penury to play this part. But neurotic depressions and anxiety co-existed with his down-to-earth qualities, and largely account for his flight into epic fantasy. He was very much attracted by Scottish folk ballads, with their laconic eloquence, their mixture of rough nature and dreamlike imagination.

Politically, before the War for Freedom, he started as a middle-of-the-roader; but by the time war came he had already turned radical. This was largely due to the influence of Petőfi, who, from the literary capital in Pest, showed rapturous enthusiasm for Arany's epic poems and very soon became his close friend. But with the war over, and Petőfi among its victims, Arany withdrew into his shell and, so far as we know, lived night and day with only one emotion: fear. As he got over it, he continued his epics about the Hun and Hungarian warriors of the Middle Ages. Parts of these versified sagas are masterly: when, for instance, two rival Hun queens quarrel lustily about their marital sex life. Puritanical in his own life and given to lofty poetic ideals, he was nevertheless at his best when he indulged the ribald peasant lad in him.

After a while he found his voice about contemporary problems as well. His main feeling was bitterness. And he vented it no less about the heroic blunders of which he felt his own countrymen had been guilty than, censorship permitting, about foreign rule and Reaction. He wrote a satirical epic about the revolt and route of a 'gypsy' tribe–with unmistakable allusions, particularly in the head of the tribe who personified Kossuth. Not surprisingly, this left many scars– mainly in his own heart. Later, in a semi-autobiographical poem, he compared himself in Byronic verses to 'the farmer who saw his young trees stricken by frost, took a club, and beat down all the rest of them, shouting "Lord, let's see what we can do between us!"'

Meanwhile, he reasserted his faith in the oppressed cause of Hungarian liberty and most spectacularly in a ballad commemorating the Welsh Bards who, so the story went, were beheaded by Edward I for refusing to sing to his glory. This was timed (in 1856) for the occasion of Franz Joseph's visit to Budapest when Arany and other poets were invited to greet the not yet constitutional monarch and his spouse with an ode. After the Compromise of 1867, however, Arany turned rather conservative; the sight of 'grocers and drunken peasants' thronging to the polls and youth 'wanting freedom without order' rather disgusted him. Yet his standards of conservatism kept him in the same humane tradition, opposed to all sorts of oppression and intolerance. With his passing, and that of his entourage, a new vintage of national traditionalists took over in poetry just as in politics: more modern on the face of it, but more intolerant, more class-ridden and biased when it came to the test. The Academy, and intellectual officialdom in general, became a conglomerate of Arany-worshippers who did not really understand what they were worshipping, and devotees of the gentry-gypsy type of nationalism. 1896, the millennium of the Hungarian conquest of the mid-Danube basin, was celebrated in a nationwide state of euphoria: Hungary at last ruled the waves of nationalities, hers was a Land of Hope and Glory. That moment marked the lowest ebb of her intellectual reserves; it was a world of mental hollowness. This millennium was followed by two decades of disillusionment, awakening, rejuvenation, and un-paralleled intellectual creativeness – but despite the leanings of the political ruling class, the gentry, and not in harmony with them.

Lights in the Shade

This being said, it is only fair to point out that that culprit of recent Hungarian history, the gentry class, was on the whole far from being either wicked or boorish and had tremendous charm, often combined with gentleness and chivalry, which understandably captivated those who came in contact with it. Though in a debased form, its ancient elegance of mind survived. Living in a world of make-believe, it was bound to cut a poor figure at the moments when sense had to be talked; but there were, after all, specific terrains for daydreams. The greatest of Hungarian professional daydreamers, the colourful and prolific novelist Mór (Maurus) Jókai (1825–1904), carried the liberal and romantic heritage of his youth into the indus-trial age where it sounded like fairy tales but sold all the better for that. In his art, he was reminiscent of Dumas *père* with touches of Victor Hugo and Dickens; he had started as Petőfi's friend and comrade, at the head of the March Youth in 1848, and ended after 1875 as the Grand Old Man of Hungarian literature in the Tisza era – not thereby betraying anything, but simply going on shaping a people's daydreams into novels. The case of his disciple, Kálmán Mikszáth (1847–1910), was even more typical. Mikszáth was an

excellent author, anecdotal, mischievous, no less readable for being
more down-to-earth than his master, as befitted an age verging more
on realism. Although elected to Parliament as a supporter of Tisza's
policy, his main activity in the House was collecting material for
sketches in which he took off members of the government and opposition alike with endearing humour. Though clever, as a rule, in avoiding pitfalls, some of his novels, by their outspokenness about the
Catholic Church or the morality of a dowry-hunting hussar officer,
alarmed the *bien-pensants*, but he did not labour his points. The public
saw him always as a clubman, stretched at portly ease with a pipe
longer than himself—which indeed remained his lifelong attitude.
One of his stories is a tongue-in-cheek eulogy of 'the fine old county
of Sáros' and bears the stylish title, 'The Gentry'. Indeed, Sáros, in
the hilly north-east of the Hungary of those days, had a particularly
large percentage of noblemen and was, as Mikszáth put it, 'the
county of good manners and—*hallucinations.*' He describes a luxuri-
ous, pageant-like wedding feast. The guests arrive in four-in-hands,
and join enthusiastically in effusions about each other's family
estates, about the princely dowry and wedding gifts, and the special
vintage wines served to each according to his age; though every one
of them knows it is all poppycock, that the beautifully bottled liquid
is *vin ordinaire*, the four-in-hands are borrowed, and the participants
posing as generous maharajas into the small hours are in fact penurious county officials who will spend the following day behind shabby
desks, dreaming up their next lordly feast. It sounds a harmless
enough pastime—but was it really? All those fine feathers, including
liveried attendants borrowed from the county hall or from absentee
landlords, had to be paid for somehow by the community; not to
speak of the way the public would be served by officials who indulged
in such pastimes until daybreak and subsequently—if they turned up
at all—lost themselves in planning the next 'hallucination'. Charming
though the gentry class was in many of its manifestations, its very
existence was based on legalized oppression and parasitism.

Free Enterprise

Who footed the country's bill for keeping magnates like maharajas
and a huge bureaucracy of idle squireens? 'Their peasants' would be
the obvious answer; but it would be a misleading one. Rural labour
was certainly kept cheap indeed and most of the peasants lived in
penury (about which more later), but this was due less to exploitation
by the landowners than to the backward conditions ruling agriculture
generally. It was convenient for the landlord to have at his disposal
labourers as ill-paid as those before the abolition of serfdom, but the
cash return for such outdated exploitation fell far short of what was

needed for state and municipal administration and for Hungary's contribution to the Austro-Hungarian armed forces. The source of money was free enterprise, which was allowed and indeed encouraged to develop and expand side by side with stagnant rural paternalism.

The boost to free trade had started, as may be remembered, under Bach in the early 1850s when national freedom was at its lowest and the fiscal interests of the Empire prompted the introduction of capitalist methods. From the Compromise of 1867 onwards, Liberalism was accepted as the guiding principle of statesmanship as well as commercially sound for the Exchequer; and from the mid-1870s, under Kálmán Tisza's guidance, quite vigorous effort was made to build up a technologically and commercially advanced network of trades. This effort was, on the whole, highly successful. The rapid growth of the urban, when compared to the rural, population, and even of the non-agricultural element in the rural districts (as well as that of the earnings *per capita* within new branches of industry compared with traditional ones) testify both to the timeliness of this policy and to its efficacy. In a roundabout way, even agriculture profited from the technological progress in other industries, so that from 1870 to 1890 the amount of arable land was increased by some 20 per cent; but the capital at the disposal of credit banks multiplied about five times, or increased by 400 per cent, during the same period. Transport—both by rail and by water—grew along with banking, commerce, mining, industrial skills, and above all, manufacturing industry. Most of these concerns were based on agriculture, as was natural in a country whose most profitable export was wheat (and remained so for decades to come); flour-mills were the first great industry of Hungary, and next came those which processed leather, wool, and sugar-beet, and breweries and distilleries; but shipyards and engineering-works—and electrical equipment factories somewhat later—also shot up at a surprising rate. Generally speaking, it was the practice of *laissez-faire* which brought these results, but enhanced by an active policy of incentives for enterprise, especially after 1881, when the government obtained practically full powers to subsidize industries either directly or by tax reduction. The customs union with Austria put a brake on the development of many industries, but this was largely offset by the influx of Austrian and also German, Swiss, Belgian, French, and British capital. The social landscape of the country was constantly changing: the number of people who earned a living from manufacturing industry increased by some 50 per cent every twenty years. It was a belated but by no means unproductive emulation of Guizot's feat; Tisza's exhortation to the mushrooming class of businessmen might well have been, *enrichissez-vous!*—which not a few of them did.

This trend in the economic and social development of Hungary was to continue after Tisza's fall right up to the outbreak of the First World War, and indeed until the end of the Habsburg monarchy in 1918. Whatever the political shifts and crises of that whole period, its stability in both political and financial structure was manifest, if only in the choice of personalities: out of the four premiers who made the greatest impact on Hungarian life, two, Kálmán Széll and Sándor Wekerle, started as Tisza's financial right-hand men; the third, Baron Dezső Bánffy, was conspicuous for his use of Tisza's methods, though with far less than Tisza's moderation, both in administration and in economics; and the fourth, Count István Tisza, who was to play a tragic and symbolic part in the fall of the Dual Monarchy, was Kálmán Tisza's son, and heir to all his basic ideas. Under all these men, Hungary's division into two worlds—one ruled from the manor house and the county hall, the other from the banks and manufacturing industries—was perpetuated; they co-existed like two countries under one nominal overlordship. It was only natural that the one which made and provided money should expand more and more rapidly, and alter the face of what was still looked upon as one country. By the time war broke out, about two-thirds of the population still depended on the land for a living, but the minority of the population employed in industry and commerce provided much more than half of the public revenue.[1] The rise in the general standard of education (of which Baron Eötvös had laid the foundations) reflected the immense social change: while in 1869, about one-third of the adult population could read and write, in 1910 the proportion was 68·7 per cent.

The Substitute Middle Class: Jewry

The trading and professional middle class which created and ran the new branches of industry came from Jewry; chiefly because all other classes of people found it either beneath their dignity or beyond

[1] Going by the figures arrived at in his analysis of the national income of Austria and of Hungary in the 1910s (*Ausztria és Magyarország nemzeti jövedelme*, Hungarian Academy of Sciences, Budapest, 1916) by Professor Frigyes V. Fellner, more than 60 per cent of the Hungarian national income came, colloquially speaking, 'from the land', which meant overwhelmingly agriculture, and grain production in particular, but including animal husbandry, dairy farming, market gardening, vine-growing, fruit farming, forestry, fisheries; while the manufacturing industries produced not quite 20 per cent of the total; the rest (roughly 20 per cent or slightly more) being divided between mining, handicraft industries, commerce, transport, banking, foreign assets. Hungary, in a word, was still an overwhelmingly agrarian country, not only on the grounds of her population figures but owing to the source of her income as well. Yet, it was a fact of life that when money was urgently needed, it could only be obtained from the banking and big industrial concerns (closely interconnected, as we shall come to see) and from commerce or, at any rate, through them.

their means to go into business and accept the strains and risks of free enterprise. Originally, it had been the liberal reformers' dream to re-educate the landlords' sons as shopkeepers; and when the poet, novelist, and Aesopian fabulist András Fáy, himself a nobleman of considerable standing, founded the first savings bank in 1825, his gesture was hailed as an example. But few followed it: it was one thing to appreciate Aesop's and Fáy's tales about the rewards of humble industry, but quite another to serve customers, folding-ruler in hand, as a beginner in trade was expected to do. The entailed office jobs were, however poorly paid, more comfortable and less humiliating. So not only the noblemen kept to the gentry form of life but also, as soon as they got the chance, the Magyarized sons of 'Swabian' and other non-Magyar burghers; so also did the heirs of the richest peasant farmers. Not more than one generation of money-making gentiles ever persisted outside the 'gentlemen's' network of employment. A few 'patrician burghers', as they were called, main-tained their, by then ennobled, 'Swabian' surnames in the trade-marks of their breweries and hardware businesses, but they were admired as special cases, almost like exotic specimens of Christian tradesmen's vegetation; the general rule was that, above the cobbler's and shoesmith's level and outside the gentry caste, membership of the middle class – of the *Bürgerschaft*, or bourgeoisie, or, in Magyar, the *polgárság* – implied Jewishness either of faith or of origin.

Another reason for this development was that while Christian gentlemen were encouraged to go into trade by Aesopian precepts only, Jews were forced to do so by the limitations of their rights in agriculture and the professions. The discriminations against Jews worked as incentives; all the more since they carried with them some strange prerogatives. This had been the case ever since the establish-ment of Christendom in Hungary – except under kings who expelled the Jews altogether or at any rate wished to do so – and most em-phatically during the early Renaissance, when the spirit of enterprise was making its first inroads on medieval rigidity. In 1436, under King-Emperor Sigismund, for instance, when lending money at interest still constituted a capital crime, Jews were specifically exempted from the prohibition; and later, when banking was legal-ized, they were allowed higher interest rates than Christians. They could not own real estate and were banned from guilds and, apart from exceptional cases, from living inside the city walls; but, despite all the discomfort and humiliation this implied, it helped them wherever a high degree of mobility was needed, so that they got a virtual monopoly of trading in certain raw materials at a time when – along with the gypsies – they were the most blatantly underprivileged group of the population. Selling spirits in the inns was another such

'Jewish monopoly', granted them by the landowners – the original licence-holders – who were more interested in cash returns than in the religion of their lessees. Of the professions, one only was open to them, and that the least respected: medicine – which, however, increased in importance and standing as science advanced. So they were really hounded into success.

The origin, or race, of the Jewish community in Hungary has often been discussed in the course of arguments on the 'Jewish question', and the sole thing that can be said with certainty about it is that an even approximately pure 'Jewish race' is as non-existent in Hungary (or elsewhere) as a 'Magyar race'. The Jews who figured among the Kabar helpers of the Megyer tribe which led the Hungarian conquest of the mid-Danubian valley in the ninth century, were dispersed and absorbed like the Megyer tribe itself; no one can say whence the 75,000 or so Jews had come who, like the Protestants, were granted human and civic rights in the 1770s under the enlightened absolutism of Joseph II. Under subsequent governments, especially after the French Revolution and the reaction from the mid-1790s onwards, these rights were again curtailed, but apparently enough of them were left to make Hungary an attractive place for Jews who fled from pogroms in the Russian empire, mainly from the Ukraine, via Galicia. Some also came from the West (Austro-Germany). Their number trebled by the 1840s and again almost doubled by the time of the 1867 Compromise; partly through immigration and partly because they were extremely prolific, with a birthrate equal to that of the Catholics but a mortality lower even than that of the Protestants. Their high standard of hygiene, in particular, amazed all observers. Thanks to it, apparently, they were practically immune to the cholera epidemics which periodically decimated the population; and although they paid for that with minor pogroms ('the Jews have poisoned our wells!'), their numbers increased both absolutely and relatively to the total population of which, in the watershed year of 1848, they represented almost 5 per cent. Most of the orthodox Jews belonged to no nationality in the sense then current in Europe; they were just 'God's chosen people', quite happy to live in a nominal or symbolic ghetto until the promised arrival of the Messiah. Their educated stratum, however, no matter what German dialect they spoke, was more fervently Magyar than the Magyars themselves; probably because the liberal ideas combined with classical dignity of the Reform Era appealed to a people fundamentally so *literate* as the Jews had been from practically time immemorial.[1]

[1] A striking analysis of the schooling of the various denominational groups which could be identified with certain nationalities was published in 1842 by the doyen

1848, however, failed to bring the Jews their emancipation; in fact, part of the mob demonstrating for national freedom at the outbreak of the revolution took this opportunity to stage anti-Jewish riots, and most of the National Guard units in Pest and Buda refused to admit Jews into their ranks. Most outspoken against anti-Jewish discrimination were the poet Petőfi and the socialist Táncsics. Petőfi accused 'the German burghers of throwing the first handful of mud on the stainless pure banner of March 15th' by fomenting anti-Jewish feelings and thus discord; an accusation not groundless, since it was the 'Swabian' shopkeepers, hitherto beneficiaries of the guild monopolies, who felt their vested interests most directly threatened by Jewish competition under free trade. Táncsics went even further than Petőfi and accepted the post of honorary president of the capital's Jewish community—a strange gesture from one so deeply sceptical of the *raison d'être* of any established Church, but understandable as a form of protest. The Jews, for their part, despite rebuffs, identified themselves entirely with the national rising and played an active part both in organizing supply-lines and on the battlefield. After the defeat they were, as a community, severely fined by the Imperial victors—but again their sacrifices paid high dividends, and this time even morally. Austrian rancour did not last long, but the Austrian quest for good business partners, particularly around the promising river ports of Pest and Buda, helped to strengthen the Jewish bourgeoisie. Meanwhile, the Jewish record in the War for Freedom gradually evolved from a crime into a merit; by 1867 the opinion was practically unchallenged among Hungarian liberals—ranging from Deák and Eötvös to the refugee Kossuth—that, in Jókai's words, 'no nationality was more loyal to us than the Jews, and none did we treat more unfairly'. Soon after the Compromise, their full emancipation was enacted; and acceptance of the Jewish religion—or rather religions, since the orthodox community was

---

of statistical research in Hungary, Elek Fényes. According to this, the percentage of primary-school students per denomination was as follows:

Roman Catholic (the majority religion, some 65 per cent of the total population, including more than 50 per cent of the Magyars)	1 per 14

. . . .

Minority religions:

Uniate (mainly Ruthenians):	1 per 80
Greek Orthodox (mainly Romanian, also Serb):	1 per 48
Reformed Church, or Calvinist (Magyar, including Székelys):	1 per 13
[Unitarian might have been similar to Calvinist]	
Evangelical Church, or Lutheran (German diaspora, also Slovak):	1 per 12
Jews (then mainly Yiddish-speaking but learning secular subjects mainly in Magyar)	1 per 10
Average:	1 per 16·66

unwilling to make common cause with the liberals, or 'neologists' – followed not long after.

Most active in bringing about these reforms was that old champion of absolute religious freedom, the 'Minister of Religion and Education' Eötvös, while the policy to be followed was laid down by the 'Wise Man of Hungary', Deák. The latter insisted that non-discrimination should be total – he was, for instance, jubilant about the election to Parliament of the first Jews – but, for practical reasons, urged that Jewish immigration be stopped. Subsequently, it did indeed sink to quite an insignificant number, which in any case was counterbalanced by emigration to Austria and further westward. Yet, the bogeyman of the new immigrant, the 'Galizianer' in contemporary slang, has persisted in the political mythology of Hungary to this day, since it suited selective anti-Semites and conformist Jews to agree that he was responsible for all the evils blamed on Jewry as a whole. To find him in person, one would have had to dig up the cemetery.

The growth of the Jewish population (which in the 1910s reached 8·5 per cent of the total) was, however, a reality; and since it was due, apart from their hygienic standards, to the fertility of, in particular, the orthodox communities, with their caftaned and ringleted men, and bewigged womenfolk, the 'Galizianer' legend could easily gain some credence.

A reality, too, was the increasingly important part played by Jewry – and particularly by 'neologist' and converted Jews, Catholic and Calvinist alike – first in the economic and later in the intellectual and public life of Hungary.

Jewish Fortunes and Misfortunes

Yet, some legends about 'Jewish riches' should also be discounted. Most of the Jewish petty traders were fairly poor, as petty traders usually are; and when political writers of even the most circumspectly anti-Semitic kind proved the economic and financial omnipotence of Jewry with such figures as that in 1910 85 per cent of commercial employees were Jewish, they ignored the fact that most of those employees were badly paid drudges. It was true, however, that as the trading middle class was Jewish, the wealth deriving from trade was earned by Jews – baptized or non-baptized – and that that wealth increased incessantly.

In the trading community, as in agriculture, a tendency towards accumulation of wealth in comparatively few hands was noticeable. The reasons were basically different – there had been no industrial capital preserved as family entail – but to the public eye they seemed comparable. A distinguishing mark of Hungarian capitalism was the enormous share of banks in the mining and manufacturing industries, which made the top flight of powerful bankers, associated and inter-married with the industrial barons, look like a second aristocracy, one that contrasted with the aulic one as the plutocratic Faubourg Saint-Honoré of Balzac's Paris did with the blue-blooded Faubourg Saint-Germain. Even within the banking world, wealth was more concentrated than in most comparable countries, the Big Two being the Creditbank (established largely with Rothschild capital) and the Commercial Bank. On the boards of directors of these and other leading banks, and of industrial and (to a smaller extent) commercial limited companies, the same set of people could be encountered, most of them Jewish, if only by origin, and almost without exception created barons or lesser noblemen, with place-names as their titles, by the early twentieth century. Except for some counts and represen-tatives of the highest gentry, retired cabinet ministers and the like, whose presence at board meetings was essentially symbolic, director-ships changed hands like a game of General Post in the world of 'Jewish' high finance; but its actual Jewishness remains a semantic question. Some financiers remained members of the Jewish religious community, but most were converted, and their sons and daughters often intermarried with those of the upper gentry. (A curious fact was that while most of the professing Jews and the Jews converted to Catholicism in this stratum rose to the baronage, the converts to Calvinism refused elevation to anything higher than the equivalent of, say, an English knighthood.) As 'race' had never figured in the Hungarian legal codes or statistics, and as the converts showed quite a natural generosity and attachment to their new religious com-munities and Churches, 'Jewish money' did not as a rule remain Jewish very long; but even what remained so temporarily was con-siderable. By the early 1900s, 'Jewish' capitalists were, without doubt, among the richest Hungarians and second only to some hereditary 'maharajas' of the land; and since they manipulated their capital more flexibly, they ruled wherever money was master. Baron Manfred Weiss de Csepel, owner of the greatest manufacturing concern, which produced arms among other things, was himself a professing Jew, with a family that included Catholic barons, Calvin-ist squires, and bank directors of all denominations; and he was supposed to be either the very richest man in the country or one of the four richest—the other three being Archduke Frederic, Prince Esterházy, and the head of Count Károlyi's family. He was, inci-dentally, the only industrialist and the only Jew to be allowed an entailed estate.

After the 'non-gentlemanly' trades, Jews began to interest them-selves in agriculture as well, and were most successful in it, mainly as land-stewards and tenants of big estates. Later, however, the number of Jewish landowners also increased, and in the 1910s it was reckoned that almost 20 per cent of the larger estates were owned by Jews, and more than half of the big rented estates were leased to them. Again, there was neither magic nor a devilish plot in their achievements, though the gentry suspected both; their secret was simply that, as the buying and selling of agricultural products and of the land itself, apart from entailed properties, was open to all, management by men skilled in commerce and applied science paid higher dividends than did reliance on feudalistic traditions. The Jews, in a word, owed their success to the fact that among the white-collar population of Hungary they were the only layer of society not to be 'gentrified'.

For this they were not wholly responsible. They did in fact try their best to be assimilated to the squires and dispossessed ex-squires and 'Swabian' neo-squires, but they were knocking their heads against an impenetrable wall. Whether because there were too many of them for the gentry strongholds to accommodate, or because of certain racial characteristics peculiar to the Jews—often effaced, no doubt, but still more identifiable than the distinctions, say, between middle-class Slavs or Germans and the Magyar gentry—it is a fact that the Hungary of Kálmán Tisza and his followers, so conspicuously tolerant towards Jewry where moneymaking and social distinctions were concerned, strictly excluded them from certain fields of professional and social activity regarded as the province of a 'genuine' Hungarian gentleman. Jews, particularly if converted, could become members of the Upper House, and cabinet ministers, generals, and privy councillors (to be addressed as 'Your Excellency'), not to mention Roman Catholic bishops born as Jews; but there could be no question of electing a Jew or ex-Jew to what in England would be the poorly—very poorly—paid post of Justice of the Peace. In the county hall, the drabbest and poorest job was unobtainable by anybody of Jewish extraction. I knew one such official, son of an ancient nobleman and an ex-Jewess, who was pointed out to me as a dazzling exception. Since the 1880s, the gentry, like the magnates, had their own 'National Casino', or club; but while that of the magnates in very exceptional cases admitted some converted Jews and even two—but no more—professing Jews, that of the gentry remained an absolutely closed shop. You could be the richest, the best educated, even officially the highest-ranking man in the kingdom, but if you had Jewish blood you could not hope to play *chemin de fer* in the premises reserved for the upper-middle-class gentry in the centre of Budapest. I knew a converted Jew, gentleman farmer, and ex-member of Parliament, titled and dandified, who could out-duel, out-ride, out-serenade all the Hungarian gentry of his circle; and he married a dowerless, most attractive girl of the ancient lesser nobility, the 'belle of the county hall' and of gentry parties in Budapest. After their wedding, she was still invited to the county balls, but they received a tactful warning that *he* had better plead public duties on that occasion. And he–and she–agreed; after all, she must not lose her old friends and there was no way of getting round such limitations.

Why should the Jews have minded? That is the obvious question today and was so, indeed, at the time. At the prosperous businessmen's club, let alone that of the millionaires, both the cooking and the surroundings were superior to those of the gentry. Those much-coveted county jobs, however brightened by leisurely and companionable interludes over a glass of apricot brandy, still tied the official to a wormeaten desk and the drab business of reading and pondering over masses of applications; why not prefer making fortunes at the stock exchange instead? And however handsome some of the male and female dancers at the county balls, they could not appear sensational to anyone with access to the worldly pleasures of the Lido and the Riviera and Ascot, which the banking barons certainly had. It seemed puzzling that a rich Jew should ever wish to join the gentry. Let us disregard the fact that it was more difficult to make fortunes at the stock exchange than the non-initiated gentiles thought, and that Jews were on the whole less rich than they seemed. It remains true that the yearning for absorption by the gentry haunted even the baron millionaires. Patriotic nostalgia mingled in that yearning with snobbery, and with the belief that nothing was secure outside officialdom. This belief was in fact encouraged by the government in order to reassure its needy dependents, the dispossessed noblemen: let the 'gentleman' bureaucrat be content with his status and let the Jewish textile merchant be content with his money, that seemed to be the ideal of government-sponsored middle-class happiness. But reality was less happy: the bureaucrat responded with envy, and the merchant with a feeling of humiliation.

The first momentous eruption of anti-Semitism since emancipation was prompted by the disappearance in 1882 of a fourteen-year-old peasant maid, just as the Jewish Passover was approaching, which led to the usual accusation of ritual murder in the village of Tiszaeszlár. The kosher butcher of the village and a few Jewish boatmen were arrested to pacify the excited masses, and the government–Kálmán Tisza's, with its crude pragmatism–turned a blind eye on what at first seemed no more than a dismal local affair. So also at first did the élite Jews, who disliked involvement in the troubles of ringleted boatmen; but as incitements to pogrom spread, they hired Károly Eötvös, the brilliant lawyer, author, and member of Parliament, to look into the matter and act as Counsel for the Defence if satisfied that he could prevent a miscarriage of justice. It was not an easy trial, as the prosecution's chief witness was the adolescent son of the kosher butcher who testified to having seen his father through the keyhole just as he was holding the peasant maid's head and collecting her blood in a vessel. Under Eötvös's paternally conducted cross-examination the boy confessed that he had been bribed by the magistrate with sweets and cajolements to tell this story; and, since the corpse was also recovered from the river Tisza – without any 'ritual cut' on it, of course – the accused were acquitted. Yet, an Anti-Jewish Party, though small, lasted for some years in Parliament: the first, albeit frustrated, attempt to institutionalize racial hatred in Hungary.

Liberal Progress

Liberal Hungary thus survived, and in some ways ahead of most European countries and certainly of her senior partner, Austria, in enacting reforms suited to the requirements of a scientific age. Most important of these was the one legalizing civil marriage, a step urged by Protestants and practically all liberally minded layers of society, but viewed with grave misgivings by the King-Emperor, Franz Joseph. By 1894, however, this reform was pushed through. The premier then was Sándor Wekerle, a benevolent and cynical finance expert, who, after searching his countrymen's hearts, had come to the conclusion that, in his country, patriotism rejected denominational intolerance, even at the risk of losing favour with the Court. So Wekerle, assisted by his Minister of Justice, the magnificent lawyer and debater Dezső Szilágyi (not the first in Hungarian history but in gifts second to none), managed to push and manoeuvre the bill over its hurdles in the Houses of Parliament and the Royal Assent. Szilágyi lost his portfolio to appease the Imperial and Royal wrath, but it was a small price to pay for his triumph in a matter of principle.

In reaction to this important liberal success among uncompromising Catholics, a clericalist 'People's Party' was formed which, though on the whole obscurantist, showed in welfare policy and the treatment of national minorities (mainly the Slovaks whose votes it solicited) more understanding than the ruling Liberals and their Nationalist ("48-ers') opposition. But as it professed belief in Authority even more than the believers of "67' and "48', it was unable to go to the roots of Hungary's striking social inequality; the Roman Catholic Church was after all one of the greatest entailed landlords, and the People's Party was committed to extending its influence still further.

The Peasants' Misery

That striking social inequality had of course always existed; but developments towards the end of the century made it more striking still by pushing it into the limelight. Small peasant farmers got into debt and lost their properties as did the landed gentry; and having no sinecures in the county halls to comfort them, they swamped the cities and mining districts where demand for labour was increasing, or else emigrated, in great numbers, to the United States where life had hard trials in store for them but also possible rewards undreamt of in Hungary. The proletariat of the cities never sank lower in penury than the rural labourers who, in lean years, faced literal starvation; but misery in the slums is denser and more conspicuous than the misery in mud-hovels scattered about the countryside. And industrial workshops foment labour movements by their very nature, as Marx and Engels knew only too well; so a wave of trade unionism swept over the capital and other cities as soon as they became centres of industries requiring highly skilled labour (printing-works being always among the first). Trade unions on a national scale were not actually legalized until the turn of the century, but sporadic labour activities started much earlier and spread so fast that by the mid-1890s even rural areas were affected and a wave of 'harvesting strikes' caused many a headache to the authorities. The then premier, Baron Bánffy, an illiberal Liberal if ever there was one, handed the social problem of the rural areas over to the gendarmes, and there was practically no protest from either the government or the parliamentary opposition benches when rumours got about that here or there a tramp thought to be one of 'those godless mavericks', i.e., socialist agitators, had been shot.

In 1898, under Bánffy's premiership and in reaction to rural un-rest, a bill was passed which put the land labourer at the mercy of his master more completely than he had ever been since the abolition of serfdom or even, in some respects, since Maria Theresa's acts of paternalistic goodwill in the 1760s. Unionism and strikes on the land were declared illegal, contracts approved by the assistance of the authorities were made enforceable by arms, and some measures in effect curtailed the migratory rights of the agrarian proletariat. Nine years later, in 1907, renewed emphasis was given to such measures by a second 'Slavery Law' (as labelled by socialists) which put the children of farmhands between twelve and eighteen years of age under their respective landlords' authority and entitled the latter to mete out corporal punishment among them. In 1907, unlike in 1898, a coalition government was in power; but the Minister of Agriculture (that is, the politician mainly responsible for the two laws) happened to be one and the same man, Ignác Darányi. Stranger still, Darányi was not only in his old-fashioned way an honest Liberal (much more principled than, say, Bánffy) but a man sincerely disturbed about the miseries of the poor and an initiator of measures calculated to help them. He was, above all, a competent agriculturalist, given credit even by his opponents for the intensification of farming. Today, he figures in Marxist-Leninist Hungarian history as the devil of neo-feudalist exploitation; whereas a counter-myth given credence in Western scholarly literature makes him appear as the champion of social justice.[1] The truth is, apparently, too reasonable to be believed on either side: that he was, in both his abilities and his limitations, very much a man of his time.

The living standards of farmhands, daily and seasonal land labourers, and other strata of the poor peasantry–altogether the majority of the population–were accordingly low, very low indeed but less so than would appear from statistics. To quote just one example: statistical surveys of the mid-1890s, made in the spirit of scholarly detachment and certainly not intended to show things as darker than they were, concluded that an average person in an average agricultural worker's family of the Hungarian Plainland consumed in food the equivalent of 3 *krajcár* a day. This amount corresponded to the purchasing value (if a guess may be risked) of sixpence in the Britain of the late 1960s; in Budapest at that time it might have been the average price of a tram or omnibus ticket. Consider, however, that in the Plainland even the poorest were known to be better off than their opposite numbers in the mountainous areas; and that in a labourer's family the wage-earning males ate much more and better than the rest; which would leave a Transylvanian poor peasant's wife with about one *krajcár*'s worth of foodstuff a day– though there was no beggar, even in the most poverty-stricken areas, who could not collect more than that. The statistics took no account of hidden incomes, without which the poorest wage-earners would simply have starved to death. A labourer who out of his declared annual earning of 134 forints (much below what could be considered subsistence level) had to give up 15 forints in direct taxation would indeed have been a fool to declare the occasional tips and presents (given to him and his dependents) which in his household might have amounted to more than what he was known to earn. Another, and even more important, additional income was a certain amount of tolerated theft. The bailiffs, gendarmes, and magistrates were prepared to turn a blind eye on a degree of poaching and of stealing brushwood or fruit, even wheat, so long as the offender behaved with

[1] Examples of Darányi's diabolification are too numerous to be quoted; practically all historians dealing with the subject in present-day Hungary (including well-balanced and undogmatic minds) are inclined to slip into it. As for the counter-myth, C. A. Macartney (*The Habsburg Empire*, London, 1968, pp. 705, 720, 721, 763), while endorsing the harshest criticism ever made of the 'Slavery Law' of 1898, refers in terms of unqualified eulogy to Darányi–simply ignoring that that law and that man had any connection.

the humility appropriate to his station. It was a complicity between masters and servants in moderate lawlessness.

All this said, it is still true that the life of the landless peasants and the 'dwarf-holders' (those whose plots were insufficient to sustain a family) was one of dour penury; and we should dwell on it the more as it was to remain fundamentally unchanged for another half-century, that is, until the end of the Second World War. Let us forget the very darkest sights, those of cave-dwellers and of servants and their families crammed together like cattle in and around courtyards, which inevitably became breeding-grounds of sickness and hysteria, if not incest and murder. Even a comparatively well-balanced and well-groomed average peasant household stank of privation. The houses themselves were often quite pleasant to look at: one-storied buildings mostly of mud, whitewashed, thatched, hump-backed like penned sheep, facing sideways to the road, with tiny windows decorated sometimes with geraniums, but hardly ever opened for airing. Of the two rooms which most of them contained, one served as bed-sitter and dining-kitchen for all, whereas the other, often referred to as 'the clean room', the one with its window to the road, had one bed or two, finances permitting, with a number of cushions and eider-downs heaped in exemplary neatness. These beds were indeed waiting for Godot–unless a stranger hired one for a night or, in search of country air, for a holiday. Dust in the village streets was overpowering, but the meadows were only a short stroll away.

Is it a habit of the poor to make life even harder than it need be? In many cases, yes; privations develop a sort of inertia which in turn numbs the will to make the best of things. The feeding habits of the Hungarian poor peasantry, like their housing habits, often showed such a tendency. The Hungarian peasant's wife was certainly not lazy; for one thing, under her husband's thumb, she would not have dared to be. Yet, her cooking seemed often calculated to worsen with monotony what poverty had made bad anyway: when, for instance, it consisted of boiling a cauldronful of beans in thickening for a week, warming it up every evening, and doing the same with some soup in the morning. At midday, when working in the field, her husband had his ration of lard on him, with bread, onion, green paprika; the rest of the family had more often than not to do with this diet short of the lard. During the compulsory idleness of the winter months bread was the staple diet, at any rate in the wheat-growing areas of the Plain and Transdanubia, until the critical spring period when it might have run out and millet or maize or some poorer substitute had to do instead–as happened more frequently in the mountainous districts. One should not generalize, however; in certain districts, varieties of *gulyás* and what may be termed the freshwater and paprika-flavoured version of *bouillabaisse* were superbly prepared even among the poor; and to be gorged with rich food and wine and marc was an evil, no less typical of the countryside (although less frequent) than to suffer from the poor, monotonous diet.

Poverty and privations for most of the rural population were not merely economic facts but part of the natural order in which the many were born to serve the few.

The Glory of Budapest

This was sad, no doubt, but not so shocking as it may sound. Kálmán Tisza's and Dezső Bánffy's practices were no more corrupt or despotic than those of Sir Robert Walpole some 150 or two hundred years before. They were 'Whigs', if this implies a preference for free and enlightened ways to dogmas and hierarchies, a basic liberalism which, though sincere, was often compatible with arbitrary use of power, and which took rule-by-the-few for granted. Did Hungary then lag some 150 or two hundred years behind England in every respect? By no means: in certain fields she was a match for the most advanced, most educated, and reasonably organized societies. This made her backwardness appear the more glaring; but it also to some degree compensated for it.

One might say without perverse oversimplification that what was advanced in Hungary, disproportionately so, was the new capital of Budapest; and what lagged some 150 or two hundred years behind was the rest of the country, and mainly the rural areas under county rule.

Budapest, formally merged into the one city from Buda, Óbuda (Old-Buda), and Pest in 1873, and absorbing the villages around her as industrial suburbs or vegetable gardens, represented, if ever a capital did, a synthetic product of will, intellect, and obsession; but she was all the more lively, enterprising, and imaginative for that. Her Magyardom and middle-class character in the eighties were a marvel of patriotic determination: it had sprung from the resolve of the Magyar gentry to become middle class; of the German-speaking middle classes to become Magyar; and of the Jews to become both.

Her two main parts, Buda and Pest, showed contrasting facets of the national character: Buda built on hills, with large forests in the background, and turning her rocky face with its old citadel, her Royal Palace, and Gothic Coronation Church towards the Danube; and Pest, built on plainland and reclaimed marshes, as the northern vanguard of the Great Plain, the *puszta*, but urbanized at frantic speed, with boulevards that emulated modern Vienna and Paris in their elegance, ugliness, and vigour, centre of the Houses of Parliament, the Stock Exchange, the University, and the National Museum, and conspicuous for her wharves and cafés teeming with trade, gossip, and literature. Buda was all ancient glory: Pest all revolution, business, and intellect. Between them they combined the national and democratic upsurge of the century. Both were overwhelmingly German-speaking when the upsurge started; but the metropolitan Budapest that emerged from them was already a bulwark of Magyardom, Magyar in language, in habits, in phantasies. She was the pride of the country, the monumental proof of its advancement. The panorama she offered to the visitor arriving from Vienna via the Danube destined her for the symbolic display of grandeur, and in the last decades of the nineteenth century the Hungarian rulers did their best to enhance this spectacle: the 'Fisher's Bastion', a Gothic labyrinth of stairs, arches, and alcoves, was erected at the foot of the Coronation Church, and facing it, on the Pest bank, arose the largest Parliament building ever seen in Europe, housing Lords and Deputies visibly on the Westminster model, but capped by an agreeable cupola (unsuited to the Gothic edifice, but impressive all the same), under which the two Houses met on solemn occasions. Between the Buda and the Pest banks, and, as it were, cradled by them, lay the little island park named after Saint Margaret, hiding the ruins of a medieval convent behind bulky chestnut and plane trees, and offering a rose-garden, a cafeteria with brass band, and sulphur springs to the visitor. The feudal prerogative of a Habsburg archduke over Margaret Island kept it free both from the real-estate speculators, who were rapidly expanding along the two banks of the river, and from the common people who were unable to pay the entrance fee required from visitors. Buda, Pest, and Margaret Island thus formed an ideal synthesis of aristocratic and democratic aspirations. Budapest lay like a coronet upon the country – a coronet set with mostly false jewels: slum houses old and new, bug-ridden and overcrowded, and smart apartment blocks overdecorated in the motley architectural style of the period; but still a glittering coronet, and ravishing when not too closely inspected. No wonder the ruling classes of Hungary were proud of it.

At the same time, they grew uneasy about it; mainly about Pest, the left bank. The literary cafés of Pest, which in 1848 were the vanguard of nationalism, carried on as a vanguard in the eighties and nineties, but rather as that of cosmopolitanism. They still had their centres of folk-patriotism, with gypsy music and lachrymose pan-Magyar jargon; but this could not be their last word. They had to recognize and express the changes that took place in Hungarian life, changes ignored by the rulers who encouraged architectural and technological progress without realizing their social implications. In glittering, metropolitan Budapest the rulers still expected people to behave like squires and labourers in the provincial mud. The fact

was, however, that by the time Budapest became Magyar the character of Magyardom itself had changed. The bourgeois and the proletarian might not have noticed this, but the café population did—
and the café meant literature.

The weekly *A Hét* (The Week) performed the historic feat of combining Budapest's colloquial language with literary standards. Its
editor, the poet József Kiss, a tireless little man from a family of very
poor village Jews, kept to the country-bred traditions in his poetry,
but made them more flexible; his folk-ballads had a touch of the
chanson. His young men, influenced now by Heine and Börne, now
by Zola or Baudelaire, and by Russian revolutionaries as well as
French naturalists, groped their way towards creating a language in
which Budapest could mirror herself. And they went further: they
held a Budapest mirror over the countryside.

A Hét, though it set the tone in new literature, was not the only
journal, nor the most violent or potent in denouncing the falsities of
the ruling system; socialist sheets were published, and even dailies
of conformist outlook would print outspoken reports on the horrors of
slums, the corruption of county rule, the terrorism of the county
gendarmerie. Hungary's rulers were trapped by their own Liberalism, which, if compromised in the politics of power, took its revenge
by developing a most sceptical and often hostile mood in the cafés,
in the streets, on the printed page. In the competition for an audience,
no one could afford to be uncritical of the prevailing state of affairs;
the humorous weekly *Borsszem Jankó*, a government Liberal publication, often outstripped opposition invective with its nonconformist
irony.

The conformist answer was 'Let Budapest have her fun; Budapest
is not, after all, the country'. Budapest night life was steeped in the
Yiddish sense of humour which provided sustenance for the music
halls; and whenever a landowner wished to 'have a good time' in the
capital, he heartily joined in. Political jokes were enjoyed with the
same sort of joviality so long as they could be dismissed as jokes; but
they could not indefinitely. Where joviality ended, irritation began;
the 'spirit of Pest' was constantly denounced as 'rootless', as 'unpatriotic' and therefore unauthentic about anything that concerned
national life—it was 'essentially non-Hungarian'. The pride of the
nation, the glory of her advancement, essentially non-Hungarian?
The Hungary of the Liberal and squirearchic era had to live with
this paradox.

Yet both the paradox and all calamities and crises springing from
the awkward make-up of the country could somehow be ironed out,
at any rate until the turn of the century. Irritation with the 'spirit of
Pest' did imply some anti-Semitism, but of a most selective kind, one

which on the whole the majority of Jews themselves endorsed, from orthodox village grocer who saw no reason to disturb his *modus vivendi* with the county authorities right up to the bankers and industrial barons in the capital who, no less than the magnates and the gentry, resented attempts to undermine their privileges. Town and country, "67' and "48', Liberals and clericals, Papists and Calvinists, Christians and Jews and Freethinkers could equally be persuaded to bury the hatchet and join in collective euphoria when a bottle of wine, a gypsy group, and a sufficiently highflown patriotic excuse were forthcoming. A godsend was the millennium in 1896–officially, and perhaps really, the thousandth anniversary of the Hungarian occupation of the mid-Danubian valley. It was a tremendous festivity: constitutional liberties and royal authority enshrined together, industrial and urbanizing progress celebrated in the same breath as the leopard-skinned horsemen who had conquered the banks of the Danube. A celebration in which 'all ruling classes united', as the Marxists would say; to which one need only add that the oppressed or exploited classes joined in no less enthusiastically. The peasants, if the crisis of a harvesting strike was over, and if they could still raise the mental energy to feel anything about politics at all, were certainly no less traditionalist than the city-dwellers; and the industrial proletariat, in which Marxist propaganda had already begun to take root, could not ignore its indebtedness for its very existence to that complex of old-fashioned patriotic slogans and modern capitalist interests which exulted in the display of gala-dresses, gala-speeches, fireworks, dances, monuments. The deliberately careless and proud mood ever since then associated in Hungary with 'millenary optimism' was foolish of course, but to ignore the achievements behind it would have been still more so.

Chapter 5

The Second Reform Generation

THE TURN OF THE CENTURY marked the beginning of a Golden Age for Hungary, a beginning which was to be stopped abruptly before it could lead anywhere. Is it, then, right to call it a beginning? Was it not rather an unfulfilled promise only? From the point of view of political and social development, yes: but not in the fields of culture. The Second Reform Generation of Hungary which emerged in those years failed to remodel the country even more pathetically than had the First, that of the 1830s. Yet it achieved lasting results, both directly and indirectly. In arts, letters, science, and in forming attitudes receptive to a large variety of beauties, ideas, and discoveries, the Hungary of that generation forged ahead at a pace never seen in her history before or after, and rarely anywhere else. An enumeration of the works of art and scholarship, scientific findings, technological and medical innovations which date from the Hungary of the early twentieth century would add up to quite an impressive total; but, more important, their increase continued after 1919–the year when the atmosphere which had inspired them came to a sudden end. The types of people moulded in that era of intellectual excitement outlived the period of their conception and have never ceased to make their mark on successive trends of life in and outside Hungary.

The branch of intellectual activity least disturbed by the division of Hungarian white-collar society into 'gentry' and 'bourgeois' (or 'Jew') was science in the English sense: that is, mathematics, natural history, and engineering. Science, after all, dealt with tenets whose validity could rarely be questioned on the grounds that they were 'essentially un-Hungarian'. The scientific life of Hungary had a leading figure of undisputed authority in the person of the physicist Baron Lóránd Eötvös (1848–1919), son of József of the First Reform Generation. Lóránd Eötvös had a mind absorbed in a multitude of physical experiments; yet, as a dutiful son of his father and of the humanitarian nineteenth century, he took an active part in promoting public education. For a short period he even acted as Minister of Education in a Liberal government (under Wekerle); for many years thereafter he was President of the Academy of Science; and practically throughout his adult life he was a professor at the Uni-

versity of Budapest, now named after him. Nobody doubted, however, that his heart lay with the soulless matter which spoke to him
in so many languages. We should leave it to the historian of science
to describe what, for instance, the 'Eötvös pendulum' was like and
why it broke new ground in exploring the secrets of our planet. Of the
many scientific perceptions connected with his name, let us only
point to the one which seems most revolutionary in retrospect – that
he was one of Einstein's predecessors in noticing that the mass of
minuscule bodies changed in relation to their speed of movement.

The universities of Hungary had a number of world-famous
mathematicians on their staffs at that time; her clinics and hospitals
could boast of doctors and surgeons who gave a lead to Western
colleagues in introducing improved methods; and in the laboratories
of manufacturing concerns (among which the Ganz shipyard and
factory of Old-Buda might rank as the most prolific) novel methods
for converting energy to industrial purposes were devised. Hungary
was still too poor and too small a country fully to exploit her own innovations, but she made what she could of them. From the point of
view of social history, it should be noted that most of the scientific in-
ventors and theoreticians, as well as of the business managements
sponsoring them, came from the three main strata of 'white-collar'
Hungary: the Magyar middle nobility; the German ('Swabian' and
Saxon) burghers; and, increasingly, the Jews. About such questions
as electrification there was no ideological difference between them –
once they accepted the Liberal principle of industrial progress, as
they all more or less conscientiously did.

Two Unhappy Dissenters: Grünwald and Mocsáry

It was an entirely different matter when it came to applying
scientific methods to social research. The impetus towards that, too,
had come indirectly from the First Reform Generation, and chiefly
from its 'doctrinaires', who encouraged learning of all kinds and a
more rational approach to questions either buried under traditional
myths or obscured by the revolutionary myth of nationalism.

From the seventies onwards, however, the ruling gentry class,
despite its commitment to Liberalism, became increasingly obsessed
with its own taboos; and those of its members unmindful of such
tacit prohibitions ran a risk of social ostracism which was deadlier
than any sentence passed by a court of law.

The fate of two very able and dedicated men who both came from
the county squirearchy exemplifies the fate of unwitting dissenters:
that of Béla Grünwald (1839–91) and that of Lajos Mocsáry (1826–
1916). Grünwald, coming from a Saxon, or 'Zipser', family of north
Hungary, ennobled and more Magyar than the ancient-stock

Magyars, was a devotee of national and rational progress on the (originally liberal) Prussian basis. He was a first-class county administrator and an important historian. In the course of his researches and of his own experience, he came to the conclusion that the counties were not (as asserted by conventional patriots) the safeguards but rather the parasites of the nation. He accordingly favoured the idea of centralizing the administration; and Kálmán Tisza, with his usual astuteness, appreciated Grünwald's advice, but not to the extent of standing up for him against outraged 'national' opinion. Grünwald, all too sensitive to the reactions of his fellow-gentlemen, took refuge from ostracism in Paris, where his body was one day identified in the morgue–he had drowned himself in the Seine.

Mocsáry, who started as a political writer at the time of the War for Freedom, had a mind less sophisticated but more direct; he believed in justice and tolerance and in speaking his mind without tactical qualifications. Basically, he was a moderate; he supported Deák in 1861 and, later, Kálmán Tisza; but when he realized that official Liberalism was far from genuinely liberal, he became in 1874 the founder and first President of the Independence Party, the parliamentary group committed to the refugee Kossuth's ideas. Mocsáry fought with special fervour for the rights of national minorities; if federation was impracticable, he argued, at the very least the existing Nationalities Law of 1868 should be observed. His views inspired such unanimous horror among parliamentarians, government and opposition alike, that he was physically thrown out of the Chamber, and his own Independence Party expelled him in 1887. One year later he was elected to Parliament by a purely Romanian constituency which he had chosen as a demonstration of national equality; and that finished his career so far as his fellow-Magyars were concerned. Isolation turned him into a political mummy. In the twentieth century, the Second Reform Generation did respect him for his erstwhile valiant fight, but by then he was too old to catch up with the new trends in social philosophy; he died, a venerable museum piece rather than a statesman, in the middle of the First World War which vindicated his foresight so tragically.

These two fine men, though equally cold-shouldered, and for similar reasons, by their class, did not see eye to eye with each other, since Grünwald insisted on the compatibility of Magyarization with liberal ideas, whereas Mocsáry was convinced that his vision of a democratic and federal Hungary could be realized by means of the traditional county autonomies. In fact, an interesting public debate– probably the most valuable outcome of their respective solitudes– took place between the two men in 1889. Their fate illustrated the hopelessness of scientific and, indeed, honest thinking in a Hungary whose foundations had been laid by the noblest and most enlightened of men in the 1830s.

The Birth of 'TT'

Yet there were renewed efforts to bring social science in Hungary up to date, even among the ruling gentry. A family outstanding in such endeavours and rich in romance were the Pulszkys, Hungarian noblemen of Polish extraction. Ferenc Pulszky (1814–97) was for years the right-hand man of the refugee Kossuth, a highly polished mind and a contributor to many Western publications (including the *Encyclopaedia Britannica* of those years); but after the obvious failure of refugee conspiracies he accepted the Compromise of 1867 and returned to Hungary to do what he could to make qualified independence and liberty work, and, in his spare time, to devote himself to his lifelong passion, archaeology. Kossuth resented his apostasy; and, in Hungary, a group of "48-er' chauvinists concentrated their fire on him with special gusto—pretending to expose the Habsburg lackey in him while really aiming at the cosmopolitan liberal. The irritation he aroused was also wreaked on his sons—Ágoston, a legal philosopher and politician, and Károly, an art historian. The latter, though less involved in public affairs than his father and elder brother, offered a better target: as the organizer of what was to become the National Gallery of Hungary, and responsible for the purchases of *objets d'art*, he was accused of financial improprieties; and although the investigation cleared him, his nerves were so shattered that he fled the country and, in 1899, killed himself in Australia. But his Gallery, beside the City Park of Budapest, has ever since been a showpiece of Hungarian culture, and rightly so; one of its gems being the beautiful portrait of a man by Sebastiano del Piombo—the acquisition of which cost Károly Pulszky his nervous balance and his life, when no more than forty-five years of age.

Ágoston Pulszky, in his theoretical writings, tried to represent law and society by methods free of myths and metaphysical preconceptions; while in daily politics he simply tried, like his father after 1867, or like Lóránd Eötvös, to make the best of things. He was a deputy in Parliament of the ruling Liberal Party and, for a short while, a junior minister (in Hungarian: 'Secretary of State') for Education. As his relations with both the liberally-minded within the Establishment and the intellectuals outside it were cordial, he seemed the ideal person to lead a movement to bring them together in research and debates. He made a notable step in that direction in a year which should be remembered, because it is from then that the birth of modern Hungarian intellectualism can be dated. In 1901, under his presidency, a Society of Social Sciences was formed

('Társadalomtudományi Társaság' in Magyar, and thus soon to be known as 'TT'). Its initial aim was to help society to know itself; and from the highest-ranking theoreticians of outspoken conservatism (e.g. Professor Victor Concha, for whom the state was a metaphysical entity) to lonely anarchists such as a Count (Ervin) Batthyány, all shades of opinion were represented in it. As an intellectual exploit, it was wonderfully promising. But no sooner had it started than, in that very same year of 1901, Ágoston Pulszky died. Had he survived, his personality might or might not have altered the course of events; but now in retrospect his death seems to have sealed the fate of an all-too-beautiful unity of Hungarian thinking, an honest unification of the most diverse elements.

There had been another reason, rooted in economic and power politics, why that unity could be established for the moment and maintained, at least superficially, for some further years. In 1899, Bánffy lost the premiership; and strange though this may sound after what has been said about his methods, his downfall was a setback to Liberalism. His group of stalwart Liberals, which included Kálmán Tisza and his impressively firm and energetic son Count István Tisza (1861–1918), then already a prominent figure, was, for all its corrupt administrative practices and its chauvinism, strictly faithful to its political principles – such as resistance to any infringement of Hungary's independence beyond the line drawn by the Compromise, and furtherance of Hungary's progress in industrialization and general education, in a spirit of expanding free enterprise, free competition, freedom of thought and worship. With Bánffy's successor, Kálmán Széll, a clique came to power which compromised on these issues both with the Court and with the extremists in clericalism and agrarian vested interests. The leader of the big landowners, and himself one of the biggest, Count Sándor Károlyi (1831–1906) – scion of the famous, or infamous, insurgent general who led the capitulation to the Habsburgs in 1711 – had, though on and off in the government Liberal Party, launched since the early 1880s a campaign against 'mobile capital', which he depicted as a parasite on the country and a menace to her very existence. To remedy the evils of capitalism, he wanted more feudalism. A shrewd and well-read reactionary, he put forward his suggestions on the grounds of social conscience, the urge to help the destitute and the poor. As the non-entailed landed properties were in debt, by the end of the nineteenth century, up to more than 70 per cent of their assessable value, anybody putting the banks (and by implication the Jews) in the pillory for it could count on popularity with the farmers, big and small; and even the idea that more entailment and less freedom in moneylending might be a public benefit could be sold to them.

Added to this was bait for the landless, both in the Civil Service and among the labourers; the neo-feudalists hoped simultaneously to capture the sympathy of the aulic aristocracy and of the proletariat in their drive against liberal capitalism. There is no reason to doubt that to a large extent they meant what they said; the plight and misery to which they referred were realities. But, as has always been the case with reformers who endeavour to improve matters by putting the clock back, in the heat of manoeuvring they forgot about their own social conscience and only succeeded in obtaining further concessions for the privileged few, never for the many. Sándor Károlyi's signal successes, too, were of this kind. From him dates the initiation in Hungary of a 'co-operative movement directed from above', under which a section of commerce was 'appropriated by' specifically subsidized concerns ('Hangya'–that is, 'Ant'–being the best known), which were run as appendages of the county halls. These privileged bodies, assuming for their managers the advantages of both private capitalism and state enterprise, were to play a decisive part after the downfall of Liberalism, from the end of 1919 onwards. A more noticeable success of the agrarian pressure-group at the turn of the century was the raising of the duties on farm products, a measure which could only be adopted with Vienna's consent and in exchange for which Széll's government bargained away Hungarian interests in finance, defence policy, and industrial progress.

Such neo-feudal successes created an atmosphere propitious for the union of all those opposed to them; and this facilitated Pulszky's venture. Not that traditionalist anti-Liberals were in principle excluded from 'TT'; in fact, the liveliest minds in Roman Catholic cultural life, such as the priest (later Bishop) Ottokár Prohászka, figured from the outset among contributors to its debates, as did conservative believers in the state-for-its-own-sake theory; but it was, at the same time, a foregone conclusion that outright reactionaries such as the followers of Sándor Károlyi would not have a chance in such an ensemble; this was the reason why, from 'mobile' capital (including barons of industry and the most diehard of Liberal gentry) down to radicals and Marxists, so many different tendencies could unite in it. A monthly periodical devoted to the social sciences and called *Huszadik Század* (Twentieth Century) was started in 1900, edited by a very moderate Liberal political writer and economist, Dr Gustav Gratz, who was later to become Director-General of the Hungarian Industrialists' Association (GYOSZ–[Magyar] Gyáriparosok Országoks Szövetsége). For all his moderation, Gratz quite passionately attacked the big landlords, such as Count Sándor Károlyi, at the head of the Hungarian Agriculturalists' Association (OMGE–Országos Magyar Gazdasági Egyesűlet) for subordinating the country's interests to those of their own class. At that moment, indeed, so ready-made for the imprint of Pulszky's personality, traditionalist Liberal Hungary was essentially united behind Progress against the forces of neo-feudal reaction. *Huszadik Század* was adopted one year later by 'TT' as its official journal.

The 'TT' Moderates

Pulszky was succeeded as 'TT' President by Count Gyula Andrássy, junior (1860–1929), one of the best brains and worst speakers in Parliament, the refined and inhibited son of an ebullient father. According to those who knew him intimately, he was an enchanting companion; he certainly looked captivating with his slender, aristocratic limbs and clear-cut, sophisticated profile made even wittier by his beard. As an historian, though serious, he was unimportant; and as a public figure, destined to respectable failure. He could see all those anomalies in his country, and all those dangers hanging over her, which were plain to the radicals; but he recoiled from any step which he felt might impair the dualist structure of the monarchy or, in foreign affairs, the Triple Alliance–the two political structures which his late father had helped to build. The essence of the latter consisted of co-operation between the Austro-Hungarian monarchy and the German Reich, with Italy as a third but never entirely trusted partner; a co-operation favoured by forward-looking patriots of that time mainly because Prussian influence could be channelled into support of the Magyar and Liberal cause. By the beginning of the twentieth century it became fairly clear that the dualist idea (that Austro-Germans and Magyars alone were complete 'nations' within the Habsburg Empire) and, even more, the reliance on a German power driven by Prussian militarism, had degenerated into a backward-looking attitude which necessitated the use of brutal and oppressive methods in public life and administration. Andrássy junior abhorred such methods. His objection to blatantly unconstitutional proceedings pushed him into opposition to the ruling Liberal Party and involved him in a lifelong feud with its strongman, Count István Tisza. People seeing the wide field of agreement between the two men could not always understand what divided them, and were ready to suspect that on Andrássy's side it was peevish hurt pride–which, after his failures, became partly true despite his nobility of mind. Thinkers labelled 'utopian' are as a rule obsessed with extremist visions; Andrássy was a utopian of moderation, who wanted things drastically improved without upsetting the applecart.

Besides Pulszky, Andrássy, and Gratz, the most important orthodox Liberal among 'TT' leaders was Lóránt Hegedüs, a strange mixture of romantic impulses and the sort of abilities one expects from a governor of the Bank of England. His career embraced strange vicissitudes: he was to become Minister of Finance (in a 'Christian' or White government, but with the clear understanding that he had nothing in common with its 'ideology'), an inmate of a 'nerve sanatorium' (or glorified lunatic asylum), a lay preacher in Calvinist churches, a witty newspaper columnist, and a less witty but quite imaginative playwright. In the early 1900s, however, he was still young and comparatively unromantic, one of the upper gentry who meant business when urging the cultivation of 'bourgeois' or 'Jewish' virtues. He was soon to become Director-General of the Industrialists' Association, a bank director, and a Liberal deputy in Parliament.

The 'TT' Radicals

Against such moderates, there were the radicals–the radicals of Liberalism, like the professor of law Bódog Somló, a disciple of Herbert Spencer; and the sociologist and publicist Dr Oscar Jászi (1875–1957), at that time an official of the Ministry of Agriculture; and there were the socialists, among whom the theorist and historian Dr Ervin Szabó (1877–1918) achieved the highest scholarly renown. Ideologically, they were far from a 'united Left'. Jászi in particular, with his temperamental pedantry and English nonconformist-style dedication to Moral Values, crusaded as passionately against Marxian materialism as he did against Jesuitical authority. Ervin Szabó, who, although disagreeing with him, was his intimate friend, edited the Hungarian selection of Marx's and Engels's works. These radicals and socialists only spoke with one voice when they denounced the system of *latifundia* (particularly the entailed ones) as the main source of moral and economic degradation in Hungary–and even on this they only differed in emphasis from their moderate partners. They expressed themselves on a subject which everybody was allowed and even encouraged to be outspoken about–so long as he talked in Budapest, and not directly to the peasants. Liberalism was blatantly selective, but for all that not a complete sham.

'TT', and in particular its radicals, ran extramural universities in Budapest which attracted a large number of the working-class élite, both manual and clerical, and provided them with tuition in a great variety of subjects ranging from the new trends in natural history, philosophy, anthropology, and genetics (it was still the aftermath of the Darwinist revolution) to sociology, history, and law. They did so quite openly in co-operation with the budding labour movement, i.e. the Social Democratic Party and the trade unions, and with the silent or explicit approval of their moderate and conservative 'TT'

fellow-members; and all this in spite of the fact that Social Democracy was not only unrepresented either in Parliament or in the town
and county councils, but considered outside the pale of respectability
and only just tolerated by law. Hungarian Social Democracy, like
its older German and Austro-German counterparts, professed
orthodox Marxist theories but concentrated in practice on wage
claims and other minor demands. Its masses of manual workers,
however captivated by verbiage about a Proletarian World Revolution, knew instinctively that their interests and moral hopes were
inseparable from those of enlightened Hungarian capitalism. This
was co-existence at its best–so long as it lasted; but it was too good to
last long.

It was followed by an eruption in the academic world against the
purely scientific spirit prevailing in 'TT'; and then by an eruption
within 'TT' itself.

The personality who cast the strongest spell over liberal-
socialist 'TT' members, and became correspondingly odious to their
opponents, was Professor Gyula Pikler (1864–1934), himself neither
a socialist nor very much of a liberal. He was a legal philosopher
with a keen interest in natural sciences and psychology, who stood
for a rational and pragmatic interpretation of law–'the theory of
insight' as he called it–according to which Law was essentially a
codification of what the common good demanded, as conceived by
the social class wielding power. About the value of freedom he was
rather sceptical; he distinguished it from, and subordinated it to, the
common good and scientific truth. Jászi attacked his doctrine as no
more than a middle-class restatement of Marxist truisms and fallacies,
which, Jászi urged, belonged already to the limbo of sociology, since
recent developments had once more proved the validity of ethical
principles and the importance of liberty. Pikler was in any case more
conspicuous for his curiosity about the nature of social phenomena
than for any desire to adjust them to an ideal; he differed from
Jászi rather like Hobbes did from Locke, or Taine from Lamartine–
being, that is, a revolutionary in his refusal to accept illusions while
rather conservative in his acceptance of facts. But the reactions to his
teachings were nonetheless vociferous. As early as 1901, demonstrations
were staged against him at the university by clericalist and extreme
nationalist students; he was several times prevented from lecturing,
amidst scuffles which unleashed, in the Hungarian way, a chain
reaction of duels. At that time, from conservatives such as Professor
Concha down to the 'Red' undergraduates, all believers in academic
freedom stood up for Pikler. Parliament, too, however class-ridden,
abhorred any gesture that might have appeared to put a muzzle on
scholarship. There were a few exceptions: for example, a spokesman

of the Catholic People's Party, Count Aladár Zichy, who urged government interference to silence Pikler and said: 'I know I shall be called a defender of darkness but I confess I should be glad to see less knowledge, less science, and more godliness, more attachment to the fatherland'. Disarmingly straightforward though this statement was, it cut no ice, and even Baron Gyula Wlassics, the Minister of Education of the day and known as a most conservative and nationalist kind of Liberal, made completely clear in his reply that he found interference neither practicable nor desirable. Pikler, meanwhile, became the idol of radical youth, though more on account of the mud thrown at him than of his doctrines.

The Unbridgeable Gulf: The Nationalities Question

Within 'TT', a fatal showdown was precipitated between radicals and moderates by political developments. In 1905, for reasons and in circumstances which will be explained later, the rule of the Liberal (Tisza) Party was interrupted, first, for not quite a year, by an extra-parliamentary government of soldiers and bureaucrats, only responsible to the monarch, and then, for three years, by a National Coalition government based on the main parties of the parliamentary opposition to Tisza's and, later, to the monarch's autocracy. At this juncture, it should suffice to point to one lamentable paradox of the coalition government: that although it had come in with the promise, honestly believed in by most of its supporters, to extend the rights of the common people, it was pushed by its nationalism into an intolerance more arrogant *vis-à-vis* the nationalities – one-half or more of the total population – than that of its notoriously oppressive predecessors. At the same time, a purge was launched against those civil servants who in the previous short period of *ex-lex*[1] had urged a more equitable treatment of nationalities, and typical of the nationalist colour-blindness, even public figures of tolerant outlook could involve themselves in such silly vendettas. The Minister of Education, Count Albert Apponyi (1846–1933), was a highly polished, polyglot orator who with his straight, tall figure, flowing beard, and bass-baritone voice was to become an attraction on such international platforms as the League of Nations. In 1906 he was the leader of one of the "48-er' factions – a party label which everybody knew might in his case be exchanged for any other as convenience required. Not that he was a cynic: rather the contrary. He was an opportunist of lofty ideas, which he worshipped so indiscriminately as to confuse and emasculate them. An extremist he had never been in anything; yet his School Law (enacted in 1907), crudely aimed at Magyarizing the teaching staff and through them the pupils, surpassed in intoler-

1 Suspension of parliamentary government.

ance any comparable legislative act in Hungary. Meanwhile the Minister of Agriculture, Darányi (a well-meaning man, as will be remembered, and by then a member of Andrássy's Constitution Party, most emphatically committed to tolerance), removed Oscar Jászi from his staff and practically expelled him from the Civil Service for daring to warn his compatriots about the dragon's teeth sown by chauvinism. Jászi by then had emerged as the apostle of an 'Eastern Switzerland' of nationalities which he hoped to see established on the banks of the Danube. This concept outraged the whole of National Opinion–that is, everybody interested in public affairs except minority nationals, socialists, and the group of radical intellectuals rallied around Jászi.

National Opinion versus Intellectualism

In this turmoil, controversies were bound to come to a head within 'TT'. Its highest office-holders, linked despite all their liberal reservations with the Establishment, tried to prevent the left wing from calling the society's tune. But the Left had an overwhelming majority; Andrássy, Gratz, Hegedüs resigned their posts, seceded, and formed another, *Hungarian*, Society of Social Sciences; while in 'TT', Pikler was elected President, Ervin Szabó Secretary-General, and Jászi took over as editor of *Huszadik Század*.

This in itself would not have mattered very much but for two reasons. The first can be demonstrated by a few genealogical facts. Of the seceded 'TT' leaders, Andrássy had come from the aristocracy; Hegedüs from the gentry; Gratz from the Swabian middle class (he had started as a German-language journalist); whereas the new leaders–Pikler, Jászi, Ervin Szabó–were racially Jews. Did this, then, imply a division on pro- and anti-Jewish lines? Not in the least. One could even argue that those three moderate gentiles were not only liberal but emphatically pro-Jewish, vesting great hopes in the progress of that free enterprise represented in Hungary mainly by Jews; whereas, of their radical opponents, Jászi in his puritanical zeal often attacked the Jews for their profit-mindedness and ultra-Magyarism, and Ervin Szabó, like many a socialist of nineteenth-century upbringing (including Marx), stood for an austere and closed economic system, not in the least favouring Jewish interests. Nor did their followers outside 'TT' divide as Jews and gentiles. Jewish (and ex-Jewish) capitalists were Gratz's and Hegedüs's patrons, while the masses of the humbler Jewish middle classes either accepted the orthodox wisdom of siding with any government which left them alone in their shops and synagogues or, even if bellicose in their fight against the remnants of feudalism and the monopolies of big capital (as was the small Citizens' Democratic Party, based on

Budapest), kept strictly to the tenets of private ownership and traditional patriotism. Organized labour sided of course with socialists and did include a considerable number of Jews, but these were no more representative of Jewry than their gentile comrades of Roman Catholicism, Calvinism, or Greek Orthodoxy. No one could therefore have suggested that the moderates, or liberal-conservatives, had left 'TT' because they found it *too* Jewish. And yet, that was the way it sounded in the country. The conventionally Liberal gentry were left with the impression that among all Jewish sects there was just one that no honest Hungarian could ever stomach: the agnostic intellectual who talked sociology in 'TT'.

The second reason why the 'TT' eruption had fatal results was that it left its seceded leaders without any following. Money was with them, status was with them, national opinion was with them, but no audience interested in the social sciences was with them. Just as the sociologists got isolated in the country, the liberal-conservatives got isolated amongst the sociologists; the average white-collar Hungarian was sufficiently disgusted with radicals to boycott their lectures on, say, the social implications of Lamarckian and Darwinian evolutionism, but not sufficiently to attend lectures on a similar subject at a rival society when he could spend his time listening to gypsy bands instead. The specifically 'Hungarian' anti-'TT' was killed by boredom; to the detriment of the radical 'TT' group, of course—for a 'dialogue', to use the fashionable word, might have kept its contact with circles wider than the Jewish intelligentsia alive. As things turned out, knowledge of social problems became the monopoly of a section of the community which had no chance to use that knowledge.

The Renaissance of Literature

The birth of Hungarian sociology was followed by the upsurge of Hungarian arts and letters, the theatre, and journalism—esoteric and experimental on the one hand, showy and sensationalist on the other, but equally at home in the media of social and intellectual innovation, and most of all so in the cafés. Today, what is most remembered all over the world of the creative output of those years is the works of certain composers; but at the time it was literature, and especially lyrical poetry and controversial aesthetics, that made the greatest impact on Hungarian minds and prepared the way for a general renaissance. It had grown out of *A Hét*, but itself outgrew *A Hét* in the early 1900s when the charm of *chansons* and the wit of columnists no longer seemed adequate to express the modern Hungarian's reaction against the mental sloth of the ruling classes.

This process was reflected in, and to a large extent initiated by, the activities of the poet, critic, essayist, and political journalist Hugo

Ignotus (1869–1949). Ignotus was the son of Leo Veigelsberg, leader-writer and, for a short while, co-editor of *Pester Lloyd*;[1] a man much admired for his beautiful German, modelled on Goethe's prose. His son Hugo, though Magyar by mother-tongue, took after his father in the cult of Goethe, as he did in the Liberal faith, though he had little use for the limitations of Liberal middle-class attitudes taken for granted at that time, which included sexual puritanism and indifference to the plight of the 'non-deserving poor'. As he was shy of basking in the radiance of his father's name, he always used pen-names when submitting his writings to various journals; and eventually his most usual pen-name, 'Ignotus', stuck to him.[2]

Hugo Ignotus was provoked into the role of literary leader by a casual remark made in a review of his first book – a versified love-story written under Byron's and Heine's influence, set in typical Budapest middle-class surroundings. It was kindly received by the critics and one of them, an eminent poet and Liberal columnist (and, incidentally, an elderly friend of the young Ignotus), remarked that it was sad to see such powerful talent wasted on 'un-national' subjects: the young author should, he suggested, spend some years in the countryside so as to steep himself in a genuinely Hungarian atmosphere. But why should Budapest be considered less national than the country she represents? Ignotus retorted, gently but firmly. Why should the register of nationally sound thoughts and feelings be confined to those of the peasants, he continued as the argument developed; and why pretend that townspeople could be happy on the peasant's diet when in fact even the peasants no longer could? Such were his battle-themes. Truisms, one would say, if a conspiracy had not then existed to ignore them; a conspiracy the more futile since meanwhile, by the turn of the century, the 'town' had won its decisive victory over the 'village', on battlefields such as the bookshops and the box-offices. What were hits in Paris became hits in Budapest; Maupassant's *Bel-Ami* was published in Magyar (and, indeed, by the fairly conservative house of Singer & Wolfner, known for its trade-mark 'Hungarian for the Hungarian!') on the morrow of its success in France; and though pseudo-folklife still held its own in anecdotal literature and a special branch of musicals, the most popular new Hungarian novelists and playwrights looked rather to urban life for

---

[1] *Pester Lloyd*, the leading German-language Hungarian newspaper since its foundation in 1854 until its cessation at the end of the Second World War. Its two most important editors were, from 1867 for some twenty-five years, Max Falk – the intimate of Széchenyi and Deák, the Magyar tutor of Queen-Empress Elisabeth, and member of Parliament – and, throughout the inter-war period, until *gleichgeschaltet* under Nazi pressure, the publicist József Vészi (see below, p. 131).

[2] It became his surname, and that of his children, astonishing many who (for instance, in Britain during the Second World War) were unwilling to believe that 'somebody could *really* be called that'.

their subjects. In practice there could not, of course, be any rigidly maintained distinction between 'town' and 'country' subjects. The poet, playwright, and humorist Jenő (Eugene) Heltai, for instance (originally, also one of *A Hét*'s young guard), was as famous for conjuring Petőfi's legendary shepherd 'John the Hero' onto the operetta stage as for his charming *chansons*, often spiced with Budapest slang, which were sung in the literary cabaret. But it was one thing to mix the two, and another to take notice of the fact that it was done. For the Academy, the facts of life were at best diversions, pardonable but against the rules. It was precisely these *rules* that Ignotus challenged: 'There is only one rule in art', he wrote. '"Do what you like so long as you know how to."'

Endre Ady

This declaration proved a green light for greater audacities than Ignotus himself imagined at the time of writing it. A powerful new poet emerged in Endre Ady (1877–1919), whose personality could accommodate itself as little to urban and sophisticated conventions as to the folksy and the academic. He did owe a great deal both to national traditions and to cosmopolitan modernism, but their fusion in his poetry was not only original, it was unique in its sensuous and visionary intensity; it electrified the young Hungarians of his time, and has remained ever since inimitable in world literature. Ady came from the impoverished Calvinist county squirearchy, and started as a conventional Liberal journalist and conventional poet by settling in Nagyvárad–of all Hungarian country towns the one most like Budapest and most worshipful of Paris; today it is a frontier town of Romania, called Oradea Mare. As a provincial young man, he was happy just to play at cosmopolitanism. In time, however, his own experience of the life of capitals made him a revolutionary in politics and a poet so original in style as to be almost incomprehensible. In Paris, as a press correspondent, accompanied by 'The Lady Leda' of his songs–a stout, auburn, middle-class Jewess from Nagyvárad, who helped him to skim the dailies and read French literature in the original–he came face to face with his dreamland. What did he really know of Paris? Nothing, on the face of it, that he could not have learned from books and pictures. He had only a smattering of French and made no effort to get into French society; most of his time was spent in the fug of cafés frequented by second-class tourists, third-class estate agents, immature artists, and ageing prostitutes; and whenever he betook himself towards either the palaces or the slums, his reactions (as his writings show) were perfectly honest: envy of the rich, brotherly compassion for the needy. He had, that is, no illusions about Paris. Yet for him it was the city of lights and songs and perfumes and liberty, a 'forest' hideaway for the Hungarian highwayman hounded by the pandoor –'highwayman' standing for personality, and 'pandoor' for parochial conventions.

In Paris, Ady dipped into *Les Fleurs du Mal*, even translated a few of them; and a shade of Baudelairean 'satanism' is traceable in his own erotic poetry, sensual and exhibitionist by the standards of his time. He was also attracted to the fantasies about *Paradis artificiels* (although personally given to ecstacies less 'artificial' – mainly drink and careless whoring for which he paid with syphilis, never totally cured). The licentious strain in both Baudelaire and the later vintage of *décadence* poets appealed to his longing for sensations, as did their play with symbols and their levelling of the frontiers between areas of mental perception. But all these things were simply in the pattern of lyrical modernism, though slightly more 'decadent' than the output of some older Impressionists and Symbolists: they were arresting in degree rather than in kind. All this super-modernism, however, appeared in the passion and wrath of ancient Magyar preachers and bards; contact with Rimbaud and the proletarian *argot* poet Jehan Rictus induced Ady to dig deeper into the Bible, and the songs of the fugitive Kuruc warriors, and his own childhood memories. His prosody became an amazing alloy of new and old, verses starting with iambic cadence but evolving in a rhythm more akin to ancient psalms and primordial Magyar songs than to the established metres of westernized Hungarian poetry. In other words, contact with modernity sparked off archaic notes in Ady. His poetry invested carnal experiences with solemnity. Most staggering were his poems to and about God. Among Hungarian poets of comparable stature, he was the first to make no bones about his disbelief in the existence of God; he was also the first (at any rate, since the Papist-Protestant confrontations of the seventeenth century) to give adequate poetic form to religious experience. Whether he believed in God or not, he always struggled with Him and often prayed for His forgiveness and protection. All this betrayed more than average self-pity, self-glory, and recklessness of obscurity. Good taste, restraint, and clarity were none of his virtues.

But he was absolutely clear about politics. In this respect he was as far as man could be from the play-acting of Baudelaire, Verlaine, and the rest; he would not trifle about human rights. His interest in public affairs was no less passionate, even compulsive, than his interest in wine and women and God. His political poetry, accordingly, often ran to cosmic visions; yet he was unequivocal and matter-of-fact (too much so for a poet, some of his critics would say) in his opinions on any piece of legislation and any government reshuffle, either at home or abroad. Although all his life an uncompromising Liberal, his attitude underwent a decisive change in the first four or five years of the twentieth century. Having started as a believer in the Tisza brand of National Liberalism, then supported the *ex-lex* administration which promised universal suffrage and other democratic reforms, he finally turned against the whole Establishment, dynastic and nationally-minded alike, and with particular vehemence against Count István Tisza: they were all, he felt, betraying the Liberal heritage. In Paris, the statesman who fascinated him most was the socialist Jaurès; and when, in 1905, the organ of Hungary's Social Democratic Party, *Népszava*, was turned into a daily, Ady made a point of regularly contributing both articles and poems to it. He never actually became a socialist; but he came to the conclusion that without the help of organized labour the progressives of the Hungarian middle classes had no chance of building a viable democracy. He was most outspoken and provocative on the nationalities issue, joining with Jászi in hopes for an 'Eastern Switzerland', and indeed going further than Jászi–for instance, in his *Hungarian Jacobin's Song* (1906) which appealed to the 'Magyars and non-Magyars' of the Danube basin for united action to rid their common land of the rule of 'squires and thugs'.

In the turmoil which Ady provoked, Ignotus took his part unreservedly, and became Ady's foremost champion. There were differences, mainly of temperament, between the two men: Ignotus was less of a radical than Ady (or Jászi, for that matter), mainly because, while agreeing with practically all his demands, he saw no hope of achieving them without making common cause with some at least of the influential magnates such as, for instance, Andrássy.

Ady the poet captivated Ignotus the critic mainly through what was least akin to the latter's own poetry: metaphysical disquietudes, the broadening of neurasthenic fears into a personal mythology.

'*Nyugat*'

In 1908, Ignotus, assisted by a dedicated discoverer of new talents, Ernő Osvát, and by the lively polemicist and organizer Max Fenyő, started a literary magazine called *Nyugat* (West), with Ady from the outset as its leading contributor. The title was significant, but so was that of Ignotus's leading article, 'The People of the East', by which he meant the Magyars. The *Nyugat* guard were determined to create a totally European Hungary, delivered from parochialism; but, at the same time, to assert the national personality and to dig deep into the Magyar heritage of images, concepts, and melodies, and refurbish what had been debased by usage and foreign influences. Thus *Nyugat* not only went one step further than its predecessors in making

Hungarian literature metropolitan: it also brought about a synthesis of that metropolitan spirit and pre-urban, primordial Hungary—a synthesis which today's Western audience can probably apprehend more clearly through Bartók's and Kodály's music than through any other medium.

Nyugat brought forth a host of lyrical poets, dedicated linguists, and translators from five or six languages, and virtuosi in all forms of verse. They were personalities very different from Ady's, and at first often hostile to him. The two most generally accepted now as classic Hungarian writers, Mihály Babits (1883–1941) and Dezső Kosztolányi (1885–1936)—the one a schoolmaster, the other an undergraduate in the early 1900s—exchanged letters in which they lamented that 'a blown-up ape has been crowned Prince of new Hungarian poetry in the person of Endre Ady'. His strident imagery, his uneven prosody, his self-glorification and the passion with which he denigrated his own country were all 'nauseating' to them; his left-wing crudity revolted Kosztolányi, and his bombastic addresses to a 'Lady Leda' exasperated Babits. Yet in the end they capitulated to Ady's power: 'He's head and shoulders above the rest of us', admitted Babits, with mingled resignation and excitement. And side by side with Ady, the acknowledged intuitive genius, Babits was to appear as leading intellectual lyricist in the *Nyugat* set-up: outstanding in his interpretation of medieval Latin, medieval German, early Italian poetry (Dante), and of English literature from Shakespeare to Swinburne and the Pre-Raphaelites. In the *Nyugat* kaleidoscope all trends in modern Western arts and philosophy were reflected, even those still only foreshadowed in their countries of origin. Ignotus was the first layman (i.e., writer outside the medical profession) on the International Committee of Freudian psychoanalysts; Babits was an early propagator of Bergson's philosophy; young György Lukács (1883–1971), on the extreme idealist fringe of the *Nyugat* movement, a herald of such thinkers as Kierkegaard, Simmel, Stefan George; Kosztolányi, relatively conservative, specialized in Rimbaud and Rilke; others acclaimed Wagner and Nietzsche, Henry and William James, Ernst Mach and Russell, Wilde and Shaw, Claudel and Francis Jammes, Wells and Galsworthy; and even Ady, who was far from an assiduous reader of foreign literature, discovered in André Gide (notably for the latter's tragic struggle with a God in whom he did not really believe) 'a man closer to me in human and literary development than anyone I have ever come across', at a time when Gide's name was hardly known to Frenchmen.

In the novel and short story, *Nyugat*'s break with tradition was more social than artistic. The greatest novelist of that circle (and, indeed, of Hungary), Zsigmond Móricz (1879–1942), emerged as a

Zola of the Hungarian countryside at a time when Zola's novels had been selling in Magyar translation for decades. It was the power of truthful narration rather than any novelty of style that excited his audience and, inevitably, horrified the conservatives. His most important fellow-writers were Margit Kaffka, a cross between George Eliot and Turgenev in her sensitive but ruthless chronicles of the decaying provincial gentry, and J. Jenő Tersánszky, creator of a twentieth-century type of Magyar picaresque fiction about vagabonds of the suburbs, highroads, and Transylvanian mountains. Such traditional styles still contributed to a literary 'revolution' because, in one way or another, they highlighted facets of life ignored by officialdom.

Bartók, Kodály

This same wave also achieved a synthesis of 'East' and 'West', of folklore and metropolis, of Hungarian landscape and Montmartre-Montparnasse techniques in all the visual arts, especially painting; and finally, and with the greatest impact of all on international culture, in music. The pioneers of the musical renewal were Béla Bartók (1881–1945) and Zoltán Kodály (1882–1967), both of them folksong-collectors as well as composers, whose efforts have perhaps been best defined by Bartók when he wrote to a friend that 'we must isolate the very ancient, for this is the only way of identifying the really new'. It was a declaration of war on the Gypsy-Hungarian style, so corrupt, artificial, and sloppy in their view, even when adapted by Brahms and Liszt; a declaration of war, too, on the Austro-Hungarian operetta valse, such as Lehár's melodies. The highbrow music-lover has ever since then had no time for such 'trash'. This writer, though not claiming to know much about music, must however express his belief that such scorn was not only unjustified but, to some degree, intellectually dishonest. The denigrators of the conventional *csárdás*-valse cult were often themselves secretly addicted to it; still worse, they remained unaware of their own hypocrisy, since the whole dividing-line between 'genuine folk-tune' and 'fake' was rather artificial. Kodály (who, admittedly, was less uncompromising than Bartók in his search for the most ancient and the most modern) made ample use in his comic opera *Háry János* of tunes which derived from the fairly recent musical hybrids of recruiting dances. The slogans encouraged by Bartók's and Kodály's success were therefore often smug and hollow, as revolutionary cries usually are; but to say so does not detract from the broad vistas their music opened to modern art, or from the stimulus they gave to ethnographic research. And to this modern music *Nyugat* gave a platform ahead of practically the whole cultural world in and outside Hungary

–just as it did, among the scientific disciplines, to psychoanalysis (Sándor Ferenczi, Freud's most intimate contributor, was a Hungarian attached to the *Nyugat* circle); which may give some idea of how and why that literary magazine, with only a modest number of subscribers, played such an important part in Hungarian history and is remembered more than half a century later as the high-water mark of national culture.

Jews and Gentry; Intellect and Genius

Another, and perhaps paradoxical, significance of *Nyugat* was, that through it the decaying gentry expressed their artistic aptitudes with more brilliance, penetration, and originality than their glorious forefathers had ever shown. Whatever the reason, the early twentieth century, which rang the knell of the Hungarian lesser nobility as a class, brought to the surface the brightest creative faculties of exceptional individuals in that class. *Nyugat*'s protagonists and intellectual leaders (Ignotus among them) were Jews; but its most creative artists were gentiles and mostly of the provincial 'gentry', such as Ady, Babits, Margit Kaffka, Tersánszky, Kosztolányi, Bartók, and Kodály. Móricz, with his mixed peasant and lower-middle-class background, and the sardonic storyteller of the Budapest cafés, Lajos Nagy, illegitimate son of a peasant maid, were (since neither of them had a Jew or a nobleman in his family background) rather exceptional among men of letters at that time.

The meeting of Jewish intellect and gentry-begotten genius, enhanced by the rise of workers' and peasants' élites, would have seemed ideally qualified to heal the breach within Magyar white-collar society and amalgamate the trading class with the professional middle class dreamt of by the great liberal reformers. In fact, the opposite resulted. The great majority of the middle-class gentry were more alienated by Jewish intellect than by Jewish commercialism; and, more than anything else, by gentile genius.

Stagecraft and Press: ahead of the World

'TT' and *Nyugat* were highbrow Hungary; an average filing clerk or gentleman farmer, let alone a peasant farmer, could have lived in Hungary for decades without being aware of either. Yet, as we shall come to see, they were at the root of what has distinguished Hungary and the Hungarian people ever since the mid-1950s. A history of contemporary Hungary would be misleading that did not point out their significance. But it would be equally misleading to ignore those other trends of taste and opinion which concurrently stirred up large masses of Hungarians on the eve of and during the First World War. The Hungarian theatre deserves attention, if only for its international impact. On the stage, spiritual renewal had a less esoteric background than in the magazines. There were in Hungary, as in practically all civilized countries, little experimental theatres; but in Hungarian play-writing and play-acting, the breakthrough of the modern mind consisted in mastering and ingeniously applying technical skills rather than in feats of social and artistic hypersensitiveness. It was, in a word, a middle-brow revolution. But few important talents can be pigeonholed as high, middle, or low so far as their 'brows' are concerned. The most important playwright of twentieth-century Hungary, Franz Molnár (1878–1952), successful also as a novelist and satirist, showed sparks of genius in his short and biting sketches, as indeed in the funny stories he liked to dramatize in conversation, but owed his world reputation to his plays, which were monumental achievements of clever and entertaining mediocrity, and to his charming and sentimental adolescents' novel *The Paul Street Boys*. His comedies were a roaring success all over the world – more than anywhere else, in German-speaking Europe (until Hitler intervened) and in the United States; and least of all in the United Kingdom.[1]

Film was still in its infancy at that time, and as an art not yet past the embryonic stage; but when, after the First World War, it emerged as the most important mass medium for decades to come, Hungarian stagecraft turned out to have been its unsuspecting pioneer. Hollywood owed much to its immigrant Hungarians; scriptwriters such as Melchior Lengyel and Lajos Biró, whose work keeps turning up even today, actually imported and processed for cosmopolitan use those techniques of drama and reportage which had developed for home consumption in the Press and theatre of pre-1914 Hungary. In Britain, the film productions mounted by Sir Alexander Korda probably made the greatest impact of that same kind and derivation.

Pre-1914 Budapest was, above all, a city of self-induced excitement, and lacked neither the inventiveness nor the vulgarity to develop her techniques faster than any other city of Europe. In her social and architectural foundations, she took after Vienna, and in her cravings for wit and grace, she pursued the image of Paris, but in enterprise and sensationalism, she resembled New York. The tricks of advertisement, of splashing news, of mixing reports on

[1] Let me quote an example of how far apart the two greatest English-speaking countries can be in such matters. Chaplin in his memoirs (*My Autobiography*, London, 1964) mentions Molnár, in one breath with Chekhov, as a household name. As his book was published in the U.K. before appearing in the U.S.A., it was for the British indexer to look that name up, and he understandably settled for the first Molnár he found. Consequently, in Chaplin's book, a late Hungarian communist cabinet minister and historian, Erik Molnár, figures as Chekhov's partner in illustrating some trends of dramaturgy.

world affairs, bedroom scandals, and business rackets, and of combining a crusade against corruption with unscrupulous gossipmonger-
ing and smear campaigns—in short, the typical techniques of modern
sensationalism—were exploited in the Hungarian Press on a scale
second only to the American. The Budapest evening paper *Az Est*
(The Evening), launched in 1910, with a former city reporter, Andor
Miklós, as editor, made European press history with its rich display
of these characteristics. It was altogether a magnificent venture,
sophisticated even in its vulgarity, dedicated even in its opportunism.
Its prime inspiration was the belief that what sells must be true; and
to a large extent, it *was* true. Society saw itself mirrored in the im-
provisations of such crack journalists as the highly intelligent and
unstable Pál Kéri and the implacable and quixotic racket-exposer
László Fényes, or in the vivid and often satirical sketches of Molnár,
later a war correspondent of *Az Est*. By the end of the World War,
its circulation had risen to 480,000—which meant that at that moment practically everybody who read Magyar saw it. As to its politics:
Andor Miklós thought, and made no bones about saying, that he
'directed public opinion'. In fact he ran after it; but he did so most
efficiently.

Chapter 6

The End of Habsburg Hungary and a Year of Eruptions

Unshakeable Count Tisza

THE DECADE LEADING UP TO the World War was in Hungarian public affairs one of constant dramatic changes which resulted in cancelling each other out–a period typical of *plus ça change . . .* In 1904 the Prime Minister, Count Tisza, broke the filibustering of the "48-er' opposition by means so flagrantly unconstitutional that, in reaction, even conservative and "67-er' opinion turned against him and a group of outraged "48-ers' smashed their benches to pieces in Parliament. In early 1905, the unbelievable happened: in spite of the strongly restricted suffrage and open vote, the Tisza government was defeated in a general election. Tisza dissolved his Liberal Party: it was, apparently, the end for him in public affairs.

The victorious National Coalition of "48-ers', dissident constitutionalist "67-ers', and clericals (People's Party) was not, however, able to hide its fundamental identity of views with the routed Liberals, standing as it did for Free Trade and free thought in the towns, but sanctity of ecclesiastical, squirearchic, and landlordly prerogatives in the villages. The "48-er' filibustering had been aimed at obtaining more meaningful tokens of Hungary's independence than those previously granted, particularly in the affairs of the army; and the National Coalition, including its "67-ers', now concentrated on these. But Franz Joseph refused to make concessions on such issues; so he banned Parliament and imposed government by decree, appointing as Prime Minister a soldier of unquestioned obedience to the crown, General Baron Géza Fejérváry. The National Coalition appealed for help over the head of the government to the counties; the government in its turn appealed over the heads of the counties to the common people. The Minister of the Interior, József Kristóffy, formerly one of the Tisza Liberal deputies, consulted the leaders of the non-Magyar nationalities and the 'godless, maverick' Social Democrats, and came forward with a franchise reform plan, under which the secret ballot was to be introduced and the number of voters more than doubled. This implied a threat to the gentry's

128

rule over the poor peasantry, and to Magyar supremacy over the non-Magyars.

The National Coalition panicked; they had clamoured for democratic progress, but in the conviction that the Court would never take them at their word. Kristóffy, however, seemed to mean business. They therefore capitulated to Franz Joseph (after obtaining some face-saving concessions), and a National Coalition government took over, headed by the adaptable Sándor Wekerle, as non-party premier and Minister of Finance. Count Andrássy, leader of the Constitution Party, became Minister of the Interior, burdened with the impossible task of devising a franchise reform which should be both democratic and a safeguard of Magyar supremacy; the Catholic People's Party was represented in the government by Count Aladár Zichy; and the "48-ers', besides Count Apponyi (with whose nationalities policy at the head of Education we have dealt in a previous chapter), by the nominal leader of their, at that moment, nominally united party, Ferenc Kossuth, the son of Lajos, who, after his father's death, had returned to Hungary and been elected to Parliament. The name Kossuth still had a magical effect on Hungarians; it had on Ferenc himself when he yielded to the temptation to head the Hungarian Independence movement; but even this ambitious step he took as an act of obedience to public opinion rather than a venture on his own. He was neither a fighter nor a thinker; and not even in good health. According to some ill-wishers of his, his doom was gluttony; he certainly liked fried fowl. Whether this sole ascertainable passion of his did fundamentally contribute to his early collapse (as his ill-wishers suggested) may be left for decision to history; but he did not cut an impressive figure either as an independence leader or as (what he actually was in the coalition government) a Minister of Trade. In the latter capacity, it was his good luck to rely on the abilities of his deputy (or Secretary of State), the most assiduous pusher and expert economist of the Dual Monarchy, the ex-Jew and Baron-to-be József Szterényi, who laid the foundations of an industrial welfare policy comparable to what had been initiated in advanced western and Central European countries. As to the independence issue, Kossuth was torn between the efforts of his lieutenants. Apponyi was sitting on the fence between 'National Opinion' and the Court; whereas Gyula Justh, the then most dynamic personality of the "48-er' camp, actually the President of the House of Deputies under the coalition government (this being in Hungary, like in most of the continental countries, a party political appointment), was sitting on the fence between the passion of nationalism and the drive for democracy. Ferenc Kossuth sat on the fence between Apponyi and Justh – an understandable attitude but uninspiring.

The National Coalition government had come with the double aim of progressing, simultaneously, towards Hungarian independence and universal suffrage. But the Court would not hear of the former; and neither coalition nor Court was keen on the latter. The 'non-compromising '48-ers', led by Gyula Justh, went into opposition, the coalition government fell, and, by early 1910, Count Tisza was back in power—although as the leader of a party renamed 'Party of National Work' and not yet as head of the government but as President of the House of Deputies—a post he filled with unconcealed partisanship.

The opposition, ranging from the former National Coalition government parties to their greatest former enemies, the Social Democrats (still not represented in Parliament), turned the heat on against Tisza, now regarded as the greatest obstacle to suffrage reform. This belief was to a large extent justified. Other political groups may or may not have kept their promises in the matter and wondered what sort of compromise to accept and when to accept it; Tisza was the man who opposed it from whatever quarter and with whatever qualifications it was put forward. Even in his own Party of National Work, many would have liked a more conciliatory attitude, but he overruled them. László Lukács, for instance, his Prime Minister in 1912, was fundamentally a financial politician and inclined to suffrage reform. Yet it was he who paid most dearly for the anti-Tisza campaign. Admittedly, he was involved in corrupt dealings—not for his own benefit but in aid of the government party funds. An opposition deputy, Zoltán Désy, declared at a banquet that 'it is an open secret that the head of government of our country is the greatest racketeer[1] in Europe'; and when sued for slander the court acquitted him. This judicial triumph was largely due to the brilliant performance of Counsel for the Defence, the deputy Vilmos Vázsonyi (1868–1926), who led a minute party in Parliament (the purely Budapest-based Democratic Citizens) but was a formidable speaker and scathing wit, destined to play a paramount role in public affairs. A pot-bellied, flatfooted, grocer-type Jew, he could capture all audiences from the platform: and was, indeed, on the morrow of the Lukács-Désy trial, worshipped as a champion of justice, not least by the Catholic People's Party and the Catholic traditionalist counts who made common cause with Marxists in using any stick to bring down the tyrannical parvenu Count Tisza. So Vázsonyi won a glorious victory but with ironical result: Lukács (in 1913) had to resign and Tisza took over once again, with extended powers, as Prime Minister. *Plus ça change . . .*, as already noted.

---

[1] 'Panamista' in Hungarian political slang—deriving from the corruption scandal connected with the building of the Panama Canal.

Court and Gentlefolk Intent on Outmanoeuvring Each Other

This decade (1904–14) could be seen as a modernized and condensed repetition of the hundred-or-so years leading from Maria Theresa's rule to the eve of the 1848 War for Independence. The dynasty and the gentlefolk tried during both periods to outmanoeuvre each other, throwing popular slogans into the battle: abolition of serfdom (or at any rate reforms pointing towards it) in 1748–1848, and universal secret suffrage (or its approximation) in 1904–14. In both cases, each party relied on the *other's* fear of a popular rising; but scared of it themselves, came to terms with the other intermittently. Meanwhile, in both cases, events were brought to a head by international developments, and a revolution came about which overtook both its dynastic and squirearchic planners.

At the beginning of the twentieth century, the radical intellectuals and the Social Democratic workers (the latter led by Ernő Garami) sided with the dynasty rather than with the counties and their National Resistance. Under the guidance of József Vészi, an extremely clever Jewish journalist who combined dynastic loyalties with an urge for social reforms, quite a number of republican and socialist intellectuals, such as Endre Ady and Lajos Nagy, served the Habsburg administration and turned against its nationalist opposition. The Democrat leader, Vázsonyi, on the other hand, sided with the nationalists; he had agitated for franchise reform but would not accept it from the hands of an unconstitutional government. In other words, the Left split into extremists sympathetic to Habsburg rule and moderates who indulged in rebellious gestures – an ironical division of loyalties but not unprecedented: the position had been similar under Joseph II in the 1780s.

In Vienna, the moving spirit of the policy of enforcing democracy on Hungary was the heir to the Imperial throne, Archduke Franz Ferdinand – another ironical fact, as he was by nature and philosophy anything but a democrat. In Hungary, he was intensely disliked even by those who occasionally made common cause with him; the one matter in which the diehard county squire saw eye-to-eye with the bohemian radical of the Budapest cafés was their angry aversion to their ruler-to-be whose dead serious face, looking like a square dumpling with a great moustache, struck them as a challenge to the liberal and easygoing traditions of their country. The main reason for his unpopularity was nationalist bias and the sort of sectional interest that can usually be spotted behind it. Franz Ferdinand stood behind Kristóffy in his attempts to mobilize the support of non-Magyar paupers against the Magyarizing county administrations; and this was an offence not only to the squires but, by implication, also to cities such as Budapest which owed their size and importance to the Magyarizing drive. Franz Ferdinand and his advisers recognized the evils and dangers of a Magyar supremacy which could often be equated with the power of the gentry over the peasants and labourers; and this was his main crime in Hungarian opinion. It would, however, be wrong to disregard his addiction to authoritarian views which made nonsense of his democratic sympathies. In foreign affairs, his preference was to make common cause with militarist and traditionalist powers against subversive liberals. A devout adherent of the Pope, a friend and admirer of Kaiser Wilhelm II, he hoped he could win active support from Romanov Russia and at least passive support from Britain so as to hold Republican France and Cavourist Italy at bay. Within the Habsburg monarchy, he experimented with schemes such as a so-called 'Trialism' instead of the existing dualism, by making Bohemia a third equal and extending the autonomy of the Croats and other Catholic Slavs so as to counterbalance both the Magyar influence and that of the Greek Orthodox Slavs (Serbs, etc.) and Romanians. In his abhorrence of chauvinist class rule over Hungary, three elements seem to have mingled: a realistic diagnosis of social facts; a militaristic aversion to any national force endangering, as he saw it, the discipline and readiness for combat of the Imperial army; and impatience with Calvinism, Jewry, Freemasonry, and the cult of rebellion for which Hungary and her lawyers and Press had always been conspicuous, even when making it up with the 'tyrant' behind padded doors. Franz Ferdinand was a man of higher education and more serious moral responsibility than Hungarians (and historians influenced by them) liked to admit; but, true enough, he was a humourless pedant, unbearable to all shades of Hungarian taste. This, more than anything else, doomed his attempts to failure.

Count Michael Károlyi and his Drift to the Left

In the 1910s (as in and after the 1830s), the hopes for a Habsburg-sponsored radicalism were dissipated; and a national Independence movement more and more sympathetic to the internationalist Left played first fiddle in the opposition to Tisza's rule. A universal secret suffrage league was formed, under the umbrella of which the intransigents of the traditionalist "48-ers' co-ordinated with Marxists, anarchists, and other ideological representatives of the 'scum of the fatherland' their attacks on the ruling oligarchy. The radicalization of "48' was precipitated in 1913 when the ailing Justh handed over leadership of the Independence Party to young Count Michael (Mihály) Károlyi (1875–1955).

Michael Károlyi was one of the wealthiest aulic magnates of his country (second in riches only to Prince Esterházy) and started his career very conscious of his remarkable family background.[1] He was the descendant of General Sándor Károlyi, who was rewarded with fabulous estates for deserting the rebel Prince Rákóczi and helping to consolidate Habsburg rule over Hungary; he was a grandson of Countess Caroline Zichy, mistress of the martyr premier of 1848, Count Lajos Batthyány, and an outspoken and implacable hater of the Habsburgs; son of a Count Gyula Károlyi who in 1860 smuggled money from Cavour to the Hungarian conspirators against Habsburg rule; and nephew of the agrarian leader Count Sándor Károlyi who, at the end of the nineteenth century, made his notable attempt to stem the Liberal trend by initiating a co-operative movement directed against free trade, free professions, and Jewry. The Károlyi family history was crisscrossed with ties of indebtedness and loyalty to the Court of Vienna, but also with memories of many a *fronde* organized against it; with pride in their prominence in the fight for national independence and liberal reform, but also with desire to reassert such traditional authorities as the Roman Catholic clergy, the hereditary King-Emperor, and the hereditary aristocracy; with a mixture of paternalistic condescension to, and romantic belief in, the common people. How could all these impulses be reconciled? Only at the expense of logic, of course. As to young Count Michael, he never had a good word to say for his notorious ancestor, the General, and blushed for his way of founding the family fortune, though he could not help enjoying its benefits. He was, on the other hand, deeply moved, albeit amused, whenever he recalled his Habsburgophobe grandmother.

Mind you, after the *Ausgleich* of '67, we became a family of courtiers again, loaded with honours. But they had to be hidden from my grandmother. 'What's that trash on your chest, another gift from *that murderer?!*' she would bawl her sons or nephews out; 'that murderer' was of course Franz Joseph . . . and, in full Imperial Royal rule, no one dared to contradict her.

Michael Károlyi's recollections of his notoriously reactionary uncle Sándor were kindly and respectful. 'He was really the most clearsighted man in the aulic aristocracy', he would say.

---

[1] I had numerous talks with him in wartime Oxford and London and in post-war Paris and Budapest; in the course of these, we often discussed the impact on him of his family entourage and of the acquaintance he made on his early trips abroad with people of quite different background; and in his portrayal I largely rely on my personal recollections. But most of the facts referred to can be found in his autobiographical works such as *Egy egész világ ellen* (Against a Whole World, Munich 1923, republished by Gondolat, Budapest, 1965) and the posthumous *Memoirs of Michael Károlyi—Faith Without Illusion* (translated into English by Catherine Károlyi, London 1956).

He was caste-bound, no doubt; convinced it was God's will that our lot should be masters of the rest. But at the bottom of our hearts, we all thought so. We professed to be Liberal because it was the fashion, and trusted that history wouldn't keep us to our word when liberal principles were implemented. My uncle Sándor at least saw the problems we were up against. And although for reasons of his own, he recognized the abyss into which the nineteenth-century version of liberalism was pushing the people. '*Laissez-faire* doesn't provide the final answer', he would say. 'It plays into the hands of the Jewish bankers and not into those of the poor masses. Read *this* if you don't believe me: it's not by a Catholic priest or a feudal landlord but by a revolutionary socialist, and a Jew at that. But whatever his errors, he did see how liberal capitalism worked', my uncle said, and he was the first man to put Marx into my hands. And Marx did impress me at once with his subtle logic. But the final outcome was somewhat different from what my uncle had been hoping for.

One reason for his getting a leftish slant from the Marxian injection rather than a neo-feudal one was, as he later explained, the impact made on him by socialist intellectuals whom he met first at international co-operative congresses and later also in private. He was on friendly terms, for instance, with Sidney Webb and the Belgian leader Vandervelde; his family background was an excellent introduction, wherever he travelled, whether at sumptious receptions for, say, the Duke and Duchess of Connaught in Ceylon, or at the informal Western dinner parties where trade unionists and academics and stockbrokers and artists met the blue-blooded more or less as equals. To the west of the Austro-Hungarian monarchy, Károlyi mixed freely with all sorts of people in whose ideas he was interested; while in his native country he never, until his rise to power on the wave of a democratic revolution with his wife, 'Red Katinka', at his side, mixed socially with anyone outside the aristocracy. He would have referred to a number of left-wingers (''48-er' deputies coming from the 'petty gentry', and journalists and intellectual socialists of Jewish extraction) as his 'intimate friends'; the countess was quite enthusiastic about them; yet the two would never have dreamt, say, of inviting their wives. 'Friends', yes, and geniuses perhaps, but still a lower animal species, in Hungary. 'Don't think it was arrogance', Michael Károlyi would say, decades later, when recalling those times;

in Habsburg Austro-Hungary, it was simply impossible to behave otherwise. If I entered a middle-class home, I was stared at like an idol, and women stood up and those who knew how to curtsey did so as to royalty. Our world was so far apart from ordinary men, even from the ordinary 'gentlemen' . . .

This was the way he recalled 1900 and 1940, and with more than a grain of truth. Yet there seems to have been from the outset a quite genuine haughtiness, indeed truculence, in him; and he himself was not always sure when he was acting out of generosity and when out of malice. He was a fighter and gambler by nature. No sooner had he followed his uncle in the presidency of OMGE, the association of great landowners, than he fell out with practically the whole association and, after resigning, was rapidly attracted towards the opposite camp. Idealistic passion did play its part; but so did resentment at the effrontery of his fellow-landowners in opposing him when they must have known, most of them, that they lagged far behind him in both wealth and standing. In the 1910s, his bugbear was Count Tisza; 'for being a reactionary or for being an upstart?' I would ask him. 'Actually for both', he answered; and he described how Tisza would snap his fingers and click his heels to the music of the gypsy band as no real magnate, not one of the aulic set, would have done. In fact, it was a group of aulic magnates, of ancient aristocratic stock, which rallied against the diehard and parvenu gentry, represented by Tisza, in and around 1910: Apponyi, Andrássy, several Counts Zichy and Esterházy, and the young Marquis György Pallavicini, though adhering to various parties, agreed that *some* step towards demo-cratization must be taken; and they associated themselves openly with the lower-middle-class democrat *par excellence*, Vázsonyi. Károlyi belonged to this group and was particularly friendly with Count Andrássy (whose niece and stepdaughter, Catherine, he was to marry in November 1914). But he very soon found Vázsonyi too much of a tactician and too cautious as an oracle of democracy. Nor was he always happy about the Social Democrat leader Garami, reminiscent in his restraint (as Hungarians would see him) of an English Labour politician. Károlyi's favourite among the plebeian firebrands was another Social Democrat, Zsigmond Kunfi, a colour-ful intellect and fascinating orator but lacking exactly what Károlyi lacked: patience and a sense of balance.

Károlyi, though his adversaries would deny this (and many of his supporters would secretly agree with his adversaries), was a highly intelligent man, and one of broad vision. When he could forget his passions, both political and personal, he emerged as a most pleasant conversationalist and wise *raisonneur*; and he displayed a rare faculty for combining interest in the events of the day with speculation on the possibilities of the future. In some of his initiatives he was almost prophetic, though at the time he may only have seemed a meddler: for instance, when, shortly before the First World War, in spite of his 'Pink' commitments, he sought friendly links with the Court and government of St Petersburg, as well as with the republicans of France and the United States, because he felt all avenues should be tried that led away from his country's fatally close entanglement with the expansionism of the German Reich. He was a good and important man. But he cut a hopeless figure on the public platform, where the passion with which he apparently tried to surmount his disability of a cleft palate led only to incoherence. Was he 'compensating' all the time, in the Adlerian sense? Whatever the psychological explanation, the fact is that owing to his elegant appearance, fluency in foreign languages, physical courage, and, above all, family name and fortune, he managed to overcome his limitations and was thought of by many as a Louis Kossuth of the 1910s. He had just taken off for a lecture tour, accompanied by Kunfi and others, to raise support among the Magyars of the United States for a democratic independent Hungary when on 28 June 1914, Franz Ferdinand and his wife were murdered in Sarajevo.

1914–17: Plunging into War, Yearning for Peace

For Hungary, and indeed for Hungarians of all shades, nothing could have been more absurd than the idea of taking up arms to avenge the death of the archduke. To die for a Habsburg? For a clericalist archduke? For a Magyarophobe? Before his assassination, all would have ridiculed such an assumption. Yet when it happened, practically all parties, all politicians, all newspapers appeared to compete in bellicosity. The reason? Apparently a general malaise from which everyone tried to escape into military adventure. *Az Est* rode the wave of military gaiety, in tune with the boulevards of Budapest which echoed to a march composed on the spur of the moment, threatening 'Serbia, you cur!' and warning her 'you will never have Bosnia!' Few really cared about Bosnia but no one cared to say so. In *Világ* (World), the daily paper of the radical intelligentsia, anguish was expressed, as also in the visionary poems of Ady and other *Nyugat* poets; but the masses at that moment felt none, and neither did the politicians. Károlyi, on his way back from the United States, was interned in France when the war broke out, but, after being allowed to return home as a well-known Francophile, even he felt he must volunteer to go to the front; while the socialists tried to strike a balance between dislike of their warlords and satisfaction that, after all, they were fighting the most reactionary Great Power, the Russia of the Romanovs. Behind the scenes, only a few days after the Sarajevo murder, Tisza, the Hungarian premier, expressed misgivings about rushing into a war; whether he feared the results of un-preparedness or the possibility of an increase of Slav population in the Habsburg Empire as a result of possible annexation may be arguable, but the formal reassurances he received on both issues were sufficient for him to throw in his lot with the war party. Subsequently he was considered the model last-ditcher of the Central Powers, and it was a great surprise to learn, years after the war, of his initial warnings.

But it became an utterly unpopular war as soon as its character became manifest. Military setbacks were only one reason and not a decisive one: sufficient to dispel some rosy illusions but, until the phase of active American intervention, amply compensated for by German and Austro-Hungarian victories. The horrors of the battle-front, with columns of crippled and mutilated soldiers limping out of the hospitals (a sight more heartrending even than the casualty lists), did make an impact, of course, but could not be called a sur-prise. The surprising element was the *boredom* of war. For most people it was anything but adventurous; it meant the limitation of one's range of activity, the squalor of the trenches in the front line, and the drabness of rationing and price control and *ersatz* materials on the home front. Many lived better than before as a result of the emergency regulations and the devaluation of currency (which meant a general liberation from debts in town and country); but not sufficiently better to be grateful for it. There were really only two categories for whom it was, or could seem, a worthwhile adventure: one, those who developed from petty traders into millionaires (whether 'war profiteers' is debatable—their code of conduct did not substanti-ally deviate from that of farmers, manufacturers, or shopkeepers in general); and the other, the penniless lower-middle-class man who, as a military officer, could indulge his lust for power, ordering sub-ordinates about and practising jurisdiction over a population at his mercy. They were two very different categories, and though the life of a megalomaniac lieutenant would seem to anyone in his senses a far shabbier fulfilment than making millions and spending half of them, the shabby variety of war beneficiary cherished the source of his advancement more tenaciously than did the other, more enviable, one. And it is easily understandable why that should be so. The war millionaire was anxious to see a peace with prospects of carrying on as a peace millionaire; but the railway clerk acting as wartime pasha over occupied territories or militarized home districts could not hope to carry on as a peacetime pasha once hostilities were over. He was in fact able to, as it later turned out, under Fascism, but no such notions existed during the war: military rule then was confined to the military.

Except for this layer of potential *Gauleiter*, it was for all Hungarians a period of stagnation, frustration, aimlessness. 'What are we fighting for?' they wondered, as they should have done when hostilities broke out. To 'teach Serbia a lesson' would no longer do, once the very first stage was over, and to repeat the war cry 'Gott strafe England!' imported from Berlin made no appeal even to those willing to believe that 'perfidious Albion' was the main villain. If Anglo-German rivalry was at the bottom of the war, why not let *them* fight it out? The German alliance grew more and more unpopular even among nationalists. The Hohenzollern military were efficient, no doubt, and made notable sacrifices to redeem the blunders of their allies, but the more their superiority was flaunted the more irritating it seemed. Meanwhile, from the late summer of 1915, the pacifist Left of the Socialist International found its voice again, and the early war-weariness and disappointment of the general public were reinforced by the revolutionary breeze across the frontier. Károlyi, with his characteristic mixture of modish and apostolic fervour, led the combined nationalist and internationalist campaign against Prussian overlordship, a campaign that often expressed itself in leg-pulling. On leave from the Front to attend Parliament, he swung along the *Corso* in his hussar officer's uniform and when a German officer asked him the way he answered 'Pardonnez-moi Monsieur, mais je ne parle pas l'allemand'. Then he hurried to the magnates' club, the National Casino, to tell the story. Most of his fellow-members were incensed by it and particularly his cousin, Count Imre Károlyi, who with German counter-intelligence agents tried to frame him as an *Entente* agent.

On 21 November 1916 the eighty-six-year-old Franz Joseph died and was followed on the throne by his twenty-nine-year-old great-nephew Karl,[1] a man of goodwill, rash decisions, and blatant inexperience which seemed due to his character rather than to his youth. The first phase of his rule happened to be marked by the most aggressive moves of the Central Powers (occupation of Bucharest and subsequent annexationist policy; declaration of unlimited U-boat warfare); but he quickly acquired the reputation of a peace-loving man, and was looked on with corresponding suspicion by the Prussians. He also showed some interest in furthering democratization of the Dual Monarchy. He abruptly sacked Count Tisza (23 May 1917) and appointed a minority coalition government under the premiership of young Count Móricz Esterházy (an intelligent and serious, though little-known, member of Andrássy's Constitution Party) with the aim of preparing franchise reform. This was, by the standards of the day, a definitely left-wing government, embracing

[1] Karl I, as Emperor of Austria; Karl IV ('IV. Károly') as King of Hungary.

representatives of all the parliamentary groups who wanted franchise reform, including Károlyi's Independence Party (which was openly opposed to U-boat warfare), and with the leader of the Democratic Citizens, Vázsonyi, as Minister of Justice in charge of the proposed suffrage bill; it also enjoyed for a while the support of the Social Democrats[1] and Jászi's radicals (neither of them with seats in Parliament), and the qualified support of most of the nationalities parties.

The unpopularity of the war was aggravated by the abdication of Nicholas II of Russia on 15 March 1917; the 'most reactionary Great Power' could no longer be located in the enemy camp.[2] The scramble for supreme power by all revolutionaries from Palest Pink to Black–from constitutional monarchists to anarchists–was watched with excitement and bewilderment. For a while, it was the determined left-wingers who put their faith in Kerensky, whereas trust in Lenin offered the most comfortable posture for having it both ways– breathing Revolution and praising the genius of Hohenzollern diplomacy at one and the same time. And he was the hero of Peace, of course; 'Lenin, Lenin!' ran the refrain of a dithyrambic poem in *Az Est*, hitting all imaginable birds with one stone.

Within less than a year, however–that is, by early 1918–things had changed a great deal. Tisza, firmly opposed to suffrage reform but chary of using his parliamentary majority to overthrow the government, manoeuvred the reformists into piecemeal retreat, thus deepening the cleavage between those who were willing and those who were unwilling to make concessions to him. On 20 August 1917, Esterházy resigned and the most often-tried master of compromise, ex-premier Sándor Wekerle, took over once again as head of the government. Vázsonyi stayed on for a while but Károlyi's party pulled out. On 7 November, Lenin established his power; and on 3 March 1918, in Brest-Litovsk, the Central Powers forced Soviet Russia to accept a most humiliating peace treaty.

After the sabre-rattling German speeches at Brest-Litovsk, by no stretch of the imagination could the Kaiser and Lenin be any longer represented as heroes on the same front. The 'most reactionary Great Power' having disappeared, the Hohenzollern Reich took its

[1] On 6 June 1917 the radical adherents of the Reform integrated in a suffrage bloc under the misleading title of 'Suffrage Committee of Budapest Citizens and Workers', with Michael Károlyi as president, and Vázsonyi and Sándor Garbai, a former bricklayer and a representative of the Social Democrats, as vice-presidents; thus, though the Social Democrats held no portfolio in the government and Károlyi did not personally participate in it either, they could be regarded as its supporters. Esterházy formed his government on 15 June.

[2] In fact, the leftish nationalist consolation that 'we are fighting the Romanov tyranny' had always been based on a fallacy, as the diehards of the Tsar's reign (including even Rasputin) were not particularly war-minded–certainly less engaged in the *Entente* efforts than moderate liberals such as the Grand Duke Nikolai Nikolaievitch; but slogans need not be accurate to spread.

place as the main buttress of outdated institutions, even in minds conditioned to find excuses for German nationalism.

Simultaneously with the appeal of social revolution there was the inrush of a very different and even more powerful pacifist influence personified in Woodrow Wilson: his Fourteen Points, promulgated on 8 January 1918, became the rallying cry of evolutionary left-wingers. The nausea with war and craving for peace had become a national religion, pointing the way to instant redemption: no matter whether it was to be Lenin's peace or Wilson's peace, the average citizen in his blissful ignorance felt that either would do since neither threatened any country with national subjection. King Karl, too, was known to want peace; his efforts to extricate his empire from the war were betrayed and foiled by both his Foreign Minister and intimate, Count Czernin, for whom he was going too far, and the French premier, Clemenceau, for whom he did not (as no Habsburg ruler could) go far enough; but he remained the hope of masses yearning for an end to the bloodshed.

As had happened at previous crises of social tension, highbrow poets and thinkers emerged as the interpreters of mass feelings, along with the champions of press exposure and open-air oratory. Not only radical poets such as Ady, and socialists such as the leader of the avant-garde, Lajos Kassák, and the Social Democratic Party minstrel Zseni (Jenny) Várnai, but the high priest of the Ivory Tower, Babits, cried frantically for *Peace! Peace!*; and equally passionate pleas for peace came from the utterly non-political elegiac poet Árpád Tóth and the philosopher-humorist Frigyes Karinthy.[1] Among the Károlyi party orators, Márton Lovászy, an imposing and remarkably single-minded offspring of the humanitarian gentry, and János Hock, a worldly Catholic priest, spoke with greatest effect; among Social Democrats, the intellectually brilliant Kunfi, the sturdy and persuasive Garbai, and an ex-mason outstanding for his fiery rhetoric, Dezső Bokányi. But more popular than any of them—more perhaps even than Károlyi—was the reporter of *Az Est*, László Fényes; his name was a household word in the remotest hamlets, and any eavesdropper on the gossip of farmhands' and labourers' wives would hear the constant refrain of their: 'I'll write and tell László Fényes . . .' In spite of the gendarme terror, and his deficiencies as a speaker (which included a shrill voice), he was elected a member of Parliament in the most critical phase of the war.

Meanwhile, stories of the massacres in Russia gained some credence, and a horror of Bolshevism began to infiltrate circles not usually scared of revolutions. Minister of Justice Vázsonyi became

---

[1] Whose fascinating description of his operation for a brain tumour, *Journey Round my Skull*, had quite a success in 1939 Britain—about one year after his death.

the embodiment of that, then rare, variety: a determined democrat, amicably inclined towards socialists but bitterly opposed to communism. On 21 December 1917 he submitted to Parliament a Suffrage Bill the acceptance of which might have amounted, in those circumstances, to a revolution; but only six weeks later, on 6 February 1918, it was he who promulgated on behalf of the government the tightening of wartime press censorship, adding in his impetuous way, 'as for Bolshevism, I'll stamp it out'. Between these two dates, on 12 January, the Galileo Circle of radical undergraduates was dissolved. Was it a nest of subversion? Yes and no; originally, with Professor Pikler as its Founding Father, it had only aimed at applying scientific methods to social as well as natural research; politically, it had not been committed to even the mildest variety of socialism; but, by the late war years, it had become the gathering-place for long-haired youths (à la Montmartre) and crop-haired girls (à la University of St Petersburg) for whom no pacifist movement was belligerent enough, no socialism revolutionary enough. Surely not everything dubbed Bolshevism then (or since) has been Bolshevik; it has often been either too mature or too immature for such a name. But the cleavage between democrats who abominated Bolshevism and democrats staking everything on the overthrow of the Hohenzollern-sponsored edifice became unbridgeable and final; Vázsonyi and Károlyi parted company for good. (The Social Democrats sided with Károlyi–committed to the 'Left', they had no choice; though some of their leaders, and particularly Garami, did not conceal their opinion that Vázsonyi would really be a more dependable 'bourgeois democratic' partner.)

1918: Commonsense too Late

While Vázsonyi and Károlyi were quarrelling, power *de facto* slipped back into Tisza's hands; Wekerle continued to preside over a much reshuffled government which yielded to Tisza's parliamentary majority by going back on everything the monarch had initiated in his lenient mood–franchise reform, separate peace moves, more liberal nationalities policy. The fact of the impending defeat of the Central Powers played, on the eve of final collapse, into the hands of the hard-liners: since all ideas of compromise were overtaken by events, the non-compromisers were called upon to do their best once again. This was Tisza's final and tragic chance. The edifice of the Central Powers was crumbling under the hammer-blows of an *Entente* amply compensated by American help for the fall of Russia; in early July 1918, even the notoriously weak Italian army succeeded in crippling the Austro-Hungarian invaders at the Piave; on 13 July, a Czech National Council was founded in Prague, in defiance of the

Germans and Austro-Hungarians; on 8 August, a shattering
Entente offensive started against the Germans on the Western Front;
on 16 August, a Southern Slav Committee (later renamed National
Council) was formed, demanding autonomy for the Southern Slavs
within the Dual Monarchy. On 20 September, Count Tisza arrived
in Sarajevo, as delegate of the King-Emperor Karl, to talk to the
Yugoslav representatives. He came in his hussar colonel's uniform,
cracked his whip as he talked, and at a crucial moment struck the
table with it, shouting: 'Whatever may happen to us, we shall still
have the strength to eat Your Lordships for breakfast!'[1] Five days
later, Bulgaria capitulated; two more days and General von Luden-
dorff recommended to the German Reich government that they
accept the Fourteen Points. On 17 October Tisza declared in Parliament, 'Michael Károlyi was right, we have lost the war.'

Though he added qualifications and reservations, the admission
spread like wildfire. Soldiers were streaming back from the front
lines, soldiers of all nationalities and the most varied character, many
simply as deserters, others as highwaymen, others again as guerrilla
fighting for freedom, of what kind they hardly knew. The Habsburg
monarchy was disintegrating into its 'national' units, as historians
might put it; although no one either then or now could decide
whether, and to what extent, the Czechs and Slovaks, for instance, or
the Serbs and Croats and the 'Bunyevci' of the Voivodina were one
and the same nation. It was a débâcle everywhere; and for Hungarians, losing hold of what they felt had been Hungary for a thousand
years, it was Doomsday. But make-believe can turn any doomsday
into kingdom come—at any rate, for the moment. The moment of
Deliverance was heralded, on 25 October, by the formation of a
Hungarian National Council, presided over by Károlyi and consisting of members of his own Independence Party and of extra-
parliamentary left-wing groups such as the Social Democrats and
radicals. The day before, the Press of Hungary had already (with a
gesture recalling 15 March 1848) refused to submit its material to
censorship. The death-knell of what the German Reich and the
Austro-Hungarian monarchy had stood for since the 1870s was unmistakable, and it was pathetic to see how, in the last remaining
week of these two empires, the stalwart upholders of a decaying order

---

[1] This at any rate was the version of the story going round about that meeting
According to eye-witnesses more sympathetic to Tisza, he banged the table with his
fist, not with his whip, and the authorized version of his most dramatic sentence was
'Hungary is strong enough to exterminate her enemies before perishing', pointing
unmistakably to the delegates. 'Hajdevo!'–'Let's go!'–one exclaimed, and the
delegates left in the middle of Tisza's statement. 'This is the cleverest they could
do!' Tisza shouted after them. (Cf. Nádasdy, Béla, *Az utolsó kisérlet* ('The Last
Attempt'): *1918*, Budapest, 1938; and Tonelli, Sándor, *Tisza István utolsó utja*
('The Last Journey of I.T.'), The University of Szeged, 1941.)

tried to catch up with the cataract of events: the advocate of peaceful reforms, Count Andrássy, was *now* appointed Foreign Minister of the Dual Monarchy, and similar moves were made within Hungary; on 30 October, Andrássy's second-in-command, Count János Hadik, formed a government with Max Fenyö, the Director of GYOSZ (the association of industrialists) as Minister of Commerce; a choice that broke with orthodoxy since Fenyö, a man of letters, had been a member of the initial editorial team of *Nyugat*. At a moment which must have represented for him the most tragic concession of his life, Count Tisza declared in Parliament that, so as not to bar the road to a possible peaceful settlement, he was willing to agree to universal suffrage and the secret ballot. Every demand, in fact, was conceded when it was obviously too late.

A People Jubilant in Despair

The National Council set up its headquarters in the fashionable Hotel Astoria, in the heart of the capital, and the rush of people offering it their support made more trouble for the councillors unable to see all their enthusiasts than any difficulties they may have had with a nominally still existing central power. On 29 October, the State Police joined the National Council. Who was there to resist it? Not a soul. And euphoria gripped the country. It culminated on 31 October. Soldiers with bunches of chrysanthemums stuck in their gun-barrels, and red-white-and-green rosettes over their Imperial and Royal emblems, roamed the streets of the capital in lorries diverted from public utility works to revolutionary demonstration. 'Long live Károlyi!' could be heard everywhere. And 'Peace', 'Democracy', 'Equal Rights', 'People's Welfare', and 'Land for those who shed their blood . . .' Paradise seemed round the corner. The victory of the Revolution was a foregone conclusion before it was proclaimed. Among those hurrying to take an oath to the Council, one of the most eager was Archduke Joseph, the head of that branch of the Habsburg-Lotharingen dynasty domiciled in Hungary; he also applied for permission to Magyarize his surname to 'Alcsuti', but Károlyi thought this would be overdoing it and tried to dissuade him: 'Beware, Your Highness, Habsburg is still a surname one doesn't throw away . . .'[1]

Tisza, too, sent a message that he was willing to support Károlyi's experiment, but accepted with dignity the answer that no good could now come of using his name for any purpose. Unlike other victims of popular hatred, however, he was unwilling to leave his residence which stood in the middle of Pest, surrounded by a dutiful

[1] I heard the story from Károlyi and could not check the fate of the application; in the subsequent White years it was allowed to lapse.

but unenthusiastic armed guard and a surging throng of booers and sightseers. On the night of the 31st, a group of armed men entered and shot him dead. 'Worse than a crime, a blunder' could well have applied to this tragic and shameful incident on the day of what passed for a Bloodless Revolution.

A Budding Democracy Snubbed by the Established Democracies

Hungary, within the frontiers she hoped to retain unaltered,[1] declared her independence and on that basis Károlyi accepted his appointment to the premiership from King Karl. His government included the most popular deputies of his party (such as Count Tivadar Batthyány, a former minister in the Esterházy cabinet; Márton Lovászy; Barna Buza, Minister of Agriculture, a most important post in view of impending redistribution of landed property; while János Hock took over as President of the National Council) and the most highly respected leaders of the extra-parliamentary Left: Garami for Commerce and Industry; Kunfi for Public Welfare; Jászi as Minister for National Minorities. Jászi's appointment was tragi-comic: entailing the offer, in full solemnity and good faith, of complete equality to the national minorities–who by then had decided no longer to remain national minorities. In charge of Finance was Under-Secretary of State Pál Szende, Jászi's second-in-command among the radicals and, like his leader, a highly intelligent blunderer: one of his memorable acts was to promise his countrymen a capital levy 'such as the world has never seen'–a speech readily advertised by agitators of the neighbouring nationalities to their minorities in wavering districts of Hungary. Justice had been offered to and accepted by Professor Károly Szladits, an unquestionably high legal authority who, however, because of the Tisza murder, declined it after all; so another meritorious lawyer, but far less important personality, Dénes Berinkey, filled this post (and was promoted in a later reshuffle to Prime Minister). No preparation had been made to take care of the Ministry of War in this most peace-minded government–so an honest and humane field officer of the General Staff, Colonel Béla Linder, was given the portfolio in haste. His most urgent task was to demobilize and disarm the roving gangs of a disintegrated army, and to strike a nobly pacifist note he launched the slogan, 'I want to see no more soldiers!' He had some justification; no one was glad to see the roving soldiers; but still, a Minister of National Defence whose most urgent message to his soldiers is that

---

[1] With the exception of Croatia, whose secession had already been granted before Károlyi's accession to the premiership; but retaining claims to the 'corpus separatum', the Adriatic harbour town of Fiume (or Rijeka), later a bone of contention between Yugoslavia and Italy.

they should cease to exist! And particularly at a moment when they might well be required to defend the frontiers and secure internal order. No wonder this unfortunate utterance has often been quoted against the minister and the whole Károlyi set-up.

They did make blunders, no doubt about it; yet it is true to say that in both honesty and breadth of vision they were second only to the Batthyány government of 1848. Their task was impossible: they inherited a shipwreck and dreamt it had the wind in its sails. Monarchy was an early casualty of the revolution. No sooner had King Karl received the oath of the revolutionary government than he was persuaded to absolve them from it and to accept in principle the result of a proposed plebiscite on the form of government. What that result would have been is anybody's guess; the majority of the white-collar classes and of the peasantry, particularly the Roman Catholics, might have stayed loyal to the legendary crown when face to face with the ballot-box; but the thunderous cheers for the Republic all over Budapest were unopposed in public, and the leftish impetus inside the country was encouraged outside by the hostility of the victors (or of their most dynamic spokesmen, such as old Clemenceau) to the idea of even a reformed Habsburg rule. Under the pressure of events, King Karl issued on 13 November a statement which to all intents amounted to abdication ('I withdraw from any participation in State affairs', etc.); and on the 16th, in the House of Parliament, the National Council declared Hungary a republic,[1] while in Parliament Square several hundred thousand people enthusiastically applauded republican speakers such as the socialist Garbai. A moving, though pathetic, scene inside Parliament was the arrival in a wheelchair of the poet Ady, crippled by the illness which was to finish him off in a few months' time; he was greeted with impressive but old-fashioned oratory by János Hock. The meeting of minds was as genuine as the cheering of the crowd.

A very short carnival it was, followed by a lean time without end. The jubilation, even at its peak, was threatened by a rude awakening. The rebuff to Minister Jászi's offer of fraternal unity from politicians who on nationality grounds (as Romanians, Slovaks, Ukrainians, or representatives of Southern Slav national groups more or less akin to the Serbs) claimed that they had really sided with the *Entente* from the outset, was only to be expected after military defeat, but it came as a cold shower all the same. Meanwhile, *Entente* forces, namely the Italians and the French, were marching on Hungary from the west and the south. In the west they were stopped under an Armistice concluded on 3 November between the still active diplomatic and

[1] Károlyi was appointed to head the Republic as Prime Minister; later, in a reshuffle of the government, he was elected President of the Republic.

military agencies of the Austro-Hungarian monarchy and, on the other side, General Diaz, acting for the Italian High Command. But the French stationed to the south of Hungary had to be dealt with separately–in the judgement, at any rate, of the Hungarian government.[1] On 12 November, therefore, a Hungarian government delegation, led personally by Károlyi, rushed to Belgrade to meet Marshal Franchet d'Esperay and sue for an armistice. The Marshal, obviously a royalist at heart, treated them like dirt, only showing some courtesy to Károlyi partly, perhaps, because he was an aristocrat and partly because 'nous savons bien qu'il est notre ami'. When the representative of the 'Soldiers' Council' was introduced to him, he reacted: 'Ah! je ne vous ai pas sus tombés si bas'–an exclamation less surprising on the part of even a republican military officer than it struck the Hungarians who had expected comradely embraces and toasts to Wilson's Fourteen Points and *la réconciliation des peuples*. 'Well, a French general is no better than a Prussian general', the disappointed Magyar republicans consoled themselves, 'but it will be different when the politicians from Paris have their say . . .' It was different indeed; and worse. Marshal Franchet, however cavalier his manners, would have allowed the Hungarian territories, even when militarily occupied by others, to remain under Hungarian administration until a final decision was made; but the refugee Czechoslovak pressure-group, close to Clemenceau in Paris, and mustering such influential friends in London as Professor R. W. Seton-Watson, head of the Research Department of the Foreign Office, speedily obtained a reinterpretation of the Armistice terms to the effect that dismemberment of Hungary, in the name of 'self-determination', could be accepted as a *fait accompli* before the peoples concerned were given a chance to 'determine' anything. The Liberal caucus, in other words, behaved even more illiberally than the avowed militarists.

What remained of Hungary was reduced to a lamentable state. Trainloads of refugees from the territories occupied by Romanians, Serbs, and Czechs delivered crowds of emaciated ghosts, their skins purple and teeth chattering with cold and bitterness, to the railway sidings of the capital. With Hungary's coal supplies cut off, the whole country shivered through the winter months. Meanwhile, the two epoch-making reforms promised by the Károlyi government were still not implemented: a general election, to be held under a law

---

[1] Károlyi has often since been criticized for not keeping to the Diaz terms but making another armistice move. According to his most severe critics, he acted out of vanity, unwilling to recognize any Austro-Hungarian government decision after 31 October. According to himself, the Diaz terms had not applied to the southern frontiers and the French would have marched on Budapest unless specifically approached. The truth seems to be that the French did not know themselves how far they were intending to march; the Károlyi government might have manoeuvred more cleverly with them but acted in perfectly good faith.

more democratic than anything seen before, was put off again and again, partly because it was argued that an election held in a rump-country would imply renunciation of the occupied territories; while Land Reform, which was to split up all big estates amongst the peasantry, had not got beyond the stage of consulting all sections of opinion. Ultimately, the date of the election was fixed, and the Land Reform started in the early spring of 1919 with President Károlyi's personal attendance at the distribution of Count Károlyi's estate in Kápolna among his labourers. It was Michael Károlyi's finest hour. Unluckily, a long-drawn-out anti-climax was to follow.

The Béla Kun Escapade: Enlisting Lenin's Help to Save St Stephen's Kingdom

Since the return of a large number of soldiers from Russian captivity, a Communist Party had been operating under the leadership of Béla Kun (1866–1939), an ex-prisoner-of-war initiated by Lenin and his entourage into the craft of subversion. He was a plump little man, in pre-war years a cross between a Social Insurance clerk and a journalist, and endowed with an inexhaustible capacity for puffing out Marxist slogans. He was by no means stupid, but lacked imaginative statesmanship. In the turmoil of a defeated and disorganized country, with the aura of Red Russia behind him, he could not fail to attract attention. There were many eccentric movements mushrooming in the streets of Budapest (and some vicious ones, too, such as the Awakening Magyars, who cashed in on anti-Semitism), and by any reliable estimate, Kun's brand of nation-redeeming only appealed to a minute fraction of the working classes. After provoking many disorders he was imprisoned together with several of his lieutenants, and though his position caused some legal and administrative headaches, his party was far from the chance of an actual fight for power. Yet there was Russia behind him; and as disappointment with Clemenceau's imperialism and Wilson's helplessness grew, more and more Magyar hopes were vested in Russia. Kunfi, a hater of Bolsheviks if only for their massacre of the Mensheviks, took to the morphine needle in despair, muttering 'Terrible, our only refuge is in alliance with Russia', and then, 'Whatever happens, we can't shoot at workers'. Other non-communists pondered about the prospects of upheaval less despondently; the brilliant and over-impressionable journalist Pál Kéri, an intimate of Károlyi's, urged that, according to his contacts in the West, revolutionary changes were in the offing everywhere and 'Hungary must be secured a good foothold in the World Revolution'. Into the prevailing mixture of despair and messianism fell the bombshell—a note from the French Colonel Vyx, on behalf of the victorious Powers, ordering Hungary to withdraw still further and leave vast districts of purely Magyar territory to be 'neutralized' under *Entente* and Romanian supervision. This step was, apparently, prompted by the reports of formerly pro-German, *ancien régime* refugees who denounced Károlyi's coalition government as 'fundamentally communist'; an allegation which, however absurd, was given some colour by Károlyi's refusal to let Hungary be used as a base for operations against Russia.[1] Czechs, Serbs, and particularly Romanians seemed much more worth bolstering up in the drive to overthrow the Soviet Union.

The result was to push Hungary into Bolshevism. In the all-pervading confusion and stupefaction one idea stood out clearly and gained the upper hand: 'Russia will save us!' Károlyi thought of appointing a purely socialist government, with Kunfi as premier, in the hope of getting communist support both at home and from Russia. On 21 March, Kunfi and his comrades, in panic, went even further than Károlyi: calling on Béla Kun in prison, they agreed with him on a merger between the two 'Workers' Parties' and the proclamation of a Hungarian Council Republic; those socialists who, like Garami, opposed this adventure to the last, withdrew. Although the Council of People's Commissars, presided over by the former bricklayer Garbai – a robust, engaging, and reassuringly old-fashioned hero of the Social Democratic soap-box – consisted overwhelmingly of socialists rather than communists, it was unavoidable in the circumstances that the tune should be called by its link with the Soviet government, the Commissar of Foreign Affairs Béla Kun. No one dared, or even wished, to challenge his power: one had to see what could be salvaged of St Stephen's Kingdom under the Hammer and Sickle! It was a patriotic duty to be unpatriotic (because, let us not forget, 'proletarian patriotism' had not yet been invented, and communist doctrine ran on strictly internationalist lines). Kun was at first visibly embarrassed by the power handed to him on a plate, but quickly convinced himself that it was due to his political genius. In his telegram to Clemenceau he stated that 'the Hungarian Council Republic does not base itself on Hungary's Territorial Integrity' and then hurried to the journalists' club, Otthon (Home), where up till then he had only been admitted as an outsider, to measure the impression he had made with this formula. 'Don't you see, I cornered old Clemenceau', he explained with glittering eyes, 'now he won't have any more excuse to pester us'. Whatever the journalists thought, Clemenceau did not seem to be worried by lack of 'excuses'; he went

---

[1] In the course of our informal conversations, in wartime London, Károlyi told me about *Entente* feelers put out to him about possible Hungarian assistance to anti-Bolshevik intervention. 'I ignored them or brushed them aside – we had had enough of war, I felt, apart from my dislike of Interventionism', Károlyi said; but, unfortunately, he was unable to recall details of the relevant exchanges.

on pestering Hungary with increased gusto. But the Hungarian public, which still clung to the concept with bigoted piety, though realizing by then that much would have to be given up of 'Hungary's Territorial Integrity', was dismayed at Kun's ingenious diplomatic stroke.

The *Entente*'s continued high-handedness made it clear enough to Hungarians that their Petty Russia on the Danube would not be tolerated; and the shadow of impending failure made disgust as general overnight as enthusiasm had been the day before. Peasants hoarded and hid what they could, no goods were available except on the black market, cadets indulged in counter-revolutionary risings and civilians in a flood of anti-Soviet puns, and prominent patriot gentlemen volunteered to assist the foreign occupiers. Co-operation with the enemy was found to be, after all, less treacherous than internationalism – once internationalism turned out to be wanting in guns.

Nationalist Terror Rule Imposed by Foreign Arms

Yet miracles should never be ruled out – such as that the Hungarian Red Army, scraped together in haste, beat the Czechoslovak forces and penetrated deep into lands held by them. Clemenceau ordered a Hungarian withdrawal; if this were done, he promised, the Romanians would withdraw from the Magyar territory they were occupying on the Great Plain. 'Let us not budge from the north until we see the Romanians moving east', many suggested, but Kun was determined to play Lenin in Brest-Litovsk; he would exhaust the capitalist enemy by cunning tactical surrenders. He withdrew and then gave orders to push the Romanians back. Within a few days the Romanians were in Budapest. On the eve of their entry the communists resigned and fled, handing over power to a purely Social Democratic government. On the morrow of their entry an armed group of Whites (mainly of the police force) ousted the Social Democrats and put a purely 'national' government in power, with Archduke Joseph as provisional Head of State, and István Friedrich as premier.

This happened on 6 August 1919. White terror gangs, known as 'officers' detachments' and recruited under French Senegalese occupation during the Kun régime, were by then let loose over the unoccupied territories of Transdanubia and the western slice of the Great Plain. Regarding Rear Admiral Miklós (Nicolas) Horthy von Nagybánya (1868–1957) as Supreme Commander of the Hungarian National Army (which he was formally proclaimed in Siófok, on Lake Balaton, on 9 August), they indulged in mass killings of workers, peasants, and Jews accused (with or without reason) of having participated in communist activities. Red terror, no doubt, had existed, and some of its victims were fine men indeed; but the subsequent White terror surpassed it many times over both in cruelty and in the numbers of its victims. Budapest, under the combined rule of the voracious Romanian occupiers and Friedrich's *putsch*-makers in the government, soon seemed an oasis of lawfulness and tolerance when compared with that part of the country under the absolute jurisdiction of the Hungarian 'National Army'.

How far was that army really National? It certainly stood for nationalism. No sooner had it obtained from the French and their allies the means to 'restore order' in its own way than it started persecuting Hungarians for showing sympathy towards the French and their allies; the standards it had taken over from the Prussian officer class were integrally upheld by it. Most ambiguous of all was the National Army's attitude to the Habsburg and Austrian heritage. Many of its officers had come from the Austrian Imperial officers' corps and only talked some pigeon-Magyar picked up in army life. Horthy himself, though a man of the Calvinist Magyar county squirearchy, protested against being called a Hungarian instead of 'a subject of His Imperial and Royal Majesty' so long as the Dual Monarchy was in existence; and he persisted in this faith insofar as he never parted with his Habsburg admiral's uniform, even after losing all contact with the sea. In his broken Austro-Magyar, he always recalled tenderly the beautiful days of his youth, passed in the radiance of the Court of Vienna. But horse-sense prompted him to adopt a different style, that of a Magyardom proud of its pre-Habsburg and even pre-European ancestries, denying commitments to any centre of power outside its own frontiers and cherishing rituals and symbols calculated to stand for National Independence; his soldiers in 1919 wore braided military caps, named after the erstwhile Prince of Transylvania, Bocskai, and ornamented with a white 'crane-feather'.

In spite of all its implied aggressiveness against the victorious Powers, and even more against their East European *protégés* and the Jews, Horthy's style of 'restoring order' could be 'sold' to the *Entente*; British, French, Italian, and United States emissaries (including a Jewish American colonel sent to Hungary to investigate charges of anti-Semitism) condoned the White terrorists on the grounds that they were National and Christian and therefore basically honest folk.[1] To disarm liberal and socialist critics in the West, a so-called

[1] Cf. *The White Terror in Hungary*. Report by the British Joint Labour Delegation in Hungary, London, May 1920.—A shattering revelation of the blindness, deliberate or not, of the British high officials in Budapest, H.E. Sir Thomas Hohler and Admiral Sir Ernest Troubridge, in face of the murder of the Social Democratic journalists Béla Somogyi and Béla Bacsó, and many others, known to be committed

Coalition Government was set up in Budapest which disintegrated on the morrow of its formation; while, at the command of the *Entente*, and with the consent of the withdrawing Romanians, on 16 November 1919—exactly one year after the proclamation of the Republic under Károlyi—the 'National Army' marched into Budapest. At the head of his pogrom-happy, dandified, crane-feathered warriors rode Horthy in his admiral's uniform on a gleaming white horse, and he proclaimed in his address to the Lord Mayor:

We shall forgive this criminal city.

'Budapest spirit' was thus authoritatively made the whipping-boy of Hungary, and 'Budapest spirit' implied, with varying emphasis, Jews and industrial workers, free trade and organized labour, Freemasonry and Bolshevism, Land Reform (*à la* Károlyi) and 'Eastern Switzerland' or Danubian Federation (*à la* Kossuth and Mocsáry, Jászi and Ady).

On 1 March 1920 some 'Officers' Detachments' entered a subdued National Assembly (elected in a state of terror and panic on 25–27 January and further browbeaten since) and, holding the deputies practically at gunpoint, made them elect Miklós von, or de, Horthy the Regent of the Hungarian Kingdom; for the kingdom was restored although the king was kept in exile and later (after his second unsuccessful *coup*, in October 1921) formally dethroned.

---

by detachment officers enjoying Horthy's favour. The Labour Delegation was led by the M.P., Josiah C. (later: Lord) Wedgwood, who on other occasions also intervened on behalf of persecuted categories in Hungary; but successive British governments, including the Labour one (under MacDonald), refused to heed his warnings.

Chapter 7

The Admiral's Kingdom

THUS BEGAN THE HORTHY RÉGIME which was to last for a quarter of a century, with profound effects on the Hungarian character and a greater impact on world affairs than is generally realized.

Varieties on a Counter-Revolutionary Theme

That régime had many contradictory features and changed character several times. Starting with some two years of instability and acute White terror, it then had a decade of consolidated, slightly permissive reactionary rule under the premiership of Count István Bethlen (1874–1947), which came to an end at the height of the World Economic Crisis; then came one year under the more moderate, thrifty, and conservative Count Gyula Károlyi (1871–1947), who experimented with a coalition on the model of the MacDonald-Baldwin government; and from 1 October 1932 onwards, when the pro-Nazi General Gyula Gömbös von Jákfa (1886–1936) was appointed premier, a series of administrations were headed in turn by active Nazifiers, and traditionalist opponents of Hitler, and some who started by opposing him but, impressed by Hitler's successes, ended up as Nazifiers. Towards the end of the Second World War, from 19 March 1944 onwards, Hungary was under German military occupation and on 15 October 1944 even the semblance of Hungarian national independence was scrapped when Hitler's German and Hungarian commandos deported Horthy and replaced him with the most paranoiac of quislings, Major Ferenc Szálasi (1897–1946). The latter nominally acted as 'Leader of the Nation' until 4 April 1945, by which date the whole territory of Hungary had been liberated from Nazi overlordship.

Horthy's rule was eminently a *counter-revolutionary* order in both senses of the word: it aimed at crushing and eliminating what had up to then been known as revolution; and it was, technically speaking, a revolution in itself.

Restoration (though not of the Monarchy)

It had been installed to restore traditional values, institutions, and authorities, belief in the God of the Churches, in the army of the

152

crown, in the sanctity of family ties and of private property. The big landed estates (including entailed family and church properties) were handed back to their previous owners; since under Béla Kun they had been kept in large units, although 'socialized', a simple administrative gesture was enough to reconvert them from 'common' to 'private' properties. Thus the communists themselves, by foiling Michael Károlyi's 'petty bourgeois' Land Reform, enabled their White successors to give feudalism another lease of life. The only former landlord whose dispossession was declared final was Count Michael Károlyi himself–by then a 'Red' refugee.

In banking, industry, and commerce, the pre-1919 owners were equally empowered to take possession of their old properties, and the monopolistic position of the intermarried and otherwise interconnected princes of big banks and mining and manufacturing concerns was further strengthened *vis-à-vis* competitors, consumers, and labour alike. Part of this process was unavoidable and, in the final analysis, beneficial to the Hungarian economy: once the Habsburg monarchy had been dismembered, it was natural for Hungary to strengthen her existing industries and develop new ones by establishing high and often prohibitive tariff walls. No sensible government, whatever its ideological colour, could in those circumstances have done without a drive for industrialization that involved both protection and incentives for the capital which was most willing and most well-equipped to do the job. Yet the fact that the profits of big bankers and industrialists soared to heights hardly ever witnessed in Hungary before and surpassing–under both the Bethlen and the Gömbös administrations–the returns in practically any European country at that time would seem to indicate that government-sponsored facilities to exploit workers, employees, and consumers also constituted an essential feature of the counter-revolutionary Hungarian economy. Measured by cash returns, the Horthy régime was a capitalists' paradise.

Like the landed aristocracy and the industrial plutocracy, the county squirearchy were saved and rehabilitated by government decrees which in roundabout ways reaffirmed the 'gentleman's' superiority over the common people. Throughout most of the régime, open voting was practised in most constituencies and linked everywhere with fairly harsh property qualifications; at the very beginning (January 1920) a nominally democratic election was made unrepresentative by a crude White terror which induced the Social Democrats to abstain altogether; and in 1939, when the secret ballot was technically re-established, Hungary, seeing Horthy's authoritarianism as the only alternative to Hitler's, was already halfway towards becoming a German colony. In other words, the secret ballot was only experienced under admittedly abnormal or noticeably satellite conditions; and the hierarchy typical of the 'noble' counties, headed by entailed office-holders and based on the pandoor force, remained unaltered during the inter-war period. The larger cities, which had enjoyed a more genuine form of self-government, were meanwhile forced under government tutelage. In Budapest, a striking feature of Liberal conservatism used to be until 1918 the sharp contrast between the eminently liberal Town Hall and, in its vicinity (since the head offices of Pest County were also housed in the capital), a diehard, caste-ridden County Hall; but from 1919 onward the difference was forcibly reduced. Through blatant manipulation of constituency boundaries, Budapest was made 'Christian'; her Lord Mayor István Bárczy, famous for his imaginativeness, was ousted; and the Democrat leader Vázsonyi, previously the most powerful politician in the municipality, was superseded by the Christian Party leader, Karl Wolff von Wolfenau, who combined Roman Catholicism with racialism, and incidentally sided with the German Reich after 1933 when the incompatibility of the two doctrines could no longer be ignored.

The restoration of big estates, big business, and big officialdom thus marked the conservative and reactionary aspects of the régime, and also what was slightly liberal in it—the observance and cherishing of at least some time-honoured freedoms. Part of this liberalism was manifest in such concessions to Western constitutional principles as the influx of peasant farmers (though not of peasant labourers) into Parliament and the limited representation granted to organized labour (i.e. Social Democracy) both in Parliament and in urban councils.

But the technically revolutionary character of the régime was even more manifest. It was revolutionary insofar as it had seized power by armed force and was prepared to strike at traditional authorities such as the dynasty; it was this revolutionary character that conditioned Hungary to act in the inter-war period as the forerunner of racialism and Fascism in Europe—as the birthplace of the 'Rome–Berlin Axis' concept.

The Treaty of Trianon Sowing the Seeds of Nazi Power

And this retrograde revolution was itself conditioned and almost imposed by the policy of the World War victors, and by the consequent changes in Hungarian class-structure and outlook.

Foreign military occupation was followed by the Treaty of Trianon (June 1920) which deprived Hungary of roughly two-thirds of her territory and population, including more than 3 million Magyars: some 1,700,000 of them lost to Romania, one million to Czechoslovakia, and 500,000 to Yugoslavia. An influx of refugees, estimated at 350,000, and coming almost exclusively from the Magyar land-owning class and state and county bureaucracy, enormously inflated that part of the population for which 'gentlemanly jobs' had to be found or created; they included also those members of the former Austrian Imperial officers' corps who found republicanism in Austria intolerable; and the sons of government commissioners, railway signalmen, and N.C.O.'s who in the counter-revolutionary gang warfare had risen to near-equality with their officers. Such a socially degraded and numerically swollen 'gentry' is the ideal breeding-ground for communal violence, military adventures, and arbitrary discrimination against both oppressed majorities and branded minorities.

This new vintage of gentry was organized, and secured preferential treatment, in various bodies—para-military, social, economic, academic. In addition to the existing strata of noblemen, for instance, a new kind of lesser nobility was created, the Order of Heroes (Vitézi Rend), with the Regent as its Captain-in-Chief. It was supposed to reward 'persons who have specially distinguished themselves in the war, the counter-revolution, and other patriotic services', but no bones were made about its chief aim: to create a 'backbone' stratum of military character which could unite the most soldierly elements of the ancient nobility with the new vintage of gentlemen and the most reliable among the well-off farmers. Members of the order were granted inalienable landed property (as lesser noblemen had been before 1848): to the ordinary folk just enough to secure the subsistence of a peasant family, but to officers four or five times as much. Members of the order were entitled 'vitéz' (heroic or brave), and the title as well as the 'hero's plot' was inheritable by the eldest son. Horthy, even at a time when he already felt the necessity of defending Jews, and particularly his own friends among Jewish heads of industry, against Nazi pressure in the Second World War,[1] recalled with pride that he had never allowed even the most patriotic Hungarian of Jewish extraction to join this order, as he was determined to keep it racially as well as morally pure.

In economics, the late Count Sándor Károlyi's 'co-operatives directed from above' were given greater scope than before, and added to them were government-sponsored monopolies, such as 'Futura', in charge of the corn market: institutions which skimmed the returns of commerce though they did not expropriate substantial sectors of it. Orthodox private enterprise (colloquially referred to as 'Jewish capital') could operate, and in years of boom

[1] Cf. his letter to Premier Count Pál (Paul) Teleki, on 1 October 1940, *Admiral Horthy's Papers*, Corvina, Budapest, 1965, p. 150.

expand, but at the price of financing in various ways a large number of 'Heroes' or other well-placed sleeping partners.

The para-military organizations ranged from the very respectable enterprise of civil aviation (with which there was nothing wrong except that its organization was not 'civil') to government-sponsored secret societies whose very names and rituals suggested a sort of black magic deriving from practices of the ancient Magyar warriors, possibly the tribes who had conquered the mid-Danube basin. Such bodies were the EKSZ or 'Etelköz Association', most infantile in its mythology but a diligent fomenter of subversion across the frontier, and efficient at securing high and lucrative positions for its members in post-Trianon Hungary.

In academic life, similar trends prevailed. The Academy of Sciences and the literary Kisfaludy Society and Petőfi Society working under its patronage, together with the universities and government education authorities, entered the counter-revolutionary period with a vendetta against Jews and ex-Jews for their mild liberal opinions described as 'Bolshevik propaganda'; and, regardless of race, against members of the *Nyugat* and 'TT' circles unless they were prepared to buy immunity by joining in anti-Semitic propaganda. A notorious case was the expulsion from the university of the distinguished philologist of Jewish extraction Zsigmond Simonyi, a conservative in general outlook but guilty of considering that a certain variety of the Magyar conjugation taught in schools was ignored by the common people, and of labelling it half in jest the 'gentlemanly conjugation'. This was branded as 'incitement to class hatred', and the old scholar was practically hounded to death. Of the *Nyugat* writers, Babits and Móricz were among those victimized at the outset (the former for his pacifism, the latter for his propaganda for Land Reform–though ostensibly for other reasons); later, the uproar against national figures like these calmed down. Ignotus, though not prosecuted, was ostracized so ruthlessly for his ultra-liberal record that he chose voluntary exile. Professor Pikler was expelled from the university although he had played no active part in the revolutions. Among the exiles, and not even a voluntary one, was Professor Jászi. Ady, Margit Kaffka, Ervin Szabó, and Professor Bódog Somló did not live long enough to see what their fate under the Whites would have been. All in all, the teaching staff and senior membership of academic institutions came under the control of the outright reactionaries of Horthy's régime.

The undergraduates, on the other hand, came under the control of the subversive racialist wing of White power. By tacit and hardly conscious agreement it was decided that, while respectability was the domain of upholders of Christian, national, royalist, and moderately liberal traditions, the guidance of youth should be left to preachers of intolerance – and since internationalist intolerance had failed, it must now be that of militarist adventures, racial discriminations, dictatorial methods, and the cult of pre-Christian tribal divinities of the Hungarian nation. Students' movements thus became the virtual monopoly of 'comradely associations' formed on a racialist (i.e., anti-Jewish) basis, with a view to securing the gentlemanly jobs all over the country for their own members (as distinct from workers' and peasants' sons and other intruders). These associations were grouped in branches named after divinities from the pagan Magyar sagas (mostly invented in the nineteenth century), and their social rules and rituals were mostly taken over from the German *Burschenschaften*.

Horthy, Bethlen, Gömbös

Horthy, Bethlen, and Gömbös, the three men who stamped their personalities most strongly on that quarter of a century, embodied its two alternately conflicting and combining trends: the will to restore and the will to subvert. Horthy was at heart a courtier, more so than any aulic magnate; but, perhaps just for this reason, he was haunted by a feeling of inferiority to the magnates, and only felt secure with the gentry and pseudo-gentry to whom he owed his Regency. Bethlen, of very ancient aristocratic stock, was yet bound, as a Transylvanian and Calvinist, to have some sympathy with the gentry; being also a tactician *par excellence* who did not hesitate to drop the Habsburg cause when expedient, he was therefore Horthy's ideal right-hand magnate. Gömbös, for his part, was the very essence of pseudo-gentry: son of a 'Swabian' primary-school teacher called Knöpfle, he endowed himself not only with a Magyar surname and the title of nobility 'jákfai', but also with military distinctions of dubious origin; while always combining an attachment to hereditary rank with resentment against those at the top – notably the Habsburg dynasty and the Roman Catholic aristocracy (he himself was a Lutheran). Yet he seemed willing to postpone, as it were, the satisfaction of his rancours almost indefinitely; he changed sides with ease and there was no shade of political opinion in the broad spectrum between conservatism and extreme racialism which he did not profess during his short career. After organizing a most brutal open-vote election under Bethlen, he overthrew him by promising to introduce the secret ballot, and then jettisoned his promise with a shrug; after founding a violently anti-Semitic Racialist Party, he proclaimed when appointed premier that he had 'revised his attitude about the Jewish question', and made a great show of friendship with some Jewish industrialists; at the same time signing a secret agreement with Goering (in September 1935) under which Hungary was to be

transformed into a Nazi-like state 'within two years'. Hatred of the
Habsburg hierarchy, hatred of Marxism, hatred of the spirit of free
criticism which he identified with Bolshevism and with everything
coming from Paris and Prague, were his lifelong obsessions; but
otherwise he was prepared to do anything for the sake of his career
and to promise anything to his friends and associates. Possibly he
even believed his own promises, at any rate in the matter of personal
favours. Like Hitler he aspired to supreme leadership, but unlike
Hitler he aspired also to being a jolly good fellow. His most memor
able gesture, however, was to coin the expression 'Rome–Berlin Axis'
and to commit Hungary on 20 June 1934 to supporting it; at a time
that is, when Hitler and Mussolini were still ready to cut each other'
throats. He made this prophetic utterance out of pure ignorance
believing simply that Blackshirts and Brownshirts and his own
fellow-members of the Order of Heroes must be fundamentally the
same sort of men, destined to come together and to set the pace o
history.

Non-dictatorial but Strictly Authoritarian

During his régime, Horthy was the country's dictator insofar as he
had unquestionable power to overrule any other person or institu
tion; but as, fortunately, he was interested only in a very few things
he made sufficiently little use of his power to appear a constitutional
ruler. A public life consisting mainly of the tug-of-war between
cliques such as Bethlen's and Gömbös's proceeded mostly without
interference from him while he ruled; and on issues about which the
three of them were either divided or indifferent, it was even possible
for leftish opinion now and then to exert some modifying influence
In other words, it was a non-dictatorial but strictly authoritarian
régime. It allowed, and indeed allotted, a token existence to Liberal
ism and Social Democracy; the former being practically confined to
the districts of Jewish traders, and the latter to industrial suburbs and
mining districts. (Trade unionism was banned in rural areas and in
public services including the railways, previously a stronghold of
Social Democracy.) Communism was the sole political idea to be
expressly outlawed, but publications known to be in touch with
émigrés in Moscow were often tolerated – if only because they pro
vided the political police with clues in their search for conspirators
At the outset, some efforts were made by unrepentant democrats to
topple the authoritarian rule; and, particularly where the call for
liberty was combined with that for Land Reform, they evoked a
lively popular response. After a few years, however, it became accep
ted as a quasi-divine law that, in Hungary at any rate, the authori
tarian rule of the few would never be shaken unless by its own

extremists; a belief naturally strengthened later by the dawn of National Socialism in Central Europe. Hitler's victory was in fact hailed in Hungary as a landmark on the road opened up by Hungary under Horthy's leadership. Tactical reasons played a part in this claim: extremists arguing that it was in the Hungarian spirit to go further along Hitler's road, while moderates urged that since Hungary had already preceded Germany in her moral self-renewal, there was no need to import inspiration from even a friendly foreign power. Among the extremists were Wolff and, less outspokenly, Gömbös; among the moderates, Bethlen and, to the surprise of many, the former counter-revolutionary premier, Count Pál Teleki (1879–1941) who, to add weight to his anti-Nazi reservations, claimed to have been 'the first racialist head of government in Hungary'.

Allowing for tactical exaggerations on all sides, there was sufficient truth in such claims to warrant the question: how could a country with Hungary's record have been perverted to play this part? 'The Magyars', wrote the harshest scholarly critic of their chauvinism, 'were unquestionably the torchbearers of constitutional liberties and had behind them in this respect a tradition such as no people of Danubian Europe could boast'.[1] Indeed, whatever their past follies and crimes against themselves and others, they had never made a virtue of tyranny; they had never shared obscurantist beliefs in the need for more authority and less discussion. Their two Reform Generations had been in the vanguard of what was most enlightened and humane in Europe; and even their reactionaries believed in a sort of liberty. How, then, could their country have become protagonist of the crusade against humanism, reason, and freedom in Europe between the two wars?

The blatant injustice of the Trianon Treaty, engendering nationalist bitterness and creating a whole class of refugees, provides one part of the answer; the forgiveness and indulgence granted by the victors to the White authoritarian rulers of Hungary, the other. On the Trianon frontiers the ruling Powers of Europe were adamant, and the Magyar people were given no chance of a plebiscite in the name of 'Self-Determination'; but thereafter all foul deeds of the Hungarian rulers and their extremist *protégés* were condoned on the grounds that much should be forgiven to a country which had been so cruelly damaged. Whenever the Magyar people stood in the dock, the unrelenting rigour of the Trianon-makers prevailed; but when it came to judging the Hungarian rulers and those who did their dirty work, leniency won the day, prompted by a combination of bad conscience and solidarity, even across the frontier of diplomatic hostilities, with

[1] R. W. Seton-Watson, *A History of the Czechs and Slovaks*, London, 1943, pp. 194–5.

whoever went in for nationalist passions. The Magyar people were taught the lesson that whereas they as a people were always punished, their White rulers could get away with anything; and he who succeeds cannot be entirely wrong.

Western Doublethink about Trianon

Horthy's first boost from the Western Powers came in 1919–20 when the White terror inaugurated by him was raging in Hungary; an international stevedore boycott against the Hungarian government for its violation of civic rights was neutralized by the attitude of the Western rulers. Horthy, in later years, mellowed from a glorified butcher into an enthroned Blimp, and his premier, Count Bethlen, boasted as justifiably about public security in the streets of Budapest as did Mussolini about the punctuality of his trains; but liberty of the Press, of speech, of public life, and trade unionism remained severely restricted even in the relatively most liberal years under Bethlen or his successors, and the Western guests of Hungarian ruling circles turned a blind eye to it. Most conspicuous in this respect was the anti-Jewish *numerus clausus* established in the universities, in violation of the Hungarian government's undertaking to refrain from any discrimination against any racial or religious community. When Bethlen was taken to task for this at the League of Nations, the *numerus clausus* law was amended by substituting for 'Jewish' certain vague terms which nevertheless betrayed anti-Jewish intentions while enlarging the arbitrary powers of administrators to reject or admit students. And this was accepted as satisfactory by the guardians of human rights in Geneva.

The field, however, in which the methods of the 1919–20 thugs survived longest was that of relations with other countries. The Austrian and German *putschists*, reactionaries, and *Feme* (extreme Right, underground) murderers were from the very beginning helped by Hungary's political rulers. Even such a moderate and worldly-wise diplomat as the minister in Berlin, Kálmán Kánya (later, when Hungarian Minister of Foreign Affairs, as anti-Nazi as he could afford to be), exhibited his contempt for republican institutions and associated with those gravediggers of the Weimar Republic, the *Herrenklub*; the German Social Democrats and their Roman Catholic and liberal partners were prepared to put up with this as they had put up with the attitude of their own diplomatic service. The Kapp *putschists* received active help from Budapest. The murderers of Erzberger, leader of the German Roman Catholic *Zentrum* Party, were hidden in Gömbös's villa in Tétény (near Budapest) with the connivance of government authorities, including the political police; and when the Liberal daily *Esti Kurir* revealed this

1 Miklós Zrínyi

4 Louis Kossuth

2 (*opposite*) Ferenc Rákóczi. Painting by Ádám Mányoki

3 (*opposite*) István Széchenyi

5 Chained serf doing punitive labour, watched by pandoor. Illustration from Jószef Eötvös's book on prison reform

6 Louis Kossuth at a banquet in his honour at Southampton, October 1851

7 Sándor Petőfi. Painting by Petrich Soma Orlai

8 Endre Ady

10 Hungarian soldiers returning from the battle-front, autumn 1918

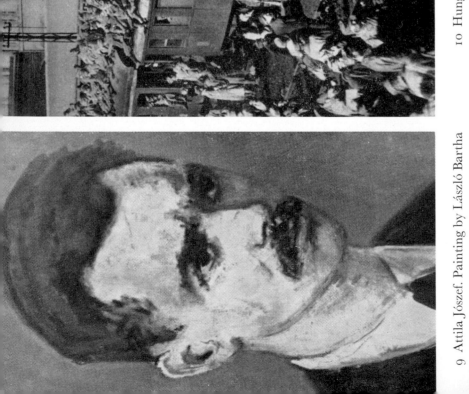

9 Attila Jószef. Painting by László Bartha

11 Count Michael Károlyi in the garden of his mansion during the Council Republic, 1919

12 Ribbentrop (*left*), and Hitler and Horthy. Hitler made Horthy his ally and later had him deported

13 The Arrow Cross puppet ruler Ferenc Szálasi (*left*) with two henchmen in the yard of Buda Castle, late 1944

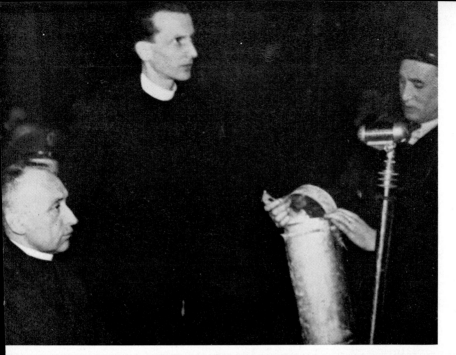

14 The Roman Catholic Church 1949. Cardinal Mindszenty confronted by 'damning' evidence at his trial

15 The Roman Catholic Church 1969. The bench of bishops taking the oath of allegiance to President Pál Losonczi

16 László Rajk (*left*) with General György Palffy-Oesterreicher at their trial, September 1949

17 Julia Rajk and her son at the unveiling of the plaque in honour of László Rajk, Budapest, March 1969

18 Imre Nagy addresses Parliament during his first premiership, flanked by Rákosi (*to his right*) and Gerő (*to his left*)

19 Refugees. The aftermath of Revolution

20 October 1956. The fate of Stalin's statue

21 May Day 1969. Losonczi, János Kádár, and Prime Minister Jenő Fock waving to participants in the parade

22 Budapest. Parliament from the Chain Bridge

23 A street in Buda

24 Peasant House in Milejszeg, Göcsej region, south-west Hungary

25 György Lukacs

26 Large-capacity machines sowing maize, Enying State Farm, west Hungary

fact, they were helped to escape further while the German Legation in Budapest practically ignored the whole affair.[1] One activity of the semi-official Hungarian irredentists was to forge money in the currency of states disliked by Hungary in order to undermine their governments and, incidentally, line the pockets of good patriots. The forging of Czechoslovak and Yugoslav banknotes as well as of the rapidly deteriorating Soviet rouble blew over without much ado, and possibly did not involve substantial sums. The French Franc Forgery, however, grew into a world scandal in 1926. The publicity started in a Brussels bank when two well-dressed foreign gentlemen were caught red-handed trying to sell forged French franc notes. The gentlemen, when searched, astounded the Belgian police by (a) 'wearing women's stockings' (Belgium had never been informed of the Central European code of elegance under which silk socks or, indeed, stockings reaching above the knees could be worn by gentlemen without suggesting any 'queer' association); (b) turning out to be Hungarian military officers on leave; and (c) having on them several packets of forged banknotes. They were only minor agents, however fatally incompetent, of a wide association of patriots determined to topple the French Republic by hitting her citizens where it hurt most. It was never discovered whom the idea originated with, but among its protagonists were Count Pál Teleki, by then ex-premier, Professor of Geography, and Director of the military Cartographic Institute whose printing-works were placed at the disposal of forgers; Prince Ludwig Windisch-Graetz, once Minister of Food to the former King Karl and an unrepentant Habsburg loyalist after the dethronement, but willing, in his own words, 'to make common cause with anti-Legitimists as well as Legitimists in the service of patriotic aims'; Imre Nádossy, the Chief Captain of Police (a post created under Horthy to control all the security forces) –an attractively tall, slim man, and withal tough, romantic, and bloodthirsty; and the Roman Catholic Bishop István Zadravecz, previously a Franciscan friar who, through his association with the Officers' Detachments, had risen to an army bishopric. Both Nádossy and Zadravecz were leading members of the racialist (and by implication anti-Christian) Etelköz Association. The packets of forged French banknotes were ceremoniously blessed by Bishop Zadravecz (in a partly Christian, partly tribal pagan ritual); whereupon Nádossy took a truckload of them to the Foreign Ministry and asked the officials in charge to seal them for transport to Belgium in the diplomatic bag. 'What do they contain?', an official asked.

[1] A report (unconfirmed) maintained somewhat later that Rathenau's murderers were in Hungary. I, as a reporter of *Esti Kurir*, called at the German Legation for a statement. A dandified young man received me. 'Die Erzberger Mörder sind wir glücklich los, nun kommen Sie mir mit den Rathenau Mördern', was his answer.

'Forged money, of course', was Nádossy's reply. The officials guff-awed over 'old Uncle Imre's' wit, and the goods were dispatched to the West. Count Bethlen, then premier, knew of the venture but managed to turn a blind eye to it. Some Legitimist aristocrats got wind of Prince Ludwig's involvement in a secret government-sponsored adventure and warned him against associating with such 'cads' as Bethlen and others who had been instrumental in dethroning King Karl; but Windisch-Graetz paid no heed to them.

When the scandal exploded, the Hungarian constitutionalist opposition (and notably the Legitimists, led by Count Andrássy and his son-in-law, the foolhardy young Marquis György Pallavicini; the Liberal Democrats led by Vilmos Vázsonyi, Károly Rassay, and Rezső Rupert; and the Social Democrats led by Gyula Peidl, Károly Peyer, and Anna Kéthly) launched an all-out attack on the Bethlen government and the whole Horthy régime. Although most of these opposition speakers were either conservative or very moderate in outlook (among the leaders enumerated, Rupert and Anna Kéthly alone would have qualified in the West as 'radicals', and 'Victorian radicals' at that), they were all convinced that the country must get rid of a set-up which landed her in such dangerous adventures, otherwise the whole nation would ultimately have to pay the price of international brawls fathered by Hungary. It was, in fact, the last attempt by democratic Hungarians to placate the democratic West by eliminating the remnants of White terror from the Hungarian state. But the democratic West was not interested in exporting Western democracy. Of the Western Powers only France, the one directly affected, showed some displeasure–for a very short while. Jules Sauerwein, Diplomatic Correspondent of the very popular and nationalist Paris daily *Le Matin*, arrived in Budapest with the loudly-voiced intention of teaching the Horthy-Bethlen régime a lesson: he left Budapest a mild commentator on the affair. 'The forged francs cost us some thousand genuine francs but we survived', a Hungarian government official remarked in confidence. Nádossy and Windisch-Graetz, together with some junior military officers, were ordered to accept the roles of very mildly chastized scapegoats; the rest, including the government, survived; because, as Western ruling circles agreed, much should be forgiven to a country that had been so cruelly damaged . . . .

The Trianon frontiers were thus sacrosanct, but so were the gangster methods of retaliation against its defenders and beneficiaries. The constant violations of the Trianon Treaty, and particularly of its clause forbidding military conscription, were regarded with equanimity by the League Powers, and Hungarian democrats had divided feelings on the matter: while worried about the implied duty of

Hungarian citizens to endorse any arbitrary act if it could be presented as a 'patriotic' circumvention of the law, they could not but admit that the *Entente*-and notably France, as the author of Trianon-and the Little *Entente* (Czechoslovakia, Romania, Yugoslavia), as Trianon's arrogant parasite, had really asked for it by denying the Magyar people equal rights to those of their neighbours. Hungarian government circles deliberately maintained bad relations with those neighbours because, whether they really hoped for a readjustment of frontiers or not, hostilities gave them the excuse to hold their own subjects down. Besides, friendly relations with the neighbours would have encouraged bad examples: Austria was a parliamentary republic (with 'Red Vienna' as her capital); Romania and Yugoslavia, although under royal rule, had carried out a radical Land Reform; and, worst of all, Czechoslovakia was guilty of both these crimes, having become a parliamentary republic *and* implemented a radical Land Reform. Understandably, Czechoslovakia was vilest of all the bogeymen in Hungarian political mythology. Yet, as it happened, the most dangerous international clash brought about by Hungary's para-military technique involved the one Little *Entente* country which, on other occasions, Horthy and his entourage thought worth trying to lure over to the anti-Czech side-namely Yugoslavia.

On 9 October 1934, in Marseilles, King Alexander of Yugoslavia and the French Foreign Minister, Louis Barthou, were killed by Croat marksmen, members of the Ustasha organization. They turned out to have been trained in the Hungarian camp of Jankapuszta. By then, Gömbös was already premier, and his leading diplomatic adviser and representative with cabinet rank (who at the same time led the opposition Independent Smallholder Party) was the former racialist politician Dr Tibor Eckhardt (1888-). The latter had the uncomfortable though rewarding task of countering Yugoslav accusations at the League of Nations. The authenticity of the Jankapuszta photographs could not be denied; but Mussolini's envoy vigorously supported Hungary (the marksmen in fact could just as well have been trained in Italy), and Laval, for France, did his best to get accepted a resolution which both parties could present to their own camps as their own achievement. 'We have brushed elbows with war', Laval was later quoted as saying; and his reason for pacifying Mussolini at all costs might have been his desire to isolate Hitler's already rampant Germany. Italy was still committed to preventing the *Anschluss*. But whatever the diplomatic implications of the bargain, the moral of the story for the Magyar people was once again that they would be fools to trust in legality: Fascist-minded swashbucklers could get away with murder. Gömbös, after all, was known to be Hitler's admirer as well as Mussolini's. (He preferred Goering to both.)

Progress in spite of All

A country governed so irresponsibly must go to the dogs. Hungary did worse by going to the Nazis. She did so, however, with quite a surprising detour; for under Gömbös, chief architect of her satellite status, she was still progressing. The fact of this progress was paradoxical and so, even more, was its character. The principle throughout Horthy's rule, and particularly under Gömbös, had been to keep down 'this criminal city' of Budapest, because, apart from political animosities, it had been self-evident for decades that the precipitately enlarged capital was a 'hydrocephalus' on so small a national community. Yet Budapest went on growing, not only in absolute numbers but relatively to the total population as well. Was this an unsound development? Not if soundness implies the improvement of living conditions; and since Budapest gradually and almost unnoticeably relapsed into her pre-war liberal practices, she created much more attractive jobs and amenities than the provinces did. One reason was the rapid growth of new industries for which the capital and her suburbs, placed as they were on the banks of the Danube, offered far better prospects than did economic experiments in far-away corners of the country. The proliferation of factories, admittedly, does little to make a city more attractive, but the stench of rapid industrialization was neutralized by another process: it was in the inter-war period that Budapest developed into a spa city of international repute. She made ample use of her sulphur springs (once frequented by gouty Roman high officials) as well as of the Danube; she conjured up a record number of glamorous and popular open-air swimming pools; she created public parks, luxury hotels, and restaurants halfway between gypsy romance and Champs-Elysées cosmopolitanism. Her night clubs were a match for Montmartre and certainly less expensive; the Prince of Wales (now Duke of Windsor) with Mrs Simpson visited them as frequently as he could during his short stay in Hungary and conquered all Magyar hearts by always calling for 'barack!' (For the benefit of the reader: 'barack', pronounced 'bawrawtsk', is the Magyar word for apricot and abbreviation for apricot brandy, one of Hungary's proudest national drinks.)

If few could afford to visit the night clubs regularly, comparatively many could form little groups to buy and maintain rowing-boats on the river; and the inter-war period witnessed the erection of a whole township of 'wild-boatmen' (as distinct from the long-established and socially exclusive regatta club members), among whom practically all social classes found recreation and the pleasures of nature only a short distance from the city centre. As one walked along the western bank of the Danube towards the boatmen's township, the well-kept road suddenly changed into filthy, weedy mire: it was precisely at the point where Budapest's local authority ended and that of Pest County began. Except for the rivers and lakes, the forests and meadows, themselves, everything that was provincial remained hopeless.

Among economic phenomena most frequently discussed was the so-called 'widening of the agrarian scissors', by which was meant the high price of industrial goods compared to that of farm products. It was and has been ever since a world phenomenon which we need not dwell upon here; but the remedies applied differed from country to country and were typical of their ruling ideologies. In Hungary, the main remedy consisted of subsidizing those engaged in grain production; and since it went without saying that for small farmers it was more rational to switch over to animal husbandry and market gardening, the government's policy implied a free gift to the big estates and to the least enterprising, most blinkered of the small farmers, at the expense of the rest of the rural and non-rural population. There was, undoubtedly, progress in agricultural technology for all that; never before, for instance, had the fruit-growing farms round the market town of Kecskemét mastered the technique of producing and packing their products for export; but it was progress achieved in spite of, rather than because of, the prevailing policy.

The manufacturing industries (once recovered from the setback caused by the World Economic Crisis, which lasted approximately until 1932) progressed much more rapidly and even though penalized by a one-sided system of taxation, paid higher returns than agriculture. Consequently, they expanded all the time; in the 1920s, the sources of national income developed accordingly;[1] and by the end of the 1930s, Hungary had become a semi-industrial country, not only in terms of her sources of income but her social composition as well. From 1934 to 1937, imports (of manufactured goods) from Germany doubled, and exports (of overwhelmingly farm products) to Germany trebled; growing economic dependence on Germany thus gave a boost to agriculture, but helped manufacturing industries at the price of imposing a war-economy pattern on them.

Beyond the Pale: Workers and Jews

The two social categories branded as 'destructive' since the 1919 counter-revolution, namely Jewry and the industrial working class,

[1] On the territory of post-Trianon Hungary, from the late 1910s to the late 1920s, the share in national income of all primary products sank from 61 to 49 per cent, that of agriculture proper from 54 to 43 per cent, whereas that of manufacturing industry rose from 21 to 28 per cent, that of handicraft industry from 6 to 8 per cent, and of commerce from 4 to 7 per cent; transport fell from 5 to 4 per cent (disregarding decimals) according to F. V. Fellner, *Csonka-Magyarország nemzeti jövedelme* ('The National Income of Rump Hungary'), Hungarian Academy of Sciences, Budapest, 1930.

did not fare so badly throughout most of the inter-war period as the outcries against them might have suggested. They were treated as outcasts, or at best as second-class citizens, with painful consequences, but without being subjected to mass starvation. The economic strength of the industrial workers lay in trade unionism, which implied affiliation to Social Democracy since all other types of labour organizations (mostly under 'Christian-National' labels) were demonstrably run by stooges of either the capitalists or the privileged gentry bureaucracy, and never won the confidence of even the most devout or most patriotic workers. Social Democracy, for its part, implied membership of the (Second) International as does membership of the British Labour Party; a connection tantamount to treason in the eyes of the White rulers. The fact was, therefore, that the industrial workers owed their comparatively tolerable living standards to their persistence in an attitude semi-officially branded as criminal. Under Bethlen this state of affairs was taken for granted; since Social Democracy had been expelled from the rural areas and the state-controlled services, the souls of the factory-workers, bricklayers, and shop assistants were abandoned to the internationalist devil without much fuss. But Gömbös made a bid for the souls of 'our brethren, the workers'; they could, he proclaimed, easily rise to be trusted members of the community if only they would 'place themselves on a national footing', by which was meant that they should quit the International. The workers refused to do so, but Gömbös did not give up hope and, to please them, introduced a system of collective bargaining. This, again, strengthened the hands of the Social Democratic trade unions, since no alternative organization to represent the workers could be found; and the Social Democratic leaders were careful to conceal what they gained through Gömbös's manoeuvres, lest it should provoke more violent action against them under the growing Nazi menace. This, at any rate, was the position when Premier Gömbös died (6 October 1936) and for a while thereafter.

Even more awkward was the position of the Jews. To all the anomalies inherent in their functioning as a second middle class, mostly better off than the gentry but never totally admitted to the 'national' and 'gentlemanly' communities, were added the measures calculated to avert their 'destructive' influence. The *numerus clausus* at the universities, aggravated by recurrent Jew-baitings under the auspices of the privileged 'comradely associations', but alleviated by the practice that degrees obtained abroad were accepted without too much trouble at home, resulted in a widening of the gulf between rich and poor: to the rich Jew all free professions were open, as he could afford to spend years educating himself in the West, while the poor Jew, if admitted to higher schooling at all, had to put up with constant harassment. At the same time, a *de facto numerus nullus* kept young people of Jewish origin out of even those state-controlled jobs (for example, the railways, the schools) where the percentage of their elders had formerly been quite high. The selling of landed property was made conditional on government permission–again, with the unwritten proviso that while it would be unrealistic to deny Jews the right to buy real estate for housing and industrial purposes, their expansion in agriculture must be contained. The outcome was a dividing-line sharper than ever between the 'gentry' (i.e., gentile) and 'bourgeois' (i.e., Jewish and ex-Jewish) white-collar classes; their mutual envy and hostility were bound to deepen. Then, certain remedies were applied which only worsened an already hopeless situation. Under Gömbös, even more than under Bethlen, privileged government supporters of the 'gentile middle-class' variety were helped to lucrative sinecures and, indeed, with German assistance, made large fortunes overnight; while government supporters of the 'Jewish capitalist' variety were allowed higher honours than ever before, but strictly and humiliatingly outside the field reserved for 'pure' Hungarians. The relationship between Roman Catholics and Protestants also worsened. Roman Catholicism had an overall majority among the population–and even more among the magnates. In the political and military hierarchy, however, Calvinists and Lutherans were conspicuously more numerous than Catholics. To assuage Catholic susceptibilities, the often violent proselytizing methods of the Catholic clergy in the villages were given silent government approval, and large areas of education were placed under exclusively Catholic influence. 'There is one thing that unites all citizens of this country: the reciprocity of their grievances', commented a witty writer; he was, incidentally, one of the old *Nyugat* guard, Zoltán Szász by name, a staunch left-Liberal who was imprisoned for his outspokenness both under Béla Kun and under Horthy. In the old Liberal Hungary, he had been regarded as the glass of fashion; in the inter-war period, he was reduced to carefully groomed rags, but his monocle, courage, and wit remained immaculate. His imprisonment did not last long, but the mental fug in which people like him found it difficult to breathe did.

The Intellectual Reaction; Servility Canonized

In one respect the Horthy régime was certainly successful: it moulded the erstwhile Liberal intelligentsia into a priesthood of servility. Servile people had of course always existed; but since 1919 (the year when, in quick succession, Béla Kun, Archduke Joseph, and Miklós Horthy emerged as embodiments of the national ideal) servility has been regarded as a virtue in Hungary, its philosophical vindication accepted as proof of promising young intellects, and the very idea of mental independence kept in limbo. The two leading intellectuals of the counter-revolutionary era, Dezső Szabó (1879–1945) and Gyula Szekfü (1883–1955), were for all their differences in temperament and outlook at one in their crusade to discredit Liberalism. The former acted as an inverted revolutionary; the latter as a conservative *enfant terrible*. They both had careers chequered with political scandals and rapid changes of opinion which strangely converged on the anti-Liberal theme.

The milestones in Szabó's career were: starting as a passionate Calvinist (of the Transylvanian 'petty gentry'), he then contributed to a provincial Roman Catholic gazette of Ultramontane views in which he made slanderous anti-Jewish propaganda; turned against both Church and state to lead the radical grammar-school teachers' movement for better pay, causing scandal by his jokes about those 'who sing the National Anthem with their stomachs rumbling with hunger'; became a *Nyugat* author–not in the front line of talents, but appreciated for his colourful style and personality as a writer of short essays and stories–and was given space in it to attack the premier, Count Tisza; under the Károlyi republic, clamoured for another revolution; after the declaration of the Council Republic, welcomed Béla Kun's government wholeheartedly; at the same time, published his first substantial novel, *Elsodort falu* (Swept-away Village), with communist blessing; immediately after the fall of the Council Republic, led the extreme White writers' and university youth movements, both of them anti-Semitic; achieved a sensational success with *Elsodort falu* (which was to head the lists of bestsellers for decades to come); sold all rights in his works, including *Elsodort falu*, to a Jewish publisher; became the idol of the racialist Awakening Magyars; fell out with the Awakening Magyars and attacked them for not being real Magyars but Slavs, Romanians, and mainly Germans in Magyar guise; offered to stand for Parliament in Rassay's Liberal Democratic Party; fell out with the Liberals and practically everyone else; swore he would emigrate from Hungary and join the Romanian nation with which he had blood ties through his mother, then forgot his vow; was subsidized by one of Count Bethlen's cabinet ministers (Mgr Vass) to attack another cabinet minister (Count Klebelsberg); accused his most devoted disciple, the National Radical deputy and editor Endre Bajcsy-Zsilinszky (1886–1944) of having embezzled part of the subsidy; campaigned against his publisher, 'the conquering Jew', for not paying him more; came to terms with him; extolled Mussolini's Fascism and, in the face of Nazi expansion, headed a group of young men who planned to counter German imperialism with a combination of anti-Jewish and anti-Swabian propaganda; died, a hero of Magyar racialism, during the siege of Budapest. The interesting thing about his tergiversations was that they never altered the style, with all its mythical catchwords, of his rhetoric. His *Elsodort falu*, smacking partly of newspaper reportage, partly of supernatural legends, showed the decayed gentry and the wretched peasantry in the grip of the First World War while the bourgeoisie of the towns gave themselves up to profiteering and intellectualism. Was this a declaration of faith addressed to the paupers of the world, with a hopeful eye on the Bolsheviks, or to the Magyar race as represented by the poor peasantry exploited and fooled by the cities? Either interpretation could hold good. Dezső Szabó's lifelong bugbear was what he termed 'Freecompetition-Democracy' (he was a resourceful coiner of words), and through all his strange twists and turns, he went on exorcizing it, whether fighting on the extreme Left, the extreme Right, or even in the middle-of-the-road Liberal camp. He was a very bad novelist, unreadable today, and a shallow and confused thinker; but a magnificent demagogue, of torrential puns and thundering emotions.

The historian Szekfü, a state archivist in Vienna under the Habsburg monarchy, shocked national opinion by siding with Habsburg authority even more than the conventional Habsburg loyalists thought permissible. He wrote a book, careful and scholarly though riddled with malignant innuendoes, on *Rákóczi, the Exile*, pointing out how pathetic and self-deceiving, if not hypocritical, that great hero of Hungarian liberty had been in his efforts to kindle the idea of independence from abroad. Rákóczi's sources of income, including the gambling club he had run in Paris (the Hôtel de Transylvanie which figures in *Manon Lescaut*), were also recorded by Szekfü with relish. The Establishment, which liked to let sleeping national heroes lie, was embarrassed; while the nationalist ("'48-er') opposition was almost as glad to accuse a Habsburg official of lack of patriotism as was Szekfü to demonstrate the human failings of a national idol. The left-wing intellectuals were divided: most of them found the outburst of nationalist indignation unpalatable, but some expressed even graver misgivings about Szekfü's devious super-loyalism. These latter were proved right after the 1919 counter-revolution, when Szekfü in his pamphlet on *Three Generations* supplied scholarly vindication to the White authoritarians, denouncing the first generation of national and liberal reformers as noble-minded but naïve, the second as drunk with wishful thinking, and the third as the one whose blindness landed Hungary in the tragedies of a lost war and Bolshevism. Did Szekfü, then, advocate the restoration of the Habsburg monarchy? Not since it had become impractical; Professor

Szekfü, like the German champions of *geisteswissentschaftlich* historiography whom he so admired, combined metaphysical idealism with a pragmatic belief in success and the established power, and saw not only necessity but also virtue in siding with authority. He became the chief adviser on culture to Premier Count Bethlen and his Minister of Education, Count Kuno Klebelsberg; and co-author with Professor Bálint Hóman of a new comprehensive *Hungarian History*, the standard book of enlightened (or, at least, disillusioned and moderate) reactionaries in his country.

From the mid-thirties, however, the bastion of moderate authority on which Hóman and Szekfü liked to rely no longer existed. They had to choose some dynamic force to ally themselves with. Hóman opted for Gömbös (becoming his Minister of Education) and later for the Nazis; Szekfü turned the other way. He first came forward with a strange mixture of conservative and reformist ideas, but when war broke out, he slipped further and further into the Popular Front and ended, after the Allied victory, as Hungary's first ambassador in Moscow. His point of view was in a way unchanged; simply, the established power to be relied on was now the Soviet Union. Yet he never gave up his faith in Roman Catholic authority.

Dezső Szabó and Gyula Szekfü thus ended in absolute disillusionment with the counter-revolutionary régime whose intellectual content had been their own creation; and both of them were horrified at the prospect, for which their own counter-revolution had paved the way, of Hungary becoming a colony of the Nazi empire. But neither they nor their disciples (including many communists and anti-communists in the Magyar white-collar classes of the 1970s) have ever recognized that the cult of illiberalism which they upheld was bound to yield such results. It was their teachings (Szabó's *voelkisch* mystique and eulogy of violence, and Szekfü's authoritarian outlook) which conditioned the generations that followed them to prefer, in one form or another, a master of slaves to a leader exposed to criticism and dependent on consent.

The Peasantry: Eulogized, Betrayed, and Kept in Misery

And there was the peasantry: at the beginning of the Horthy régime, definitely more than half of the total population, and towards its end, roughly half. Despite constant industrialization, it was still *the* common people. Is it correct to call it 'peasantry'? When referring to the Anglo-Saxon world, from the English Channel right to the Pacific, we talk of 'farmers', 'farm labourers', 'farmhands' – the 'peasants' begin where the English language barrier ends. Whether this distinction also applies to France and Scandinavia may be open to argument, but it certainly seems meaningful to a student of Hungarian and eastern European affairs. In Hungary, peasants had a special status, different from that of any other category of people, whether upper-class, middle-class, or industrial working-class. Unlike the rest, they were extolled; and more than the rest, oppressed and exploited.

Veneration of the peasantry as sole unspoilt transmitter of the national character was a cornerstone of the patriotic creed; revolutionaries such as Dezső Szabó had launched the concept and no conservatives or reactionaries would have challenged it, least of all those who were convinced that the peasants' simplicity could be preserved by shortening their gentlemanly reins. In manipulating them, of course, the tremendous differences between one 'peasant' stratum and another had to be taken into account; their top layer, the smallholder peasants owning a plot large enough to sustain them and their families, were only too conscious of both the social superiority and the conflict of interests which divided them from the paupers of the land; so that although a 'peasant' image did exist in literature, there was and could be no such thing as a policy of the 'peasantry'. After the upheavals–revolutionary and counter-revolutionary–of 1918–19, a group of jackbooted, tieless, well-off farmers calling themselves 'smallholders' was pushed into Parliament, and István Nagyatádi Szabó, by far their most important spokesman, served as a cabinet minister in the (Károlyi) republican and various later White governments. He several times attempted to establish some qualified form of 'agrarian democracy' within the feudal framework; his last attempt being when he served under Count Bethlen. Bethlen's answer was to have his safe forced: he knew the Smallholder leader's greed for money well enough to count on finding proofs of corruption. The government Chief of Press, Dr Tibor Eckhardt, started leaking hints of 'fishy' dealings in the ministry. Nagyatádi Szabó capitulated. 'What next?', the Press Chief asked Bethlen; 'Shall I wash him white?'–'Wash him grey', Bethlen answered. A couple of years later, in 1924, another corruption scandal exploded and forced Nagyatádi Szabó to resign. Almost immediately after, he died of a stroke. In front of the Ministry of Agriculture, scene of his privy dealings with public funds, a statue was rapidly erected, immortalizing Szabó in peasant's jackboots, and Count Bethlen, aristocratically slim, at the historic moment when they shook hands, with an inscription saying that this was the Rock on which to build the Future of the Fatherland. If communists had one spark more sense of humour, that statue would still be standing today.

Nagyatádi Szabó was a smallholder and, politically, a Smallholder; the rest of the smallholders and Smallholders entering public life with him differed from him mainly in being less bright. The jackbooted, tieless deputy, his belly protruding from under his waistcoat, tottering forth from a night club on the arms of blondes employed by government to entertain him, was a familiar sight of Budapest night life; the layer of peasantry they represented could on the whole be trusted.

But smallholders only amounted to about one-third of the rural population; the rest were either totally landless or 'dwarf-holders': compelled, that is, to sell their labour on a market where manpower was cheaper than anything else. Much has since been written about the misery of these 'three million beggars', as they were generally called – numbering, together with their dependents, roughly one-third of the population of Hungary. Statistical data were gathered to illustrate their standard of life, but I submit that these were largely based on arithmetical illusions. Whether the daily income of an average 'beggar' was estimated to equal $\frac{1}{2}d$ or $3d$ in 1938 Britain simply did not matter, as the whole £.s.d. system was inapplicable to the conditions under which he lived. Such a beggar, say a digger in a vineyard or an orchard, may have earned a pint of wine or a beautiful peach quite frequently, which would be delicacies in London beyond the reach of modest income groups; on the other hand, he may never in his life have had one simple garment other than the rags thrown out by others, and may never have had a bed which he could call his own – items difficult to evaluate even in $\frac{1}{2}d$'s of the Britain of those days. The living conditions of those 'beggars' varied considerably from one district, from one year, from one season, to another; they certainly did not starve to a man all the time, not all their children were rickety and undernourished, a few in fact developed into well-built, sturdy individuals; but with all caution against sweeping generalizations, it is a fact that their poverty was appalling. There *were* cave-dwellers among them; there *were* villages where the poor chewed the bark of trees; even if it happened only in some districts and some seasons, does this not bear out in essentials what the purveyors of universal-hunger stories were trying to convey? Starvation was a familiar feature of life for the people who tilled the land.

The petrification of the big estates, covering roughly half of all the productive land, was but one cause of their penury; more important was the fact that practically the whole rural population suffered from underemployment or a degree of constant and hidden unemployment. There was simply not enough land to feed all its labourers, particularly since emigration to the United States – an alarming symptom of pre-1914 dearth but a relief in itself – had been severely cut under the American 'national quota' system. Nothing short of a drastic reorganization of the whole economy on more rational, more businesslike lines, and in co-operation with some or all neighbouring countries, could substantially have improved the lot of the peasantry.

This would have meant tackling the monopolies of the big landlords, particularly the entailed ones. But the aim of attaining a multitude of small estates would not in itself have improved matters very much. It was dependence on uneconomic farming methods that lay at the root of the trouble. Exploitation of the peasantry, or of their needy majority, was due less to ruthless profitmaking than to the social factors which kept rural life stagnant; underemployed labourers may not have been a source of particularly large incomes but were nevertheless welcome servants to underemployed squires and county officials.

Yet, progress from *latifundia* towards smallholdings seemed clearly in line with the national interest, and the question was not so much whether this should be encouraged but rather how and to what extent and, mainly, under whose leadership it should be done. The Social Democratic Party accepted an agrarian programme (devised by a committee consisting of two long-standing peasant members, Ferenc Szeder and József Takács, and the party's lawyer and economist, Dr László Faragó) which pressed for the splitting-up of big estates; as did also the rearguard of the erstwhile Károlyi Independents and Jászi radicals: Rezső Rupert, Vince Nagy, Barna Buza, Rustem Vámbéry, and the author and journalist Béla Zsolt (1898–1949), most eloquent of their younger generation. But once the régime was 'consolidated' and trade unionism and the secret ballot expelled from the villages, such left-wingers did not have a chance of approaching the peasantry direct; communists did not even try to, although their illegal 'cells' cropped up spasmodically in factories and even in universities. The most powerful figure among the Liberal deputies, Károly Rassay (1886–1958), urged the ending of entailments and of subsidies to big estates, but would not commit himself to inciting the paupers on the land. This task thus devolved upon the extreme Right – the more so since the 'Divide and Rule' strategy of both the Bethlen and Gömbös governments actually favoured any move calculated to show how much the 'pure and unspoiled Magyar peasantry' disliked both liberal and socialist manifestations of the 'Budapest spirit'. Subversive literature about rural conditions became a monopoly of the extreme Right. Consequently, some quite good reports on the peasants' misery were published in the late twenties by journalists notorious for their hatred of Western ways, of parliamentary democracy, and of what was always associated with it – Jewry. The reports were good, that is, in factual reporting, though their interpretation of the facts would have disgraced a primary schoolboy.[1]

[1] 'Three million beggars' was originally the title of a book by an able right-radical (later, pro-Nazi) journalist, György Oláh. (The Magyar title was *Három millió koldús*, Miskolc, 1928.)

Chapter 8

In a Literary Melting-Pot

The Stupid Man Fooling the Clever

IN THE THIRTIES, after Gömbös and Hitler had come to power in their respective countries, the handling of agrarian pauperism was given another twist. Gömbös proclaimed his 'Reform Policy'. He never made quite clear what he meant by that; but his idea was to give a general impression that he was going to break up the *latifundia* while at the same time reassuring the Regent (who was more conservative than even the multi-millionaire aristocrats about agrarian policy) that he had no such subversive intentions and only wanted to give philanthropic help to the needy. He achieved a similar ambiguity about putative schemes to curb the already limited freedom of the Press; to 'Aryanize' banks, industrial concerns, commercial networks; to replace trade unions (as well as employers' federations) by Fascist-like corporations. His talk was a kind of ignorant blustering which, strange to say, fooled for a short time such far more intelligent and sophisticated partners or opponents as Bethlen, Eckhardt, Gyula Károlyi, even Rassay for a moment. He also fooled a number of intellectuals.

The author László Németh (1901–), who in the thirties was regarded as the leading ideologist of the young intelligentsia, was extremely versatile, prolific, and receptive, a remarkable but unselective transmitter of every idea which in that part of Europe could be attributed to the *Zeitgeist*. His prophetic zeal, which inspired him for a while to write a periodical on his own, was reminiscent of Dezső Szabó, to whom he owed the populist belief in mysterious forces of racial rejuvenation; but he was a more polished artist, a better-informed thinker, and a less daring man than his master. Politically, his great gesture was to publish in the government gazette, *Budapesti Hirlap*, an article welcoming what he called the 'Third Side' in Hungarian public life; an expression which sounds awkward in English but which should be retained as he used it in the political jargon of his country, lest it be confused with what, for instance, was called 'Third Road' or 'Troisième force' in post-war Britain and France. One 'side' of Hungarian public life was conservatism, or the Right as exemplified in Bethlen's supporters and the

Legitimists; the other, the no less outworn Left of Liberals and socialists. The new Era of Reform must come from the Third Side, as did Fascism in Italy and National Socialism in Germany. Perhaps, Németh speculated, the young *literati* gathered in the capital could stage a March from Budapest to shake up the dreamy provinces with the same determination as had gone into the March on Rome. He never advocated outright dictatorship for Hungary, nor indiscriminate anti-Semitism; he rather flaunted his association with a number of Jewish authors and, as literary director of the Hungarian radio, encouraged rather than fenced in nonconformist minds; and among the Western 'élitists' he popularized, the liberal Ortega found his place along with Spengler and other right-wing authoritarians. Yet, in the light of political examples he quoted for inspiration, it was clear that his 'Revolution of Quality' was devised as a Hungarian brand of Fascism.

'New Spiritual Front'

Meanwhile, the well-known playwright Lajos Zilahy (1891–), who had very vague ideas about political problems but an insatiable urge to solve them, came forward with a similar scheme in a daily of the largest Hungarian newspaper combine, 'Est Lapok', Jewish-owned and professing Liberal principles. In a manifesto-article, 'New Spiritual Front!' (*Pesti Napló*, 14 April 1935), he urged the participation of young intellectuals in politics to support the 'visible government', headed by General Gömbös, against the 'invisible government', or 'Holy Triple Alliance of clerical big estates, secular big estates, and big capital', in order to bring about 'the Reforms'. As inspiring examples he mentioned 'reform movements abroad such as Fascism and Hitlerism'; a statement which he did his best to qualify, and even neutralize, in later articles by adding alternatively communism and the New Deal; but as Gömbös, his chosen leader, relied on a 'Rome–Berlin', and certainly not on a Washington–Moscow, Axis, the basic tendency of his proposal could not be mistaken. The Jewish Liberal combine then put one of its dailies, the evening paper *Magyarország*, entirely at Zilahy's disposal, and the paper carried a special page under the title 'New Spiritual Front', with László Németh and other able young writers as contributors, some of them with a revolutionary tendency, others with a leftish record which ill-suited their appearance in those columns. Both Zilahy's editorship and Németh's belief in Gömbös and the whole Front came to an early end, but the hostilities it stirred up have long persisted, with sad results.

Village Exploring

By the early thirties, an important literary movement had developed which was generally referred to as 'village exploring': a branch of informal sociology, centred on the depressing conditions of the countryside. Its forerunners ranged from *Nyugat* authors such as Zsigmond Móricz and Lajos Nagy, outstanding for their objectivity, to Dezső Szabó, with his racist oratory, and from the 'TT' left-radicals of the 1910s to the 'Awakening' right-radicals of the 1920s. Equally varied were the 'explorers' themselves, both in style and outlook; they ranged from poets to agronomists and, judging by their later record from the 1940s onward, from crypto-Nazis to crypto-communists. In the early 1930s, they hit the Budapest readership like a bomb; many of the townsmen apparently had not realized sooner what rural penury was like. The pro-Fascist régime hesitated between treating the village explorers as subversive and using them as trump cards against conservatives, left-wingers, and the 'Budapest spirit'. Similarly hesitant were the village explorers themselves. But most of them settled for at least trying it: could one after all neglect such a chance, however small, of bringing about 'the Reforms'? Unrepentant left-wingers, however–Liberals as well as socialists, and also democratic Catholics–bitterly resented this attitude and for three main reasons: firstly, because they refused to put their faith in any reform that was left undefined; secondly, because ('timeo danaos et dona ferentes') they were convinced that no good could come of any gift from Fascists and Nazis; and thirdly, because above all it infuriated them that authors and intellectuals–that is, people committed to clarity of thought–should allow themselves to be misrepresented in this way.

The man whose appearance in the New Spiritual Front caused most disillusionment among left-wing intellectuals was Gyula Illyés (1902–), on account both of his outstanding abilities and of his previously flawless record of opposition to White rule. Illyés had as a secondary schoolboy been a communist, and after the defeat of the Hungarian Soviets, was helped by his relatives to get to Paris as a safety precaution. This was at a time when the dividing-line between political and artistic revolution was still rather blurred–so it was natural for him to get in touch with the French 'Dada' movement (including, among others, Tristan Tzara) and join Kassák's circle of the *émigré* avant-garde. It was no less natural for him in later years to return quietly to Hungary with a mellower political attitude and style, take an important place among the new generation of *Nyugat* poets, and discover, as it were, the world of Transdanubian shepherds and farmhands from whom he had come. His essays at that time mainly centred on his fear lest the Magyar race should be extinguished–a recurring theme of his ever since. The thing which then estranged part of the left-wing intelligentsia from him was his equivocal appearance in company with Gömbös supporters. Meanwhile, in 1936, his book *The People of the Puszta*[1] won him the admiration of all educated readers, and with good reason. It was, without any doubt, the best work to come out of the vogue of village exploring: a masterpiece of observation and description, reflecting the fate of peasant labourers and rural artisans through the history of his own family and his own youth, recalled with warmth and a beautiful sense of balance. It was ironical that its publication should have coincided with hostilities between its author and some of his most sympathetic colleagues. Two of these unrepentant left-wingers should be mentioned at this point: the eloquent spokesman of middle-class radicalism, Béla Zsolt; and Attila József (1905–37).

Attila József

Attila József was a tremendous personality, a beautiful poet and entirely individual in his art, although the story of his vicissitudes verged on the melodramatic. A weird story it was, though not without picaresque humour. He was sprung from the very depths of poverty, slum and *puszta* combined: born in Budapest, the son of a washerwoman from the Cumanian plainland and of an itinerant soap-boiler, probably Romanian, who had come from the Transylvanian mountains and disappeared when Attila was still a toddler. The farcical element in Attila's story began with his Christian name, which in his walk of life sounded even more bizarre than it would in Britain or North America; for, although Hungarian noblemen had been accustomed since the Romantic rebirth of nationalist myths to baptize their sons with such a name, it was unheard of among the common people. The fanciful soap-boiler Áron József, however, had a dream during his wife's pregnancy that their son was to conquer the world, and therefore insisted on calling the baby after the world-conquering King of the Huns – 'The Scourge of God' as he was remembered in Hungary. Indeed, his name was the sole thing Attila József owed to his father; everything else came from his mother the washerwoman, who worked day and night to keep her two daughters and her son, crammed in one-half of a damp room except when the boy was placed in the country as an infant herdsman or the like. She died when Attila was on the verge of puberty.

It was a proletarian childhood, a textbook case of infant misery; and yet intermittently classless. For all their misadventures and penury, the three orphans displayed the sort of liveliness of mind which filters irresistibly through class barriers, even in the most class-ridden of countries. Attila was a bright schoolboy; and, more im-

---

[1] 'Puszta' in Magyar is mainly associated with the steppes of the plainland, but Illyés uses this word, as is customary in his native Transdanubia, to denote the world of the big estates, ruled by the manor houses, outside towns and villages.

portant, his elder sister was a strikingly pretty young girl who, as a cinema usherette, soon headed towards middle-class smartness. She was picked up Pygmalion-wise by a Jewish banker and lawyer called Ödön Makai, who supported and later married her, and at her request allowed her younger sister and the still younger Attila to live with them, their identities concealed, as small servants. When strangers were about, they had to call their elder sister Madam. Attila was thus given more square meals, and access to a more interesting library, than his classmates of similar background could have dreamt of, but, as may readily be imagined, such a situation tends to sharpen rather than assuage one's consciousness of class differences. His brother-in-law fully appreciated Attila's budding talent, but he could not, after all, conjure back the József parents whose memory unceasingly obsessed Attila. It would have been an intolerable ménage for him even if 'Sir' and 'Madam' had lived in harmony. But they did not; their conflicts ended with Makai divorcing the elder József girl and marrying the younger, who bore him three children; while the divorced elder became an inveterate remarrier, gambler, would-be suicide, and, incidentally, quite a clever authoress.

Attila was still a grammar-school boy when he was first prosecuted (for 'blasphemy' in a poem), but he succeeded in entering the university as a philologist. When planning to apply for a grant, in 1921, he answered the question about sources of his earnings as follows:

I was a private tutor, newsvendor, cabin-boy,
bookseller, book-keeper, bank clerk, publisher's
agent, newspaper boy, shorthand typist, maizefield
keeper, poet, translator, critic . . .

and it was, for all its self-dramatization, a factually true statement. It also set the pattern of his life: even ten years later, when his name already figured in the Hungarian encyclopaedias, he still now and then earned his living as an errand boy. Circumstances in a cant-ridden universe conspired to keep him downtrodden and unhappy; yet the causes of his fate lay as much in himself as in circumstances, and as much in his unstable temperament as in his uncompromising search for truth. At the university, after he published a song-like poem which started with the lightheartedly scanned lament:

I have no father, nor mother,
I have no god, nor country[1]

a professor rebuked him and warned that after voicing such views he would never get a job as schoolmaster; whereupon Attila left the

[1] The original is not in free verse.

university and turned up in Vienna as a newspaper boy and cleaner. Was the lack of freedom in Hungarian academic life his reason, or only his excuse, for this adventure? It was both. In Vienna he joined the group of avant-garde *émigrés* whose defiance of political and artistic conventions strongly appealed to him, but soon found himself at loggerheads with the leader of the group, Kassák, and for a reason very typical of them both: Kassák insisted that poetry in definable metres had become 'barrel-organ', that is, mechanical, doggerel; while Attila, after some attempts to suppress the versifier in himself, decided he could express his thoughts more fully within the 'shackles' of traditional forms – a bit like Ovid, who had tried his hand at prose in vain because 'Whatever I tried to write became verse'. Two compulsive urges beset Attila: he breathed poetry, scanned and rhymed poetry, often against his will; and he incessantly searched for truth, probing the world as a riddle to be solved at all costs while at the same time obsessed with the importance of minute details. Although by now one could fill a library with what has been written about him in Hungary (and in many another country as well), it was this double compulsion which only a few could recognize and many, even among his admirers, have misunderstood. His early Maecenas, Baron Lajos Hatvany, for instance (an author of distinction himself, originally of the *Nyugat* guard), maintained that the author of *I have no father, nor mother* was violating his own nature plus the rules of beauty by struggling with cosmogonic and para-psychological problems in his poetry; whereas modern critics who know him only in translations have wondered, on reading stanzas more reminiscent of Byron or Wordsworth than of Eliot, whether, for all his charm and pathos, there was not something old-fashioned in him and in the Hungarian intelligentsia who looked upon him, right into the 1970s, as the most contemporary of poets. The fact is that in the Vienna and Paris of the early 1920s, where Attila József spent much of his self-imposed exile, practically all the trends of latter-day modernism were foreshadowed; and Attila himself was among the first to be fascinated by them. Guillaume Apollinaire was part of his ambience no less than King David of the *Psalms* or the *Kalevala* of the Finns; his imagination was fertilized by all, but the style of his self-expression dictated by none. In Paris, incidentally, he joined an 'Anarche-Communiste' society; politics were part of the universe whose riddle he was determined to solve, and a synthesis of the strictest order and fullest liberty seemed to his juvenile mind the most promising starting-point.

On returning to Hungary, Attila (who was almost universally known and referred to by his Christian name) continued, police and his dire finances permitting, to search the universe to the tune of his poems, and after several attempts at unorthodox 'syntheses', landed, by the early 1930s, in the communist underground movement. But, unable to toe the line, he soon fell out with his Moscow-controlled comrades, and mainly on two counts. First, he became interested in psychoanalysis and wished to combine the Freudian 'liberation of the inner self' with the Marxian 'liberation of the means of production'; second, recognizing after Hitler's victory in Germany that the Muscovite strategy of denouncing Social Democrats as 'traitors' only played into the hands of Fascists, he urged the working class to unite and ally itself with all liberally-minded sections of opinion, in resistance to the right-wing authoritarian trend. His communist comrades replied that he must be a *provocateur* and a police spy.

Psychoanalysis has always remained anathema to Marxism–Leninism as interpreted by the Kremlin, although slightly less so since Stalin's death; but as to Attila's second heresy, events very soon took an ironical turn. No sooner had he been condemned as an opportunist, to say the least, for his deviation, than the cry for a Popular Front went up for reasons virtually identical with Attila's. But to see the light prematurely is a sin rarely forgiven by authoritarians. Moreover, Attila had in the meantime come to the conclusion, and expounded it in the Social Democrats' monthly journal of political sciences, that no dictatorship could be reconciled with socialism; he agreed to the Popular Front but his estrangement from Kremlinist communism remained final.

An additional stumbling-block between him and his ex-comrades was that once the green light for fraternizing with non-communists had been switched on, some 'illegal revolutionaries' used the new doctrine simply as a means of currying favour with established authorities. Their eagerness to find allies outside the Marxist camp was too unselective for Attila to stomach. The Populist venture to help Premier Gömbös implement 'the Reforms' was a case in point. Attila József had, in fact, had a Populist period himself and argued for the urgent need of village exploring; but once he saw the shadow of Hitlerism growing, he rejected any idea that could be interpreted as a compromise with authoritarian fashions. He sharply attacked the New Spiritual Front. This marked, in 1935, his estrangement from his old friend, Gyula Illyés, with whom he had so much in common; and also a split among the progressive intellectuals of the post-*Nyugat* generation. The highbrow centre of the Populists became the monthly *Válasz* (Answer), launched by László Németh, with Illyés as one of its chief contributors; that of the unrepentant left-wing radicals, an unlicensed but tolerated periodical (a phenomenon typical of the semi-dictatorial Horthy régime) named *Szép Szó* on the initiative of one of its founding editors, Attila József. Literally translated, 'Szép Szó' means 'Beautiful Word'; but, in a Magyar idiomatic phrase, 'beautiful word' stands for persuasion, *argument*, as distinct from violence; 'Szép Szó' thus denoted, as Attila pointed out, not only the literary medium of his magazine but its political aim as well: 'we are aiming at a social order in which argument prevails'.

Válasz had a very limited circulation, and that of *Szép Szó* was even more limited; they did not reach the masses and only rarely the men in power; Admiral Horthy is unlikely ever to have heard of them. Yet whenever since then, in the short breathing-spaces between one and another kind of authoritarian rule, anything emerged that could be identified as the will of the Hungarian people, it was a continuation of the ideas set forth by these two groups of young intellectuals. It has become a commonplace that their hostilities sidetracked resistance to the authoritarian régimes which few would openly defend today – Horthy's, Hitler's, also Stalin's; although the cause of hostility is still a moot point and often discussed in Hungary. In the mid-1930s, indeed, it was the communists (illegal, but identifiable) who urged 'all progressives' and 'all anti-Fascists' to make common cause, but with their crude jargon and pontification alienated rather than attracted the putative partners. There was one exception among them, György Lukács, then a refugee in Moscow, whose intelligent criticism of the young intellectuals could have helped them to create a platform for thrashing out their differences in a spirit of comradeship – if it had reached them in time. But his relevant book, *Responsibility of Literati*, was only published in 1944 and was not available in Hungary before the Nazi defeat.

Cultural Links with Neighbouring Countries

Perhaps the most memorable efforts of the *Válasz* and *Szép Szó* groups were those to establish links with the neighbouring nations, including, of course, their Magyar minorities. Their approaches were different, the *Válasz* ideologists encouraging belief in the magic of mid-Danubian destiny without challenging the principle of national sovereignty, whereas *Szép Szó* – less pragmatic and more rationalist – argued that nothing short of a federal arrangement could settle the nationalities problem in that area. Attila József expounded this idea in his ode *By the Danube* which starts with lyrical contemplation of the river, goes on to meditate on race and history, and ends with an appeal to all peoples of the Danube to work together:

> I want to work; sufficient 'tis to endure
> The battles of the past I must confess
> Past, present, future linked together are

Here where the Danube's billows soft caress.
The grim wars that our ancestors were waging
Have melted into peace in memory's sight;
A general settlement, past wrongs assuaging,
Is now our task to make; it is not light.

(translation by Neville Masterman)

The roads to popularity are strange; *Szép Szó*, as already pointed out, had only a modest circulation, and Attila József's volumes practically none (his last volume before his death sold less than one hundred copies); yet, some of his verses, including *By the Danube*, immediately spread like wildfire, and were chanted in chorus several years later by anti-Nazi demonstrators. Between these two dates, in October 1937, his colleagues from *Szép Szó* made a lecture tour in Czechoslovakia, for which they were denounced as traitors by the German and Hungarian government Press. Attila had been one of the planners of the tour but was by then too ill to take part. His characteristic recurring bouts of craziness and melancholia took the unmistakable shape of paranoia and schizophrenia. In his fixed ideas, senseless though they were, he seemed to continue struggling to resolve the world's riddle and his own, to conjure his mother back to life, and to decipher a deep meaning in every triviality. Was it sheer hardship that unhinged a mind as lucid as his, or was his genius from the outset florescent with incipient lunacy? The present writer, who was sadly privileged to be the closest colleague of his last years, must regretfully accept the second assumption, the one that holds no comfort for spirits such as he was. Attila had a strong sense of fun and pleasure, and in the course of his life he could certainly often have done with more sympathy, more understanding, and more money; but his ultimate madness revealed depths from which nothing could have saved him. He took his life by throwing himself in front of a goods train in December 1937.

All Hopes Gone

His departure, though it had nothing to do with politics, seemed symbolic: it coincided with the collapse of hopes to extricate Hungary from the spreading Nazi swamp and to find a place for her in a society 'in which argument prevails'. The *Anschluss*, the capitulation at Munich, the outbreak of war and its extension to Yugoslavia and Russia, with Hungary's avowed participation on Germany's side, made an exchange of clearly defined views in the *Szép Szó* spirit both impossible and irrelevant; a cruder and more highflown style was needed for protest against the Nazis. As a result of measures to control the Press more strictly, which made regular newspaper work dependent on membership of a Fascist-like Chamber of Journalists and did away with the category of hitherto 'unlicensed but tolerated' periodicals, *Szép Szó* was banned and by the outbreak of the war many of its contributors had sought refuge in the West. These included the socialist historian François Fejtő, well-known as a political writer in France today, the literary essayist Andor Németh, an early Kafka admirer associated with the French and German avant-garde, and Baron Bertalan Hatvany, Lajos's cousin and Attila's Maecenas in his last years, who described himself politically as a 'Tory radical'. In Budapest, two Liberal men of letters, the sociologist Zoltán Gáspár and the economist, historian, and sagacious polemicist Géza K. Havas, were the most active in attempts to carry on *Szép Szó*, even though disguised in 'sheep's clothing', to the bitter end. They both fell victim to the Nazi massacre.

The *Válasz* group and the movements growing out of it were destined to play a larger part in public affairs of the war and post-war years; in March 1937 some of its authors, supported by a section of university youth (the latter led by crypto-communists, as is known today), inaugurated a 'March Front', with claims to kinship with the March Youth of 1848, and with a clear-cut programme of democratic reforms. This narrowed the gap between Populists on the one hand and Liberals and socialists on the other; but it tore wide open the rifts which had always existed within the Populist camp. While one of their leading agronomists, Mátyás Matolcsy, made a deputy by Gömbös, joined the Nazis (and eventually became a speaker on the Donausender), another, Ferenc Erdei, plunged into the communist underground (to become Minister of the Interior after the war), and a third, Mihály Kerék, the most erudite advocate of Land Resettlement, joined the staff of the big landlords' federation, OMGE. As for the village explorers, Illyés concentrated on literary work; Géza Féja, author of the book that had caused the greatest stir in this genre, attempted to adapt his vision of a peasant's revolution to the requirements of a government newspaper sponsored by Count Teleki; and another successful village explorer, Imre Kovács, was foremost in the fight against the Nazis and, though on the staff of a conservative daily, showed sympathetic interest in the Soviets as well as the Western democracies. A most interesting personality among the village explorers was Péter Veres (1897–1970) – a genuine dwarf-holding tiller of the land who first appeared as an author in the pages of socialist and left-Liberal periodicals, for which he was kicked and clouted by the village pandoors. Thanks to the spell of Populism, he was later spared maltreatment; in fact, pro- and anti-Nazi centres of publicity vied for his adherence, especially from the late thirties onwards when he voiced some irritation with the 'Budapest spirit'. He tried to reconcile dialectical materialism with a sort of 'Turanian' (Turco-Ural-Altaic – by no means Aryan or German) racialism. His equivocal ideological position did not, however, save him from enlistment in a 'punitive battalion' during the war. 'And what did those Nazi officers say when they learned you were there?', I asked him later. 'None of them had any idea who I was', he answered; by then he was already Minister of War as a coalition partner of the communists.

László Németh, after his disappointment with Gömbös, made a dramatic gesture of withdrawing from public life, but then redoubled his efforts to make his mark on it. He agitated for 'Garden-Hungary' and the 'Revolution of Quality'. He introduced a distinction between 'deep-Hungarians' and 'shallow-Hungarians' as a refined form of racialism; he did not exclude anybody from the 'deep' category merely on account of his race, nor did he advocate inhumanity towards the 'shallows', but it was nevertheless the characteristics associated with 'pure Magyar blood' that he wished thus to single out. In the war, his attitude was what would have been called *attentisme* in France, but he felt it to be rather like that of the Hungarian patriots of three hundred years before him who had fought 'between two pagans for one fatherland'.

In the meantime, the March Front had disintegrated almost as soon as it was inaugurated, and *Válasz* had stopped publication in 1938, handing over the Populist case to periodicals more adjusted to the public taste. The fate of its last editor, György Sárközi, however, should be noted as a tragedy exemplifying the illusions as well as the gallantry promoted by this interesting movement. Sárközi, a delicate poet, accomplished author, and efficient business organizer, served the Populist cause devotedly and as a Jew (by race, though not by religion), he fell under the spell of its nationalist mystique even more than his 'racially pure' gentile associates. When towards the end of the war he was enlisted in a 'Jewish labour battalion' and some friends urged him to try and escape before being dispatched to an extermination camp, he merely shook his head: 'We are in the hands of *Hungarian* Nazis and however blinkered they may be, they won't do *that*'. The *Hungarian* Nazis then directed his battalion towards the Austrian border whence he never returned.

Chapter 9

The Nazification of Hungary

Capitulating to Hitler

IN THE YEARS FROM THE *Anschluss* to the defeat of the Third Reich (spring 1938–spring 1945) more happened to the mid-Danube basin in general and to Hungary in particular in terms of warfare, massacre, political upheavals, and redrawing the map than in earlier periods ten times as long; yet, when summing up these events, the only surprising thing in them is lack of surprise. Everything was perfectly preconditioned: with a social structure, foreign relations, and official mystique such as Hungary's, no country could have reacted differently to Hitlerite expansion and the subsequent World War. This applies as much to the kind and extent of anti-Nazi resistance, such as it was, as to the Nazi drive that prevailed. The shock of the *Anschluss* made Marxists and Habsburgists mourn together over past glory and fear together for national independence and the ancient constitution; even the Regent joined in and found braver words to express his grief for the Austria of his youth than one would have expected from an usurper. The bulk of the gentry, however, led by Premier Kálmán Darányi, hurried to reinsure themselves against the advent of World Hitlerism. Anti-Jewish, anti-Press, freedom-restricting legislation was the first step; headlong rearmament the second. Dynamism as well as opportunism lay irretrievably with the Nazis; left-wing revolutionaries could only put their faith in conservative values.

Munich helped Hungary to recover the Magyar strip of Czecho-slovakia (with a few dubious Slovak-Magyar districts thrown in). This was bound to play into the Nazis' hands; no Hungarian could have refused that bonus from the Axis Powers, whatever his foreboding about the price to be paid. The premier by then was a former President of the National Bank, Béla Imrédy (1891–1946), known as a devout Catholic, a believer in high dividends and soldierly obedience, a 'Salazar type', as his admirers said. He was the great hope of the magnates, bankers, priests, and other respectable anti-Nazis. But under the impact of Munich he turned Nazi overnight. Parliament outvoted him but he stuck to power–and the Regent, following cautious advice, did not dare to drop him. In support of a Second

Anti-Jewish Law which he publicized, with a picturesque touch of cruelty, on the eve of Christmas 1938, he declared that 'one drop of Jewish blood' was enough to infect a man's character and patriotism. No sooner had he said so than he turned out to have more than one drop—a Jewish great-grandmother in his German–Bohemian ancestry.[1] When the Regent at a dramatic audience showed him the relevant document he fainted. The Regent now plucked up courage and dropped him, appointing Count Paul (or Pál) Teleki as premier in his place; while Imrédy, after recovering, emerged as the leader of a Nazi opposition party (there were always more than one).

Count Teleki: A Machiavellian Romantic at the Helm

Teleki, who thus headed the government on the eve and at the beginning of Hitler's war, was a mixture of Machiavellian feudalist and romantic patriot. He was determined to squeeze out of German friendship and international turmoil the maximum in terms of territorial gains without giving up Hungary's independence, that is, her freedom to leave the Axis when her interests required it. Simultaneously with the German occupation of Bohemia–Moravia and the establishment of the German puppet state of Slovakia, he occupied Ruthenia (or Carpatho-Ukraine—the eastern province of what used to be Czechoslovakia); and, while promising Hitler all facilities in this territory in return, he assured the British through confidential channels that this annexation was aimed at establishing a common frontier with Poland and thus enabling Poles and Hungarians and possibly others to unite in stemming German expansion. Yet, it was no surprise that when subsequently Germany invaded Poland, there could be no question of Hungary helping the Poles—she had neither the determination nor the strength even to attempt it—although the Poles fleeing to Hungary, and especially those connected with the Catholic clergy and aristocracy, were sheltered and treated generously.

Hungarian–Romanian hostility continued irrespective of the World War, in which it took the form of competitive sycophancy towards the Germans while at the same time confiding to Western wellwishers that the hearts of the Hungarians (or Romanians) were with the Allies. In this rivalry Hungary came off best until nearly the end of hostilities, mainly because, reluctant though she was to give up the tokens of her symbolic independence and sovereignty, the commitment to revisionism which welded her to the Axis could always be counted on. Italy, in particular, pushed Hungary's revisionist

[1] The Liberal leader Rassay and his valiant Legitimist friend, Count Antal Sigray, dug out the document and passed it on, through Count Bethlen, to the Regent. By doing so they not only rendered a great service to their country and the anti-Nazi cause but provided a world audience with one of the most amusing and instructive farces of history.

claims. Consequently, on 30 August 1940, under German–Italian arbitration, the northern half of Transylvania was returned to Hungary. In this award, unlike that affecting Czechoslovakia after Munich, ethnological frontiers could not be even approximately observed, as the purely Magyar 'Székelyland' lay in the eastern tip of Transylvania; so, to recover it, big intervening chunks of ethnically Romanian territory had also to be attached to Hungary, while in order to sweeten the pill for the Romanians, considerable Magyar districts in the south were left under their rule. But Trianon was eradicated: most if not all Magyars were returned to Hungary, together with masses of Romanians, Ukrainians, Slovaks, Germans (Saxons), and Yiddish. And all this aggrandizement had been achieved by a 'sovereign' nation: it was too good to be true. Indeed it was untrue. In exchange for her gains, Hungary had to be more subservient to Berlin than she had ever been to Vienna. Teleki was a professing Roman Catholic prone to diabolist imagery. 'We may have to sell half our soul to the Devil', he intimated to some of his scholarly young associates. He forced himself to believe that the second half of 'our soul' could be kept stainless so as to rescue the whole. He reasoned in true nationalist style: surely his followers would understand that if patriotism demanded support for Germany up to a point, it demanded the very opposite beyond it?

A memorable and typical manifestation of this concept was his Pact of Eternal Friendship concluded with the Kingdom of Yugoslavia on 12 December 1940. Prospects of peaceful revision of frontiers hinted at in the pact were combined with belief in an unshakeably solid Yugoslavia, to be relied on in all circumstances. Yugoslavia, under Prince Paul's regency, had already slipped halfway into the status of a German satellite, and Teleki wanted to oblige the Germans by making this bond tight and final. Yet it was common knowledge that Teleki's chief aim was to create a near-neutral core within the Axis orbit, a stronghold against total domination by Germany.

The jubilation about an Eternal Friendship that offered Hungary the best of both worlds lasted barely longer than three months: on 27 March 1941 the Serbian military overthrew Prince Paul's Vichy-style regency. Was Eternal Friendship still valid? It was, urged Teleki, since deplorable though the estrangement between two of Hungary's friends might be, the pact had been concluded with a country, not only with her rulers, and should therefore be honoured. But neither German nor Hungarian government circles were impressed by this argument. In early April, the German army made an onslaught on Yugoslavia, in which Hungarian forces readily participated without waiting for Teleki's consent. Teleki shot himself. He felt his comrades had betrayed him. Yet how could it have happened otherwise? The men whom he allowed to act in key positions were all, with the exception of the honest diehard patriot and Minister of the Interior Ferenc Keresztes-Fischer, committed to serving the German cause. The nationalists had thought they could sup with the Devil without a long spoon.

The next premier, László Bárdossy, was a Nazifier; and the one after him, Miklós Kállay, another resister. Bárdossy seemed a civilized human being and had started as an Anglophile. He had been Press Attaché in London, but returned from Britain with a chip on his shoulder, and Hitler's dazzling successes encouraged him to take his revenge on the British Empire. Like Darányi and Imrédy before him, he meant at first only to be a wise and patriotic opportunist (or 'realist', which comes to the same thing) when he tried to outpace other satellites in assisting the Nazis; but then, having thrown in his lot, he added his heart and was unable to extricate himself. It was under his premiership that Hungary (using the fiction of a Soviet attack as excuse) joined Germany in invading Russia at the end of June 1941, an act which by 6 December brought her into a state of war with the United Kingdom. Then came Pearl Harbor – which induced Bárdossy, as well as the Romanian and Bulgarian governments, to declare war on the United States. Finland alone among anti-Soviet belligerents refused to do so.

Horthy as Hitler's Prisoner

The Regent and his aristocratic advisers were quick to realize that Bárdossy had been rash; in March 1942 he was sacked. His successor, Miklós Kállay, was a scion of the most ancient county squirearchy, and embodied its merits as well as its limitations. He was skilled in running a county or, for that matter, a country of whose problems he had no idea. He was caste-bound but not inhuman; and an honest patriot who thought it quite natural to equate love of his country with defence of her social structure. He sincerely disliked the Nazis, as well as the Bolsheviks, and both of them for the same reason. His double task from the outset was thus to extricate Hungary from the war and, at the same time, to reassure the Western Allies (namely the two Anglo-Saxon Great Powers, for the rest hardly counted at that moment) that Hungary's help to Germany was barely more than nominal and aimed merely at keeping the Russians off the Danube basin; an objective which he presumed could only please the British gentlemen with their top-hats and the Americans with their bulging wallets. In warning the West against Stalin, Kállay was of course right, like all other Blimps; his blindness only consisted in thinking that to rely on Horthy's Hungary as 'a factor of order in

Europe' was a workable alternative. This in fact was the idea popularized in pro-Axis terms by his pressmen and offered for Anglo-
American consumption in Christian and democratic jargon by his
secret agents via Ankara, Lisbon, and the Vatican. The man whom
it could have been least expected to convince was Hitler; and in fact
Hitler put up with the spectacle of a secret diplomacy so diligently
advertised only until the Allied successes (fall of Mussolini, Anglo-
American advance from the South of Europe, Russian advance from
the East) made it too risky for him to base his army on a territory
controlled by such Vichy-style neutralists. On 18 March 1944, he
received Admiral Horthy at Klessheim and informed him that, in
order to protect his realm against both Asiatic Bolshevism and
Judeo-American plutocracy, German troops had crossed, or were
about to cross, the Hungarian frontier with a view to occupying the
country, dismissing the treacherous Kállay administration, and
replacing it with a reliably patriotic one.

Admiral Horthy, on his return, had to rule with the Nazi stooge
and former minister in Berlin, Döme Sztójay, as premier, while the
deposed premier, Kállay, sought and found refuge at the Turkish
Legation in Budapest. There was one man, and one only, who
received the German intruders with firearms: the National Radical
deputy Endre Bajcsy-Zsilinszky, last and most genuine of the romantic patriots. After a skirmish, arrest, release, re-arrest, and torture, he
was executed by the Nazis on 23 December. Today, a main boulevard in Budapest is named after him – an ironical fact, but creditable
to all concerned including the communist rulers. Bajcsy-Zsilinszky
had started on the extreme Right, and his emotional bias remained
largely unaltered throughout his life: his posthumous apotheosis
shows that admiration for humanity, patriotism, and courage can
bring people together irrespective of their ideologies.

Under Sztójay's premiership, the by then familiar features of
Nazi terror rule set in. Most conspicuous of these, in the capital, was
the Yellow Star on Jews and 'Jewish houses', while from the provinces practically the whole of Jewry (including Christians of Jewish
origin, in some cases even gentiles of 'mixed blood') was deported for
'final solution'. The work of Parliament, purged of leftish parties and
anti-Nazi conservatives, was restricted to rubber-stamping government decrees; political dissenters, including well-known journalists,
capitalists, and trade unionists, as well as politicians proper, were
deported *en masse*. The split which had existed for quite a while within
the political police widened into a showdown: József Sombor-
Schweinitzer, the chief of the department, was deported and his
deputy, Péter Hain, took over. Originally, both had been stalwart
supporters of the Horthy régime, the former a sophisticated snooper,

the latter the coarsest beater-up of detainees; two complementary types of authoritarian policing which necessarily fall out when the urbane surface of such an order can no longer be maintained. Yet, as Horthy was still supposed to be Regent, he managed to exert some moderating influence and stop, for instance, the deportations before Eichmann (who was on the spot) could capture the majority of Budapest Jewry. At the end of August 1944, after Romania's sudden and cleverly-timed change of sides, Horthy even succeeded in getting rid of Sztójay and appointing a new government, led by General Géza Lakatos, who renewed the attempts to get Hungary out of the war. With the Russians already on Hungarian territory and the pro-German camp falling into the hands of types who might have been recruited from the lunatic asylum or the underworld, the formerly unthinkable combination of all political shades from Horthy to the communists was formed as a last and inescapable resort.

The question remained *when* to strike together; and Horthy managed its timing most unfortunately. It seems today that he had come comparatively early to the conclusion that to save Hungary he must unequivocally go over to the Russian side, but few among his adherents were willing to go so far; even his new Prime Minister, Lakatos, went on hoping for a neutralist way of extricating Hungary. Whatever the reason, Horthy had appeared to be temporizing until he learned that his son, Miklós junior, was kidnapped by the Nazis; which prompted him to make a public, and completely unprepared, announcement of his Armistice with the U.S.S.R. on 15 October. Within a few hours he was deposed and taken prisoner by the Germans. In his place ex-Major Szálasi, the leader of the most extreme Nazi party, the 'Hungarists' or 'Arrow-cross Fascists', was appointed 'Leader of the Nation'. All points of strategic importance in the capital, including the vital broadcasting centre, were occupied by the Gestapo and other German formations practically without a shot fired. Most of the Hungarian army units obeyed the German occupiers like automata. The few generals and bodyguards who sided with the Regent—first of all, General Béla Aggteleky, commander of the army corps stationed in the capital—were overpowered by traitors who, headed by General Iván Hindy, performed successful commando raids against their own headquarters under cover of German tanks. If quite a number of Hungarian soldiers had a bad conscience about betraying their Regent and country, they were reassured by forged orders issued by the leading Nazi Hungarian agents, which declared the Armistice terms null and void.

Devastation

The ease of the Nazi takeover surprised all parties concerned. It was, after all, a retreating German army, known to be in the grip of total defeat, which annihilated a nominally still sovereign state in an immeasurably short space of time. Even more surprised than the Germans and Horthy's associates were the Hungarian Nazis. On hearing the announcement of the Armistice, their leaders panicked and sought refuge at the German Legation–some, indeed, fled right to the Western frontier of the country, putting themselves directly under German military protection; but once they learned of Horthy's removal, they met as a 'Hungarian government' in Budapest and felt safe in the saddle. No matter that the Hitlerite empire, including *their* Hungary, was visibly shrinking day by day; they were hypnotized by the roar of German tanks and Nazi rhetoric promising them fantastic secret weapons and fantastic bloodbaths. The latter did in fact materialize. While the German regular army dismantled and transported westward all that was movable in factories and trade combines, the armed Arrow Cross gangs were roving the streets and knocking up households at will with demands for jewelry, cash, and lives. As winter set in, with ice-floes blocking the Danube, and the people of Budapest shivering in cellars beneath the thunder of Soviet gunfire and Allied air raids, the Hungarian Nazis took their final toll in blood and property, no longer bothering themselves about deportation when railway waggons were not available, but shooting their victims on the spot and shovelling them into the river–from which, miraculously enough, quite a number managed to crawl out, their wounds staunched by ice, and survive. The hunt was directed against political dissenters and Jews, but in the general disarray, with a colossal influx of refugees from the East (estimated at 300,000 to 400,000 in the capital alone) discrimination and identification became rather difficult, which was perhaps the only lucky feature of the mass *grand guignol*, since it helped well-known anti-Nazis to get away with false beards and false papers. Needless to say, many were murdered all the same, and particularly many Jews; by the end of the war some two-thirds of Hungary's Jewish population (practising and converted), including some 40 per cent of those in Budapest, were exterminated. On the whole territory which during the war was supposed to be run by Hungarians, about 600,000 Jews lost their lives.

The Nazis left behind a wholly devastated country, and a moral vacuum. The fine bridges of Budapest had all been blown up by the retreating Germans, and their pillars, with dangling ribs and chains, looked like the carcasses of ice-age monsters when the victorious Soviet army entered. 4 April 1945 was the day when the last German unit left Hungary, but a Soviet-appointed Hungarian government had been in existence since the Christmas of 1944. Horthy was trans-

ferred from German to American custody, but no charge was brought
against him, and after a short while he was allowed to settle peacefully for the rest of his life in Portugal. Hungary did not apply for his
extradition because when the question arose, Stalin shrugged it off:
'Leave him alone, after all he did ask for an armistice . . .' For whatever reason, restraint on the matter was justified; Horthy had committed his war crimes years before the war, in a period to which the
competence of the Nuremberg court could hardly have been extended. After the *Anschluss*, he had no choice. Horthy's anti-Nazi high
officials such as Kállay, Keresztes-Fischer, Sombor-Schweinitzer (the
latter employed by the Americans to sort out war criminals from
among the masses of Hungarian refugees), were also granted the right
and opportunity to live and die quietly in the West; Dr Tibor
Eckhardt, whom Budapest ruling circles planted as an anti-Nazi
émigré leader in the United States in the middle of the war, is still
alive and fit in New York.

The politicians and soldiers prominent in leading Hungary into
the war and Nazi terror (Bárdossy, Imrédy, Sztójay, Hindy,
Szálasi, and the most notorious promoters of mass murders such as
the former county bureaucrat László Endre, the former pandoor
officer László Baky, the former Detachment officer Emil Kovarc, etc.)
were shot or hanged by sentence of the People's Court in Hungary;
many were imprisoned and some (Professor Hóman for example)
died in gaol.

The former spokesmen of anti-Nazi opposition views – whether
Catholic, agrarian, Liberal, or socialist – were allowed a comeback
to Hungarian public life, some being jubilantly welcomed by the
Russian generals, until some years later they were driven into exile
or confined to deportation centres, when not gaoled and tortured, on
the orders of the Moscow-trained communist leadership. Yet they
fared better, even under torture, than the non-Muscovite communists, scores of whose leading personalities were murdered.

This, however, is part of a different story though not *so* different
as is generally thought.

Chapter 10

The Stalinization of Hungary

SINCE EARLY 1945 THE RUSSIANS have been masters in Hungary. Insofar as Soviet Russian overlordship can be equated with communism, it is natural to ask: 'How does the communist takeover of 1945 and after compare with that of 1919?'

They were, in fact, as different as two political actions could be. The '1919-ers', after clamouring for Red terror and dictatorship, slipped into power to their own surprise; the '1945-ers', after presenting themselves as advocates of parliamentary democracy and offering co-operation to all freedom-loving citizens, established a fully-fledged tyranny, coupled with decimation of their own ranks. The '1919-ers' owed their power to a wave of messianic patriotism, but fought shy of everything explicitly national and only pledged loyalty to the 'world proletariat'; the '1945-ers' appealed to patriotism with a jargon so shameless as to beat even the mythmakers of gentry Hungary, but were in fact from the outset only concerned with turning Hungary into a Russian colony. 1919 stemmed from hysteria, 1945 from military conquest.

But surely the way a military conquest can be exploited is as typical of the conquered country as it is of the conqueror? Hungary, while being turned into a colony of the Soviet empire, has kept on repeating and combining the policies which characterized her in comparable circumstances, from the Habsburg and Ottoman intrusions in the sixteenth century down to the German infiltration and occupation in Hitler's time.

In communist jargon, the military occupation of 1945 was a *liberation* of Hungary. Jargon or no jargon, the claim implied in this expression is definitely justified. Whatever was to follow, Nazi rule could not be surpassed in horror; and in most of the Danubian countries, the Red Army was its chief destroyer. No Hungarian could fail to recognize this. Yet the entry of the Red Army was a nightmare as well as a relief–though a nightmare very different from the one that had been expected.

A Wild Eastern Free-for-all

A Bolshevik retribution had been dreaded by many and hoped for by a few; instead, there came a horde of primitive youngsters with a rage for sex, alcohol, and wrist-watches. Their rapings and lootings have often been recalled, and even exaggerated, since; stories of their tenderness towards children and 'granny'-type old ladies are also on record; 'ideology' did not make them better or worse and could only be spotted when they sacked, for instance, a caretaker's apartment amid shouts of triumph that this must be a 'burzhui's' since it contained such luxuries as family photographs on the wall. As to their generals and political emissaries (with the skeleton staff of an embassy), these proved equally insensitive to 'progressive' ideas and values, and, if interested in art, surprised the artists by their conservatism. In the workshop of the able and conventional sculptor Zsigmond Kisfaludi-Strobl, they discovered the model of a statue which impressed them very much: a lofty female figure, raising the palm branch of Peace and Glory in her hands towards the sky. 'Whom is this for?', they enquired. It had really been intended as a memorial in honour of István Horthy, son of the ex-Regent, the artist apologetically explained; but one should take into consideration that István Horthy was said to have been killed by the Nazis, and thus his memorial in those past years would have implied a demonstration against Hitler. The apologia was correct but the Russians did not care anyway. 'Why not have this as a war memorial in honour of the Red Army?', they suggested. Everybody, including the artist, found it an excellent idea, and the lofty female figure has stood ever since on the most conspicuous point of Gellért Hill, as the symbol of Soviet triumph and Liberty.

A stereotyped 'Denazification' drive did of course take place: Arrow Cross gangleaders and prominent anti-Soviet propagandists were rounded up if still found in Hungary—for the majority of them, together with some tens of thousands of displaced persons with a background less clearly political, had fled to Austria—and no prompting by the new masters was necessary for everybody to realize that the heroes of the day before had become 'Fascist beasts', while the victorious invaders were 'glorious'. Over and above this, however, the Soviet diplomatists and generals were not interested in differences between right- and left-wing Hungarians; they did business with whomever they could. There was no question as yet of liquidating capitalism in Hungary; on the contrary, a boost to free enterprise seemed the only way to get things moving and lure hidden commodities to the surface. Zoltán Vas (b. 1903), one of the Hungarian communist refugees who had returned in the wake of the Red Army, was particularly well qualified to galvanize the market with his boisterous, happy-go-lucky style allied to the aura of a martyr who had spent some sixteen years in Horthy's prisons. He was known to be a Jew and looked it unmistakably, and his Muscovite background made people suspicious of him; yet he became a popular figure overnight, thanks to his ability to provide food and crack jokes. He made friends easily with *ancien régime* bureaucrats, company directors, and black marketeers – the latter not being always distinguishable from the champions of legal trade – and Soviet generals and diplomats were ideologically even less fussy than he. Joint stock companies, dubbed 'Soviet-Hungarian', shot up and helped many a Russian Marxist-Leninist to high profits which they shared with old-fashioned exploiters. Some of the Soviet officials pressed hard for 'compensation' (factories were dismantled and removed, though on a smaller scale and less efficiently than by the Germans) and if some prisoners-of-war escaped from the waggons heading for Siberia, others were caught at random in the streets to make up the complement. It was far from being a cosy affair. A Wild Western free-for-all had been imported from the Wild East; or the Turkish pashas with their passion for loot had re-emerged in jeeps with five-point stars. But whether for good or evil, the 'doctrine' of communism remained invisible.

While the war was still on, the first 'Provisional Hungarian National Government' had been set up by the Russians under one of Horthy's generals and included two more of them, together with Count Géza Teleki (Pál's son) – an insultingly crude tactical move, even as bait for Hungarian nationalist opinion. The Russians or their advisers also secured representation (partly sham, partly genuine) for the 'four democratic parties' who were allowed, and indeed ordered, to compete and co-operate as befits a parliamentary democracy engaged in struggle against the Fascist enemy. These four parties were: the Independent Smallholders, inherited from the Horthy era as a pool of mild and colourless agrarian and middle-class forces; the Social Democrats, who could not be ignored without provoking the Western world and mainly Britain; the communists; and a National Peasant Party. The latter was moulded from the pre-war village explorers movement and comprised some writers of outstanding quality but without wide backing among the agrarian population; yet the communists encouraged it as a rallying-point for the poor peasantry which they could use for their own ends. There was at the start also a Citizens' ('Bürgerlich') Democratic Party, but though the communists made a point of snubbing it as 'bourgeois', its commitment to liberalism was too definite to attract the masses of conservatives still under the Horthy era's spell; so its existence was quickly reduced to a symbol.

Rákosi

The leader of the communists, Mátyás Rákosi (1892–1971), was an able, quick-witted, and extremely ambitious operator. Son of a well-off Jewish country grocer, he had worked in his youth as a bank clerk in London and been involved with radical movements; under Béla Kun he rose to a junior ministerial post and, after Kun's fall, succeeded in escaping to the U.S.S.R. He was a squat little man with an early tendency to plumpness and baldness, who compensated with energy for the gifts that nature had denied him. Like a commercial traveller obsessed with his job, he hawked his commodities indefatigably no matter under what trade-mark or by what confidence tricks, provided the going seemed good enough. Characters like this often started out as revolutionaries and, on the threshold of their thirties, came to terms with the established power, to become its agents at forty and its millionaires at fifty. Rákosi, with his total indifference to principles, could well have made such a career. But there were two modifying factors: his encounter with Stalinism, which presented the strictest of state hierarchies as the sponsor of World Revolution; and his conviction that power is a currency more stable than money.

Can a man profess to be a revolutionary and at the same time compete in servility and sycophancy with the most timid of bureaucrats? 'You can't have it both ways' would be the normal answer. Under Stalin, however, this combination was not only possible but essential at the higher levels of power. It appealed to Rákosi's active, enterprising, and businesslike mind, and as he was a man of physical courage he may have been quite pleased to accept a commission in 1924 to travel to Hungary, illegally and under a false identity, in order to reorganize the underground Communist Party. He feared nothing so long as he felt that one of the greatest Powers, and the one he believed to have the brightest future, stood behind him. His commitment to the Soviet Establishment was total, and so was his hope that he would be richly rewarded if he survived this venture. It was a great but calculated risk.

He was arrested and maltreated as all communists were under Horthy unless spared for some special reason; and behaved in court as practically all Moscow-trained Party organizers did, that is, with discipline and courage, although the legends later promulgated about his superhuman 'heroism' can be dismissed. In prison he was given a job in the administrative office, which in its turn raised the suspicion that he was acting as a police spy. This, too, can be dismissed insofar as it concerned his unshakeable loyalty to the Party and the U.S.S.R.; but denunciation of 'Trotskyites' and other deviationists conformed with directives from the Kremlin, and a local leader was free to pick and choose such victims as he pleased. We cannot know whether, or to what extent, he used this freedom of choice to curry favour with the prison authorities; though one circumstance clearly pointing to it is the fact that later, as dictator of Hungary, he was at pains to get rid of all those former gaolers and former cellmates alike who had been close witnesses of his prison career.

When his sentence of eight and a half years expired he was tried again, on new charges, and sentenced to life imprisonment. This legal farce understandably shocked Western opinion and gave Rákosi an aura of martyrdom beyond the circle of his communist comrades. After fifteen years of captivity he was saved by the Nazi-Bolshevik partition of Poland. The U.S.S.R. obtained a stretch of common frontier with Hungary, and as both countries were, if not strictly neutral, at least non-belligerent in that phase of the World War, it was expedient for them to bury the ideological hatchet. When the Russians expressed their interest in a few Hungarian political prisoners such as Rákosi and Vas, in 1940 the Hungarian government readily extradited them. By the time Rákosi arrived in Moscow and joined the crowd in the Lux Hotel where the communist top refugees were established, the hottest phase of the Stalinist purges was over and most of his Hungarian comrades had been gaoled or exiled to Siberia, while scores of them, including his erstwhile leader Béla Kun, had been murdered. The mantle of leadership thus fell on him.

Some five years later, his triumphant return to his mother-country gave him the opportunity to gratify all his passions and nostalgias. He came as a Workers' Leader but not only that; he posed as a benign father-figure and traditionalist patriot, dedicated to the task of softening the powerful victor's heart towards the misguided and recovered people of his native land. 'All forces unite for reconstruction of our country!' was the slogan he launched, without any reference to 'class struggle'; he paraded at state-organized hunting parties side by side with Soviet generals and diplomats but also with emissaries of the Western Allies and the survivors of the Hungarian squirearchy. He played up his 'lack of sectarianism' and often sided with the defenders of national myths against left-wingers. 'We must take what we need from both the Soviet democracy and the Western democracies', he declared, 'but our own democracy must be rooted in Hungarian soil'. Though couched in a flatulent cliché, this expressed what every sensible person thought and, indeed, a promising start was made on these lines. Most of the institutions smacking of feudalism, Fascism, and racism were abolished. The two long overdue reforms, universal suffrage with secret ballot and the distribution of the *latifundia* among the landless peasants, which had stood first in the programme of the Károlyi republic in 1918, were at last implemented. A republic was presently declared; as a step towards mixed economy, mines were nationalized; and Workshop Councils elected by the workers (on the whole, Social Democrats and communists *pari passu*) were secured a share in the control of industrial concerns. All this with crude imperfections, and crowned with an inflation unparalleled in history: while you were eating your dinner in a restaurant, the bill you had to pay for it rose by several billion *pengő*. It was a topsy-turvy world, but no monolith.

Yet, in barely more than four years (that is, by the late summer of 1949) Hungary was totally enslaved by Stalin's imitators, with Rákosi in command, and with no pretence of seeking a compromise between the Soviet, Western, and traditional Hungarian ways of life. How could this change have been brought about?

'Slicing Salami'; the Soviet Forces and the Ávó

Rákosi himself supplied a lively metaphor, most helpful in answering this question, when he publicly boasted after the enslavement that he had 'sliced off like salami' all parties and factions other than his own. He had indeed the appetite, the cruelty, and the knife to do it.

The knife was, first, the presence of the Soviet army. Its apparent lack of commitment to any doctrine did not make it a less formidable threat. Its police force (whether termed N.K.V.D. or otherwise) kidnapped, even from Austria, Hungarian anti-Nazi resisters who had links with the Western authorities; a Swedish diplomat, Wallenberg by name, with the finest record of sheltering Jews and anti-Fascists in wartime Budapest, was known to have been murdered by Soviet security agents; and 'non-interference with Hungarian home affairs' was erratic, to say the least, as the Soviet authorities could always justify their clamping down on a particular Hungarian politician as reprisal for an armed anti-Soviet conspiracy. However sporadic the use made of the latter possibility, it was enough to know that, in the final resort, 'no trifling' would be tolerated with the Soviet power—or with the ex-refugees under its protection.

Then there was the newly established Hungarian political police, generally referred to as the *Ávó*.[1] This was the one organization over which the communists claimed control from the outset; any institution could be run on a coalition basis, approximately or seemingly in proportion to the votes received, except this. There was general murmuring against one-party rule in this field, but on the whole it did not seem too high a price to pay for having been defeated by a communist

---

[1] Abbreviation, originally, of the name of its civilian branch, 'Állam *védelmi* Osztály' (State Security Department), which had its counterpart in the army, *Katpol*, standing for 'Katona-politikai' (Military-Political). After the former absorbed the latter, it was renamed 'Állam*védelmi Hatóság*' (State Security *Authority*), abbreviated 'A.V.H.', but the more easily pronounceable 'Ávó' has stuck in people's minds.

power. A certain widespread feeling of guilt also played into the hands of the communists; as they had been the political category most severely persecuted before, it seemed almost the fulfilment of a natural and moral law that their turn should now have come to pay off a few scores. Many of the *Ávó* officers were recruited from among the survivors of Auschwitz, with memories of gassed parents and babies, and hearts dedicated to the power which gave them a chance of revenge. Their headquarters were set up at 60 Andrássy ut, formerly the headquarters of the Arrow Cross Fascists. Again, there was a general revulsion; the radical writer Béla Zsolt–a Jew himself–was acclaimed for commenting that 'the pandoor's jackboot ill becomes a Jew'. Yet, 'what else could you expect?', people said. The bill had to be footed. To make things even more awkward, the N.C.O.s of *Ávó* were largely recruited from among former White gaolers and the Nazi rabble–generally known as 'the Arrow Cross small fry'– who were keen to work their passage home in the service of Hungary's new masters. 'Jews and Nazis idyllically united', the facetious comment ran. The head of *Ávó* was General Gábor Péter, a Jew, formerly a tailor who specialized in the illegal communist movement as a 'security' chief and had thus been in touch with the White police; his deputy, Colonel Gyula Décsi, was a Catholic ex-seminarist of 'Swabian' origin.

Thus, to return to Rákosi's metaphor, the *Ávó* served as the knife for slicing the salami. He used it, at the beginning, economically– that is, only when his persuasive powers failed. He could, however, always brandish it; and its glitter, combined with his cajoleries and threats, did most of the job. His technique was the time-honoured 'Divide and Rule' or 'One by one'. To illustrate this in some detail: as a result of the general election of November 1945 (free and fair by the standards of the country and of eastern Europe), the Small-holders held an overall majority of almost 60 per cent in Parliament, while the communists with their powerful backing only obtained 17 per cent of the seats, as did the grudgingly admitted Social Democrats; the National Peasants held 5 per cent. Accordingly, the President of the Republic (Zoltán Tildy, a Calvinist parson) and the Prime Minister (Ferenc Nagy, at one time a peasant farmer, later a barber) were Smallholders; two vice-premierships were created and filled, one by Rákosi, the other by the newly elected leader of the Social Democrats, Árpád Szakasits (once a bricklayer, later a journalist); the fourth coalition party, the National Peasants, was less strongly represented, but one of its leaders, Ferenc Erdei, known to be a communist in all but name, was for a while entrusted to lead the Ministry of the Interior with its nominal or potential authority over the *Ávó*. This was the picture early in 1946 when Rákosi started his slicing operations. The two top communists who apparently helped him most were Ernő Gerő (1898–) and László Rajk (1909–49). Gerő was, like Rákosi, a Muscovite and, like most of the Hungarian Muscovites, of Jewish middle-class background, but in appearance and style he was the very opposite of his leader. He was a dry and lanky man, suggesting a cross between an inquisitor and a cash register. He worked hard, and his activities in the Ministry of Transport and elsewhere gave colour to the communist build-up of him as architect of the newly erected bridges and railways. Yet it was difficult to make him popular – and, beyond advertising his efficiency, the communist *apparat* did not even try: he was sold as a character commanding respect rather than confidence. Rumour had it that he was 'Moscow's eye', even on Rákosi; and neither he, prizing Soviet connections above everything, nor Rákosi, parading his native Hungarian character, seemed to mind this assumption. Rumour also had it that Gerő had acted in the Spanish Civil War as an N.K.V.D. agent, responsible for the deaths of 'deviationists' real or so-called, including Hungarian fighters of the International Brigade. Thus Gerő's presence as Rákosi's alternative was a threat rather than a promise.

With Rajk, it was a mixed proposition. He was an arrestingly handsome young man, a gentile (in fact, coming from a German minority group, the Saxons of Transylvania), and, most important, a non-Muscovite. He had been a Hungarian illegal communist, active in the cell of 'conspirators' in the Eötvös College (the 'Hungarian École Normale Superieure'); in the International Brigade in Spain; in the Peace Party of wartime Hungary; and had suffered heavy sentences and internments in Horthy Hungary, Vichy France, and Hitler Hungary. Such a record was at that moment an emphatic recommendation, only slightly weakened by the story that he had practised some sentimental nepotism to rescue one of his brothers who had been in the Arrow Cross. There was an engaging youthfulness about him – but fanaticism as well. He could be violent in attack; 'his eyes flashed all the time', a Social Democratic opponent, Imre Szélig, used to recall; and precisely on account of his background, he was the man to take on the tasks most repellent to national opinion. Rákosi, while using his services, cautiously dissociated himself from the man; confidentially he complained that he himself would favour a more moderate course if only 'that bigot Gerő' and 'that firebrand Rajk' would not force his hand. Yet it was undoubtedly he, Rákosi, who directed tactical moves.

Slicing Political Dissenters

The 'right wing of the Smallholders' Party' (though not right-wing by pre-1945 Hungarian standards) was the first important victim. Its leader, Dezső Sulyok, was among the very few Small-holders who had unequivocally opposed racialist legislation, and one of his lieutenants, Vince Nagy, remained undeviatingly loyal to the programme of the 1918 revolution throughout the years of White oppression. But their outspokenness about communist malpractices made them a target; and neither the bulk of the Smallholders nor the Social Democrats (the rest did not really count) felt inclined to stand up for them. They were expelled from their party to become (for a while) the leading right-wing opposition group in Parliament.

The 'right-wing Smallholders' removed, who would hold a brief for 'right-wing Social Democrats'? Their visible leader was Károly Peyer, known as the leader of the party in the last decade of the White régime, an energetic and on the whole sound but somewhat peevish personality, who played a little into the communists' hands by his open bitterness about no longer being political first fiddle. After various tactical manoeuvres he left the party, then Parliament, and finally the country–an escape which, with those of Sulyok and Vince Nagy, started a long stream of refugees.

In early 1947 the alleged revelation of a 'counter-revolutionary conspiracy' (possibly with a minute grain of truth in it) served as a pretext to switch on the slicing-machine against the bulk of the Small-holders, led by Premier Ferenc Nagy; the Catholic priest and President of Parliament, Mgr Béla Varga; and the Party Secretary, Béla Kovács, member of Parliament. Rajk, by then Minister of the Interior, accused Kovács of complicity and demanded that he be handed over by Parliament to the police. While the tug-of-war between Smallholders and communists was going on, the Soviet military police arrested and deported Kovács as an 'anti-Soviet spy'. His followers panicked; and a few months later Ferenc Nagy and Mgr Varga joined the refugees in the West. So, among others, did Imre Kovács, leader of the 'right wing of the National Peasants'. As a rule, the communist authorities turned a blind eye on such attempts to escape–it was simpler to have them outside the country than to bother with putting them in gaol.

With the Smallholders sliced off, and only their rump of intimida-ted yesmen in government, came the turn of Social Democracy for liquidation. In early 1947 new elections were held, brutally rigged by the communist-controlled Ministry of the Interior, which struck off masses of declared Social Democrats from the electoral register and then further falsified the results by pouring fake votes into the ballot-boxes. Consequently, the communists emerged as the largest single party in Parliament, with the Social Democrats as the main losers. The Social Democratic Minister of Justice, István Ries, known as the earliest advocate of co-operation with the communists (for whom, as a lawyer, he had valiantly stood up under the Whites), resigned in protest; but the head of the Soviet mission in Budapest promised some corrective action and persuaded him not to leave the government. The workers, particularly in what had been known as the Red Belt of Budapest, were not, however, reassured. In the suburb of Ujpest and the island of Csepel, centres of the largest manufacturing combines, the workers, proud of their old standing in the 'Red' movement, felt insulted by communist pontification about 'Workers' Unity', and resented what they witnessed of Soviet intrusion and appropriations in the factories. They demanded the resignation of the nominal head of the Social Democratic Party, Szakasits, and the removal of his close advisers, known as fellow-travellers; they put their faith in their 'centrist' leaders, Anna Kéthly (since 1946 Vice-President of Parliament) and Antal Bán (the young Minister of Industry). Thereupon the *Ávó* intervened with threats against the protesters; the workers' resistance was paralysed; and by the spring of 1948 there was no more Social Democracy in Hungary. A 'united' Hungarian Workingpeople's Party ('Workingpeople' having a less sectarian tone than 'Workers') established its dictatorship over the country, under communist leadership, with the well-known features of a Politbureau, etc., and a number of fellow-travelling ex-socialists in the Unity show-window. Anna Kéthly, Bán, and the whole leadership of committed socialists were simply deprived of their seats in Parliament–and this was only the beginning of their ordeal.

Expropriation of Capital, Shops, and Land

According to communist cant, 1948 was the 'Year of the Turning-Point' which transformed Hungary 'from a bourgeois democracy into a people's democracy'; to which Rákosi added the formula that a 'people's democracy performs the function of the dictatorship of the proletariat without a Soviet form'–that is, calling its Supreme Soviet its Parliament. This was correct, except that the 'proletariat' had nothing to do with it; Lenin and Trotsky in 1917, Béla Kun in 1919, Tito in 1945, Mao in 1948, though never properly tested by democratic elections, could muster an impressive degree of popular support behind them, but the foundation of communist power in post-1944 Hungary was fear and nothing but fear–fear handled deliberately, in salami-slicing style.

In 1948, at Easter (with a display of cruelty reminiscent of Imrédy's 'Christmas present to the Jews' in 1938) the manufacturing industries and bigger companies were nationalized by decree overnight, without compensation and without allowing the expropriated owners and directors to set foot in their premises again. Gerő headed this operation with characteristic inhumanity. Insult was amply added to injury by unleashing a hate campaign against the dis-possessed – on the assumption that no pity would be felt for people thus degraded. A similar campaign was launched against small traders and shopkeepers so as to compel them to give up their proper-ties. The workers, at the same time, lost their right to participate in control of the workshops through their councils; 'the factory is theirs anyway', explained Ferenc Biró, newly appointed head manager of the Csepel combines and incidentally a brother of Mátyás Rákosi.

The drive for collectivization of the land started simultaneously and the same spirit, the 'kulak', was made the bogeyman of village life – first to be turned out of his property and then to be held up to contempt and suspicion, without hope of redemption, as a potential saboteur of collective farming if admitted to it at all. But the bulk of the peasantry, holders of little plots, who were, in communist jargon, 'the allies of the working class, though under the latter's guidance', had equally to forfeit their land; the old dream that 'the land should belong to him who tills it' came true in 1945 to last only some three years.

The Mindszenty Trial; Religious Persecution

In cultural life, Roman Catholicism and first and foremost its visible head became the main target. Cardinal Primate József Mindszenty (1892–) was an honest, brave, and narrow man who owed his high office, so it was assumed, to the conviction of Pope Pius XII that in countries overrun by communists the strength to face martyrdom was required from a prince of the Church rather than intellectual brilliance. His bravery did indeed make him popular with the masses in Hungary; while his lack of sophistication aroused the misgivings of many a Catholic intellectual (leading Jesuits, for instance) who felt the Church should take a more flexible and pro-gressive line. Whoever was right, it made no difference in the circumstances; the Stalinist apparatus was eager to see priests in the torture-chamber – no matter how reactionary or progressive they were. In 1947, the liberal Catholics, led by Dr István Barankovics and backed by the Jesuits, contested the elections as a Democratic People's Party and won a surprising number of votes, to emerge as the leading opposition party, with facilities granted (temporarily) to act as such. Its efforts to bring about a *modus vivendi* between state and Church, however, were doomed to fail. Predominant among the issues debated was, on the surface, the impending secularization of schools, but its details are not worth recording: the underlying question by then was whether a citizen professing to be a Roman Catholic should be allowed to live unmolested. In 1948, after the 'turning-point', the Cardinal Primate, in spite of his barely concealed misgivings about previous compromise attempts, himself made some vaguely conciliatory overtures, but these were not even acknowledged, let alone reciprocated, by authority. The attacks on him became more and more venomous. As his imprisonment seemed a foregone conclusion, he declared in a sermon that if ever, deprived of his freedom, he was to 'confess' to having committed seditious or other illegal acts, his statements to this effect should be attributed to the frailty of human nature under duress. It was a timely warning. The *Ávó* raided his residence in the Archbishopric of Esztergom, and while arresting the cardinal, his secretary, and other prominent Roman Catholics, the Party Press advertised with maximum publicity that conclusive evidence of Mindszenty's guilt had been revealed. In fact, there were found buried in the park of the archbishopric some rather pointless and incoherent handwritten notes by the cardinal, which included a mild criticism of the 1945 Land Reform (in any case outdated by the drive for collectivization). The reaction to such ramblings by a detached observer could only be to wonder why they need be (i) written and (ii) if written, kept, and (iii) if kept, hidden at all. But no one concerned was in a mood for joking. The clamp-down on the 'Mindszenty gang' was staged by the *Ávó*, in the Imrédy-Gerő tradition, as a Christmas present, this time to the Catholics; and in early 1949, at a trial to which only a carefully selected audience was admitted, and whose records were tampered with, the cardinal was sentenced to life imprisonment. A Yellow Book subsequently published by the Hungarian government supplied more convincing proofs that the whole affair had been a frame-up than anything the anti-communists printed or could have thought of printing. There was, for instance, the facsimile of a statement by the cardinal in his own handwriting, produced while under arrest, which starts by stating

> I am a Hungarian nobleman. My original surname was Pehm. The Pehm family was declared noble in 1732

and then carries on 'confessing'

> My aim is the aim of the monarchist movement in Hungary; a Federative Central European Monarchy with a personal union between Hungary and Austria and with other Catholic States

and

> I only thought this possible by overthrowing the Hungarian Republic with foreign and in the first place American aid

and further 'confesses' to having furthered his aim

> by constantly urging their [the Americans'] interference by a regular service of facts and by espionage

and finally

> I acknowledge that from the days of my youth I opposed every democratic policy of the Hungarian people and supported right-wing movements. –József Mindszenty.[1]

Whether he consented to put this down in writing or whether the manuscript was actually forged (as some of the relevant documents turned out to be) is immaterial: it took the astounding stupidity of Stalinism to imagine that this could possibly sound genuine.

If a Cardinal Prince Primate can be arrested, there is nothing to stop communist power: this was the lesson driven home, in particular, to the masses believing in ancient authorities. The simultaneous pulverization of all other religious and quasi-religious centres thus roused but little emotion. No one was astonished to see Barankovics's party removed from Parliament and its Jesuit fathers (together with Archbishop József Grősz and a steadily increasing number of other priests) follow the primate into gaol. The arrest of a Lutheran bishop, Lajos Ordass, gave the green light for persecution of all Christian denominations (although the Calvinists enjoyed relative tolerance, due to the fellow-travelling manoeuvres of some of their church dignitaries); and special emphasis was laid on the persecution of rabbis and other Jewish community representatives, partly in a futile effort to divert public attention from the great number of Jews in the communist leadership, and partly in support of the 'anti-Zionist' drive initiated in Russia. Freemasonry, psychoanalysis, Esperantism, and all other breeding-grounds of 'bourgeois cosmopolitanism' were similarly proscribed. 'Marxism-Leninism' might as well have been declared the state religion; dissenters were at best tolerated, though with less complacency than centuries before by the conquering Moslems.

The Rajk Trial; Hunt after Titoists and other Heretics

Yet the worst was still to come. Until the spring of 1949, the slicing-off operations aimed at ideological streamlining. But then the strange gadget went berserk and chopped around in a diabolical

---

[1] Quoted the official Hungarian translation in the government publication *Documents on the Mindszenty Case*, Budapest, 1949.

frenzy. Woe to him who incurred the displeasure of a Muscovite quisling or a leading *Ávó* gangster! The witch-hunt had been in the nature of Stalin's rule ever since its purges, and been given additional fury by the expulsion of Yugoslavia from the communist fold in 1948. 'Titoist-Trotskyite' victims were required in the docks. Rákosi decided to victimize Rajk as 'the Hungarian Tito'. His motive was simply fear of Rajk as a potential rival; and he could safely assume that Stalin would be only too pleased to learn of the revelation of such a Titoist conspiracy, which would correspond with his most recent paranoiac suspicions. Rajk had not been trained in Moscow, but, fighting among Trotskyites (genuine and so-called) in Spain, and interned in Vichy France, must have been exposed to the influences most abhorred by Stalin. Rákosi, to make his haul more impressive, ordered a large number of International Brigade veterans and dispossessed *ci-devant* notabilities to act as 'accomplices' in the coming trial. Rajk, who (presumably in preparation for this) had already been removed from the Ministry of the Interior and put in charge of Foreign Affairs, was raided in his home by three *Ávó* toughs; he refused to go with them but was overpowered. The *Ávó* chief, Péter (with personal grudges against Rajk, who as his nominal chief had on a few occasions overruled him), started on the 'interrogations' with gusto: torture of Rajk himself, torture of his wife and friends in adjoining cells, threats of, among other things, running over his baby son 'in a car accident' were set in motion at once, combined with promises that any sentences on Party members willing to co-operate loyally would only be nominal. Péter, as a reward, was allowed similarly to liquidate his own rivals, among whom General György Pálffy-Oesterreicher, the chief of *Katpol*, was most important. *Katpol* was simultaneously absorbed by *Ávó* or, as it liked to term itself, A.V.H.[1]

There was only one snag. Rajk and some of his most conspicuous 'accomplices' were gentiles. Rajk was in fact the only gentile among the communists to be well known to the general public; with him removed, there would be no mitigating the fact that the country was ruled by four Jewish Muscovites (Rákosi and Gerő; the Minister of Defence, Mihály Farkas; and the Minister of Culture, József Révai), with a 'little Jewish tailor' (Péter) at the head of the most formidable body of armed terror. This could not be helped but could (so Rákosi and his henchmen seemed to imagine) be neutralized by including as many Jewish defendants as possible, pointing out their Jewishness and dubbing them Zionists. It was not difficult to do so, since the middle-class communists who had spent the war years as refugees in the West were overwhelmingly of Jewish extraction; and some of

[1] See above, p. 198n.

them were put in key positions after their return to Hungary (Tibor Szőnyi, for instance, head of the Cadre Department of the Party, who decided about the distribution of jobs), although it was common knowledge that, following the Kremlin's instructions, they had made contact and common cause in the fight against Hitlerism with Western agents (such as the American Allen Dulles in Switzerland). Now this was levelled against them.

Added to the victims were left-wing socialists who, though in favour of the merger with communism, had irritated Rákosi by their assumption of superior understanding of 'dialectical materialism'; and an avalanche of fake trials, partly *in camera*, was unleashed to expose the sinister plots of Titoist-Trotskyite-Clericalist-Zionist-Fascist-Racist-Nationalist-Cosmopolitanist-Imperialist-Capitalist scoundrels who had been in the pay of American, British, French, Yugoslav, and (before 1945) German and Hungarian secret agencies. The Muscovites were the sole category of left-wingers to be spared to some extent in these purges. The very few among them who betrayed, though inadvertently, a slight degree of dissent, came under unpleasant pressure; the agronomist Imre Nagy (1896–1958) who, as Minister of Agriculture in 1945, had administered Land Reform, being accused by Rákosi and Révai of 'Bukharinist' deviation and forced to make 'confession of error'; the philosopher Professor György Lukács (1883–1971), being publicly grilled about his Western cultural sympathies, forced to make a similar 'self-criticism'; the practical economist Zoltán Vas put into cold storage by Gerő, actually for being too practical; the two Szántó brothers, Zoltán and Béla, with their highly respected record of participation in the 1919 Soviet Republic, confined to insignificant jobs. Yet these men survived without imprisonment. The reason became obvious when a communist general, Sándor Nógrádi by name, was clearly singled out for liquidation: his mistress and her former husband, of the old gentry military caste, being arrested and several of their relatives killed, in 1950–51, while armed *Ávó* men shadowed the general himself. Then, armed Soviet soldiers arrived to drive off the *Ávó* men. Connections in Moscow were some help, but nothing else. To be in the hands of *Ávó* was known to be hell, and the dependents of the arrested were avoided like lepers. A typical case was that of Péter Mód, formerly Rajk's colleague in the Eötvös College, his associate in illegal communism, and sent after the war as a diplomat to Paris. He was arrested together with Rajk, as a '*2ème Bureau* agent'. His young wife who had known him from illegal communist days ran from pillar to post to find out what had happened to him. 'Get the hell out of here, Fascist whore!', was the reply she got from the security chief at the Foreign Ministry, Mátrai, whose name seems worth remembering for such acts. She killed herself.

Many others killed themselves. A general nightmare descended on Hungary.

It was, in a way, paradoxical: why should the fratricidal massacres of a minority sect such as the communist in Hungary affect the whole population? Indeed, the first reaction to announcements of such arrests was, understandably enough, a kind of wry gaiety, a *Schadenfreude* that emerged in jokes. The communist cry on the morrow of nationalization of industries had been: 'Yours is the factory, you've built it yourselves!' This was now paraphrased for Rajk's case: 'Yours is the political police, you've organized it for yourself!' But not even this consolation worked. The caretakers of apartment blocks were expected to report on visitors and on random political remarks by the tenants. Schoolchildren were encouraged, if not ordered, to report on their parents. Dossiers based on such information were compiled on everybody. Everyone knew that no one was safe.

No more 'Classes', only 'Layers'

Meanwhile, three characteristics of the régime became prevalent. One (which is often ignored by Westerners of all kinds) was the brazen jettisoning of any egalitarian pretences. 'Class difference' was abolished, but differences between the more and the less 'deserving' layers of society were stressed all the more. The Stakhanovites were not a 'class' but a 'layer'. So also were the heads of nationalized enterprises and the *kolkhozi*; so also the intellectual aristocracy of scholars, scientists, doctors, artists, authors (a mixture of Party hacks and genuinely important practitioners of their disciplines), who were generously paid and systematically referred to by, say, radio announcers with their full titles and honours conferred by the People's Republic. The most conspicuously privileged layer was, however, the Party oligarchy. Politbureau members were entitled (even under law since 1950) to draw as much as they liked from the Exchequer without giving their reasons. They and their higher subordinates lived in luxury villas, grouped where possible in specially enviable areas; by Lake Balaton, rows of villas were expropriated for them and surrounded with barbed wire; there were special shopping centres, sanatoriums, and schools for them and their children to which the general public were not admitted; not to mention their privilege of being watched day and night by rifle-carrying *Ávó* guards—whether for their own safety or to make sure that they didn't escape was anybody's guess.

Connected with the stratification of society was its second dominant feature, the one later denounced by post-Stalin communists as Personality Cult. This had to be seen to be believed. Whether in a theatre, ballroom, classroom, or in Parliament, the first mention of Rákosi's (or Stalin's) name had to be acclaimed with a standing ovation, in rhythmical applause never practised in Hungary before. In the shameless mass-produced eulogies 'the great Stalin and the wise Rákosi' was the recurring theme and Rákosi did not hesitate to make clear that it was the sole authorized version. Once he reprimanded a hack for praising a 'wise' Party decision: '"Correct" would have been the right word, let us not bestow wisdom on everyone'. The adjective 'wise', that is, was reserved for himself and, if need be, for the great Stalin. Officially he was then vice-premier and Secretary-General to the Party, making clear that the Party was above the government (although in 1952 he took over the premiership as well). Such a spirit permeates down to the last hamlet – the Hungarians were to be turned into a nation of slaves.

Thirdly, there was Russification. Magyar as the general vernacular was not challenged and some nationalism (termed proletarian patriotism) was even encouraged to counter 'cosmopolitan', that is, Western, influences. A measure of racism, too, was allowed, in 'rubbing in' the German origins of Rajk and Mindszenty (called originally Pehm) and the equally foreign-sounding surnames and ex-names of the Jewish victims. The Hungarian should feel himself first among the ordinary nations, ran the implication, but the U.S.S.R. politically, and the Russians ethnically, were a nation too great to be measured as simply human. That Russian became the second language in schools, with crash courses to produce Russian teachers, with Russian street names that twisted the Magyar tongue and Soviet emblems that broke the Magyar heart, and with Lenin–Stalin quotations scattered all over the country, was the most obvious manifestation of this trend. More surprising was the rehabilitation, to a large extent, of military and cultural Tsarist traditions. On the centenary of the death of the poet Petőfi on the battlefield, newspapers were instructed to ignore the fact that he had been killed by Russians. As the Romanovs' invasion could not be entirely ignored, it was played down and the merits of a previously unknown Russian lieutenant, Gusev, were given wide publicity: he was said to have revolted against the Tsar in defence of the Hungarian cause. A street in the centre of the capital was named after him in haste. Some years later that noble-hearted Russian turned out to have been invented by socialist-realist fiction-writers such as the Magyar novelist, Soviet major, and editor of the Red Army's Magyar journal, Béla Illés.

The style of uniforms and distinctions, the system of teaching and examinations, were made similar to the Soviet (and largely to the former Tsarist) models. The wearing of hats was discouraged,

Rákosi paraded with a Lenin-cap on his fat bald head, and so, in atonement for his heresies, did even poor György Lukács, who looked, with his bushy hair and frail scholar's face, quite ludicrous in it. The idea was, as Rákosi once casually remarked, that anything striking people as strange or exotic was liable to provoke laughter even if admired. Russian ways, therefore, had to be made familiar as well as being admired. Meanwhile, Western films and contemporary literature, including works by Western communists, were to all intents and purposes banned. Cinema-going to admire Soviet films became a general duty, like attending ideological seminars.

The development of this state of affairs was completed on 20 August 1949, St Stephen's day, named since time immemorial after the first King of Hungary. It was renamed Constitution Day after the rubber-stamp Parliament (elected by then on a single-list basis) passed without fuss the Constitution Bill submitted by Rákosi. Appalling though this law was, the main trouble was that not one word of it could be believed. All citizens, for instance, were assured of the 'secrecy of their postal communications' when everybody knew about the photostats kept by the *Ávó* of letters opened and sealed again. One paragraph of the constitution was, however, perfectly truthful. The old Hungarian coat-of-arms, with red stripes on a white field on the left, and a double-cross on three green hills on the right, was overnight replaced by one which it took an expert to distinguish from those of most Soviet republics. A heraldic device is of course a convention, and the old Hungarian one enshrined a mixture of misunderstandings. But from Christmas 1944 until August 1949 no one could worship that symbol of 'Hungarian national sovereignty' more than Rákosi and his followers. What induced them to do away with it? And why did the West tolerate this whole process?

The West Stands by; Hungarians Pray for a Thermo-nuclear Holocaust

With Rákosi, it was his way of reacting first to his own memories of prison and exile and secondly to the Tito breakaway. Ordeals such as his affect different characters in different ways. His response to tales of anybody's suffering could be summed up as 'So what? And what about *my* past experiences? Why should it be easier for him than it was for me?' He bore a universal grudge for his past and, typically of a careerist, he turned it with greater heat on those who could claim to have shared in his struggles than on his ex-persecutors. The latter, after all, could be kept in check by holding their record against them. But ex-cellmates and the like were unpleasant witnesses and potential rivals. Communist dictatorship adulterated with some old-fashioned nationalism would have suited his snobbish desire to act as 'the Wise Leader of the Nation'. But the break with Tito clearly pointed to 'Double your money!' for him: he could either run ahead of all rivals (his own lieutenants and the other Soviet satellite leaders) in subservience to the Kremlin and in the cold war on Belgrade, or else it was the end of the road. He knew he had no indigenous communist masses, as Tito had, to back him; 'I don't want to spend the rest of my life in the Lux Hotel', he once casually replied to a hint that there should be some tuning-down of the anti-Tito campaign. But what he feared even more was Béla Kun's fate; his counterparts Ana Pauker, Gomułka, and, particularly, Slansky, were facing that. Rather let others perish, was his simple remedy.

He turned Hungary into a Soviet province without the slightest qualification. The Western countries behaved like horrified but stunned onlookers. At the beginning, they made much of their sympathies with anti-communists; they even did so, in this writer's view, too much. The first British Legation (until the Peace Treaty, a political mission) in Budapest was headed by, and largely consisted of, men known for their attachment to the Hungarian *ancien régime*; and following their advice, the Labour Foreign Secretary, Ernest Bevin, expressed his unqualified disapproval of the events in Hungary, Romania, and Bulgaria, in the course of which 'one kind of totalitarianism was substituted for another'. This he said in 1945, when the national coalition in Hungary (unlike in Romania and Bulgaria) was still a reality and when such remarks were calculated to suggest that the sole alternative to Soviet penetration was a restoration of the pre-war power structure. But after this attitude had been fortunately revised, the British simply did not lift a finger to stop Rákosi, except at times expressing 'The deep concern of His Majesty's Government', etc.[1] The Americans started with less

---

[1] I was Press Counsellor of the Hungarian Legation in London at the time of the Mindszenty trial, and once I entertained for luncheon an official of the Foreign Office Northern Department, responsible for political matters concerning Hungary. 'Care for some sherry?', I asked my guest, to which he replied, 'First of all, forgive me, I must make clear that my government take the very gravest view of the way affairs are being conducted in your country'. A similar warning was repeated after every course and when (if I recall the details precisely) after the cheese the official told me, 'But really Mr Ignotus, I should like to impress on you that I do mean it, my government take the very gravest view', etc., I answered 'Of course, you want me to report on this and I shall be reporting on it. But, *entre nous*, I don't think they care by now about any "grave view" unless it is taken by Russia. They would care, because the Russians would care, about a threat of armed intervention, but about nothing else. What can *I* do besides reporting? I could resign but what would be the good of that?' My guest answered with a helpless shrug and a glance of sympathy. (I suppose that what I told him *entre nous* was passed on to some of his colleagues, and later, when one got the impression that through Kim Philby the Russians must have had access to any information about unreliable diplomats of their own camp, I wondered why my remarks were not held against me by the *Ávó* in September 1949 when I was arrested and grilled by them. The answer is, I am sure, bureaucratic muddle. What the Russians won by efficient spying, they lost by inability to make proper use of their material.)

nostalgia for the past, continued with more table-banging, and their minister in Budapest wrote friendly letters to 'Dear Mr Cardinal' which, though not actually committing the United States to saving Mindszenty from the tightening noose around his neck, yet made clear where American sympathies lay. Ultimately no one did a thing. Why not? The ready answer in an embittered Hungary (as well as among Western onlookers) was 'Yalta'. In Yalta, so it was assumed, Hungary had been made part of the 'Soviet sphere of interest', and though the implications of such sphere membership were debatable, this much was clear: on the basis of the agreement between Stalin, Churchill, and Roosevelt at that historic meeting, the Kremlin was to have more say in Hungarian affairs than the Western Powers combined. This at any rate was the reason to which Hungarians attributed the passivity of the West and which convinced them by at latest the summer of 1949 that any resistance to Rákosi was futile. It may have been futile–but, as we know today, their underlying assumption was erroneous. Prior to Yalta, in Moscow, on 9–10 October 1944, Churchill (as he later described and quoted the document to prove it)[1] agreed with Stalin that where post-war spheres of interest were concerned, Hungary should be 'fifty-fifty'; and this was tacitly endorsed–certainly not revoked–at the Big Three meeting in Yalta. It must therefore have remained valid. Yet I doubt if Rákosi was told this. I doubt if Bevin was.[2] The fact is, Hungarians felt they had been sold down the river and could only vest their hopes in a Third World War, whether thermo-nuclear and genocidal or not.

Impoverishment of Town and Country

In almost four years that followed, nothing happened to allay this feeling. Every night was spent in horror and panic; at the sound of any fast motor-car or lorry after midnight the guessing started: 'Whose turn is it now?' The fast motor-cars took the victims to Ávó headquarters; the lorries took them to deportation camps. The deportees had to leave at a few hours' notice, with no more luggage

---

[1] Winston S. Churchill, *The Second World War*, Vol. VI (*Triumph and Tragedy*), London, 1954, p. 198.

[2] I, with friends in the British Labour leadership as well as in the whole spectrum of post-war Hungarian politics, from 'right-wing Smallholders' to Muscovites, was never given a hint of such an agreement. In early 1946, revisiting Hungary after the war, I gave a talk at the Anglo-Hungarian Society, and risked the depressing guess that, according to current British opinion, in the balance of Great Power influences to be established after the war 'Hungary will come mostly under Russian influence although, let us be clear, priority does not imply exclusiveness'. Had I used the symbols of the Churchill-Stalin scrap of paper in Moscow, I might have said 'sixty-forty'; and still fail to understand why the 'fifty-fifty' was not clearly explained to us. Bureaucratic muddle in the U.K. as well as in the U.S.S.R.?

than they could carry; the rest of their belongings, including their apartments, were taken over by the *Ávó*. In the deportation camps, as in the prisons and internment camps, the inmates were kept in appalling conditions, fed on swill and refuse. The former upper and middle classes (always excepting the few who belonged, sometimes for their real merits, to the particularly favoured 'layers') were branded in an openly racist spirit: schoolchildren had their 'class background' marked in their documents, and the child with the former 'exploiters' blood' in his veins was expelled from higher education and frequently pilloried in front of other children for the 'crimes' of his parents or grandparents. By including the 'kulaks' and making it a rather elastic category, the race of the damned-forever was substantially enlarged, though the skill in lying and in forging documents which had saved thousands from death under the Nazis was applied to reducing it. Masses of professional people and well-off traders produced 'workers and working peasants' (the latter standing for a peasant too poor to be classified 'kulak') in their ancestry: an inverted social snobbery became obligatory.

The large masses of people, the 'proletariat' which was supposed to be dictating, and its ally the 'semi-proletariat', saw their living standards constantly sinking after 1948. Drabness and privations became the general rule. In the early fifties, bread-rationing was reintroduced, and long bread-queues became a familiar sight in towns and villages alike. In factories the working hours were increased ('now it no longer harms the worker as he works for himself'), piece-rates introduced wherever possible instead of hourly wages, working norms constantly stretched, sweated labour obtained through 'socialist competition', and levies made on earnings, however low, through incessant 'voluntary' contributions to such causes as Peace Loan, Save the Korean Children Fund, Rehousing 'Free People'[1] Fund, etc. If things went conspicuously wrong, 'saboteurs' were easily caught.

In the rural areas, things went even worse. Whatever the possible merits of a farming co-operative (for instance, in Israel), nothing can make it work with methods such as those applied in Hungary. The peasant's sole consolation for his troubles in lean years used to be that he was 'master in his own house' which included the plot big enough to support him. Once deprived of it, no technocratic genius could persuade him that he was going to 'own' it – but in economically sounder conditions, even if he had to pool his resources, including his plot, with his neighbours, under the paternal supervision of a socialist state. The peasants hated the whole idea; and not surprisingly, therefore, the *kolkhozi*, or 'co-operatives', which after the

[1] 'Free People', *Szabad Nép*, was the official Party daily.

'turning-point' had taken possession of by far the greatest part of the arable land, fared even worse than the state farms proper. Whoever could flee from the land did so–particularly the young–and in a few years time large areas of previously fertile soil (approximately one-tenth of the total) became neglected and eroded or devoured by weeds.

Concentrating on Heavy Industries: Gains and Losses

It is no good consulting statistics about the impoverishment of the people in 1949–53–that is, under fully-fledged Stalinism; since statistics were declared to have been rescued from the lies of 'bourgeois objectivism' and turned into the 'weapon of class warfare', they could no longer be expected to supply even roughly reliable figures. But two things should be made clear on the balance-sheet of those years: the intentions behind the deeds; and the achievements among the failures.

The idea was, without any doubt, 'to build socialism'. Lenin said, 'Socialism equals Soviet system plus electrification'; for Rákosi and Gerő it equalled slavish imitation of Soviet Russia. In a sequence of Three- and Five-Year Plans, most ambitious schemes were embarked upon; power plants and foundries were naturally given key roles; and Dunapentele, the large village on the Danube renamed Sztálin-város, was made the symbol and centre of such efforts, with an entirely new population of skilled and unskilled workers, housed in shacks, moulded into an instant metropolis. The manufacturing plants of Csepel, known as Manfred Weiss Works until taken over by Nazis, and renamed Mátyás Rákosi Works under Stalinism, were further developed; and the exploitation of Hungary's bauxite and crude oil resources was forced on at an unprecedented pace. The heavy industries and capital investments absorbed a much increased proportion of economic resources; which was supposed to account for (and to a large extent really did) the shortage of commodities, of consumer goods produced by light industries, as well as of food and other farm products. Wine sold on the market was atrocious, made of maize according to most consumers, and opinions differed as to whether this was because the vineyards had been ruined or because 'the Russians took the wine'.

Building socialism demands sacrifices–no bones were made about this by the rulers; and if the 'sacrifices' were heavier than foreseen, whipping-boys were at hand. Rákosi admitted 'inflationary symptoms', but due, he added, 'to the manipulation of bourgeois and right-wing Social Democrats infiltrated into our ranks'; and 'saboteurs' were imprisoned by the hundred, not a few being hanged. A signal failure was met with in the crude oil industry, which had formerly had Shell and Vacuum Oil connections. A simultaneous and forced drawing on oil-wells and gas was decided upon; 'bourgeois' experts who expressed misgivings were imprisoned; and many of the oil-plants subsequently swamped. After a hitch at Mátyás Rákosi Works, the head manager Biró sent a 'bourgeois' head engineer straight to the gallows. The fact that the Sztálinváros project had been too precipitate and over-ambitious was already recognized before Stalin's death in 1953. In other fields, the most notorious construction failure was the collapse of houses over the extending underground lines in Budapest, the building of which had been started with a triumphant flourish under Gerő's auspices. On the Castle Hill of Buda, instead of the old-fashioned but quite handy 'funicular' train, which had been used for decades until its destruction in the siege, a gigantic escalator was projected in an early Plan; and then shelved, without restoring the funicular train either. Among the most notorious of heroic Stakhanovite achievements was that of a worker highly decorated for producing two or three times the amount of buttons produced by his colleagues. He turned out to have bought them in a shop. The buttons were up to standard, and it was legal to buy them. So high were the rewards for champions of 'socialist competition' that it paid to be dishonest within the law.

Yet it would be wrong to think that nothing was achieved. Heavy industry did expand, and this did strengthen the potential of the Hungarian economy as a whole. By the end of this era, the industrial population had almost overtaken the agrarian in numbers–and gruesome though the conditions were which had speeded up this process, the process itself was in line with technological progress. The protectionist economic politicians under Count Bethlen, Gömbös, and their successors, the economic tactics of the German quislings themselves, and finally the forced pace of industrialization under the Russian quislings, notably Gerő, willy-nilly resembled each other in furthering a sound process by unsound means. Hungary grew, technologically speaking, more civilized, under Stalinism possibly at higher speed than ever before. She did not yet have a chance of making much use of this gain, but it was still a gain.

Achievements in Two Fields: Children's Welfare; and, in a way, 'Kultura'

And apart from this, in at least two fields, improvements began to be apparent, although, as will be seen later, with most paradoxical consequences. Child welfare was one; respect for *kultura* the other.

'He who conquers youth has conquered the future' was one of Lenin's truisms incessantly quoted. And communists were prodigiously resourceful in providing amenities for youth, especially for the under sixteen age-groups. Many of the former lordly castles were turned into their recreation homes, swings and slides shot up in great variety in the public parks, and a special 'children's railway' was run by adolescents in the mountains of Buda. A sort of Punch and Judy show now included scenes where the Villain was clad in stars and stripes, while the radiant fairy wore a hammer and sickle, but who cared? Children's lives became healthier and more colourful.

The communist reverence for artistic and scientific genius, combined with the urge to violate and distort it, continued even through the darkest years. Research in genetics was crippling owing to the influence of T. D. Lysenko, Stalin's favourite biologist, and use of the Theory of Relativity only allowed provided warnings about its dangerous 'idealistic' implications were given adequate space. In aesthetics, A. A. Zhdanov, Stalin's ideological Grand Inquisitor, was infallible, and some of his obsessions have outlived both him and the 'sectarian' era – 'naturalism' and 'formalism' have remained dirty words though with qualifications, even for György Lukács right to the end. But the classics were hardly affected. Nor were the skills of artists such as surgeons, pianists, opera singers. Beethoven and Verdi were 'progressive by the standards of their time'; so were Homer, Shakespeare, Walter Scott, Goethe, Dickens, Hugo, Balzac . . . . And Zola, admitted with some reserve. Russian classics were more progressive than others, but this did not harm anybody. In Hungarian classics there was practically a boom. They could be bought cheaply, were edited with care, printed in good taste, and given only as much ideological rigging as to add a piquant flavour of absurdity. They sold like hot cakes and were absorbed as substitutes for real wine, jazz, 'Westerns', and George Orwell as well as for their own sakes. Whatever the reasons for it, the spread of general knowledge and of popular interest in intellectual values was enormous. And no artist starved (except when in gaol).

Kádár's Fall; Péter's Fall; a Jewish Dictatorship Engineering anti-Jewish Pogroms; Paranoia Rampant

In the field of policing and politics proper (the two being closely knit), the liquidation of suspect categories never came to a stop. Coalition partners tame enough to swallow everything, such as ex-President Tildy and his successor in that symbolic Presidency, Szakasits, together with many of their crypto-communist advisers, were destined to share the stench of prison with practically all the Smallholder and trade union personnel, including Anna Kéthly (the lawyer István Ries being beaten to death shortly after his arrest). There they were crammed together with pro- and anti-Nazi ex-Horthyite generals, and priests, magnates, and bankers. The National Peasants were the sole political category to be spared in these purges (except for confining some of their distinguished scholars to drab ill-paid jobs in the country), but the hunt for 'presumably dissenting' communists never relaxed. And this had some strange results.

1951 brought the arrest of a 'gang' headed by János Kádár (1912–). Kádár held a key post and, even more, stood for a symbol in the Party hierarchy. Coming from a proletarian family in southern Transdanubia, having started as a manual worker–first unskilled labourer, later toolmaker–and involved since his teens with the illegal communist movement, he was the character most suitable to bear out the Stalinist myth that the body and soul of both underground and victorious communism in Hungary were the Hungarian working classes. True, his original surname (Csermanek) rang Slav, which did count under Stalinism, with its latent racism, but still it was much less 'compromising' than the painfully hidden Yiddish or German ex-names of the Jewish leaders, or, for that matter, of their lieutenants coming from the Magyarized German middle classes. Kádár seemed a conscientious and devoted Party worker, without brilliance but of engaging manners, and seemingly without qualms about the mass murders and tortures which had been the rule since 1949, though he certainly showed no sign of pleasure in them. From 1948 he acted as Minister of the Interior because he was told to do so. Sharing in the leadership of wartime underground communism, he had been particularly close to Rajk and his wife, and must have felt unhappy when ordered to play his part in their arrest. But 'the Party above everything'–and he conformed. According to one story, never confirmed or denied by him or anybody who could know the truth for certain, Kádár personally called on Rajk in his *Ávó* cell and, referring to Comrade Rákosi's personal message of goodwill and sympathy, implored him to 'confess' to whatever was expected of him, because this was the only way of exposing the Tito gang as the scoundrels they were; without such dramatization the general public would not understand it. Kádár is also supposed to have promised Rajk that the death sentence on him and his comrades would only be nominal; they would all survive in comfort and when the time came to make things clear they would be rehabilitated and paid high tributes for their services to the Party.

Subsequently, when Rajk and many of his comrades had been hanged, and masses of them imprisoned, and all records available to the Party centre and the *Ávó* tampered with so as to make the verdict passed on them irrevocable, Kádár was in the limelight as the undisputed Number 5 of the hierarchy, running up close to the 'Muscovite Quartet'. Clearly he looked like one of the very few who were safe so long as communism was. What happened to make him lose favour with Rákosi? Allegedly, he did express some doubts about the wisdom of treating Rajkists as they were in fact treated. And then, again allegedly, Rákosi rang General Péter on his private line and asked for Kádár's dossier. Everyone had to have his dossier, but Péter knew well that Rákosi did not want to 'see' anybody's simply to muse over it. Some incriminating details were added in haste. 'Didn't I have the right hunch?', Rákosi is supposed to have commented. What really happened has never been discovered. About the way Kádár was arrested and subsequently treated, various stories went round, which agreed in suggesting that he was cruelly tortured even by *Ávó* standards, his jaw and knuckles being manhandled, and the *Ávó* Colonel Vladimir Farkas (son of the Defence Minister Mihály Farkas) urinating in his mouth. These are widespread stories, again neither confirmed nor denied. There is no doubt, however, about his 'trial'. It was staged in *Ávó* headquarters, *in camera*, though produced as a 'trial', with a set of *Ávó*-trained 'judges' and 'attorney' and 'counsels for the defence' in attendance, and with victims readily 'confessing'. The charge, or part of it, was that Kádár, in complicity with Rajk, and with practically the whole wartime communist underground in Hungary, had deliberately played into the hands of the British Secret Service when, in 1943, they dissolved the illegal Hungarian Communist Party and substituted for it an (equally illegal) 'Peace Party'. The present writer, who had the strange privilege of attending this performance as a 'witness for the prosecution',[1] feels that, in perspective, the astounding stupidity of that charge, however tempting to dwell upon, is less interesting than what was aimed at and achieved by it. The reader is reminded of the March Front in 1937, with a section of crypto-communist university youth as its most dedicated supporters.[2] Rákosi had always affected kindliness towards these 'March Front communists', if only to flaunt his association with such 'pure Hungarian lads', almost to a man gentiles. Now this whole category was sliced off–jobs, and not a few heads, fell. The Minister of the Interior, Sándor Zöld, also a former March Front student, having got wind of his approaching arrest, killed his wife, children, and himself. That pogrom-happy, 'Zionist'-baiting set of Moscow-trained Jews, with the whole country prostrate at their feet, simply could not find one man to fill an important position as a home-grown, gentile communist. (Ex-Smallholder, etc., puppets acting as honorary presidents and the like did not count from this point of view.)

[1] Cf., for more detailed descriptions, Paul Ignotus, *Political Prisoner*, London, 1959; and 'János Kádár–Hungary's Quisling Redeemed', in *Leaders of the Communist World* University of Southern California, Los Angeles (awaiting publication).
[2] See above, pp. 183–4.

In late 1952 came another and even bigger bombshell. Hints were leaked through the Press that the malpractices of a sinister gang of infiltrators had just been revealed. Political prisoners, though not allowed to see daily papers or listen to the radio, were quicker than the general public to learn what it was all about. In the storeroom of prisoners' belongings, an *Ávó* general's uniform was discovered which could only belong to Gábor Péter. The prince of thugs had been caught. No reasons have hitherto been suggested for Rákosi's falling out with his security murderer Number 1. Was it simply the paranoid, and ultimately suicidal, automatism of the salami-slicing device? The reasons may never be known, but there was no doubt of what was in store for 'the Gábor Péter gang', as Rákosi's Press from then on referred to them. A huge trial was being prepared, *Ávó* officers, prisoners, and others interrogated at frantic speed about the 'gang's links with Yugoslavia, Israel, and Western capitalist countries'; a 'Zionist conspiracy' monster trial was to be staged, with Péter as the first defendant and (a useful element for conformist myth-mongering) his 'Swabian' deputy as chief accomplice. In Russia, the monster trial of the Ten Jewish Doctors was to start shortly; no better moment could be imagined to support it by exposing the plots of Hungarian Zionists. Everything was set for the big bang when, on 5 March 1953, Stalin died.

Chapter 11

Thaw, and Re-freezing, and Thaw again

Rákosi Dethroned, Beria Beheaded

A 'WIND OF CHANGE' was obviously coming, but at first no one knew where from. Rákosi was to learn it soon from the horse's mouth. In May 1953 he was summoned to his Kremlin masters and one of them, in fact the security chief Beria, ordered him in harsh terms not to 'play King of Hungary' any longer. He must share the supreme power with others, he was told, and if he stuck to his post as First Secretary of the Party, he must give up the other top post as President of the Council of Ministers. He was even told who the new premier was to be: Imre Nagy, a then comparatively inconspicuous figure of the Moscow-trained establishment. There was no question of not obeying Moscow.

Meanwhile, some newly coined catchwords blowing in from Moscow gave an idea of the direction to be taken. 'Return to the Leninist concept of Collective Leadership' was a fairly clear pointer. The doing-away with Personality Cult made a lot of trouble for workshops melting down their rich reserves of Rákosi busts on Rákosi's own order. (Personality Cult was 'unworthy of a communist', he declared.) 'Socialist Legality' sounded, to the masses, a most encouraging catchword, though no one knew for a while what it implied. In foreign affairs, a conciliatory attitude towards Yugoslavia was the first indicator of change; the discovery of something like a new democracy in India, the next; and there followed 'Peaceful co-existence with capitalist countries', including NATO powers, though combined with warnings against mistaking love of peace for a sign of Soviet weakness when it was really a sign of Soviet strength. (In some respects, indeed, the Soviet attitude towards the West hardened under 'co-existence': Stalin had been ready for an Austrian-type arrangement in Germany, but his successors were not.)

All in all, so much was clear: that an era less and not more 'sectarian' was to start. But its top personnel were not yet consolidated. No sooner had Beria dethroned 'King Rákosi' than he himself was not only dethroned but 'beheaded' (i.e., shot) by his own Fellow-Collective Leaders[1] who accused him of having tried to establish his

---

[1] Probably on 26 June 1953–a week before Rákosi formally renounced the premiership.

own personal dictatorship. This was a most welcome 'wind' for Rákosi's sails as he saw it. Could not Imre Nagy be held in check by hints of his indebtedness to Beria? And there was the 'Gábor Péter gang' in prison. Would it not be expedient to denounce Péter as the 'Hungarian Beria'? This in fact happened at once. Rákosi expressed admiration for Tito's Yugoslavia and declared that there was nothing but a 'misunderstanding' to be settled between Budapest and Belgrade. The misunderstanding had been created by the lies, calumnies, and forgeries of the Gábor Péter gang, and by nothing else. As the Ten Doctors[1] in Moscow were released and rehabilitated, the material of Péter's Zionist conspiracy was scrapped, together with the charge of his 'Titoism'. Instead, interrogations started about the violations of Socialist Legality committed by the gang. Whom had they tortured and how? What false confessions had they extorted from their victims? This time, the evidence did not need to be forged–there was in fact an *embarras de richesse*, the sole difficulty being to convince anyone that the gang had committed everything on their own, while Wise Rákosi and other Party leaders remained innocent as children of their crimes. Yet Rákosi insisted on this. About Rajk he took the line that his plotting with Tito had been an invention of the gang, but that the accusation of his having acted before 1945 as a White police spy was 'unfortunately true'. Rákosi stuck to this preposterous assumption and formulated it, in so many words, more than two years later, in November 1955.

Imre Nagy, Premier

'Collective leadership' could not, however, be sidetracked. Premier Nagy proved a hard nut to crack. He was very much unlike the rest of the better-known Muscovites. He did not outshine them, to be sure, in any noticeable sense. He neither seemed nor tried to seem a genius; it was rather his apparent character of down-to-earth countryman which made him an attractive proposition to many–and first of all to the Kremlin rulers, with their sometimes quite sound hankering after the despised petty bourgeois and kulak virtues. He was a thick-set man, with a farmer's moustache and a schoolmaster's *pince-nez*, with reassuringly round features, a reassuringly deep voice, carefully but unobtrusively dressed, and obviously a moderate in outlook as well as in manners. François Fejtő called him 'a reformist who lost his way in the jungle of Bolshevism', which was true. But, one may ask, what had pushed him into that 'jungle' at all? It was the

---

[1] Actually, seven were named at the time of the arrest, and fifteen at their rehabilitation; but the round figure stuck in people's minds. Some two-thirds of them were of Jewish extraction.

apparent hopelessness of 'reformism' in the world where he operated; and his (somewhat old-fashioned) loyalty to his chosen leaders.

He had come from Kaposvár, in the Transdanubian county of Somogy, from a family of dwarf-holding Calvinist peasants. This at any rate was believed about him when he entered public life as Minister of Agriculture at the end of 1944, married to a nice and houseproud wife who originally, as an illiterate maid, had learnt to read and write from him. Later, when Nagy became a controversial figure, emotive rumours were launched, simultaneously, by diehard communists and diehard anti-communists, alleging that Nagy only 'posed as a peasant' and was really the son of a well-off Jewish tenant farmer. Nagy's biographers (and admirers) indignantly rebutted this 'vile insinuation' and insisted on their hero's pure Magyar ploughman's pedigree. All the facts produced seem to substantiate the latter assertion – but more interesting than the genealogical truth is the fact that this could be a passionately discussed issue at all. The myth of Blood and Soil, worshipped under Horthy, Hitler, and Stalin alike, has outlived them in its potency and can still be identified up to the date of this book in a great many utterances both of governing circles in Budapest and of Hungarian political *émigrés*.

Imre Nagy, like Béla Kun and Rákosi, got his first decisive Bolshevik brainwash as a prisoner-of-war in Russia at the end of the First World War. The Hungarian Council Republic of 1919 and the subsequent White terror left him with the conviction that nothing short of an upheaval on the Russian scale could redeem the Hungarian people from servitude and exploitation. He took a job as a metal-worker in Budapest, although the agrarian question, and particularly as seen from his native county of Somogy, remained his chief concern; it was as an expert on agrarian questions that he achieved some standing in 1924–25, first as a spokesman of the internal left opposition in the Social Democratic Party and then as a communist conspirator. He was imprisoned, but released by 1927 and, by the early 1930s, settled as a refugee in the U.S.S.R. There, again, he tried to tackle the misery of the peasants in Somogy. He severely criticized the Kun government in retrospect for nationalizing the land instead of dividing it among the peasants 'as Lenin and Stalin did'. So they had done indeed, but not without second thoughts; and as for Stalin, he was just about to dispossess the plotholders by shovelling them either into the *kolkhozi* or into labour camps. And Kun, though involved in factional quarrels, was still an authority among the Hungarian refugees. Nagy thus got into troubled waters as soon as he met his comradely hosts face to face. A 'confession of error' was one of the first things expected of him, and he made it dutifully and loyally. Yet, his 'error' was not judged to be grave; and not even its condemnation as an 'error' seemed final. While forced collectivization was going on in Russia, the opinion won ground that communists, in their propaganda towards countries where quasi-feudal big estates still existed, should profess belief in privately owned peasant holdings and indignantly deny any intention to export the methods of the U.S.S.R., conceived in specifically bloody conditions. Did communists then deliberately spread lies about their intentions? They were certainly prepared to do so for the supreme 'End' which they cherished; but, in this specific matter, I am convinced they simply did not know yet whether they were telling a tactical lie or not. They were, in any case, holding several irons in the fire; and Nagy seemed suitable for holding as a Magyar farmer puppet. After working in Moscow for a while (allegedly, under Bukharin's guidance), he was sent as a *kolkhoz* manager to Siberia and only returned to the capital towards the end of the Second World War as a Magyar announcer on the Soviet radio–a post he owed to his pleasant baritone voice rather than to anything else. Added to this, his studies and experiences in farming made him the ideal man for Minister of Agriculture in the instant government set up while the battle still raged in Hungary. It was equally natural for him in this post to implement the Land Reform for which he had been preparing so long. But after less than a year, in November 1945, he was shifted to another government department–as nominal Minister of the Interior–so as to be 'kicked upstairs' and elected President of the National Assembly (Parliament) on 16 September 1947. The reason was, obviously, that he took his Land Reform more seriously than Rákosi liked; and that, on the other hand, in the dignified posture of 'representative of the sovereignty of the nation' no other communist could have cut a better figure. The only trouble was that, even in his high position of glorified insignificance, he went on agitating for his life-long hobby, the peasants' cause; and when, in 1948, the knell of 'the kulaks as a class' was rung, he bombarded Party leaders with warnings against inhumanities. Farming co-operatives were a more advanced system than individual farming, he urged, but they must win over the peasantry peacefully, by competition and example, not by force. The reaction of the Party leaders was to expel Nagy from the Politbureau and make him renounce the Presidency of Parliament in August 1949. It was in the heat of the anti-Tito campaign; Rákosi is supposed to have hesitated whether to dub Nagy or Rajk 'the Hungarian Tito', but decided that Rajk, as a non-Muscovite, would be more dangerous as a rival to himself, whereas Nagy's arrest might hurt susceptibilities in Moscow, where Rajk knew but few people: so it was both safer and more useful to victimize Rajk. Nagy, meanwhile, consented to make another 'confession of error' which saved his skin. He was allowed to retire to a country town, Gödöllő, and to lecture at the Agrarian Academy. Later, gradually, he was even allowed to re-enter the *apparat*; and Rákosi–relying apparently on his rustic and schoolmasterly innocence–appointed him deputy premier on 15 November 1952, in what proved to be the last phase of his own absolute despotism.

4 July 1953 was the day when Imre Nagy introduced himself to Parliament as the new premier, and he did so in a speech which, despite its temperate and stilted phrasing, struck people like a bombshell. Legality had been violated; the economic resources of the country had been overstretched; the general standard of living had been unnecessarily lowered; the industries producing food and other commodities had been neglected in an exaggerated effort to boost heavy industries; the co-operative movement on the land had been imposed at an unreasonable pace which harassed the peasantry and caused hardship to the consumers; the intelligentsia had been unnecessarily bullied and insulted; workers and employees had been exhausted by excessive working hours and humiliated by disciplinary actions; in general, 'our authorities have often disregarded the rules laid down in the constitution in defence of the rights, personal liberties, and security of citizens'. Nagy promised, on behalf of the new government, to do his best to remedy the 'grave mistakes' of the recent past. Some of these could be set right by a stroke of the pen; concentration camps could be dismantled overnight, and the unfortunate deportees could be allowed to leave their obligatory slums immediately if they found some accommodation elsewhere–which few did. The reorganization of industry, however, needed time, as everybody realized. But whatever the possible rate of improvement seemed at the moment, the very fact that, after four years of total yesmanship, such exposure of malpractices should be given an airing amounted to a miracle which not a soul could have dreamt of some weeks before. In fact, it was too miraculous to be believed even at that moment. Was it not a communist head of government who spoke thus? And was he not ordered by the Kremlin to do so? He was, in any case, authorized–since his criticism was in line with the liberal and 'co-existentialist' initiatives taken concurrently by the Soviet premier, Malenkov. This was why many (mainly among the diehard anti-communists) felt puzzled and incredulous rather than relieved: they suspected a new Soviet trap behind the surprising utterances. And, on the other hand, it was the reason why no communist thought of contradicting Nagy openly at the time; Rákosi, at a meeting of the Party functionaries in Budapest a week later, voiced qualifications and reservations to show that the Party Secretariat–and not the government–was still the supreme power in Hungary, but did not

explicitly join issue with Nagy. A clever manipulator, he was playing for time.

Two Fighting Heads: Nagy and Rákosi

For a while, Nagy's star seemed to be rising even higher: when, for instance (on 8 August) Malenkov emphatically committed the Soviet government to the new course of collective leadership and legality, adroitly combining this with the announcement that the U.S.S.R. possessed the H-bomb. On 23 January 1954, Nagy was able to report to Parliament with satisfaction on the improvement in living conditions and to announce his intention of strengthening Hungary's economic ties with the Western world. But then muddle in Hungary and conflicts in Moscow played into Rákosi's hands. Nagy's statement that no peasant should in future be forced into a co-operative against his will was interpreted by masses of *kolkhoz* members as permission – almost as encouragement – to leave their *kolkhozi* and reclaim their former plots at once; which added chaos to existing troubles. The improvement of the workers' conditions had its usual dark side – slackening of discipline, rise in prices – recorded with relish by the hard-liners and passed on to the Kremlin. A tug-of-war was going on all the time: Nagy's popularity versus Rákosi's greater skill and determination.

It was not, however, a clear-cut division between 'the nation and her quislings', as one would see it today. Liberalization had after all been launched from Moscow and the quickest to jump on its bandwaggon were some of the notorious Soviet agents: the Stalinist defence chief, General Mihály Farkas, for instance, with his record of violence and Personality Cult second to none, made a Fouchet-like attempt, quite successful for a while, to save his future by siding with Nagy against Rákosi within the Party. Rákosi, on the other hand, was no less quick in his attempts to enlist the support of right-wingers, whom he had always preferred to Social Democrats and, even more, to liberally inclined communists. For the general public this was a power game behind closed doors – the average citizen had even less to do with it than he had had three hundred years before with the intrigues of aristocrats shuttling their loyalties between Vienna and Constantinople.

Some events were welcomed with general relief: such as the announcement on 13 March 1954 of a sentence of life imprisonment on the former *Ávó* chief, General Péter, and of nine years' imprisonment on his deputy and former Minister of Justice, Décsi, for 'crimes against the state and the people'; though obviously used by Rákosi as scapegoats, these men had really so much cruelty to their discredit that their fall was felt to be the fulfilment of a moral law. But about the revision of political trials, which Nagy had promised and pressed for, Rákosi dragged his feet; he had too much to lose by it. Yet the pressure to release communist prisoners, at the very least, was too great for him to resist. On 9 October János Kádár, the former Minister of the Interior, was set free and straightway appointed Party Secretary of the largest industrial district of Budapest. As a sop to Western opinion, Rákosi consented to the release, on 21 November, of the well-known socialist leader Anna Kéthly, while masses of Social Democrats sentenced as her 'accomplices' were still kept in gaol; similarly, he allowed the release from prison (though still kept temporarily under house arrest) of Cardinal Mindszenty on 17 July 1955, when the Roman Catholic priests and laymen imprisoned for assisting him were still serving their sentences.

Nagy Ousted

A sharp setback for Nagy came from Moscow at the beginning of 1955: the fall of Malenkov.[1] Now it was the hard-liners' turn to go over to the offensive. Rákosi at once took heart, and with table-thumping insisted (on 25 January) that industrialization was more urgent than the improvement of living conditions. Arch-terrorist Mihály Farkas also took heart—and backed up Rákosi again. By 19 February Nagy was sent on 'sick leave' and in the first days of March the nature of his 'sickness' became manifest. He was condemned by the Party Central Committee and later, 'unanimously', by the National Assembly, for 'rightist deviation', 'opportunism', 'nationalism', neglect of heavy industry, dissolution of co-operatives, and so forth. In mid-April he was formally removed from the premiership and from all Party functions—later also from Party membership. Once again he was expected to 'confess errors of judgement'.

But he was fed up with that ritual by then. He flatly refused; now it was for him to play for time, though in a manner very different from Rákosi's. He accepted his status of dishonourable retirement, which meant banishment from the university as well as the political arena. He concentrated on drafting his *Memoranda*, on 'A Communism which does not forget the human being'.[2] He set forth his ideas, such as that what was morally wrong could not be politically right; that to tread on people's consciences and inflate the prison population was a poor substitute for governing; that workers could never appreciate the blessings of a socialism which was intent on lowering rather than raising their living standards. As to Hungary's

---

[1] Officially announced on 8 February but foreshadowed weeks before.
[2] 'Un communisme qui n'oublie pas l'homme' was the title under which they were published, edited by François Fejtő, after his deportation, by Plon, Paris, 1957.

place in the world, Nagy recalled Kossuth's plans to make a reality of Hungarian independence and democracy by bringing about a Danubian Federation of free and equal nations. Truisms, in a word, but their lack of originality should not have prevented sensible people from seeing sense in them. So, at any rate, Nagy seemed to think; he sent his drafts, dutifully, to Soviet politicians (Khrushchev and Bulganin were then the most important among them), with copies to Hungarian Central Committee members, and though he showed them also to friends and close followers, he was not preparing any campaign with them. He simply trusted to commonsense–and time. His successor as the nominal head of government, appointed on 8 April, was András Hegedüs, a young apparatchik. He was of peasant stock, brought up in a People's College, qualified as a sociologist. He became in quick succession Gerő's personal secretary, Minister of Agriculture, and vice-premier under Nagy. His obvious task was to act as Rákosi's home-produced and younger double. Rákosi looked like having won the game.

Yet the ball set rolling could not be stopped. Many of Nagy's reforms proved irreversible. The re-emergence of political prisoners caused a deep stir within the Party organizations, even more than outside. The stern look of tall, haggard Julia Rajk, with her young son, haunted her comrades like a spectre. Shortly after Kádár, the survivors of the communist March Front youth were set free: Gyula Kállai, a former Minister of Foreign Affairs; Géza Losonczy, a former Under-Secretary of State for Information; the agronomist Ferenc Donáth, one-time secretary of Rákosi; the former Ministry of Health high official, Dr Vilmos Tariska; their elder and editor-in-chief, Sándor Haraszti, Secretary-General to the Hungarian–Yugoslav Association; and so forth. And there came others, 'Rajkists' or 'Kádárists' in Party parlance, according to the vintage of their imprisonments, some with valiant records in the International Brigade in Spain (like General 'Pedro' Cséby) or of illegal communist activities in South America, or of participation in the British war effort against the Nazis: Professor (of economics) György Ádám, the journalist György Pálóczi-Horváth, the ex-President of the Hungarian radio, István Szirmai, and the former Press chief of the Party Endre Rosta were perhaps the most outstanding personalities among them. They were given quite important posts–in journalism, in research centres, in diplomacy–while some of them started a desperate search for the children who had been taken from them and placed under false names in various hostels at the time of their arrests. Searching for lost children was but one sombre feature of this period when the horrors of the past three or four years came to the surface. The released prisoners, to be sure, did not see eye to eye on many questions, but their accounts of the *Ávó* torture-chambers, with Rákosi's spirit brooding over them, were fairly unanimous. The communist intelligentsia were shattered. Make-believe, if not naïve fanaticism, had up to then supplied soothing blinkers whenever the Party-sponsored lie was too painful to face. But it could be dodged no longer.

Writers in the Vanguard; Tibor Déry

Hungarian life was in ferment, with writers in its vanguard, and most prominent among them the disillusioned communist writers. The key figure in the protests against inhumanities was the novelist Tibor Déry (1894–). Déry, in spite of his emotional sincerity in embracing collective causes, had really always been more of an individualist fellow-traveller than a communist proper. In his recently published, shattering autobiographical notes, *No Verdict*,[1] Déry recalls his youthful involvement with modern literature and revolutionary politics, and adds:

> As can be seen, I was a bad communist from the outset, I don't deny that. The question only is – and the answer to it has been sought for decades – whether anyone can be a good writer and a good communist at the same time, in the close-fitting uniform which the Party puts him into and which he only rarely gets permission to unbutton.

This is a justified remark but, to be fair (and as he makes clear in this autobiography), Déry was already a bad communist before becoming a good writer. He had been a young man obsessed with a literary vocation before he knew what he had to say. And throughout most of his career he remained an experimentalist *par excellence*, with the usual merits and shortcomings of this category: he was devoted to Art, and even when he slipped into the Arty, some authentic fire gleamed amid the masses of heavy and unappealing prose. Starting as a *Nyugat* young man and then joining Kassák's group round *Ma*, he underwent many influences, from Knut Hamsun and Karl Kraus through the Expressionists, Dadaists, and Surrealists of the twenties to Thomas Mann and Marcel Proust in the thirties. His life was fairly agitated. Coming from a family of wealthy and polished bourgeois, he was employed in a company under his uncle's management, and began his political activities by inciting his fellow-employees and the workers to strike against him. His ties, however superficial, with the Béla Kun régime later caused him and his relations, including the paternally forgiving capitalist uncle, some head-

[1] *Itélet nincs*, Szépirodalmi, Budapest, 1969.

ache under the White terror. Naughty Tibor and his girl wife were helped to leave the country, and he spent years of an exile, more or less self-imposed, and as a rule overshadowed by penury, in Vienna, Berlin, and Paris. He tried his hand at odd jobs and not a few times at the gambling table, with no satisfying results. In the second half of the inter-war period, he carried on a sort of internal exile in Budapest, earning his bread mainly on translations. And translating brought him ironically into conflict with the law under the Whites. He translated André Gide's *Retour de l'URSS*, the book denounced in Moscow at once as a pack of most sinister Trotskyite and reactionary lies and calumnies about the Workers' Fatherland. The Hungarian authorities, however, saw it differently: the book was confiscated for its 'eulogy of the criminal Bolshevik system', and since the author was out of reach, Déry as his translator was imprisoned for two months. This implied loss of random jobs, a burden harder to bear than gaol itself. Yet Déry survived it, and even the subsequent Nazi terror, under hidden identity of course, as he was blacklisted as a communist as well as a 'destructive writer' and a Jew.

After Liberation, it was the natural thing for him to join the Communist Party and to make an attempt to come to terms with the Zhdanovist concept of Socialist Realism. Yesterday's would-be Proust emerging as a would-be Gorky: it was a painful sight but helped, surprisingly, to mature Déry's faculties. Both in observation and in style, his writing became more direct. The immediate outcome, however, was a tremendous and well-nigh disastrous freak. He embarked on *the* great working-class novel of his country and epoch, planned as a trilogy under the title *Felelet* (Answer), in which he tried to reconcile Party directives with truthfulness. The result was a poor hybrid, contrived and reeking of compromise; while the ideological bureaucracy was outraged by the author's failure to lie more bravely. The great speech of indictment was delivered personally at a writers' meeting at Party headquarters in 1952 by the 'Hungarian Zhdanov', József Révai, who, with a past in the left-wing avantgarde himself, was over-zealous in scrapping all remnants of revolutionary spirit not kept on a short lead. Révai's tone put paid to all hopes for a communist author of expressing even fractions of what he knew to be true without incurring the wrath of the Establishment. The main objection to the two volumes of the trilogy published up to then was that although they centred on working-class life in the White era, the Positive Hero ordered by Zhdanov (that is, the communist worker in the front line of the fight against Fascism) was not to be found in them. Déry, grilled in public by his inquisitors, defended himself as best he could and announced his plan, however unusual, to take the 'votes' of his readers as to how things should develop in the concluding volume. There was no tongue-in-the-cheek in that offer. It was the wriggling of a human being pierced like an insect by a sadist's pin. The 'concluding volume', however, has remained unwritten.[1]

For communists like Déry, the whiff of freedom under Nagy was a relief even greater than for non-communists, and their meeting with the released *Ávó* prisoners a revelatory shock. Déry had been known to entertain some doubts about the authorized stories on Rajk and others, but his suspicions fell miles short of the emerging facts. Literature is indebted for Déry's perfect two short stories to the author's concern with the subject: *Niki* (1956), the longer one, is the history of a fox-terrier who dies while her master is in gaol because 'no other animal can endure as much as the human can', and *Love* (1956) is a snap of the return to his wife of a man imprisoned for unintelligible reasons and suddenly released.

With other communists, fanaticized into complete credulity for a while, the shock of awakening was mainly coloured with remorse. Most moving of these was young László Benjámin, who had started as a budding poet in the pages of *Szép Szó* and whose gift of lyrical simplicity lent itself to a style of the Socialist Realism kind–once he believed in it. He had been one of those who staked everything on Rákosi's word; and on his confrontation with the truth he reacted no less emotionally. A poem to his friend Sándor Haraszti, released after frightful tortures, was significant. In it he made a vow 'To repair what can never be repaired'. In the middle fifties, with Rákosi still at the helm, no one dared to print it, but, roneoed and passed from hand to hand, it achieved a larger circulation than most journals.

The Writers' Union

The main field of political activity in the critical period following Nagy's fall was the Communist Party section of the Hungarian Writers' Association (or Union). At Déry's side the poet Zoltán Zelk (who had a career somewhat analogous to Benjámin's) was most active in drafting and moving resolutions urging, particularly, the extension of intellectual freedom which was, naturally enough, the author's first concern. But the demand for one freedom encouraged that for others; and after a while the Writers' Party Section became notorious as a wasps' nest of (so the Stalinists maintained) 'counter-revolutionary plottings and incitements'. An official Party document in December 1955 first confidentially, then publicly, denounced the activities of 'Déry, Zelk, and Co.' in terms which in Stalin's time

[1] In *No Verdict*, Déry dismisses *Answer* as simply a 'bad novel'. 'Verdict' or not, this is too sweeping to be accurate. The novel contains, for instance, a beautifully described love-episode between a strange scientist professor and a communist girl student.

would have marked their imminent arrest; and Rákosi thought of it even now, but his dictatorial power was broken. The weekly of the Writers' Union, *Irodalmi Ujság* (Literary Gazette) sided with the protesting authors and the authorities were almost helpless against it: if one editor was removed, his successor proved to be equally unmanageable, as did the successor after that. The *Gazette* was time and again confiscated but could not be essentially changed; and though predominantly literary in character, it was waited for by large and excited queues on the boulevard—its publishers simply could not print enough copies. The communist popularization of *kultura* happily boomeranged: literature, even its esoteric varieties, had become a public affair, and the visionary poetry of young Ferenc Juhász, for instance, who had started as a Socialist Realist peasant bard, and of the inveterate Ivory Tower poet Sándor Weöres, pilloried for years as a reactionary in Party literature, reached and moved masses of readers.

So great was the commotion around the rebel communist writers that Rákosi personally intervened several times. Once he invited to a heart-to-heart talk the President of the Union, the 'Narodnik' (Populist) author Péter Veres, who since 1948–49 had been banned from politics proper but had been always held in high esteem as a writer. In fact, Veres's personal relations with Rákosi had all the time been cordial, if only because Veres had in him a certain amount of that leftish anti-Semitism which could well be utilized in 'Zionist'-baiting as well as taking the wind out of right-wing racialists' sails. In the struggle between 'Rákosists' and 'Nagyists', Veres chose to sit on a dignified fence: 'after all, it is an internal Party matter, no concern of ours . . .'. Yet, the general trend towards freedom appealed to him, and he could not conceal his sympathies. 'Don't you see you are being duped by a pack of Jewish boys?', Rákosi asked, to win him over. Then Rákosi talked with some of the unruly 'Jewish boys' in similarly heart-to-heart terms. 'Have you lost all sense of proportion, young comrades?', he castigated them. 'The former pandoor officers and county magistrates are applauding you; you are playing into the hands of the Jew-baiters! And once Péter Veres gets a bigger say, *he* won't allow Jews like yourselves to carry on in the limelight . . .'. He tried to rule by dividing once again.

Theatrical censorship became one of the most controversial issues. The communist playwright Gyula Háy (1900–) was prominent in that controversy. Háy had earned some international reputation with his historical drama *God, Emperor, Peasant,* produced on the Berlin stage in the last year of the Weimar Republic, and spent the subsequent years partly in Russia. He returned to Hungary in 1945 and became a popular playwright—as popular as a Muscovite could be.

Shaken by the revelations made under Imre Nagy, he wrote a play, *The Justice of Jasper Varró* ('Varró Gáspár igazsága'), depicting the plight of the Hungarian poor peasantry under the *kolkhoz* system; it was printed in 1955 and rehearsed in the National Theatre, but Rákosi, after his comeback, prevented its performance. At the same time, the many-sided author László Németh, who had played a leading part in the intellectual life of the late 1930s, had a similar experience with his play *Galileo* which dealt with an Inquisition unmistakably reminiscent of the *Ávó*; the Rákosi-Hegedüs administration banned it from the stage. Non-Party and de-Stalinizing communist authors thus met in the community of their grievances – and the grievances of those for whom they were speaking. Háy, incidentally, became very popular as a spirited publicist, which he had never been before; his skit on the Party bureaucrat, *Why don't I like Comrade Kucsera?*, was to become, in 1956, a piece incessantly quoted.

The '1956 Youth'

After the writers – youth. There was a Petőfi Circle, founded on 17 March 1956 – originally devised by the diehard Party ideologists as an instrument for rallying undergraduates and other young men of intellectual curiosity, giving them the illusion of free research and debate while keeping a firm hold on them behind the scenes. But this scheme boomeranged just like the loving manipulation with *kultura*. The Petőfi Circle convoked one public meeting after another – on historiography, philosophy, the natural resources of the country, on the teaching of music with Zoltán Kodály's scholarly attendance – but no subject could be too academic to stir up political emotions; especially if, for instance, Julia Rajk appeared in the audience and addressed it on the question of 'judges and lawyers under socialism'. Then came the climax. A debate 'on the Press' was advertised by the Circle for 27 June at 7 p.m. – but by 4 p.m. the hall where it was to take place was full up, and the crowds gathered in the neighbouring courtyards and parks where loudspeakers were set up to relay the speeches. The meeting lasted until after 3 a.m., with the audience blithely enduring the inconveniences of such a long session, including the risk of being photographed by the *Ávó* agents known to be placed with their cameras on the roofs. The main speaker was Tibor Déry. With his low-pitched, velvety voice, he made an impressive speaker. 'I am a writer and cannot bear to see people suffering', he said, and his audience were captivated. His concluding sentences amounted to a revolutionary appeal. He recalled the example of Petőfi and his followers, 'the March Youth' or the '1848 Youth' as they live in Hungarian memory. 'I should like to see a 1956 Youth equally worthy of being remembered by posterity.'

Within three days, Déry's expulsion from the Party and the
Circle's condemnation by the Party were announced, but the drive
for liberalization could no longer be stopped. It had in fact received
a boost from Moscow. The Twentieth Congress and the world
publicity secured for Khrushchev's famous Secret Speech, simultaneously with the repercussions of new Russian writings such as *Not
by Bread Alone*, revived the hope and belief, in abeyance since
Malenkov's fall, that the U.S.S.R. herself was on the verge of transforming herself into a democracy. Rákosi was prepared to compromise with the new trend so long as it did not affect his own position.
He renewed his favourite tactic of trying to outwit the liberalizers by
effecting a *modus vivendi* with the remnants of traditional authority.
At a comparatively early date (14 October 1955) Archbishop Grősz,
sentenced for plotting to overthrow the People's Republic,[1] was
released; and on 11 May 1956 the archbishop became Chairman of
the Bench of Bishops. The release of the Smallholder leaders and of
practically all Social Democrats was completed, presumably under
pressure from Moscow, by that same time (May 1956), although
Rákosi blocked it as long as he could. But the bitterest pill for Rákosi
to swallow was the rehabilitation of his own victimized comrades.
Yet to save his own position, he swallowed even that: on 21 February,
the Hungarian Party gazette paid tribute to Béla Kun, as a victim of
Stalin's Personality Cult; and on 29 March, Rákosi publicly ate his
own words–declaring at the very last that *all* charges against the
victims of the Rajk trial, including Rajk himself, had been trumped
up. The criminals had been Beria and Gábor Péter.

It was too late to win over the communist intelligentsia with such
admissions. Rákosi was called a Judas and, at a Party meeting which
he attended, a young schoolmaster, György Litván by name, told
him to his face: 'Comrade Rákosi, the Hungarian people no longer
trust you.'

Rákosi Ousted, Rajk Reburied

'Will he stay or go?' was the one question people debated throughout the first half of 1956 in Hungary. Rákosi insisted (and told
Moscow so) that once he was out it would be the end. His response to
the speeches at the Writers' Union and the Petőfi Circle was to draw
up a list of people who should be arrested at once: they counted some
four hundred and were headed by Imre Nagy and Tibor Déry. The
Central Committee of the Communist Party was absorbed in

---

[1] So much of this charge was true, that he had taken part, in consultation with
American diplomats, in talks about appointing a new government, as *homo regius*
('the man acting for an absent king'), in the event of a change. I learned this from
his prospective premier, the Very Reverend Pál Bozsik, in prison hospital.

thrashing out the pros and cons of such a step when, on 18 July, there came a knock at the door to announce the arrival from Moscow of Comrade Anastas Mikoyan, First Deputy Chairman of the Council of Ministers of the Union of Soviet Socialist Republics. The visitor's title was a long one, but the message he brought was short: Rákosi must resign. Rákosi turned pale and excused himself for some minutes. He rang Khrushchev: 'If I go everything collapses', he began, but was interrupted: 'Nothing will collapse. You must resign.' And Rákosi resigned. For the third time in his life he took refuge in the Soviet Union (though not in the Lux Hotel).

Rákosi's successor as First Secretary to the Party was Gerő. Gerő was less involved with mass killings and Personality Cult rituals but known to be, if possible, an even more dedicated Soviet agent than Rákosi. Other changes in personnel (Farkas's expulsion from the Party, Kádár's admission to the Politbureau, etc.) were too technical in character for the general public to appreciate. Thus the Kremlin, by dropping Rákosi, made a concession to national opinion that was big enough to whet appetites for further change but not to allay the hatred of Soviet domination. Could some bolder reshuffling—say, Imre Nagy's reinstatement—have succeeded in turning Hungarians into willing partners of the Soviet Union? Possibly not; but it seems a pity that it was not even tried.

Gerő carried on with 'democratization'—the slogan had after all come from Moscow—repairing past errors dutifully, and only cautiously dragging his feet. Tito, who had mercilessly snubbed a subdued Rákosi, was willing to turn a blind eye to Gerő's share in the Rákosi set-up at the time of the anti-Yugoslav campaign: he met Gerő several times, and friendly relations were re-established between Belgrade and Budapest. This was Gerő's one signal success in the three months of his dictatorship.

During 16–21 September, the Writers' Union held its general meeting and elected a Presidium on the basis of free nomination and a secret ballot—a proceeding unparalleled since 1947. It was an anti-Stalinist victory. The new Presidium consisted mainly of Reform communists (Déry, Zelk, Benjámin, Juhász, Háy, etc.) and 'Narodniks' (Illyés, Péter Veres, László Németh, the Transylvanian author Áron Tamási, etc.) with a few non-Party socialists (Kassák, the poet József Fodor, etc.); the Establishment communists, including the Minister of Culture, József Darvas, all lost their seats.

It was one of those dramatic moments in Hungarian history: writers, mostly highbrow writers, acting as the leaders of the nation. After the authors, kindred professions joined in—journalists, scholars, scientists, artists, educationalists—and, most passionately of all, university youth. And its ripples spread wider and wider; the names of esoteric poets became household words in industrial suburbs and far-away villages; workers' and peasants' delegations flocked to the offices of the Writers' Union. The belief in *kultura* was paying dividends; so was, even more ironically, the Zhdanovite cry that authors must regularly visit factories and *kolkhozi*, must learn to talk to manual workers, and must take notice of their problems, their desires.

On 6 October (a day chosen in remembrance of the Hungarian rebel generals hanged by the Austrians on 6 October 1849), some 200,000 people attended the solemn reburial of Rajk and his leading comrades. The speeches at the graveside glowed with bitterness against Rákosi and his close associates, against Personality Cult, against the memory of the Stalin era; and the speakers were, to a man, communists. The bitterness they voiced was not contradicted by a single soul; 'but surely', some were murmuring, 'Rajk himself was as much a murderer as those who had him hanged?' It was the murmur of a small minority: the masses, whatever their attitudes towards Rajk's politics, saw the martyr in him, and a step towards their own liberty in his rehabilitation. Yet divergence was becoming apparent between the would-be humanizers of communism and the crusaders against it. Most people were uncommitted in this controversy: they only knew they wanted a freer and better life.

Chapter 12

The Revolution of 1956

'Russians, Go Home!'

FROM 23 OCTOBER TO 4 NOVEMBER 1956, the world watched aghast what was going on in Hungary. These were the 'Thirteen Days That Shook the Kremlin'.[1] The preceding reform era had been initiated in Moscow, by Malenkov and, with enhanced impetus at the Twentieth Congress, by Khrushchev; and the determination to defy the Soviet Union was inspired from Warsaw by the example of equally staunch communists, notably the new First Secretary to the Polish Party, and former prisoner of Stalin, Władysław Gomułka. Between 18 and 21 October, communist Poland won a bloodless war of independence against the U.S.S.R.: Gomułka, in the face of Soviet troops marching on Warsaw, asserted his country's right to 'choose her own road to socialism'; and Khrushchev, after dramatic hesitation, concurred. Poland was to remain in the communist fold but with far greater elbowroom for her government and freedom of thought and worship for her citizens than hitherto imaginable. Hungary responded to such news promptly, with an outburst of meetings and resolutions. Academic youth was haunted by the memories of 1848: in that year, on 15 March, the leaders of the revolutionary marchers had formulated in 'Twelve Points' the 'Demands of the Hungarian Nation', and it was a leaflet containing them which, together with Petőfi's thrilling poem, 'Arise, Hungarian . . .', had left the press as 'the first uncensored piece of print in Hungary'. In 1956, from 18 October onwards, the drafting of similar Points, varying from five to twenty, marked the transformation of an urge for reforms into readiness to take up arms. Although conceived in a mood of elation, they make uninspiring reading today; they were mostly couched in Party jargon and congested with references to factional conflicts and with vague and florid appeals to patriotic pride and the sense of human dignity. They revealed national unanimity on fundamentals but also the lack of a programme of action. After resolutions enthusiastically passed in the provincial cities of Győr and Szeged, on 22 October, the Budapest students' organiza-

---

[1] Title of a best-selling book on the Hungarian Revolution by Tibor Méray, London and New York, 1959.

tions decided on a demonstration for the following day, to express their solidarity with the Poles. They would meet in front of the Writers' Union and march to the statue of Petőfi and that of Joseph Bem, the Polish general who fought in the Hungarian War for Independence of 1848–49.

23 October started with the usual symptoms of government hysteria in face of a threatening revolution: the march, at first permitted, was banned by midday and repermitted later on. The Petőfi Club issued a Ten-Point resolution, and Péter Veres, as President of the Writers' Union, read out a Seven-Point one from the pedestal of the Petőfi statue at about 3 p.m. But by then few could be bothered with Points. One cry electrified the thousands round the statue: 'Imre Nagy to the government!' In a few hours' time the crowd swelled to tens of thousands and as it roved from Pest to the Bem statue in Buda and back to the Pest embankment, another cry drowned all the rest: *Ruszkik haza!*–'Russians, go home!'

Nagy was attending a wine harvest near Lake Balaton when the revolt broke out. He was persuaded to return to Budapest at once: everybody expected him to act, either as a leader, or as a safety valve. In the evening, a group of his close followers persuaded him to go to Parliament Square, where the greatest crowd was, and address those gathered there. 'Comrades!' he began, and was booed. 'So you are booing me?', he retorted. 'Not you but that word', they shouted. Should an avowed communist accept the leadership of a crowd that loathes the very word 'Comrade'? There was no time to weigh such problems. He tried to reassure and calm the crowd; 'we want constitutional order and discipline', he told them, and hurried away to see the Party leaders in the Central Committee. He got a hostile reception. They reproached him with having pushed the country into anarchy; and he reproached them with the same thing. Yet he stayed on–and they wanted him to. No solution seemed possible without him. By the following morning, he was appointed premier. Hegedüs, his predecessor, became his deputy, with Gerő staying on as First Secretary to the Party.

This was announced at 8.15 a.m. on 24 October. But many things had happened by then, and it could never be established how much Nagy knew or understood of those happenings, nor how far he participated in the decisions taken overnight.

'Who Fired First?'

Early in the evening of the 23rd, Gerő gave a radio address which was like throwing petrol on fire. 'Down with Gerő!' the crowds chanted as they roamed the streets. 'He dared to call us Fascist rabble!', some furiously explained. In fact, his radio address contained nothing of the kind; it was just a rigmarole of Party shibbo-leths, flavoured as usual with adulation of Soviet Russia and diluted slightly more than usual with humanitarian and patriotic Hungarian clichés. He is supposed to have used the alleged abusive terms when talking to a delegation led by the author Gyula Háy, who is supposed to have reported on this to others, so that by the time the rumour spread, the audience believed they had heard it from Gerő himself over the radio, which may or may not have been the case. The essential fact, however, was Gerő's inability to keep track of what was going on around him. Louis XVI could not have been more unaware of the *sans-culottes* and their passions than were the Stalinist chiefs of the bitterness and yearnings that drove the masses of students and workers into the street.

Near the Bem statue, there was a barracks whose soldiers gave un-mistakable signs of sympathy with the demonstrators. And in a matter of minutes, eight hundred cadets from the Petőfi Military Academy had joined them. These were hand-picked sons of 'pure proletarians' pampered and indoctrinated and therefore trusted as the storm-troopers of Rákosi's kingdom. They had been brought up in the cult of guerrilla warfare and trained in its methods. Now was the time for them to make use of their skills to destroy the spirit that had created them. Arms depots were sacked, rifles distributed among students and young workers; even fourteen- and fifteen-year-old schoolboys were shortly to emerge, equipped with rifles and red-white-and-green armbands, as insurgents or, in the rhetorical jargon that was later codified, 'freedom-fighters'. They were quick to invent their proper flag: the national tricolour with a big round hole show-ing where the Soviet-style crest had been cut out from it. The 'Kossuth crest', too, was to reappear shortly all over the country: the ancient national one, albeit without the royal crown, just as Kossuth had used it after the dethronement in 1849. But the authentic symbol of the Revolution was and remained that black hole in the red-white-and-green stripes.

The actual shooting started in front of the Radio building at about 9 p.m. on the 23rd. The students insisted that their Points be broadcast in full; the Radio staff was bargaining and temporizing, and tempers rose high in the street below. Then–'Who fired first?' was, as usual, the question subsequently debated. Probably, as the crowd's behaviour seemed threatening, the security guards fired warning shots, whereupon some of the trigger-happy insurgents shot at them. Lives were lost on both sides. The security guards succeeded in holding the Radio building, but at about 1.30 a.m. the crowd successfully stormed the building of *Szabad Nép* carrying with them the dead body of an insurgent wrapped in the tricolour. An extra edition of the paper condemned the security guards. Révai, most militant of the Stalinists kept up to then in high positions, was helped to escape through a back door.

In the City Park of Budapest, there stood a 24-foot statue of Stalin with the inscription: *To the great Stalin, from the grateful Hungarian people.* This was pulled down the same night by a crowd which comprised, allegedly, 5,000 students. As a work of art, the statue was a typical piece of socialist-realist hero-worship, showy though conventional; but by a chance collusion between the problem of demolition and the improvisatory genius of those who tackled it, the nearly-demolished statue was turned into a masterpiece. Its two terrific jackboots remained on the pedestal.

Pavements in the suburbs were torn up, trams overturned, barricades erected. In Debrecen–the largest town of east Hungary–the insurgents seized power.

Nagy–Premier or Prisoner?

Meanwhile, at 4.30 a.m. on the 24th, Radio Budapest announced that as 'Fascist and reactionary elements have launched an armed attack . . . on our forces of law and order . . .' the government banned 'all assemblies, meetings, or demonstrations', and the law would be applied 'with full rigour against troublemakers'. At about the same time or shortly afterwards (exactly when was never ascertained) 'the government . . . has applied for help to the Soviet formations stationed in Hungary under the terms of the Warsaw Treaty' (a Mutual Help agreement signed between the U.S.S.R. and her European satellites on 14 May 1955). 'In compliance with the government's request, the Soviet formations are taking part in the restoration of order', Radio Budapest announced at 9 a.m. on 24 October–shortly after Nagy's premiership had been announced on the same wavelengths; Soviet tanks, however, had been in action since 4.30 or 5 a.m. They were received, fittingly, with 'Molotov cocktails'. Meanwhile, martial law against the insurgents was declared in a government decree. How far was Nagy responsible for this and the armed Soviet intervention? Hegedüs is on record as having threatened the rebels with Soviet intervention in the last hours of his premiership; nothing of the kind was said by Nagy. Yet he seemed to concur; and his first radio address after his appointment was an appeal to the insurgents to cease fighting. Did he act so because, as later suggested, he was to all intents a prisoner of the Stalinist rearguard at Party headquarters? Or was he convinced that it was the right course to take, and that by adding his own, mellowed voice to the provocative voices of Gerő and Hegedüs, he was doing the very utmost possible in the circumstances? It was probably a combination of both, at a moment of total confusion.

Most Genuine of Revolutions: Headless and United

There was a mixture of general internecine warfare and unparalleled unity of purpose. 'Revolutionary councils' and 'workers' councils' and 'youth councils' proliferated all over the country, five-pointed red stars and other emblems associated with Soviet domination were torn down, and a general strike was declared. Strike against whom? Against the government? The government had melted to a powerless symbol, not worth striking at. Against Nagy? Though his popularity had waned rapidly, he was still the visible leader to be won over for firm action; the 'councils' delegations' flooded his antechamber which was guarded by security police (whether with or without his consent was anybody's guess). Or was the common enemy the Soviet intruder? Indeed, 'Russians, go home!' was the cry raised by everybody, including those communists whose voice could be heard; but hope still existed that even the Soviet military would endorse the aims of the Hungarian Revolution. Rumour spread that some Soviet units had joined the freedom-fighters—and scenes of fraternization certainly took place. The identifiable villains were thus reduced to those communist leaders most conspicuously compromised by Personality Cult and the detested Ávó, equated with the security police. The latter were, indeed, the only group actively to resist the revolutionary (or, as the Stalinists called it, 'counter-revolutionary') trend; and even these did so mostly because, in their uniforms and with their records, they saw no help for it. The Hungarian Workpeople's Party with its million-or-so members had practically vanished.

The real reason for striking was psychological; as there had been no chance of doing so for some twenty-five years, it was a fulfilment to make use of this cherished right. But demagogues and adventurers were on the spot to make themselves strike leaders and claim high positions. It was ironically reminiscent of the Bolshevik Revolution of 1917: the Councils (i.e., Soviets) were determined to overrule the National Assembly (i.e., Duma). Most of the 1956 Workers' Councillors came from proletarian families and had been educated in Marxist–Leninist seminaries; but sons of the former gentry and capitalists also figured among them. Again, Rákosi's campaign had misfired: the more he denigrated the dispossessed gentlefolk, the more the workers took their part, and thus the composition of the Councils of 1956 reflected a combination of 'Soviet' spirit with nostalgia for the paternalistic Hungary of the past. The rebel army and their juvenile snipers showed a similarly chequered pattern: the initial impetus came from youths brought up in communist organizations, but former officers of Horthy's army were granted key positions, if only to make use of their skill. Within a couple of days, the streets of Budapest were littered with burnt-out tanks and sub-machine-gun nests, with bricks and splintered glass and a general shambles, and corpses lay about on the pavement until buried in haste. Passionate and inarticulate arguments could be heard wherever a crowd gathered, but if ideas were not unanimous, idealism was; no one touched, for instance, the goods behind the broken shop-windows. Honesty as a mark of national unity became a fashion so powerful that not even professional thieves felt like defying it.

The Nagy government seemed even more undecided than the masses. On the 24th, 'unconditional surrender' was demanded from the insurgents, but the surrender deadline was extended again and again, with understanding expressed for those who had up to then disobeyed orders. Kádár, one of the few communists who had still some credit with the workers, declared in his broadcast that 'the demonstration by university youth which began with the formulation of demands on the whole acceptable, has swiftly degenerated into a demonstration against our democratic order'; and he expressed 'burning anger' about the crimes committed by 'Fascist reactionary elements'. Nagy, on the following day, announced his intention to ask the Soviet forces to pull out of Hungary, but urged his countrymen to facilitate this by restoring calm and order. He remained unheeded: the killings increased, and the lust for revenge got out of hand. In Parliament Square, on the 25th, Soviet and security forces opened fire on a crowd, killing an estimated three hundred to eight hundred, and wounding five or six times as many on this single occasion. On the 24th–25th, a decisive blow was struck at the Stalinist rearguard which still claimed command over the 'Hungarian People's Army'. The Defence Minister István Bata, ordered a young field officer, Colonel Pál Maléter, a Soviet-trained former partisan whom he completely trusted, to approach the rebel soldiers in the Kilian Barracks and either 'bring them to their senses' peacefully or crush them by force. The Kilian Barracks was situated so as practically to dominate the southern part of the city of Pest, and a formation of five tanks was put at Maléter's disposal to subdue it. Maléter, after some talk with the insurgents, came to the conclusion, as he reported in a message to Minister Bata, that these 'were not bandits, but loyal sons of Hungary'; that they, as well as himself, wanted nothing but a 'free, independent, and socialist Hungary'; and that he had therefore decided to go over to their side. In fact, he took charge of Kilian Barracks at once and then swiftly rose to be commander-in-chief of the revolutionary forces.

The Ugly Features

Heroic defiance of the invader was coupled with ugly scenes. A crowd marched in front of the Parliament building in time with a shrill female voice that chanted: 'Murderous government, resign! Murderous government, resign!' So Imre Nagy had been declared a 'murderer' overnight. And in the middle of the city, in Váci utca (the traditional Bond Street of Budapest under all régimes), the main Party bookshop was sacked and a huge pile of books and leaflets and gramophone records burned on the pavement. They were mostly nauseating stuff, made for shovelling down the throats of Hungarian readers, but their flames were nonetheless alarmingly reminiscent of the Nazi bonfires of books. These smelt of 'counter-revolution' indeed. Uglier even than these were the manhunts and the lynchings. 'Ávós, ávós!'–*Ávó*-man!–the howl went up, and the unfortunate victim of mob hatred was shot or beaten to death on the spot, and sometimes hanged upside down, with one or two hysterical women spitting at the corpse. Once lynch law takes over, innocents are bound to suffer: who in that turmoil could ascertain whether the man singled out for vengeance was really an 'ávós'? Even if found in the hated, blue-lapelled uniform, he might have been innocent; quite a number of poor lads had been recruited willy-nilly for the force. Moreover, the most notorious thugs of the Stalinist years had, by the outbreak of the revolt, already been imprisoned (Péter, etc.), or at any rate moved into less conspicuous positions. As is always the case: the innocent or the little crook caught on the spot was made to pay for the absent master scoundrels.[1]

[1] I was unhappy to witness such scenes at that time in the Budapest streets. Some of the very ugliest were instantly photographed and published–not in the Soviet Press but in the West, for instance, by *Time-Life* magazines. Possibly the most revolting of these scenes was that of Republic Square, Budapest, on 30 October, when insurgents mowed down a security unit which, after clarifying a misunderstanding, had surrendered to them. A victim was the respectable communist functionary Imre Maző. Such events should be remembered and condemned, with unqualified disgust and sorrow. But this is no reason, of course, for inventing additional abominations. The information and propaganda agencies of the Hungarian government that took over from 4 November 1956 onwards have described manhunts to the cry of 'Communist!' and informed Westerners of manhunts after 'Jews!' These are, to the best of my knowledge, lies. I naturally could not inspect every district of the country, but in Budapest, where I moved about a great deal, neither 'Communist' nor 'Jew' was used as a term of abuse during the Revolution.

Personally, I tried my best to stop the hunting of 'ávós', mainly through my influence in the Writers' Union, but we did not act as quickly as we should have done. Yet, on 1 November, an appeal on behalf of our Union, signed by a number of its leaders (including myself), was broadcast over 'Free Radio Kossuth', protesting against the acts of violence and urging that the guilty be handed over to the legal authorities. On 3 November, the last night before the Soviet reoccupation, in my own broadcast I pointed out that acts of illegal revenge were not only repellent but might be fatal for our national revolution.

The Legend of a Western Plot

Spontaneity, verging on leaderlessness, was the endearing but fatal feature of this revolution. The allegation, since then parroted by Kremlin spokesmen, that it was an 'imperialist capitalist plot' is absolute nonsense. If the revolutionaries did get some outside help, at least morally, it came from communists in Yugoslavia, Poland, and even China, and not at all from 'capitalists'. The Western 'imperialists' did indeed do great damage–not by knowing and preparing for what was to come, but by their unawareness of it even after the event and by their subsequent, irresponsible meddling. This applies particularly to the American-sponsored Radio Free Europe, which disposed of far more wavelengths and broadcasting hours in Magyar, and employed a much greater advisory and technical staff, Hungarian and non-Hungarian, than any other broadcasting station talking to Hungarians from anywhere outside Hungary, from Moscow to Madrid. 'Whatever Imre Nagy does, he is a communist and not to be trusted', was the message unmistakably implied in its comments on Hungarian events; he had the 'mark of Cain upon his forehead', in the words of one speaker. And then it clamoured for proclaiming Cardinal Mindszenty the leader of the Revolution. Unfortunately but understandably, this was a successful campaign; the cardinal, with his aura of suffering at godless hands, and bolstered up by what looked like the greatest economic and military power in the world, became the centre of reverent attention. Meanwhile, he was dumb. Though his reinstatement as Primate had from the outset been a foregone conclusion, this was not officially announced until 31 October, and then his first statement was only a pledge that he would shortly broadcast a message to the nation. His hesitation was, again, understandable, but not a feat of revolutionary leadership.

The Russians proceeded even more stupidly than the Western propaganda chiefs. The luck that saved them from ultimate disaster must not deceive students of these events. Their first intervention was a tremendous military blunder: as they only sent tank units, without infantry for house-to-house fighting, they could take possession of vantage-points but not penetrate all blocks of flats and other hiding places of the snipers. They could only have won the battle by exterminating Budapest. But that was neither their instruction nor their desire. They were baffled and bewildered, restricted to defensive action while the Hungarian teenagers dictated events in the streets of Budapest. 'Budapest's schoolboys defeated the Red Army', the saying went round, and foolish though its smugness might be, facts could be quoted to support it.

Mikoyan on the Spot

The Soviet deputy premiers Anastas Mikoyan and Mikhail Suslov arrived in Budapest on 24 October and spent three days in practically uninterrupted talks with the members of the Politbureau and the government. Witnessing some of the scenes in the streets of Budapest, they could have no illusions about the feelings of the Hungarian people; and gracefully to accede to Hungary's independence, as Nagy suggested, must have seemed to them the wisest way to salvage anything of Soviet prestige. They gave way in stages. On 25 October, Gerő was sacked and Kádár appointed First Party Secretary (whereupon Gerő, together with Hegedüs, fled to Russia). To make this change appear the one thing the insurgents had been fighting for, it was heralded by a radio call early in the morning: 'Hungarians, hang out the national flag!' There was, indeed, no risk in encouraging people to do so, as they had been doing it anyhow, though for other reasons. Then came the explanation why they should be jubilant: because János Kádár had been appointed First Party Secretary! Only half a year earlier, this would indeed have electrified the country. But after what appeared to be a victorious national rebellion and the foundering of a bankrupt communist dictatorship, any concession expressed in the One-Party jargon was bound to seem ridiculous.

Nor did the reshuffling of the Nagy government help, when announced on the 27th. This was a transition between a de-Stalinized one-party government and a coalition. But it was not, and could not be, totally de-Stalinized: the régime had been too much involved with the Rákosi era. The appointment of György Lukács as Minister of Popular Culture did make a good impression on communist élite youth, which had sparked off the revolt, but meant little to the masses. Of the non-communist ministers, the two reactivated old Smallholders, Zoltán Tildy (back from prison) and Béla Kovács (back from Soviet internment), commanded some sympathy but no longer carried weight, as the former was known to be a weakling and the latter seemed unable to make up his mind about anything; while the National Peasant representative, Ferenc Erdei, with his record of eager subservience to the Stalinists, was a deterrent rather than an attraction to non-communists. Social Democrats had not yet joined the coalition.

Independent, Democratic, Non-aligned Hungary–Seemingly with Soviet Blessing

The striking, fighting, and pouring-out of Points went on. Outside the capital, the bloodiest battle was that fought in the little west

Hungarian frontier town of Magyaróvár, on the 26th, when the security police opened fire on a crowd, killing more than eighty people in a matter of minutes. Three or four security officers were subsequently caught and lynched by the crowd.

Of the provincial centres, the north Hungarian industrial town of Miskolc emerged as the most agitated and most active in drafting Points and installing rule by council. But on the whole, all districts of town and country were in the same turmoil, and by the end of the month the main demands of the insurgents and indeed of the whole population had become clear.

They wanted a return to multi-party democracy, with a Communist Party that was legal but without special prerogatives.

They wanted freedom of worship, Press, and opinion comparable to that in Western democracies.

They wanted agriculture to be based on independent peasant holdings. Co-operatives should be allowed to carry on if their members so desired; but only on that condition. No land would be returned to its pre-1945 owners; the splitting-up of *latifundia* was irrevocable.

Manufacturing industry was to remain in public ownership, with far-reaching autonomies for the large plants or the networks of smaller plants, to be run by freely elected Workers' Councils.

The Soviet troops should be pulled out of the country as soon as possible, and steps should be taken towards making Hungary more independent from the U.S.S.R.—and ultimately 'non-aligned'.

The Russians seemed to be giving in on all points. Time and again, they warned Nagy to 'defend the socialist achievements', but did not on that ground object to democratic reforms. A factor often disregarded in power politics—feelings of guilt in at least some of the Soviet politicians—might have contributed to the fact that on 30 October the Soviet government issued a statement which condemned the 'violations and errors' committed 'in the relations between socialist states' and continued:

The 20th Congress of the Communist Party of the Soviet Union has resolutely condemned these violations and errors and has decided that the Soviet Union will henceforth base its relations with other socialist states on the Leninist principles of the equality of the rights of peoples. It has proclaimed the necessity of bearing in mind the history and the peculiarities of every country which is in process of building a new life. . . . Realizing that the maintenance in Hungary of Soviet divisions may serve as a pretext for aggravating the situation, the Soviet government has given instructions to its military commander to withdraw Soviet troops from the city of Budapest as soon as this shall be considered essential by the Hungarian government. At the same time the Soviet government is ready to undertake negotiations with the governments of the People's Republic of Hungary and of other signatories of the Warsaw Pact concerning the presence of Soviet troops on Hungarian territory . . .[1]

Even what must have appeared for Russians the bitterest pill in the package, Hungary's neutralization, could be considered acceptable so long as it was not presented as a snub to the U.S.S.R. but as part of an effort towards the liquidation of 'the policy of Blocs'; an effort advocated by Nagy in his *Memoranda* with reference both to the Five Principles declared at Bandung in April 1955 and to the vital stake of the U.S.S.R. in the cause of world peace.

Kádár about the 'Glorious Uprising of Our People'

When the above-quoted Soviet communiqué was issued, on 30 October, the withdrawal of Soviet troops from Budapest and other densely populated areas of the country had actually started. The security police having been replaced by a democratic police force recruited in haste, a cease-fire was declared and implemented between the Soviet forces and the main body of insurgents which, led by Maléter, by then accepted the guidance of the Nagy government. Nagy, meanwhile, announced the end of the One-Party system and the formation of a National Coalition government which would call a general election. Tildy speaking for the Smallholders, Erdei for the National Peasants, and, most significant, Kádár for the communists announced their wholehearted approval. Kádár, moreover, claimed credit on behalf of his comrades for the Revolution, particularly in his broadcast two days later when he said:

> In their glorious uprising, our people have shaken off the Rákosi régime. They have achieved freedom for the people and independence for the country. Without this there can be no socialism. We can safely say that the ideological and organisational leaders who prepared this uprising were recruited from among your [the communists'] ranks . . . Hungarian Communist writers, journalists, university students, the youth of the Petőfi Circle, thousands and thousands of workers and peasants, and veteran fighters who had been imprisoned on false charges, fought in the front line against Rákosite despotism . . .[2]

[1] *The Truth about the Nagy Affair*. Published for the Congress for Cultural Freedom, London, 1959, p. 52.
[2] Free Radio Kossuth, 1 November 1956. Cf. *The Hungarian Revolution*, A White Book, ed. Melvin J. Lasky, published for the Congress of Cultural Freedom, London, 1957, p. 179.

Despite such apparent unanimity on essentials, and the urgent need for action, it took four more days after Nagy's announcement until the full list of the provisional National Government could be announced; factional jockeying for positions made things difficult. Among the Social Democrats, their veteran leader, Anna Kéthly, and the Secretary-General of the revived party, Gyula Kelemen, had supported Nagy ever since the crisis; but a host of their lieutenants hampered them with interminable excuses for putting off the decision. The Smallholders, acting in the 1945 tradition as the conservative wing of the coalition, had to manoeuvre a great deal to obtain for this role even the tacit approval of Cardinal Mindszenty who, since his reinstatement as Primate, made difficulties even about whom he would 'receive in audience' as a government representative. The National Peasant Party changed its name to Petőfi Peasant Party to emphasize its break with the Stalinist past, and dropped Erdei from its leaders nominated for government membership. For similar reasons, the communist Hungarian Workingpeople's Party had been replaced by a Hungarian Socialist Workers' Party.

The Democratic Coalition

When at last on 3 November a full cabinet list was announced, it comprised three communists (Nagy, Kádár, Losonczy), three Smallholders (Tildy, Béla Kovács, István B. Szabó), three Social Democrats (Anna Kéthly, Kelemen, József Fischer), two Petőfi Peasants (István Bibó and Ferenc Farkas), and one non-party member, Maléter. Nagy retained the premiership and Foreign Affairs, Maléter was appointed Minister of Defence, and their colleagues were all appointed 'Ministers of State', while other ministries were run, so far as they could be run at all, by officials appointed or elected on the spot. General Maléter, together with his deputy and the military commander of the capital, General Béla Király, had in fact acted as members of the Nagy government since 30 October. Apart from them, the most interesting new name in the leading set-up was that of the legal philosopher Dr István Bibó (1911–) who had emerged as an important writer on politics after the war. He was the spokesman of a Third Road policy which he applied to the problems of the government coalition of 1945–46, to the relations between the eastern European states, to the Jewish question, etc.; and as he belonged to the National Peasant Party and not to the Social Democrats, he was allowed comparatively great freedom even in the 'Year of the Turning-Point', 1948. In the following years of Stalinist streamlining, however, he was silenced and confined to obscure jobs in the country. The thaw under the first Nagy government enabled him to return to Budapest and gradually to public life.

As he was known to be a dedicated believer in friendship with both the Soviet Union and the Western Powers, as well as with the neighbouring small nations, his name on the government list underlined the peaceful intentions of the victorious Revolution.

After the defeat by military force of the Revolution, the victors poured out a torrent of propaganda stories to demonstrate its 'counter-revolutionary' character. One of their allegations, the hunting down of 'ávós' (who were not even always real 'ávós'), was depressingly true, though the number of victims is probably much smaller than their wild and unsubstantiated charges would suggest.[1] But all other allegations calculated to give an impression of 'counter-revolutionary' plotting and terror were either perfectly false or related only to peripheral cases. A rapid mushrooming of parties did take place, and that somewhere in the country even Arrow Cross Fascists should have been speculating on a renewal of their chances is imaginable. Ex-landlords and ex-capitalists might have cropped up, either emerging suddenly from their humble retirement in Hungary or dropping in from the West in barely concealed hopes of presenting a stiff bill for their years of exile–in fact I knew of some such cases. And I can well believe what one of the *White Books* of the post-Revolution year, the one dealing with the events in County Veszprém, alleges: that one of its former squires openly declared that in a matter of days he would reoccupy the big estates he had lost in the 1945 Land Reform, but 'the *kolkhoz* peasants have nothing to fear, I will employ ten of them as my farmhands at once and the eleventh can join them as my dishwasher.' Smug and silly people have existed everywhere, and will always be tempted to fish in the troubled waters of rebellion. But the government coalition had nothing to do with such people. Some self-appointed leaders in factories brought to a standstill agitated for a sort of military dictatorship: 'Why so bloody many parties? Let Maléter and General Király take over!' This was indeed the potential germ of a new Fascism, but then it should be recognized that a nationalist junta dictatorship is necessarily Fascist-like in character, whatever its ideological pretext. In any case, Nagy and his colleagues were

[1] 239 Hungarians were killed by the 'counter-revolutionaries', according to present-day Hungarian government estimates. In fact, however, most of those listed disappeared in conditions never cleared up, and many were actually killed as insurgents *by* the *Ávó*. The Hungarian government *White Book* enumerates altogether 84 state security men–43 officers, 10 warrant officers, 31 security guards–among the victims; of these, 20 seem to have been lynched, the rest killed in battle (cf. Gosztony, Péter, *Az ÁVH és a forradalom*–'The Ávó and the Revolution'–Munich, 1966.) Non-*Ávó* communists lynched amounted to a very small number. Of the Soviet soldiers captured not one was lynched; most were handed over to Soviet units after 1 November, while a few joined the insurgents and stayed with them, as far as can be ascertained.

unanimous in rejecting such tendencies. There were some military gang-leaders trying to snatch power, and the one who made most trouble, József Dudás, was a sort of National Communist. He was arrested, though only temporarily, on Nagy's orders and then rearrested on Kádár's orders and executed some ten weeks later as a Fascist; which indeed he potentially was.

Hungary, though beset with heavy complications, was feeling her way towards a genuine Social Democracy. But a catastrophe threw her off course.

The Catastrophe Foreshadowed

The Soviet troops had no sooner started pulling out than they prepared for reoccupation. Was it from indecision or perfidy? Really from both: they were hesitating all the time, and their perfidy consisted rather of breaking their pledges on a succession of hypocritical pretexts than of premeditated double-dealing. Meanwhile, the Soviet leaders double-crossed one another too. On 30 October, Mikoyan terminated a second, hit-and-run visit to Budapest with an assurance to Nagy that all Hungarian wishes would be met by the Russians. On that very day, however, Nagy was informed that while some Soviet units withdrew, others were advancing. The Soviet ambassador, Yuri Andropov, whom Nagy asked for an explanation, argued that these moves were of a technical nature only, since the Soviet army had to secure its own routes of evacuation, including access to the airfields. At first some credence could be given to this argument, but not when a steady flow of fresh Soviet troops from across the frontier was reported. Nagy demanded explanations more and more urgently both from the Kremlin itself and from the embassy in Budapest; the Kremlin seemed dumbfounded and Andropov's explanation vague and unconvincing. The threat of a new Soviet invasion became unmistakable. Nagy was pressed from all quarters to 'act'. After consulting his colleagues in the Party, the government, and the Foreign Ministry, on 1 November he announced Hungary's withdrawal from the Warsaw Pact and appealed to the United Nations to guarantee Hungary's neutrality.

This, without any doubt, was pure folly. Whether the Kremlin could have been manoeuvred into a gesture of benign consent to neutrality, as had seemed likely at the last Nagy–Mikoyan meeting, may be a matter of opinion, but that garnishing it with an 'appeal for U.N. guarantee' would make it less and not more acceptable to Moscow was obvious. Moreover, Nagy and his colleagues were informed of the Suez crisis which had flared up two days before and made it the most inappropriate moment conceivable for a concerted American–British–French action in the Danube valley. Despite this ill-advised Hungarian gesture, there were politicians in the Kremlin (possibly Mikoyan) who thought that a display of generosity would still pay, while some leading soldiers (Marshal Zhukov, allegedly) wanted to limit the operation to the securing of strategic bases and then come to terms with the Nagy coalition, instead of imposing a quisling government on the country. Khrushchev, a few years later, in one of his torrential public outpourings, himself disclosed the painful conflict of opinions among the Soviet leaders before they decided for intervention in Hungary. Their moderates were certainly not helped by what must have struck them as lack of moderation at the Hungarian end.

Poor Imre Nagy fell victim to the faulty judgement of his inadequate advisers. But it can well be put forward in his defence that hardly a single voice was raised against the final fatal decision. In the de-Stalinized Politbureau of his own Party, only two old Muscovites, György Lukács and Zoltán Szántó, expressed some misgivings; the rest were heart and soul for instant neutrality. As to the Party Secretary, Kádár, he not only approved but exceeded his colleagues in vehemence when facing Ambassador Andropov, who had been summoned to be formally notified of the government's decision. 'What happens to me is of little importance', Kádár is alleged to have said,[1] 'but I am ready, as a Hungarian, to fight if necessary. If your tanks enter Budapest, I will go into the streets and fight you with my bare hands.'

Non-communists may or may not have been more concerned about Soviet susceptibilities than the Politbureau seemed to be, but in any case there was no way in which they could have voiced their concern without appearing to denounce Nagy and his followers to the Kremlin. Moreover, public opinion was so overwhelmingly for renouncing the Warsaw Pact that to put in a word of warning would have seemed suicidal to any Hungarian politician or writer.

A Glimmer of Hope

Anxiety clouded many minds, but in their hopes people were more united than ever. All Souls' Day, 2 November, dawned on them in a mood that was tense but elated. The revolutionary number of the *Literary Gazette* was read aloud in the streets, with Gyula Illyés's poem *One Sentence about Tyranny*, and Tibor Déry's lyrical prose appeal, 'Respect the Dead!' Imre Nagy had regained his popularity; if possible he had even increased it. Not even Radio Free Europe attacked him any longer. The workers seemed ready not only to fight for Hungarian freedom, as they had been from the first, but even to resume work for it; negotiations between a government-

[1] *Thirteen Days that Shook the Kremlin*, p. 194.

appointed commission and the delegates of labour organizations were visibly yielding results, precipitated by the Social Democrats' decision formally to join the coalition. News from abroad? Neither good nor bad; just keeping you guessing. From the West: admiration for Hungary, immense admiration, boundless admiration. And even money for needy Hungarians: President Eisenhower said $20 million! Meanwhile, at the United Nations, the American delegate was devoting himself to quite a different cause: namely, urging Britain, France, and Israel to leave Egypt alone in Suez. Nagy's request to guarantee Hungary's neutrality (repeated on this day) was taken note of but not discussed; in any case, the Soviet delegate denied that Soviet troops had crossed into Hungary. From Moscow, there was no news; neither conciliatory messages nor threats. Kádár had disappeared, which puzzled and worried his comrades; they decided not to disclose it. Most disturbing of all was the movement of Soviet troops: they took possession of all key points of communication, especially at the airfields.

The following day, 3 November, brought a glimmer of hope in the agonizing suspense. At midday a Soviet military delegation, headed by General Malinin, presented itself in Parliament (where the Hungarian government was provisionally in session) to ask for the appointment of a Hungarian committee with which details of the Soviet military evacuation could be discussed. The Hungarian committee was appointed at once and, headed by General Maléter, started negotiating on the spot. At 6 p.m., General Király (Maléter's deputy) learned that there was agreement on essentials though not on all particulars. The Russians said they would be unable to pull out completely before 15 January; the Hungarians appreciated the reasons for avoiding the semblance of panicky haste but insisted that the evacuation could be completed in good order by 15 December. Meanwhile, it was agreed that the withdrawing Soviet troops should be given a friendly farewell; it was in the interests of both sides to recognize that the Soviet army had not sought territorial aggrandizement or loot but had only entered Hungary at the request of the then Hungarian government. Negotiations were then adjourned, but only until later the same night: at 9 p.m. a Soviet military car took the Hungarian delegation to Soviet military headquarters at the village of Tököl on Csepel Island, to continue the talks. The delegation comprised, besides military leaders, the most tenacious survivor of Hungarian public life, the deposed National Peasant leader Ferenc Erdei—a Hungarian Vicar of Bray. At eleven o'clock, Maléter rang Király in Budapest just to assure him that 'everything is going well'.

From the Parliament building (which served also provisionally as a radio centre) Cardinal Mindszenty broadcast his message to the nation. He declared that Hungary wished 'to live in friendship and mutual respect with both the great United States of America and the mighty Russian Empire' and to have no enemies anywhere. As to home affairs, notably the relations between Church and state, he emphasized at the beginning of his address that his views had not changed during eight years of silence; and, unfortunately, this was only too well borne out by what followed. Under the subsequent, Soviet-imposed government, communists made a habit of referring to this speech as a counter-revolutionary incitement to restore the *latifundia*. That is untrue; the cardinal did not 'incite' to anything; but that his address was packed with disturbing pontifications and irrelevances ('I who, by virtue of my office, stand outside and above parties', etc.) is true.[1] For all its deficiencies, however, it had at that moment a pacifying effect.

The Bitter End

This night, from 3 to 4 November, was in fact the first since 23 October which the people of Budapest could sleep through without being disturbed by, at the very least, rifle-shots. In the small hours came the awakening, to the rumble of tanks and the thunder of heavy guns. At 0519 hours Imre Nagy personally announced over the Budapest Radio:

> Today at daybreak Soviet forces started an
> attack against our capital, obviously with
> the intention to overthrow the legal Hungarian
> democratic Government.
> Our troops are fighting.
> The Government is in its place.
> This is my message to the people of our
> country and to the entire world.

Translations of the announcement, patriotic tunes, and some more dramatic short broadcasts followed. A spokesman of the Writers' Union (Gyula Háy, who was on the spot) appealed for help to the intellectuals of the world. A broadcaster on behalf of the Hungarian government appealed to the Soviet soldiers in Russian not to shoot; 'the Russians are our friends!' And then followed Premier Nagy's message to General Maléter and his colleagues, who had gone at ten o'clock the night before to Soviet army headquarters: 'Return without further delay'.

[1] I happened to be present and was struck by the following sentence in his reference to the Hungarian rebellion: 'This is not a revolution but a fight for freedom'. From the text as recorded in *The Hungarian Revolution*, A White Book, this sentence is missing.

At Tököl, the talks between the delegations led by Maléter and Malinin had in fact been going on until about midnight, when, in the words of a United Nations Report:

[they] were . . . interrupted by the entry of a personage 'who bore no insignia of rank'–General Serov, Chief of the Soviet Security police. Accompanied by Soviet officers, he announced that he was arresting the Hungarian delegation. The head of the Soviet delegation, General Malinin, astonished by the interruption, made a gesture of indignation. General Serov thereupon whispered to him; as a result General Malinin shrugged his shoulders and ordered the Soviet delegation to leave the room. The Hungarian delegation was then arrested.[1]

By about 6 a.m., on 4 November, the Parliament building was occupied by the invaders, and the Hungarian radio silenced. At the same time, from somewhere in Russian-occupied Hungary (Szolnok as we now know), the formation of a 'Revolutionary Worker-Peasant Government' was announced, with Kádár as premier and an old Muscovite, Ferenc Münnich, as his deputy. They made no bones about their being imposed on Hungary by Russian arms; not until the 7th did they return to Budapest, from whence the Kommandatura issued its orders directly to the population. Kádár later said that he 'broke with the Nagy government on 1 November'. The break consisted in his secretly accepting the invitation of the Soviet embassy to flee from Budapest with Münnich under Soviet military protection and give the invaders a helping hand. This, only a few hours after his threat to the ambassador to fight the Soviet tanks with his bare hands, was quite a brisk change of attitude; and not less so, incidentally, for Münnich, who had also voted in the Politbureau for neutrality. Hypocrisy? Certainly in their explanations after the event; but they are unlikely to have planned the show of patriotism first and the treason after. Politicians have a remarkable faculty for believing their own cant.

Imre Nagy, together with the members of his family, sought and obtained asylum at the Yugoslav embassy in Budapest. So did a considerable number of communists involved in de-Stalinization: Julia Rajk; the Minister of State Losonczy, Rákosi's ex-prisoner; other ex-prisoners such as Ferenc Donáth, Sándor Haraszti, Szilárd

---

[1] United Nations Report of the Special Committee on the Problem of Hungary. General Assembly Official Records. New York, 1957. Of the Hungarian delegates, F. Erdei was before long released; he became a staunch supporter of the Kádár régime, as Secretary-General of the Hungarian Academy of Sciences, etc. His noteworthy accounts of the 'changing village' will be quoted below. (This text was already in the press when Erdei suddenly died, at an early age, in 1971.)

Ujhelyi; old Muscovites such as György Lukács, Zoltán Szántó, Zoltán Vas; Nagy's son-in-law Ferenc Jánosi; Nagy's secretary, József Szilágyi; and others.

Cardinal Mindszenty sought and obtained asylum at the United States Legation in Budapest. He stayed at the embassy (to which it was later promoted) until September 1971.[1] Of Nagy's cabinet ministers, one happened to be abroad–Anna Kéthly. On 1 November, she had left for Vienna to attend an international labour meeting and from there urged her Hungarian comrades to support Nagy. When she heard of the new Russian invasion she hurried homeward but was held up and refused an entry permit by the Soviet frontier guard. This was a blessing in disguise; she has stayed in the West ever since and settled in Brussels. Her activities included a moving address on the Hungarian question to an informal committee of the United Nations in New York in 1957.

General Király succeeded in escaping to the West and has settled in the U.S.A. where he has become a university professor, concerned with Hungarian history.

The invaders, ten divisions[2] strong, were this time well prepared for all eventualities, including the coming winter. Yet armed resistance went on for weeks, and sporadically for months. In some districts, indeed, the bloodiest battles only started when the Revolution could be seen to be lost, and more communists of the *Ávó* category were killed in defiance of Russian arms than previously under unrestricted lynch law. In the factories and mines work stopped again, and into the two main strongholds of the industrial workers–the Budapest suburbs of Ujpest and Csepel–neither Soviet troops nor the reorganized security police dared to penetrate for quite a while. The insurgents hoped against hope and when all hope died, bitterness kept them fighting until they were disarmed or killed. The number of insurgents killed in the resistance is estimated at between 2,500 and three thousand;[3] of those executed under the era of repression, at between 400 and 450; of those imprisoned, at between ten and twelve thousand;[4] and of those who escaped to the West (mostly through Austria, but also through Yugoslavia), at 200,000–of whom, however, in the following two or three years, some 30,000 returned to Hungary.

[1] His release was a result of prolonged negotiation between Hungary and the Vatican. He went into exile in Vienna, after a visit to Rome.

[2] Approximately 130,000 troops; together with air force, M.V.D., signalling, and sapper units, about 150,000 men. Of the divisions, 75 per cent are estimated to have been armoured.

[3] As against one thousand Soviet soldiers. Hospital casualties amounted among the insurgents to 13,000; on the Soviet side, allegedly, to 1,500. (On the Soviet losses, no official figures have been published.)

[4] I am indebted for these figures mainly to Dr Péter Gosztony.

Chapter 13

Ten Years of Kádár: Repression and Let-up

THE TERRORIST REPRESSION did not develop so fast as such figures would seem to suggest.

The Russian High Command proceeded with the whimsical carelessness of life and justice that had distinguished it in 1945: on the whole it left people alone but, in a haphazard way, deported truckloads of teenagers to the Soviet Union–especially those caught fighting; and if the unfortunate deportee turned out to be unarmed and innocent, this was no reason for bothering to release him. As to the common Soviet soldier, his behaviour this time was impeccable. A strange contrast: in 1945 the Soviet troops which came to liberate the country behaved like wild animals; those who came in 1956 to do an abominable job were, in their private relations with the inhabitants, polite, helpful, and considerate.

Premier Kádár, in his first fortnight of office, definitely courted the leaders, institutions, and social categories responsible for the rising. The Writers' Union, the Workers' Councils, even the Revolutionary Councils were recognized by his government as negotiating partners; Kádár's dialogues with some leading workers' councillors were given publicity over the recaptured Budapest radio. He amicably begged the workers to resume work, while the Kommandatura asked the Writers' Union representatives to use their influence with the workers to this effect. The Hungarian will to resist, however, seemed unbroken–the peasants supported the fighters and strikers with free food supplies, and the offices of the Writers' Union were loud with the clucking of poultry waiting to be collected by the authors, together with jars, sacks, and baskets packed with all kinds of farm produce.

Kádár insisted that he had only come to prevent an outright Fascist-imperialist takeover and, in the course of his talks, promised practically everything: free elections, multi-party democracy, personal freedom; no *Ávó*; no return to the Stalinist methods of sweated labour in the workshops and forcible collectivization on the land; and as to the withdrawal of Soviet forces from Hungary, this

255

was part of his programme, and he would start pressing the Soviet government for it as soon as order in Hungary was restored. To the idea of Hungary's neutrality he was less committed but thought it worth considering. But, he was asked by workers' councillors, what about his coalition partners? And particularly, what about Imre Nagy? Why is *he* not allowed to take over? Well, Kádár answered, first and foremost because he is not on Hungarian territory but in the building of a foreign embassy. As soon as he leaves the embassy it will be possible to consult him. Kádár made no promise to restore Nagy's premiership, but did not rule out the possibility of co-operating with him either in the new Communist Party or in the government. And he assured his audience that there was no question of punishing either Nagy or anyone else for his 'participation in the great popular movement of the past few weeks'.

The uncompromising voices at that moment came from the defeated, the disarmed population. Among smouldering ruins, under the eyes of Soviet soldiers supported by their tanks, people ostentatiously walked about with the 'Kossuth crest' in their buttonholes and pasted onto walls the resolutions of various revolutionary councils and the like–some typewritten or roneoed, some printed 'somewhere', and most of them demanding the *immediate and total* withdrawal of Soviet troops as the main precondition of an agreement.

István Bibó and Anna Kéthly

Among the posters was one outstanding for its moderation as well as courage and signed by a Minister of State of the deposed coalition government, István Bibó. He did not join the popular clamour for 'out with the Russians at once!', but did appeal to his countrymen for passive resistance unless and until a constitutional government was re-established, and he emphasized that 'the sole legal representative of Hungary abroad is Minister of State Anna Kéthly'. Meanwhile, he worked out plans for a compromise solution–an attempt to combine neutrality with guarantees for Soviet strategic interests and multi-party democracy with constitutional safeguards against 'exploitation', against going back on socialist achievements, and against the persecution of communists. Even in early 1957, when armed resistance had practically come to an end, he called at the British, American, and Indian Legations and submitted to them both this plan and a memorandum in which he urged that the 'scandal' of the Hungarian case be wiped from the face of the earth by energetic action through the United Nations. Such a scheme may sound as naïve as it was wise, but it was by no means useless: it helped to make clear what course the Hungarian people were prepared to take and what the Soviet power and its satellites and appeasers turned down.

The Writers' Union proceeded in similar spirit: though anxious to remain on courteous terms with the Kommandatura (with whom it intervened to stop the deportation of youths to the Soviet Union), it nevertheless made clear its conviction that the Soviet occupation of Hungary was 'an historical error', and expressed the hope that this would sooner or later be recognized by the Soviet government itself.

Terror; the Judicial Murder of Imre Nagy and Others

Kádár's reign of terror did not start until mid-January 1957 and lasted without a let-up for at least two years. But it had been initiated earlier by the Soviet M.V.D. (political police), who overruled Kádár's decisions–whether with his willing or forced consent is anybody's guess. Kádár, in his broadcasts and talks to the Workers' Councils, had not only guaranteed the safety of Imre Nagy and his comrades, but had formally offered them a safe-conduct in his exchanges with the Yugoslav embassy. Yet, when on 23 November 1956 Nagy and his party left the embassy, they were kidnapped from the street by an M.V.D. detachment, in spite of the protests of Yugoslav embassy officials among their escort. The Yugoslavs went on protesting after the incident, but their protests–like everybody else's–grew fainter and fainter.

Nagy and his party were deported to Sinaia, Romania, and interned (at least some of them, and for a while) in the summer palace of former Romanian kings; 'so Kafka was after all a realist', one of the deportees, namely György Lukács, commented when he first saw their castle-prison. The Kádár government issued a communiqué according to which Nagy had been taken to 'another socialist country . . . at his own request', and was enjoying the Romanian 'hospitality' in a spirit of 'understanding and good humour'. Hospitality and all took a strange turn in the following eighteen months, for on 17 June 1958, it was officially announced in Budapest that at a trial in Hungary, held *in camera*, Imre Nagy had been found guilty of treason and of attempting to overthrow the 'democratic state order'; and had been sentenced to death, together with three of his accomplices: Pál Maléter; the journalist Miklós Gimes; and Nagy's former secretary, Jóhzsef Szilágyi. Other defendants, such as the police Colonel Sándor Kopácsi, Ferenc Donáth, Ferenc Jánosi, the journalist Miklós Vásárhelyi, and (sole well-known non-communist among the defendants) the former President Tildy had been sentenced to imprisonment ranging from five years to life. One of the accused, G. Losonczy, had died from 'natural causes' in prison. The death sentences, the communiqué laconically added, 'have been executed'.

Hungarians at that time were inclined to believe that these judicial murders, violating the safe-conducts given by the Hungarian government, had been forced upon the Kádár administration from Moscow;

some even sought behind them the hand of Mao's China (which between 1956 and 1958 had turned from a moderator into an out-bidder of communism). These speculations proved unfounded. Or more precisely, the sole truth in them was that the court had acted on administrative orders. But they were the orders of the Kádár government. The pattern was roughly this: that those willing to con-fess to an 'error of judgement' and also to inculpate their comrades could save their lives. Nagy, in particular, had been several times offered this chance but he refused. And he said in court:

> I have twice tried to save the honour and the image of Commun-ism in the Danubian valley, once in 1953 and once in 1956. Rákosi and the Russians prevented me from doing so. If my life is needed to prove that not all Communists are enemies of the people, I gladly make the sacrifice. I know that there will one day be another Nagy trial, which will rehabilitate me. I also know I will have a reburial. I only fear that the funeral oration will be delivered by those who betrayed me.[1]

By the time Nagy's murder was announced, the policy of the Kádár government had completed a volte-face: except for keeping the 'Rákosi-Gerő clique' out of office, at any rate as far as these two leaders and their most notorious 'Security' thugs were concerned, Kádár broke all his pledges without the slightest noticeable qualm. One-Party rule was re-canonized; he himself remained the supreme holder of power in Hungary, as 'First Secretary to the Central Committee of the Hungarian Socialist Workers' Party'; and whether he also acted as 'Chairman of the Council of Ministers of the Hun-garian People's Republic', i.e., Prime Minister, or whether a Ferenc Münnich, a Gyula Kállai, or a Jenő Fock filled that post, as in turn they did, made no difference. The retribution was savage and aimed at two categories in particular: snipers, whatever their social back-ground and ideology; and the 'revisionists', as the humanizers of communism were labelled.[2]

Clamp-down on Revisionists—Workers as well as Authors

One effect of the clamp-down on revisionists was the havoc wrought among writers: Déry, Háy, Zelk, and many other former

---

[1] David Pryce-Jones, *The Hungarian Revolution*, London, 1969, p. 115 (Magyar original first published in *Irodalmi Ujság*, Paris, June 1968).

[2] A fashion that spread at about that time all over the communist world, from Peking to Budapest. Previously, the term 'revisionist' was almost exclusively applied in discussions about labour movements to the pre-First World War efforts of Social Democrats, such as the German Dr Eduard Bernstein, to 'revise' Marxism in the light of then recent developments. As Lenin severely condemned such efforts, 'revisionism' has ever since remained a dirty word in communist literature.

Communist Party members were arrested in 1957 and sentenced to many years of imprisonment; two young journalists close to them, József Gáli and Gyula Obersovszky, were sentenced to death, and their lives most probably only saved by a wave of worldwide indignation and the intervention of such bodies as the International PEN. Of their non-communist friends, the scholar István Bibó was the most conspicuous victim; he, too, faced execution and was saved only by world opinion – from death, though not from special 'disciplinary' vexations. Actors, painters, sculptors, composers, educationalists, and historians who had shown sympathy for the revisionist trend fared no better than the authors and journalists; their punishments ranged from being silenced and put under police supervision to sentences during which some managed to commit suicide. The philosopher Lukács, who had been very cautious in 1956, was released once the hospitality offered to him in the Royal Palace of Sinaia came to an end, but remained a revisionist bugbear, criticized in the lengthy Party documents for his 'negative' influence. The Writers' Union was banned in 1957 and replaced in late 1959 by a body of authorized literary yesmen.

The Workers' Councils were dissolved without anything to replace them. Their leaders were imprisoned; some of them (for example, the Vice-President of the Szeged Workers' Council) executed. The attempt to make the workers masters in 'their' factories came to an end – although, and this must be emphasized, the slave-driving methods of Rákosi and Gerő were not reinstated either. This in fact was the Revolution's most lasting result, even after armed defeat.

But the gulf between the workers and the Party which was supposed to be dictating on their behalf has never been bridged since the Revolution exposed it. Of the million former members of the Communist Party, no more than 283,000 could be induced to join Kádár's re-formed party in the first half-year of Soviet reoccupation, and though promises of favours and every other form of amicable pressure were applied to increase this number, especially among the workers, a whole decade was not sufficient to bring it up to 600,000.

Kolkhozi, Once Again

With the peasantry, at first, a smoother *modus vivendi* seemed in sight. The peasantry, if no less 'counter-revolutionary' than the workers, were at least less 'infected with Trotskyism'; in the Revolution, they had not operated through 'councils'; their more conservative outlook made them less, and not more, irritating to a régime which based its authority on the claim that it had come to crush a reactionary plot. Moreover, it seemed possible that past experiences had induced Kádár's establishment to follow the examples of their

Polish and Yugoslav comrades and allow the peasants to carry on as
'dwarfholders' within a largely nationalized industry; since most of
the peasants had left the *kolkhozi* between 1953 and 1957, the framework for such a mixed economy existed. But hopes to this effect did
not last long; after the 1957 harvest, the collectivization screw was
put on again, and in 1961 the government could announce that
practically all the cultivable land of the country had gone over to
the 'public sector'–roughly two-thirds to co-operatives (*kolkhozi*),
one-third state-owned, and only some fanciful strips left in private
ownership. The campaign of peaceful persuasion which brought
about this result left many farmers with broken heads; yet it was still
an improvement on the Rákosi methods. The kulaks, once 'persuaded', were no longer pestered and pilloried; on the contrary: a degree
of corruption was tacitly allowed to them, a blind eye was turned to
their thefts from *kolkhoz* properties and sale of their loot on the free,
or even the black, market. This was a substantial consolation for
'socialism' but did not stop the peasantry–particularly the young–
from swarming towards urban areas; the reason being shortage of
amenities as much as of land.

Uneasy Friendship between State and Church
    The social layer which Kádár came most smoothly to terms with
comprised the remnants of the upper and middle classes. These were
the people most grateful for any gesture of benevolent despotism, if
only because it meant a quite fantastic improvement on their infernal
sufferings under Rákosi. To be precise, both Rákosi and Kádár were
inclined to enlist the support of superficially converted right-wingers
against the non-communist Left and the revisionists, but they still
differed as to their favourite type of converts: Rákosi preferred the
former Nazis; Kádár, the conservatives and the hesitants. The most
powerful and characteristic conservative force in Hungary was the
Roman Catholic Church; it was significant, therefore, that not quite
half a year after the reoccupation, on 11 April 1957, precisely ten
days before the dissolution of the Writers' Union and the arrest of
Tibor Déry, the Bench of Bishops declared its support for the Kádár
government. The head of the Bench, Archbishop Grősz (who was
more flexible mentally but not at all less of a conservative than
Cardinal Mindszenty, still in self-imposed exile at the American
embassy), was awarded a high state decoration on 7 December that
year, as were other church dignitaries at the end of the month. This
did not prevent the judiciary of the Kádár government from sentenc-
ing seventeen Catholic priests on 11 January 1958 for their activities
during the 'counter-revolution', although Archbishop Grősz tried his
best to save them. An uneasy friendship has ever since prevailed

between state and Church in Hungary: it would be an understatement to describe it only as a 'truce', but it would be equally misleading to ignore the constant tension and occasional acts of religious persecution which overshadow it. Under Archbishop Grősz's guidance and, after his death in October 1961, under Bishop Endre Hamvas's, the Church adopted a very conciliatory policy in everything outside its own narrowly defined field of activity; at the end of 1959, it emphatically supported the drive for land collectivization, and the organizers of Soviet-style peace demonstrations could always count on the Papal-style blessings of the Bench and its subordinates. In exchange, the state accepted responsibility for the livelihood of the priests: a government subsidy periodically renewed has in fact become the main income of both the Catholic Church as such and of the substantially reduced number of schools (of secondary grade) left at its disposal. Yet not a year has passed without trials which exposed the 'conspiracies' of priests and other Catholics who had read Teilhard de Chardin at secret gatherings or discussed the possibility of reviving the Catholic Democratic People's Party. State and Church thus were never completely separated, as they were, for instance, under the French Radicals of the Third Republic; it was rather a balance of patronizing and punitive gestures which characterized the post-1956 Hungarian government's attitude towards the Church, and both the Hungarian and international representatives of the Roman Catholic Church were persuaded to accept this, with all the vexations and anti-religious discriminations involved, as the least of evils threatening their priesthood and flock in a communist-dominated eastern Europe. An agreement between the Holy See and Hungary on vital outstanding issues, concluded on 14 September 1964, expressed formal recognition of this state of affairs. The 'Mindszenty problem', however, was resolved in September 1971.

With the religious minorities, namely the Protestant and Jewish communities, arrangements evolved on a similar pattern, and with far less difficulties for the government to overcome. The percentage of practising Jews had shrunk to about one-tenth of what it used to be before the war; few though they were, their existence became a sore point with the régime, but only after the Six-day War of 1967–in the latest chapter of Hungarian history.

Wholesome Pragmatism

After the liquidation of the class of peasant plotholders, only a few categories of free professionals and petty traders still functioned as survivors of the pre-war bourgeoisie; and Kádár, with his undogmatic approach, facilitated their integration into the socialist system. In a way, this had been going on ever since the 'Year of the

Turning-Point', 1948; some 'remnants of capitalism' had been tolerated both for practical economic reasons and for their uses as whipping-boys whenever 'exploiters' might be required in the dock. Kádár brought this scapegoat technique to an end. Once an occupation was legally authorized, no one had to fear persecution for earning his living by it. That much became clear even in the initial, repressive phase of his rule. Another sadistic practice of the Rákosi era which dropped out under Kádár was that of pillorying people for their 'class background'. Although the ability to boast proletarian pedigree has still remained an advantage under his rule, discrimination against the 'offspring of exploiters' had lost its humiliating emphasis. The son of an ex-landowner specializing in car repairs and supplying spare parts was not expected to be enthusiastic about the Dictatorship of the Proletariat and join its Party so much as a turner or miner, but had at the same time more reason to be impressed by the disappearance of its crudest ignominies.

The writers struck for about six months; until mid-1957, hardly anything was published unless it was by dedicated hacks of the Party or had been in print already at the time of the Revolution. But once the régime was established, it would have been both mulish and suicidal to continue abstaining. A signal development was the conversion of László Németh to wholehearted support of Soviet communism and the Kádár government, culminating in his journey to Moscow in 1959 and his enthusiastic references to it. As Németh had been the leader of that young intelligentsia which in the thirties had been searching for a right-wing élitism to fit Hungarian temperament and ambitions (termed by him 'Revolution of Quality', etc.), his coming down on Kádár's side could be taken as symbolic of the attitude of hesitant middle-class people altogether. Other writers, mainly among the revisionists, were more reluctant to capitulate, but gradually all had to accept some accommodation with the government. This was facilitated by the understanding of the government official in charge of matters concerning them, Deputy Minister of Culture György Aczél, a dedicated communist but sensitive to human values and one of Rákosi's ex-prisoners. In matters of Party ideology, however, another ex-prisoner, István Szirmai, issued directives thoroughly steeped in the loquacious jargon of his creed; their recurring theme was the necessity to fight for pure Marxism-Leninism against threats from revisionism and opportunism on the one hand and dogmatism and sectarianism on the other – a shower of hollow *ism*'s which has remained the dominant style of communist theorizing.

In foreign affairs, Kádár's return to the pre-Nagy line was total; all his promises to end foreign military occupation and loosen the country's subordination to the U.S.S.R. were ignored, and indeed to voice such demands was made a 'crime against the democratic state order'. Hungary became a tool of Russian imperialism as much as she had been under Rákosi; that she could all the same maintain friendlier ties with the West – manifested in culture, in tourist traffic, and most of all in foreign trade – and that Russian overlordship acquired more courteous forms, was due to the difference between Stalin's way and Khrushchev's, and not to any change in Hungary's satellite status. 20 March 1957 was a significant date from this point of view: a delegation led by Kádár to Moscow reinforced the Warsaw Pact, deferred the withdrawal of Soviet troops indefinitely, declared the October Revolution to have been a 'counter-revolution' and 'imperialist plot', and pledged harsh measures against revisionism. 'Another Bach era is in the offing' ran a line in an oft-quoted poem by a revisionist poet who was subsequently imprisoned, István Eörsi, and this indeed expressed the general feeling; Kádár's rule was hated not because Bolshevism was hated, but because absolutism based on foreign weapons was. It followed naturally, therefore, that, second only to the closed circle of its dedicated dogmatists, the people most willing to support it should come from the social layers typified by conservatism, political indifference, or experimental indecision – technocrats, bureaucrats, businessmen, clergymen, sportsmen, and, among intellectuals, the believers in benevolent authority.

'Those Who Are Not Against Us Are With Us'

Like the Bach Period, the Kádár era compared favourably with the savage Nazi domination of 1944 or the Stalinist of 1949–52; it allowed repressive terror to subside to a functional level which often gave it almost the semblance of a régime verging on liberalism. The first significant step in this direction was the amnesty timed for 4 April (anniversary of Hungary's liberation from the Nazis) in 1960. The amnesty, characteristically, applied to common as well as political prisoners; and to notorious terrorists of the Stalin era kept in gaol since the eve of the Revolution (Mihály and Vladimir Farkas) as well as to distinguished authors and other revisionists: the balance between the two ideological foes had to be demonstrated, and the biceps as well as the compassionate heart of the leadership put on show. But what people cared about was the fact that Tibor Déry, Gyula Háy, and even the agronomist Ferenc Donáth, an intimate of the murdered Nagy, had been set free. Another amnesty under which almost all the remaining revisionist intellectuals and also István Bibó were released, followed three years later. The Social Democrats imprisoned or reimprisoned after the Revolution were also gradually set free, partly on the intervention of the ex-Social Democrat György Marosán, one of Rákosi's most cruelly maltreated ex-prisoners and of Kádár's most violent lieutenants, conspicuous for demagogic outbursts against imperialists and revisionists in public which he counteracted by helping persecuted liberals and socialists behind the scenes. The amnesty of 1963 coincided with the first publication, after seven years of forced silence, of György Lukács's writings; which only made a landmark because he had figured, how-ever baselessly, as the arch-devil of revisionism in ideological Party papers. Thus in the early sixties even the 'pink' intelligentsia were allowed to follow the conservatives in acting as non-committed but loyal assistants of the communists.

In a speech on 8 December 1961 Kádár declared that if the Rákosi government's slogan could have been 'Those who are not with us are against us!',[1] that of his own government was rather 'Those who are not against us are with us!'

23 October 1966, tenth anniversary of the Revolution, was marked simultaneously by precautionary mass arrests, the standing on panicky alert of the political police against possible demonstrators, and, on the other hand, preparations for a New Economic Mechan-ism which was planned to revive or introduce as much of the incen-tives of a free-market economy as could be reconciled with the absolute power of the state and the ruling single Party over the property of citizens. The go-ahead for the N.E.M. was actually fixed for 1 January 1968.

The Hungary of the 1970s rests on the foundations laid in 1961–68: on the whole, a compromise between the forces that exploded in October 1956 and the Power that crushed them in November. Mean-while, the revolutionary fervour has withered away, and the Marxist-Leninist backlash has shrunk to a public ritual mechanically repeated on some prescribed occasions: the realities are Soviet tanks behind the scenes, and in the forefront, the economic factors of often-tried bourgeois consolidation.

[1] In fact, this formula was devised to demonstrate the difference between the two régimes by the refugee writer Tibor Méray (*Irodalmi Ujság*, 23 October 1961), but Kádár answered that never mind who 'kept pricking us' with this formula, he was pleased to accept it.

Chapter 14

Hungary in the 1970s

THERE ARE MORE THAN 15 million people speaking Magyar as their mother-tongue today, and barely more than 10 million of them living in present-day Hungary, the same area of 35,650 square miles (with a minute alteration about which more later) that she was allowed under the Treaty of Trianon in 1920 to retain of a territory more than three times as big.

Of the roughly 5 million Magyars outside the Hungarian frontier almost 3½ million are subjects of the communist countries bordering on Hungary. Nearly 2 million live in Romania (most in Transylvania); nearly 700,000 in Czechoslovakia (mostly in the southern strip of Slovakia); half a million in Yugoslavia (mostly in the Voivodina); and not quite 200,000 in the Soviet Union (in the Ukraine). The rest, slightly more than 1½ million, are scattered all over the non-communist world, with the largest contingent in the United States.

These are, to be sure, very rough estimates, but detailed statistical data would not make the figures more meaningful; a census, or any other survey of nationhood or the like, is controversial by its very nature. It is worth remembering, however, that one-third of the people considering themselves in one way or another Hungarian live outside the country called Hungary. The history of the Hungarian diaspora reflects European history in the twentieth century as the partitions of Poland did in previous centuries; and the impact made by Hungarian immigrants on the artistic, scientific, and economic lives of the countries of their resettlement went far beyond the limits of Hungarian national history.

Trianon and Neo-Trianon

In the inter-war period, Lenin and his followers used to denounce the Treaty of Trianon as a typical act of bourgeois imperialism, and Hungarian communists found much propaganda value in its blatant injustice; 'whatever our "crimes" against the nation' they would argue, 'it was not our leaders but the capitalist war victors who imposed Trianon on Hungary.' Even today, disparaging references to the authors and buttresses of Trianon, the *Entente*, and the 'Petty

Entente', are quite usual in communist literature. It is the more ironical that after the Second World War it should have been the U.S.S.R. who vetoed the very idea of a modification of the Trianon frontiers. In 1946, for instance, when Czechoslovakia, backed by the U.S.S.R., was engaged in dispossessing and expelling her Magyar minority,[1] some Hungarians suggested that at least a strip of the purely Magyar districts of Slovakia should be returned to Hungary so as to facilitate the resettlement of the refugees. A number of Czechoslovaks seemed agreeable to such a solution; Foreign Minister Jan Masaryk, behind the scenes, actually encouraged Michael Károlyi to bring forward the idea. But Molotov, when told of the plan, strictly vetoed it; and in the Peace Treaty signed in 1947, Czechoslovakia's share of ex-Hungarian territory was even extended by adding to the city of Bratislava an appendage across the Danube.[2] Meanwhile, Ruthenia, the eastern province of Trianon Czechoslovakia, with her more than 100,000 Magyars, was incorporated in the Soviet Union.

There was no doubt whatever that the persecution of Magyars, so welcome to the pogrom-happy ex-Fascists of Slovakia, now converted to communism, was encouraged from Moscow, while at the same time the Hungarian Stalinist leaders were authorized by the Kremlin to head the protest campaign against such acts of nationalist violence. Yet, when in 1948 both Czechoslovakia and Hungary were turned into 'people's democracies', the Kremlin ordered them to love each other; and the deportations, at least, were stopped.

In Yugoslavia, the wartime record of Hungary had been particularly bad: the treacherous attack of 1940 having been aggravated, mainly in the town of Novi Sad, by massacres of Serbs and Jews carried out mainly by the pandoors. The reoccupation of ex-Hungarian territories by the Yugoslav partisans started with equally nauseating acts of cruelty, though smaller in number; but by the time that actual warfare ended, they had been stopped, and Marshal Tito initiated a comparatively liberal rule in respect of the Magyar minority. It was sometimes even demonstratively liberal: for instance, in the establishment of a Magyar university and cultural centre in, of all towns, Novi Sad, so as to stress that the era of revenge was over. When Stalin excommunicated Tito, Rákosi made Hungary the spearhead of the anti-Yugoslav campaign, this being but one example of how he followed in the footsteps of the Nazi quislings. Since then, relations between the two countries have become

---

[1] Cf. *Hungary and the Conference of Paris*, Hungarian Ministry of Foreign Affairs, Budapest, 1947.
[2] Cf. Paul Ignotus, 'Czechs, Magyars, Slovaks', *The Political Quarterly*, London, April–June 1969.

friendly, though Yugoslavia has never given up her non-aligned status; and the treatment of the Magyar minority in Yugoslavia is, by both the ancient nationalist and the communist standards applied in the Balkans, surprisingly good. Some 450,000 of them (90 per cent of the total) live in what is termed the Socialist Autonomous Province of Voivodina where their minority rights are recognized; and even outside that province they are spared persecutions. Yet, some pressure towards Serbification is manifest in such facts as that a smaller percentage of Magyars than of any other ethnic group in Yugoslavia except the Albanians figure in the professional and higher clerical categories, although they undoubtedly used to be, and perhaps still are, one of the most educated nationalities of that area.

The worst treatment of a Magyar minority (nearly 2 million) is in Romania. It was not so at first when hostilities ended. The first of the Romanian leaders playing the Russian game, though himself no communist, the cynical and benevolent Petru Groza, liked the Hungarians; and, apart from his personal feelings, he made use of anyone he could recruit among them to keep down the Romanian majority. This added bitterness to the hatred of Hungarians which had always been prevalent among Romanians; and their moment of revenge came after the defeat of the 1956 Revolution. The minority Magyars followed with sympathetic and hopeful eyes the struggle of Hungarians across the frontier; and even if they had not done so, it was easy enough to accuse them of being the greatest troublemakers in the Socialist Camp. A persecution of Magyars followed: they were deprived of whatever minority rights they had before, their university was closed, their administrative autonomies abolished; mass deportations, mass internments, and, among Magyar academics, not a few cases of suicide marked the crusade of Romanian chauvinism. In the early 1960s, the Stalinist rulers of Romania embarked on a policy of forcible Romanization which played up to the prevalent Magyar phobia; and since in foreign affairs they played it most astutely, establishing their own diplomatic and trade links with one Western Power after another (and with China, too), world opinion was prepared to pooh-pooh the ordeal of the Magyar minority. Yet, since about 1967, possibly in response to Western liberal currents which it was thought expedient to take note of, and also in response to protests by the Kádár government, made behind the scenes but detectable in public, acute persecution has been replaced by icy containment. Today, the position of the Magyars in communist Romania is, from a nationalities point of view, on the whole neither better nor worse than it was in the inter-war period under the excesses of a Romanian chauvinism that was right-wing in every sense and blatantly reactionary, but alleviated by inefficiency and corruption.

With Czechoslovakia, while she was enjoying her reform era under Dubček's leadership, Kádár's Hungary maintained the friendliest links possible; the two leaders liked to show themselves in public side by side, all smiles, teeth, and comradeship, and it was an open secret that Kádár opposed the Soviet invasion of August 1968. Yet when it came, he ordered the Hungarian contingent to participate; of the Soviet Bloc countries, indeed, Romania was the only one that had the guts to abstain. Since then, Hungarian relations with Czechoslovakia have been like those with any Soviet republic—neither more nor less close.

Hungary's western neighbour, and her only non-communist one, is neutral Austria. Austria, too, was allotted a patch of Hungarian territory under the Treaty of Trianon, namely the province of Burgenland; but the Magyar minority in this province is negligible in number. There is, however, and has been for a long time, a substantial number of Magyar *émigrés* in Vienna, with a noticeable impact not only on Austrian but also on international developments; since 1919, Vienna has been the springboard, as it were, of the expatriate Hungarians.

Every nation's life is to a large extent determined by that of her neighbours, and so is Hungary's. History and geography provide the frame of what she is today, and this is unlikely to change in the decades to come. Let me add, however, a cross-section of her existence at this time of writing (in 1971) which may of course undergo changes between now and publication time.

The Holders of Power

Since the declaration of the 'Brezhnev doctrine' of 'limited sovereignty' on the morrow of the invasion of Czechoslovakia, there has been no gainsaying the fact that supreme power over all Comecon countries, including Hungary, is held by the Kremlin. In Hungary, this is guaranteed diplomatically by several emphatic reaffirmations of the Warsaw Pact; economically by the nature of Hungarian foreign trade and industrial planning;[1] and militarily both by Hungary's stretch of common frontier with Slovakia and Soviet Ukraine and by the Soviet forces stationed in Hungary.

The latter are estimated at four divisions, two of them armoured. Together with the Soviet air force, sapper and signal units, and political police attached to them, they may amount to 50–60,000 troops. This is less than an army of occupation but more than a token force; it may be considered a western outpost of the Soviet empire, destined to prevent anti-Soviet moves in the Danube basin and for use as a bargaining counter in potential settlements with the

[1] See below, pp. 290–95.

NATO Powers. The withdrawal of Soviet troops from Hungary has in fact been several times suggested by Soviet spokesmen as a *quid pro quo* for NATO concessions, and the idea has been echoed in Kádár's statements, but without implying any loosening of the dependence of Hungary on the U.S.S.R. Hungary's status as an imperial province is (from a strategic point of view) unquestionable. Within this status, however, she has considerable elbow room to organize her economics and culture as she thinks best. When referring to 'her' as a country, we mean, of course, the ruling communist set-up; the rest, in and outside the monopoly Party, only count insofar as the rulers choose to take notice of their feelings. When decisions are being made the President of the Presidential Council (nominally the highest official of the People's Republic) is as much a nonentity as any village tramp.

The ruling communist set-up is essentially the same as that put into power by Khrushchev in November 1956: that is, a 'centrist' group which disclaims association with the 'sectarian', etc., excesses practised under Rákosi, but even more with 'rightist opportunist', etc., deviations personified in Imre Nagy. Death and reshuffles, a few owing to quarrels (for instance with Marosán who, after the liquidation of revisionists, urged an inquiry into the Personality Cult more thoroughgoing than his colleagues were prepared to undertake), have, however, led to some modification in the top personnel; and the actual holders of power now seem to be these: János Kádár, Béla Biszku, Rezső Nyers, Jenő Fock, Gyula Kállai, Zoltán Komócsin, György Aczél.

Kádár, First Secretary, is the undoubted leader. Biszku is supposed to be Number Two and Kádár's successor; rumour has it that he would prefer a tougher line than Kádár's, but it has never come to an open clash between the two men. Yet, as the political police have often appeared to overrule permissive attitudes in other government departments, and sometimes even Kádár's own decisions, the suspicion arose the Biszku was master of the security forces and, with Soviet backing, exercised a check on Kádár's liberalizing influence.

Fock and Nyers are economic technocrats whose personalities were pushed into the political limelight when, in the middle 1960s, the planning for the New Economic Mechanism started to dominate public life. When the N.E.M. came into force, Fock was appointed Prime Minister with a view to stressing the pragmatic character of the government. Since then, not unnaturally for a communist country, Fock's profile has faded into distinguished insignificance; everybody knew, after all, that decisions came from the Party and not from the government. Meanwhile Nyers, as a Secretary to the Central Committee, a member of the Politbureau, and Chairman of the

Economic Policy Committee of the Party, has grown into the economic dictator of the country – to some extent he is to Kádár what Gerő was to Rákosi. Nyers, born in 1923, started as a typesetter. After the end of the war he joined the Communist Party and studied economics. A working-class man, quick in learning both the shibboleths of Marxism-Leninism and the technicalities to be coped with by a factory or office manager, could count on a smooth and brilliant career, particularly if he was cautious enough, as Nyers was, to steer clear both of the most blatant Personality Cult performances under Rákosi and of the revisionist attempts under Nagy. He thus filled various important economic posts in the government and Party offices until in his present capacity he became known as the chief engineer of the N.E.M.

Whether he really was *the* chief among its engineers can hardly be proved; but he was certainly one of them. N.E.M. was prepared by team work. Among the members of the team were: Kádár himself; Fock, before his promotion to Prime Minister; Professor Imre Vajda, a former Social Democrat, who was particularly active in establishing trade and industrial processing links with Austria and Great Britain; the veteran agrarian communist Lajos Fehér, used for his expertise on rural co-operatives; István Friss, head of the Economic Institute of the Hungarian Academy of Sciences; and Béla Csikós-Nagy, head of the Price-fixing Authority. These men (except Vajda, who died in 1969) still play some part in directing Hungarian economics, and though their order of importance is hardly ascertainable, Friss and Csikós-Nagy seem to be the theorist brains working behind Nyers's decisions. Friss comes from the Jewish upper-middle classes, and was a devout communist from early youth, untouched by Personality Cult and always concentrating on economics; Csikós-Nagy, of the pre-war gentry, started as an economist in the Fascist camp, but has since 1945 developed into an impeccable member of the Marxist-Leninist planning team.

Komócsin is an *apparatchik*, a lower-middle-class bureaucrat type with no profile to the public. Kállai and Aczél, on the other hand, are 'ideologists', which is tantamount under communism to having been a theologian in the time of medieval Christianity. They were both imprisoned under Rákosi (together with Rajk, Szőnyi, Kádár) but came out of prison with their belief in the basic Party tenets unshaken. Kállai has since his release filled various highly representative posts, but his significance chiefly consists in his contribution to Hungarian Communist Party literature in the shape of recollections, for example, of the resistance against the Nazis: he can always be trusted to reflect the Establishment views by rigging facts, though cautiously in lying. Aczél, of a younger vintage, presents a more interesting personality and career. Coming from Jewish pauperdom, brought up in an orphanage, he set his heart on reciting Hungarian poetry either as an actor or as a verse-reader. After the Nazi terror and its collapse under the blows of the Red Army, he turned up, in 1945, as one of the most zealous provincial Communist Party secretaries. His arrest under Rákosi was due, allegedly,[1] to his naïve championship of a friend rounded up as a 'Titoist', whom he knew to be innocent. Years later, matured by prison and office experience, he mastered the skill to balance what survived in him of his youthful enthusiasms for world revolution and Magyar poetry: he became the middleman between the communist Establishment and the literary world and, since István Szirmai's death, has been in charge of 'Agitprop' and the Party section responsible for ideological pronouncements. Though there can be no doubt about his dedication to Marxism–Leninism as he sees it, he is the man given most credit for the comparatively broad gamut of ideas and their style of presentation in book publishing, film production, academic life, and other intellectual activities in present-day Hungary.

These seem to be, in the present set-up, the names most important to the present writer–but the selection is necessarily largely based on impressions. A few names may therefore be added, to make the list more closely resemble the official hierarchy. The President of the Presidential Council (and *perhaps* quite an important personality–nobody knows) is Pál Losonczi, who started in his youth as a farm labourer, as pointed out in biographical notes. The presidency of the National Assembly has since May 1971 been filled by Antal Apró, who seems to have been 'kicked upstairs' when he was elected to this high post; until then, he was not only a Politbureau member (since 1946) but, as one of the vice-presidents of the Council of Ministers, the chief representative of Hungary at Comecon. As to his background, formerly a building contractor, Apró came from the trading middle classes and has ever since the end of the war carefully toed the Kremlin line, without being too conspicuously engaged in Personality Cult excesses. Some may see in his removal from that key post Kádár's effort to devise his trade tactics more independently of Russia as Apró was regarded as a Kremlin tool and crypto-Stalinist. His successor as the vice-premier responsible for Comecon links is Péter Vályi, up to then Minister of Finance; apparently a very active economic agent. The man outstanding in representing Hungary abroad outside Comecon is the Foreign Minister, János Péter, a former Calvinist parson.

About the invisible forces, mainly political police with direct links

---

[1] I made his acquaintance in prison and heard the story of his arrest in chats with fellow-prisoners.

with the Soviet security agencies, the only certainty is that they do exist; illiberal decisions cutting across Kádár's clear intentions are too numerous to be attributed to chance. The handling of Western visitors is a case in point. Obviously it is government policy to encourage tourism both for psychological reasons and in order to get hard currency. Accordingly, Hungarian *émigrés* are as a rule cordially solicited to revisit their native country; special Magyar periodical publications are run to win their sympathies, international conferences are organized for their benefit – the agencies in charge are generous in allotting time, attention, and money to their entertainment. Then, suddenly, and without any credible explanation given, applications for visas are refused, or a well-known writer previously welcomed by the authorities is 'advised' by them to leave the country at once.[1] Security officials, or some of them, it seems, feel their own importance diminished by the liberal treatment of foreign visitors and are therefore determined to show their strength to those of their comrades engaged in liberalizing. Another ambiguous subject is Zionism. Hungary, after the Six-day War, obediently followed the Soviet example of breaking off diplomatic relations with Israel, blaming Israeli 'aggression' and so forth; but the prescribed slogans of the anti-Zionist campaign were repeated by the general public with tongues even more conspicuously in their cheeks than on other topics; there was simply no Hungarian who took 'solidarity with the Arab people' seriously. This in a way is a godsend to those over-ambitious security officers who send denunciatory reports on their colleagues to Moscow; as attested by some Hungarian defectors to the West, even Kádár is spied upon by such snoopers, eager to detect 'Zionist sympathies'.

Power in Hungary is thus wielded through an interplay of Soviet authorities, privileged Hungarian Communist Party officials, and the Hungarian citizens at large insofar as the present-day set-up allows them to show their feelings and thereby to influence decisions. In this sense, the dictatorship is a qualified one. But what should *not* be regarded as its counterbalance is the existence of a 'democratic' machinery. In spite of the tremendous improvements in practically all fields of life since the peak period of Stalinism, the constitution is as much a dead letter today as it was when enacted on 20 August 1949. The National Assembly, nominal interpreter of the nation's will, is a rubber-stamp Parliament, elected by all citizens above the age of seventeen, but appointed rather than elected in practice. The basis of elections has, since 1948, been the farce of a Single List.

---

[1] This actually happened in 1970 to George Mikes on his visit to Hungary as the member of a B.B.C. television team which had undertaken to make a film on Hungary in co-operation with the Hungarian Ministry of Foreign Affairs.

Recently, some relaxation of the Single List system has been implemented so as to introduce an element of choice into the proceedings. At the general election held on 25 April 1971, out of 352 members of Parliament barely more than 300 were elected 'unanimously', while for the rest of the seats, the constituents could freely choose between two candidates put forward at special nomination meetings. There was even one constituency, Old-Buda, in which three candidates could stand, and the surprise result was the election of a political outsider, a twenty-eight-year-old historian, and incidentally a blind man, Zoltán Szép by name. The election of local councils may contain more of such local surprises but reflects the same ban on political dissent in authorizing the contestants. Nor is it of importance that most of the elected representatives of the people are 'non-party'—as a matter of fact, the most servile executors of communist orders have often been recruited from among those who made a show and profession of *not* joining the Party. The Patriotic People's Front, with which all sections of tolerated public life are associated (including, of course, the avowed communists), is a purely ritualistic organization, calculated to demonstrate that even non-communists accept the communist lead. And so they do, since they have no alternative. Imre Nagy had indeed tried to broaden the Front into an organization which could promote genuine debates, but this was exactly one of the acts of 'opportunism' and even 'treason' attributed to him by the present-day rulers. Whether, as time marches on, the eyewash institutions of parliamentary life and of 'non-party' participation in government will develop any reality remains to be seen; at the moment, whatever sparks of democracy can be detected in Hungarian life exist in trade, industry, culture, and not in politics proper.

It was originally the 1949 constitution which replaced the traditional coat-of-arms with a Soviet-style crest; since Kádár established his power, in 1957, both of them were abolished and a shield striped in red-white-and-green took their place—a device which can at least be credited with being simpler than its predecessors. The Red Star surmounts it as a crown used to do under the Habsburgs and Horthy, but people have grown equally indifferent to crowns and red stars alike.

A Congress of the Hungarian Socialist Workers' Party (the Communist Party) is (and should be) regarded as a more important and spectacular event than a session of the National Assembly (the Parliament). The last Congress (the tenth, as far as Hungarian Communist Party Congresses go) was held in Budapest, on 23–28 November 1970. Most of the 'sister Parties' were represented by their leaders, and the most important among them, the Soviet sister Party, by Leonid Brezhnev who was given a most enthusiastic welcome. In the front row, among the guests of honour, sat the authors Gyula Illyés, László Németh, and György Lukács, all non-sectarians.

Kolkhoz, Danubian-style

What do the 10 million Hungarians live on? Some 5 million of them are registered as 'active earners' (a percentage materially higher than only a few years ago); and as to the sources of their earnings, Rezső Nyers, the highest authority on the matter, publishes this table:[1]

| | Production of national income by economic sectors | | | |
	in 1938	in 1950	in 1968	in 1970
Industry	23·5	28·1	42·7	42·5
Construction	5·5	9·0	11·3	11·7
Agriculture	70·0	56·3	21·9	21·3
Other	1·0	6·6	24·1	24·5
	100·0	100·0	100·0	100·0

'Hungary has changed from an agrarian-industrial country to an industrial-agrarian one', Nyers comments. Indeed, barely more than one-fifth of the national income is yielded by what, not so long ago, was regarded as 'the' Hungarian industry; and although, if measured by the percentage of occupational groups, the change is slightly less dramatic,[2] the time when the common Hungarian people could practically be equated with ploughmen has definitely come to an end.

According to another statistical survey, also published with Hungarian government backing,[3] the contribution of the main branches of economic activity to the national income of Hungary was in 1967 as follows: industry, 68 per cent; construction, 11 per cent; agriculture, 15 per cent; others, 14 per cent. The reason why such noteworthy differences should occur between two official statistics is irrelevant in this context—since the latter graph demonstrates even more dramatically the same trend as that manifest in the figures quoted by Rezső Nyers.

Concurrently, the town population has increased, and is likely to increase further compared with that of the villages. In 1960, town

[1] 'Profitability and Income Distribution', *The New Hungarian Quarterly*, Budapest, Winter 1970, p. 24. (In the glossary of this table, 'Industry' of course stands for industries *other than* agriculture and building or construction works.)

[2] 'Up to 1949 around 50 per cent of all those in employment worked in agriculture, today only about 28 per cent', according to Ferenc Erdei, Director of the Research Institute for Agrarian Economy of the Hungarian Academy of Sciences, 'The Changing Village', The *N.H.Q.*, Summer 1970, p. 5.

[3] *Magyarország*, published by Magyarok Világszövetsége (World Association of Hungarians), 1970, p. 4.

inhabitants amounted to 4 million; village inhabitants to 6 million. In 1970, town inhabitants were 4·6 million; village, 5·7 million; but by 1985, it is reckoned, town inhabitants will amount to 5·9 million, as against a village population of 5 million.[1] Meanwhile, the difference between town and village narrows as towns are helped to acquire more parks, and villages more amenities.

Yet the structure of farming and its development under Kádár show a pattern somewhat different from that of other industries. Approximately 1,900,000 people work in some capacity on farms.[2] Of the cultivable land, some 30 per cent is state-owned, some two-thirds belong to the *kolkhozi* (named in Magyar, with a frightful neologism, *téesz*), and the rest has for various special reasons been left in private ownership. In fact, a *téesz*-farmer is both more and less of a cog in the collective wheel than his legal status suggests. He is more so because the Communist Party or its district agency has the final say in decisions by the farming communities; the collectives, or *téesz*, are subordinated to the state or its masters and have therefore never been able to appear to their members as the agents of 'co-operation' which they are supposed to be. The single farmer, on the other hand, enjoys some commercial independence insofar as private property, even of the land, thrives *within* the *téesz* under the name of *háztáji* or 'household plot'. The origin of the household plot is that when the farmers were induced to join the *kolkhozi*, they were allowed to keep little strips of land, preferably round their dwellings, on which to grow their own 'household' goods as part of their payment. Such arrangements, to be sure, existed in practically all village collectives set up in communist countries, but did not as a rule substantially modify the character of collective expropriation. For one thing, they affected only a small fraction of the total: a household plot was less than one acre, while an average holding pooled by a peasant farmer into the *téesz* was around 10–12 acres. But under Kádár the household plots increased their yield and significance enormously, and eventually their size as well. In the early sixties, with practically all the land collectivized, the peasants made a habit of neglecting the collectives to concentrate on their household plots. And though this practice openly bypassed the 'public ownership' system, the rulers were wise enough to accept it. The peasants acquired the right to sell their 'household' products on the free market, which worked as a natural spur; in vegetable gardening and animal husbandry, the yield of all the tiny household plots outweighed that of the collectivized land; and while the *téesz* was in the red, its members broke even by making the most of their crumbs of private ownership. A tug of war then started between the agronomists:

[1] Erdei, op cit., p. 7.   [2] ibid., p. 6.

the doctrinaire resented this state of affairs and agitated for the restriction of 'household' activities, but their opponents, the pragmatists, backed by Kádár, succeeded in saving the undeclared private sector within the public sector. The territory allotted to it was subsequently increased by allowing the members of farmers' families to acquire household plots of their own; and the 'Agitprop' machinery went out of its way to reassure the peasantry that the survival of household plots was not, as doctrinaires would have them believe, a temporary concession to bourgeois archaism but an integral part of the collective system. Collective agriculture, in a word, paid its way by not taking itself quite seriously.

There were years under Kádár when Hungary, whose main headache used to be finding markets for her grain surplus, had to import grain – but this paradox is such a well-known feature of the grain-producing communist countries that it would be otiose to dwell on it at length in a book dealing specifically with Hungary. In any case, thanks to a number of concessions to bourgeois ways, of which the handling of 'household' farming is the most remarkable, and also to undeniable technological progress, the leanest years of the *téesz* economy are over. In wheat and other grains, Hungary is self-supporting once again, although possibly in 1971 some imports may again be required – but owing to floods and other exceptional climatic conditions rather than to mismanagement. In the drive for higher efficiency, agriculture has always lagged behind other industries (at any rate according to official Hungarian statisticians who have no reason to distort the relevant figures); but a steady improvement has nevertheless been maintained even in this branch of industry, although always more noticeably in such individualistic fields as animal husbandry than in the typical collective effort of wheat-growing. The latest Hungarian Five-Year Plan[1] foresaw for 1971–75 a further shrinkage of agriculture's contribution to the national income to 13–14 per cent, which sounds realistic enough;[2] agriculture, if no longer the foundation of the Hungarian economy, is no longer its greatest liability either.

The N.E.M.

January 1968 was fixed as the date for launching the 'New Economic Mechanism', but, quite naturally, its implementation was

[1] Accepted by the Central Committee of the Hungarian Socialist Workers' Party on 15–16 July 1970.
[2] This figure is arrived at by reckoning that the productivity of agriculture would increase by 15–16 per cent in those years, but that of industry proper by 32–34 per cent and its contribution to the national income by 40–42 per cent; these may be over-optimistic estimates, but seem to be in the right proportion to each other. The increase of national income foreseen in the Plan is 30–32 per cent, and that of the average wage or salary 16–18 per cent.

spread over years before and after that date; practical adjustments had started about two years before, and to complete all the adjustments foreseen has taken all the time since then and will, presumably, take more years to come. It is a great and almost unparalleled undertaking, the results of which can hardly be assessed in the very near future. So much can already be claimed for it, that as an *experiment* it has been *successful*; few people outside the 'lunatic fringe' would deny that, on the whole, things look better as a result of this reform than they would if nothing like it had taken place. But about the character and limitations of its achievements, and the price that was to be paid for them, opinions differ widely.

Let us try, nevertheless, to point out the most important features of N.E.M. in terms as uncontroversial as possible:

1. *Decentralization.* Before N.E.M., the central planning authority undertook to determine the kinds and quantities of goods to be produced by various industrial plants, together with the number and working conditions of the wage-earners to be employed, and the prices for which their products should be available to the public or its specifically favoured sections. This, at any rate, was the guiding principle; but it is so no longer. Under N.E.M., central decision-making is reduced to the minimum, and the autonomy of individual plants (i.e., of their managements) raised to the highest degree compatible with one-party and dictatorial state ownership. In political matters, that is to say, the monopoly of the state (or rather of the Party ruling the state) is unchallenged, and the general trend of economic activity is part of politics; but as to details, the less politics interfere the better. In the words of Rezső Nyers:[1]

> There are, strictly speaking, three levels of decision-making in the use of national income under socialism: the state, the enterprise, and the household. The state determines the general principles, the social patterns, and the regulators of distribution . . . but it does not finally share out the whole of national income item by item. Decisions at the enterprise level are made on how the investment fund, the wage fund, and the profit sharing fund are used. . . .

And he comments:

> If and when the socialist state assumes the function of decision-making at lower levels, . . . then we are faced with a situation which we may call a typical socialist bureaucracy, one which is always costly and morally wrong. To avoid this, the state of

[1] op. cit., pp. 13–14.

Hungary surrenders part of the social net income to enterprises
... and leaves a decisive part of the movement of products to the
price mechanism.

2. *Profit motive reinstated.* The objective of an enterprise is profit;
as Nyers explains:[1]

> Since profit is the most comprehensive expression of economic
> efficiency, it is a pivotal factor in the system of incentives; under
> the Hungarian economic mechanism the increase in profits is a
> prerequisite for the increase in wages and personal incomes in
> general.

But no man could, of course, be more concerned with the profits of
his enterprise than with those of his country (or state, or party) unless
his own income noticeably kept pace with them. This is achieved
under N.E.M. (a) by distributing a large share of the net profit
among the personnel of a profitable enterprise, while keeping wages
and salaries in an unprofitable one down to the bare minimum,
possibly even with penalty deductions, and (b) by tolerating
inequality of private profit in the sense that higher-paid staff are
allowed higher additional payments, both absolutely and in proportion to their fixed incomes, than the lower-paid categories. A well-
informed British newspaper correspondent, clearly impressed by
N.E.M.,[2] quotes this telling example:

> The Dunai Vasmü [Danube Iron and Steel Works] made a
> profit of 1,200m forints (nearly £17m) last year. Of this 30 per
> cent went to state taxes, 58 per cent was ploughed back into the
> company and 12 per cent was shared among the employees–a
> bewildering formula for a Communist country to employ.
>
> The 30 or 40 members of the top management can receive a
> bonus of up to 85 per cent of their annual salary; the 500 members
> of the middle management can receive up to 50 per cent; and
> everyone else, about 12,000 of them, is allowed up to 15 per cent.

3. *Interplay of supply and demand reinstated.* This can be seen from the
facts and statements quoted above under (1) and (2). Market economy is the main regulator of prices. The state *may* on some occasions
interfere–as it may in practically all countries, whether they call
themselves socialist or not. The trend, however, is clear: in Czikós-
Nagy's prediction, by 1975 'most if not all prices would be freed'.[3]

---

[1] ibid., p. 12.
[2] Christopher Price, 'The profit motive goes east', *The Times*, London,
30 November 1970.
[3] Cf. Harry G. Shaffer, 'Progress in Hungary', *Problems of Communism*, Washington, January/February 1970, p. 53.

4. *Inequality remodelled* – and not, as many would say, instated or reinstated. This distinction should be stressed because communism, at any rate as we know it since the mid-1920s, is *not*, even *in principle*, an egalitarian doctrine. That on certain occasions it makes use of egalitarian emotions and slogans does little to modify the truth of this fact; after all, 'liberty' also has often been a rallying cry of communists, although few inside or outside their camp, and no one versed in their ideology, would believe that the word in fact means liberty. Classless society, abolition of the exploitation of man by man, planned and just distribution amongst all men prepared to work for it of what nature can yield to man – yes, these are communist objectives, but they do not imply, as an orthodox communist sees it, either liberty or equality. In previous chapters dealing with the stratification of society in Hungary under fully-fledged Stalinism, it has been demonstrated how blatant the differences of income (let alone differences of power and social standing) were between various social strata in the most 'sectarian' and 'dogmatic' period of communist rule. These differences were reduced after Stalin's death: the financial privileges of the Party top bureaucracy dwindled, Stakhanovite money-grubbers receded from the limelight, and so forth. Basically, however, the pattern of economic inequality did not change – until the introduction of N.E.M. The communist concept of legitimate economic inequality did not admit the rewarding of commercial acumen (or luck). In practice, of course, even this had to be tolerated so long as a private sector of economy existed, and the State Bank paid interest on savings; and for reasons of expediency a blind eye was turned to diplomats, trade representatives, and sportsmen who exploited the commercial opportunities of travel. In the 'dogmatic' peak period, *Ávó* officers used to make high profits out of barter in apartments; and when, later, communication with the West grew easier, an influx of motor-cars in the real or alleged shape of 'gifts from relatives' was the most conspicuous feature of the general scramble for bourgeois goods, pleasures, and status symbols. This could not have happened without a general respect for the capacity to make money in a 'capitalist' way. But it is one thing to tolerate an activity, and another to encourage it. N.E.M. explicitly encourages the spirit of business enterprise. A new era of *enrichissez-vous* has dawned in Hungary, reminiscent of the great upsurge of capitalist enterprise a hundred years ago under Kálmán Tisza's premiership.

These seem to the present writer the most important *integral* characteristics of N.E.M., those without which it would not be what it is. But let us add to the list four more which, though less integral, are no less important and are typical of the same spirit:

5. *More technical skill, less partisan zeal* required throughout the

whole gamut of economic activities. The apologists of N.E.M., particularly when concerned with reactions in Moscow, would argue that this is not quite correct because they have never despised expert knowledge and abilities, while political reliability is as essential today as it has ever been, but . . . this said, they would repeat in somewhat more stilted terms the same statement that they had rejected in the first place as incorrect. To be sure, they are justified in their objections: it would be foolish to think they have relaxed their vigilance over the key posts of political power. Yet, the shift of emphasis has been great enough to remodel the general attitude towards work and learning. An average Hungarian, even if ambitious in trade and business, no longer needs to demonstrate his readiness to fight for Marxism–Leninism; it is enough for him tacitly to conform.

6. *Multiplying trade links with the non-communist world* are also characteristic of though not originating under N.E.M. Certainly, trade with the West has steadily increased in the last few years, but so, even more, has trade with the countries of the Socialist Camp, and most of all with the U.S.S.R. (as will be demonstrated below). Another significant development has been the contribution of Western capital to Hungarian industrial enterprise; West German capital, namely the Krupp works, was the first to establish large plants in Hungary; but British, French, Italian, Belgian, Austrian, even American, capitalists also joined in, either by direct participation in management, or by concluding agreements for processing raw materials or semi-finished goods. This appearance of Western capitalist 'exploitation' on the map of the Socialist Camp is of course no novelty, and has not derived from the liberalization or decentralization of economic practices in the respective communist countries. But under N.E.M. the managements of individual plants are allowed to trade and make agreements (subject to security checks, of course) with capitalist partners–and this in itself materially contributes towards shaping the new managerial class into what it would be under more or less private capitalism.

7. *Landlordism has been re-established* in several respects. Again, we must make clear in what respect it was not re-established, since it had always existed. The inequalities of housing under fully-fledged Stalinism were not only great but glaring. While the defence chief Mihály Farkas gloried in his newly-built luxury villa, hardly anything was done to clear or replace the slums inherited from the Horthy régime, and new slums were added to them by establishing a system of 'co-tenancies' in formerly middle-class districts. Houses, moreover, could be 'owned', since they were not a 'means of production'. Apartment blocks were expropriated like other sizeable capital, and so were all private palaces and not a few cottages and huts for

the use of new occupiers, but without subjecting them to the same principles as those applied to agrarian, industrial, or commercial capital. Rents throughout most of the communist years have been unrealistically low in the state-owned blocks–which could be called a social benefit, except that the buildings are allowed to deteriorate. A typical sight in Budapest, even recently, was a tolerably well-repaired doorway in the street front, and a beautifully kept, re-decorated flat inside, with a decrepit, malodorous entrance hall and staircase in between. The reason is simple: the outside is looked after by the local council, the inside by the tenant, and the space between the two by nobody.

Houses could be built or bought as inheritable private property; so could flats ('eternal apartments' is the technical term in Magyar), and so with some limitations could buildings which were partly or entirely to be let, minor apartment blocks as it were. The families of the well-off classes save for 'owned' and not rented homes–say, a four-room flat in Budapest, with television set and washing machine and refrigerator, and a villa by Lake Balaton, a car for the parents, and a motorcycle for the eldest son to commute with. This has in fact been a feature of neo-bourgeois life since the early 1960s, but N.E.M. gave a dramatic boost to it. Many people (particularly of the dis-possessed, exiled, and then rehabilitated middle classes) have for quite a while been living as tenants in what used to be their own property, and not a few are today offered their ex-property for sale. Whether such deals have been concluded frequently or only excep-tionally is unknown to the present writer, but it seems clear that the main hurdle for putative buyers is a psychological one: they find it difficult to believe that what could once be taken from them without compensation should be any safer in their hands the second time. Yet they do buy similar properties elsewhere–which seem as safe as the régime itself: after all, neither a capitalist nor a communist government likes to undermine its own credit by dishonouring its promises if it can help it. Rákosi and Gerő, it is true, did not think twice about it; in fact, they rather boasted about having tricked the 'class-enemy'. But those times are definitely over; together with the trader's skill and initiative, the trader's reliability has re-entered the list of commendable virtues.

8. *Maszek extended.* The new houses are to a large extent built by *Maszek* traders. 'Maszek' stands for '*magánszek*tor', i.e. 'private sector'; and has' with its un-Magyar ring of Budapest slang, become the most popular colloquial term coined by post-war politico-economic jargon. There are *Maszek* plumbers, *Maszek* electricians, tailors, shoemakers; some are grouped in more or less close 'co-operatives' or 'work communities' (lawyers who accept private

clients are also grouped in 'work communities'); and their survival as a class, or social category, is no novelty, although the greater scope allowed to them certainly is. In and around the building trade, for example, their activities are not confined to new buildings; anyone who wants his leaking roof, his blocked gas-pipes, his blurred TV screen *quickly* repaired will call a *Maszek* trader. Or else he calls a skilled worker employed in a state-owned factory and says: 'Could you do this for me on a *Maszek* basis?' And the skilled worker will do it–either after his factory shift or (making some excuse to leave his workshop) during it, depending on his initiative. There are, needless to say, borderline cases between fair and unfair dealing in this respect; as there are among National Health Service dentists or ophthalmologists in the United Kingdom when they tell the patient, 'Sorry, this is something I can only do in my private practice'. The 'work community' system substantially contributes towards enabling people to combine public service with work for private profit. Official statistics suggest that the percentage of private traders proper, which decreased abruptly after the expropriations of enterprises in 1948, has consistently decreased further and no longer amounts to more than a minute fraction of the population, while that of traders grouped in some form of co-operative has steadily increased. This is indeed the case. What the official statistics do not–and indeed cannot–demonstrate is the percentage of work done 'on a *Maszek* basis', which has grown and is growing all the time.

These eight features of present-day economic life–or nine, if one includes the encouragement given to 'household plot' priorities in agriculture–would seem to indicate that with her New Mechanism Hungary is heading for a free market capitalism as we know it in the West, and indeed for a free-for-all as we knew it before Keynes, Schacht, and Roosevelt. But this is only one side of the picture. To see it in proportion, at least two features pointing in a different direction must be stressed with the same emphasis:

(i) *It is still a socialist economy in the sense that communists use the word* '*socialist*'. True enough, communists do not always use it in the same sense: 'dialectics' in their philosophy and tactical considerations in their daily propaganda enable them to manipulate it. Moreover, today there may be great differences between what rates as 'socialist' in Moscow, Peking, or Belgrade. Instead of trying to define in our own words what the communist-authorized version of socialism is, rather let the most authentic economic spokesman of the Kádár régime, Rezső Nyers,[1] speak for himself and themselves:

Socialism is an international idea, and this means that socialist

[1] op. cit., p. 22.

productive relations must be established on identical principles in all countries, regardless of the different state of development of productive forces and the difference in national circumstances. If we gave up this principle, we would degrade our international movement to a national one. What are the common principles? First, the interests of the working class as a whole and all working people must be effective. Secondly, socialist productive relations must become absolute, society must dispose over productive forces and national income. Thirdly, central planning and state guidance must secure the planned development of the whole economy. Fourthly, regulated commodity and money relations must bring into harmony the central plan, enterprise decisions and personal action. These are the guiding principles in every socialist country. Their joint application must be aimed at, if one of the four fails to prevail the remaining three will also be impaired.

I suggest that to most of these declarations of intent, democratic Western politicians of Left or Right could readily subscribe. Who would challenge, for instance, the pious principle that 'the interests of all working people must be effective'? And so forth. The one clause (not even a whole sentence) which to some extent betrays the real difference between the communist and non-communist world is this: *society must dispose over productive forces and national income*'; although the applicability of even this depends on what is implied by 'society'. It may be argued that if 'society' means the community of *all* human beings organized on some kind of regular basis, then society under communist rule cannot 'dispose' over anything—it is a privileged Party leadership disposing only in the name of society. Is that leadership entitled to do so? This is a matter of faith, unanswerable by rational arguments; and where arguments fail, tanks decide. The difference between a socialist and a non-socialist economy thus boils down to the question whether the man with his finger on the trigger does or does not call himself a socialist.

(ii) *Progress towards a welfare state.* But there are symptoms of the awakening of a socialist spirit in a different sense.

The main beneficiaries of N.E.M. are the new managerial and top technologist classes, as without incentives for them, incentives typical of an acquisitive society, the whole experiment would be doomed to failure. This does not rule out, however, a growing concern with the welfare of the working classes; on the contrary—as in the English-speaking world and many another country of the democratic West, where capitalism had the sense to get workers interested in its success by making them partners in affluence, the liberalizers of the Hungarian economy have created a partnership in purpose and profit between the men at the top and the lower strata of the industrial population. Even the poorest worker profits to some extent by the relaxation of communist workshop morality in general, and by the commercial success of his employers in particular. The welfare of the common workman has thus grown into an objective of the Hungarian state. In a way, of course, the dictatorship of the proletariat has always aimed at an earthly paradise for the proletariat. Increases in the workers' spending power, whether to be found only in statistics or actually in everyday life (copious examples of both could be cited), have been acclaimed as achievements of socialism. The very idea that social insurance and care for the sick must be universal brought considerable benefits to the poor, in spite of its imperfect application. Even under fully-fledged Stalinism, as will be remembered, much was done for working-class children and for mass entertainment, including the popularization of classical art. But *to leave the worker alone with his increased spending power* was a thing hardly envisaged by communist welfare officials. Under Rákosi, the very opposite was required: the worker must always be visible to a Big Brother agent— if not in the workshop, then in the seminar or even kicking up his heels at dance-halls, so long as he also sang Party marching songs and toasted Party celebrities. *Leisure*, in a word, was no part of welfare under Stalin–Rákosi; the authorized working-class ideal was compatible with striving after luxury but not with love of privacy; and de-Stalinization was slow to revise this ideal.

The Hungarian N.E.M. indicates a new departure in this field. In 1968, one-third of the industrial working population was shifted in planned stages from a 48- to a 44-hour working week. It was made clear from the outset that this was meant to be an experiment–the idea being that by 1970 the whole of industry should follow suit but that in case the reform resulted in a noticeable drop in productivity, the managers might go back on it, at least temporarily. Since in the following year (1969) the increase in national output failed to reach its target, and productivity in industry actually dropped,[1] the effort to shorten the working week suffered a setback; and since reconciling leisure and productivity requirements is a very tentative business,[2] it is impossible to foretell what the position will be when this book is published; but in any case, as an approach to Western-style welfare state concepts the experiment remains significant.

Another, perhaps even more significant, innovation pointing in the

[1] Cf. Hungarian sources quoted by Shaffer, op. cit., pp. 54, 278 n. 3.
[2] In *Hungary 70*, Pannonia Press, Budapest (Hungarian government publication), p. 36, a general reference is made to the beneficial effects (for example, in increasing the labour force) of 'the reduction of the working week to 44 hours . . . on a wide sphere' without going into the details of this reform.

same direction is the task allotted to the trade unions of voicing the workers' interests. From the communist 'turning-point' of 1948, the unions' responsibility had been the very opposite, namely to act as watchdog of the Party and the government, keeping a vigilant eye on the labour force in workshops and in entertainment or cultural centres. Under N.E.M., the unions are to regain part of their rights to negotiate on behalf of the workshop personnel with the owner of the plant–that is, with the state or its representatives, the management. It is even suggested that in a further phase of development the workers might be entitled to elect, through union machinery, their managements in the respective plants–what, in fact, the revolutionaries of 1956 demanded and what has to some extent been achieved in Yugoslavia. At the moment, these are matters of speculation and dreams rather than realities in Hungary; even the 1945–47 practice of allowing the workers' representatives some say in the selection of their managers has only been revived to a minute extent; but the trend is unmistakable.

N.E.M. thus combines Western capitalism with Eastern socialism–and with Western socialism, too. At any rate, it seeks to do so, although of course under different names. It is, so to speak, an economic policy of eating one's cake not once but twice and still having it. The result may fall short of expectations, but it is in fact the most realistic expedient imaginable so long as the map of Europe stays roughly the same.

How do Hungarians live?

After so many changes and experiments, how then do Hungarians live today? Better, certainly, than under the same régime ten years ago; or than earlier still under Stalin; or under Horthy; or under the Habsburgs. Kádár could justifiably tell his people: 'You've never had it so good'.

But as to the degree of improvement, some scepticism is justified about the impression given by statistics. Nyers, together with his above-quoted table, produces on the same page another one, on 'Per capita growth of national income', which compares several countries, for instance:

	in 1950	in 1968	Percentage change Average annual increase 1951–68
Hungary	100	273	5·7
Soviet Union	100	459	8·8
Great Britain	100	166	2·9

If this table were to be taken at its face value it would mean that an average Ivan or Natasha in Russia can spend today four and a half times as much as their father or mother could twenty years ago. Everybody who has visited Russia recently knows that this is nonsense—most observers, though not all,[1] would agree that *some* improvement has taken place, but nothing like what the figures suggest. The reason for this discrepancy is partly ideological; in a social system where 'objectivity' is a dirty word, and 'partisanship' (or 'Party-mindedness') a word of praise, statistical analysis devised so as to please the holders of power will naturally reflect the wishful thoughts of officials. An even more essential reason is that statistics tend to reflect technological improvements, but to a lesser degree the price paid for them. Shop-bought bread and tinned meat are, after all, bread and meat, often good in quality, but still lacking something that the originals used to have and which rarely finds its way into the 'national income' statistics. Full employment, extended to categories previously *ex officio* unemployed such as housewives, is on the whole a boon; but certainly not an unqualified one. The wife who works in the factory either neglects her household and children or else has to do an extra shift of work at home and is ultimately more exploited than her ancestresses in pre-suffragette centuries. To some extent, this applies to the highly industrialized and democratic West as well as to the newcomers to industrialization in eastern Europe or to their impetuous imitators in Afro-Asia; but with one great difference. The United States, to take the most telling example, is richer not only in foodstuffs but even more in gadgets than the rest of the world; and a multitude of gadgets can be quite an entertaining and hygienic substitute for a dedicated materfamilias. Without that substitute, in a far from prosperous 'industrial-agrarian' country, sweating the housewife is the only alternative to letting the household run down. In this specific phase of technological development, would political freedom be a help? Yes, because it always is; but it would not make the problem non-existent.

With these qualifications, the above-quoted economic growth-figure for Hungary may be almost correct; according to sound observers, it has in the last few years been on an average between 4 and 5 per cent. As to the present-day standard of living, Nyers writes:[2]

National income per capita in Hungary, calculated at comparable

---

[1] 'Astonishing as it may seem, every serious research—by Professor Sergei Prokopovich, Dr. Naum Jasny, Mrs. Janet Chapman and others—has shown conclusively that the real wages of the Russian industrial worker today are, at best, hardly better than in 1913' (Tibor Szamuely, *Sunday Times*, 7 February 1971).

[2] op. cit., p. 29.

prices, is about $750, as against $1,200 to 1,700 in western Europe, $1,000 to 1,200 in Italy and Austria, and $500 to 700 in Spain, Portugal and Greece, $60 to $100 in liberated former colonial countries and $200 to $300 in the less developed capitalist countries.

Again, this is not wide of the mark. 'An average Englishman has twice, an average American three times as much to spend as an average Hungarian' is the verdict of level-headed, down to earth, and observant people, Hungarians as well as Westerners, who in the last few years have travelled about a great deal in the areas concerned. But any such estimate can only convey impressions. The difficulties of comparing average standards of living are well-known even in the case of Britain and France; the qualities of housing, cooking, and pleasure do not easily translate into statistics. What can fairly be stated is that a Western visitor does not see starving or particularly ragged people in Hungary; partly because even in the old days under the King-Emperor or the ruling Admiral, penury was not so general or obvious as to catch the eye at once; and partly because the undoubted technological progress, often accelerated by social upheavals, has resulted in draining out, as it were, the most putrid morasses of misery, the multitude of rickety children, staring as if hypnotized at a glass of milk and prevented from going to school in the slush by lack of footwear. Today, most people look tolerably fed and tolerably dressed, quite tasty food is served in the workers' canteens, and chic bikinis brighten the holiday resorts. Consumption has steadily increased in practically all fields but, quite understandably, at very different speeds: since 1960, that of food by approximately 20 per cent, according to official sources,[1] while the number of TV set-owners increased from barely more than 100,000 to almost 1,400,000 (in 1969). The amenities and consolations of a lower-middle-class existence have become accessible to more people than ever before.

Salvation through Corruption and Conformism

Many, in fact, live better than their opposite numbers in the West; Western visitors are often surprised not only by the lavish hospitality with which quite humble people receive them, but also by the spendthrift snobbery which they encounter: 'Really', a Hungarian lady fresh from the Marxist–Leninist seminar would say with condescension (about the famous British chain-store, Marks and Spencer), 'you shop at Marks and Sparks? I thought it was only for the common people.' And though, of course, most knitwear in

[1] *Hungary 70.*

Hungary is much below the Marks and Spencer level, a great number of people succeed in obtaining luxuries not quite fitting their acknowledged positions; and most earn and spend slightly more than they are supposed to.

Their secret is, as in pre-war decades, a degree of tacitly authorized theft. 'To do *Maszek*' during working hours, in the state-owned factory, using factory material, is, as has been pointed out, a widespread and cheerfully acknowledged practice. It cannot (and never could) thrive without some connivance between bosses and underdogs, customers and purveyors, civil servants, managers, and workers: forgetfulness about certain obligations is reciprocal. All this would seem to prove that without such a happy-go-lucky variety of corruption, reminiscent of Kálmán Tisza's and Count Bethlen's eras, no social order can function smoothly in Hungary, even less keep up an impressive pace of economic progress. Altogether it is a benign and almost universal network of mutual bribes and backscratching, for the time being the sole alternative to the incorruptibility of slave-driving fanatics. Those categories outside its orbit are indeed in a bad way: old-age pensioners, for instance, widows of *ancien régime* high officials, etc., who, without support from relatives in the West (a most important source of income for their kind), have to try and make ends meet on a monthly sum of the purchasing value of about £10 or 25 dollars. It is hardly a consolation to know that the number of such people diminishes as death takes its annual toll and leaves the survivors lonelier still.

On the whole, the main casualty of the system of mutual backscratching is integrity of mind. And this owing to the fact that the key posts are held today (again, as in the period 1867 to 1944, almost without a break) by a privileged bureaucracy. Without the connivance of the local Party secretary, the whole cosy system of semi-illegality would break down. He, however, cannot be satisfied by your mending his refrigerator for nothing or passing fillets of veal under the counter to his wife: he insists on your putting on an appearance of political conformism, at least to the extent of not dissenting conspicuously. There are fields in which criticism is allowed—indeed, required. 'Do you know', the cabaret compère asks, 'why there are no strikes in Hungary?' Rustling and titters among the audience; everybody knows why but expects *him* to answer, and so he does: 'Because no one would notice the difference anyway'. General laughter and relief: how comforting to know that such serious questions can be discussed so genially. And when the discussion grows weightier, 'we still have our faults' is the most favoured formula to introduce a profession of faith in the ability of the leaders to remedy them. But beyond such limits, hardly anybody can afford to take a critical attitude. If he does it all the same, he is not neces-sarily arrested; only expected to *work to rule*. No extra *Maszek* facilities, no quick promotion, no permit to travel to the West,[1] let alone a fair quota of hard currency, for the tiresome dissenter!

Hungary is thus back in the rut which seemed so characteristic of her paternalistic habits when led by men such as the two Tiszas and Count Bethlen. The rules of her daily life derive from what an entailed bureaucracy dictates and what the class of entrepreneurs invents both to implement and to parry it. However shaken, her two ruling classes, the holders of power and the manipulators of money, have re-emerged as if obeying the natural law which makes oil rise to the surface of water. There are of course differences, even contrasts, between the past and the present, but the fundamental similarity is unmistakable. The ruling bureaucracy are no longer gentry and the entrepreneurs are no longer overwhelmingly Jews, but the stilted rhetoric of the erstwhile county magistrate in praise of His Serene Highness the Regent or some other representative of authority strangely survives in the ponderous and long-winded style of Marxist–Leninist rituals; as does the ironical sing-song of erstwhile ghetto merchants in the quarters where business deals are negotiated, however national the enterprise and socialist the profit aimed at. Business is there to serve the bureaucrat, but also to demonstrate that what the bureaucrat says need not be taken seriously.

Yet, 'socialism' was not imposed for nothing, and socially the gap between the ruling and the working classes has considerably narrowed since feudal and private capitalism was abolished. The belief in an almost biological difference between people born to rule and those born to be ruled has gone; everybody able to work and prepared to play by the rules can feel himself in the antechamber of power; and even if he is not, he feels he has the right to claim a stake in the ventures of his country. In other words, the common man has, and is encouraged to have, a feeling of human dignity. The advent of communism certainly had a share in bringing this about, though the 'counter-revolution' of 1956 had an even bigger share. Now, thanks to the experiences of the post-war decades and particularly to those of the N.E.M. years, the common people of Hungary are at last capable of managing their own affairs – if only they were left alone to do it.

But there is no question of leaving them alone; not even, in the foreseeable future, of going far enough in democratization to allow a

---

[1] According to a recent (liberalizing) reform, practically every Hungarian subject can obtain a passport, but an extra permit is needed to make it valid; and the amount of 'hard' currency granted on such occasions is (except to those sent on some mission) so small that only Hungarians helped by friends and relatives in the West can make use of it.

dissenter to speak his mind without looking over his shoulder. This is the saddest aspect of Hungary today. Her establishment has always been based on public servility; yet, under the Tiszas, and to a lesser extent under Count Bethlen, there were certain categories, particularly in Budapest, who could air their dissent without necessarily incurring fatal penalties. They could choose, then, between respectability and intellectual honesty. But it will take a long time before the people's right not to be respectable is restored to them.

Still a satellite but no longer isolated

Two sets of figures, both relating to Hungary's economic development, which have consistently soared in the last decade are headed 'Tourist Traffic', and 'Foreign Trade'. The latter, of course, is the more important of the two; the former may be considered as its appendage–adding a human touch to business.

Compared with the inter-war period, Hungarian foreign trade has not only increased but radically changed its character: then, two-thirds or more of the export goods were agricultural; since the 1950s, agricultural products have fallen to approximately one-third of the total. In fact, even the method of recording them has changed so much that it is difficult to compare figures for the two periods in detail.[1]

Since the consolidation of the Kádár régime in 1960, however, the pattern of foreign trade has been basically what it is today, although its size has rapidly increased all the time. 'Compared to industry or national income', we read in an official Hungarian publication,[2]

> the volume of foreign trade in Hungary is increasing at a faster rate. For instance, between 1960 and 1967, industrial production increased by 71 per cent, whereas ... imports increased by 82 per cent and exports by 94 per cent.

We learn from the same article that 'over one-fourth of the products of the industry of Hungary are exported' and 'the value of exports amounts to about 40 per cent of the national income'. Hungary is thus further from being an autarky, and is more dependent on both imports and exports, than ever before. Such dependence is not necessarily a bad thing, of course. It implies (politics permitting) interdependence; and offers the only road towards technological improvements and a higher standard of living for a comparatively

---

[1] The two approximate figures in this paragraph are based on the analyses in *Hungaria*, a comprehensive statistical survey issued under the auspices of the Hungarian government in Budapest, 1938; and *Magyarország*, a collection of statistical graphs issued under the auspices of the Hungarian government in Budapest, 1970.

[2] *Hungary 69* (a collection of documentary articles: Pannonia Press, Budapest, 1969), pp. 141 et seq.

small country, particularly if she is as poor as Hungary in some of the basic raw materials of fuel and industry. The increase in her foreign trade should on the whole be considered as an indicator of her economic progress.

But it is one thing to achieve this by freely negotiated settlements, choosing the best buyers and sellers wherever available, and quite another to do so with one eye on the probable reactions of a foreign Great Power. Which way has been Hungary's? In fact, both–but with a clear bias towards the latter. If since 1960 her trade with Western countries has steadily risen, so even more has that with Soviet Bloc countries–and most of all with the Soviet Union herself. 'On the basis of 1967 statistics', we learn,[1]

> trade with the socialist countries amounts to 67·6 per cent, trade with the advanced capitalist countries to 26·5 per cent, and trade with the developing countries comprises 5·9 per cent of the country's [Hungary's] total foreign trading activity.

Broken down geographically, European countries represent about 90 per cent of Hungary's trade partners; and one reason at least for the smallness of America's share is suggested in another paragraph of the same article which reads: 'Hungary applies punitive tariffs against countries which levy maximum import duties on Hungarian goods–for example, the United States, the Republic of South Africa, and Portugal'.[2]

A similar picture of developments, including those since the beginning of N.E.M., is given by Nyers[3] who reckons that 'commodities worth about 40 per cent of [Hungarian] national income are exchanged for other goods in international markets' and publishes this table:

The distribution of Hungary's foreign trade turnover by groups of countries
(in per cent)

	1949	1955	1969
With socialist countries	50	63	68
With non-socialist countries	50	37	32
	100	100	100

[1] *Hungary 69*, ibid.

[2] The author may or may not be trying to imply that the U.S.A. comes into the same category as the two countries most often pilloried nowadays for racial or colonial oppression, but in fairness to the Hungarian foreign trade agencies it must be admitted that, unhampered by ideology, they do all they can to strengthen their links with 'revanchist' West Germany and even with Franco's Spain–as will be seen below.

[3] op. cit., pp. 26–7.

The trend demonstrated by these figures seems particularly interesting if one bears in mind what the political climate in any of those years was. In 1949, to get an innocent personal greeting from the West was enough to cause the recipient sleepless nights; to suggest trade with the West would, for anyone outside the inner circle of Moscow's top quislings, have been courting disaster. And Yugoslavia, in spite of her continuing communist dictatorship, was not only outside the Socialist Camp but practically in a state of war with Hungary—certainly cut off from her economically. In 1969, trade with the West (and with non-aligned Yugoslavia too) was openly sought, and progress achieved in it was advertised as a successful endeavour by the Hungarian People's Republic to translate political co-existence into economic reality. Yet, in the twenty years leading from panicky isolation to *gemütlich* co-existence, the relative share of Russia and her satellites in Hungarian trade has constantly increased. This pattern leaves one with the impression that N.E.M. Hungary has won the right to trade with whom she likes, but pays for it by trading even more assiduously with those whom Moscow prefers.

This, no doubt, is only one side of the picture; the fact that Hungary has increased her trade with such countries in both the communist and the 'Third' worlds as are behind her in industrial development provides a welcome stimulus to her manufacturing industry. Yet to gain a clear idea of Hungary's position in the world, some facts illustrating the tightrope she has to walk should be pointed out.

Hungary is more advanced, and has been for about half a century, in some of the most sophisticated branches of industry (e.g. electrical engineering, precision tools) than her agricultural and *puszta* background would seem to suggest; but in others she lags surprisingly behind her contemporaries in 'industrial-agrarian' status. The shortage of computers is a case in point. As the Budapest daily *Magyar Nemzet* of 15 July 1970 reported,[1] there were at that time altogether eighty computers in use in Hungary—as against 1,200 in Holland, 1,550 in Italy, 4,500 in France, 5,000 in Britain, and 6,300 in the Federal Republic of Germany. In February that year the Hungarian Council of Ministers decided that in five years time the number of computers must be increased fivefold, but experts estimated that it would increase tenfold. Up to that time computers were mainly imported from East Germany and the West; and it seems unlikely that the pattern will change in the near future, although the U.S.S.R. also has a part to play in this development: some of the computer engineers get their training in Russia.

[1] Quoted by 'Free Europe' Service, 28 August 1970.

Among Western countries, the lion's share of trade with Hungary is held by the Federal Republic of Germany – with which Hungary has not even diplomatic relations! This is particularly manifest in a field which one would think politically the most delicate: co-operation between Hungarian and non-Hungarian enterprises. As Budapest Radio announced on 21 August 1970, an organization called 'Intercooperation Trade Development Ltd.' had been formed in Budapest with a view to assisting Hungarian enterprises to conclude and implement agreements with Western firms which go much further than buying and selling; they entail, for instance, establishing Western industrial plants in Hungary and lending Hungarian equipment and labour to firms in the West. According to the economic journal *Figyelö* ('Observer' – Nr. 19.8.70) 85 co-operation agreements of the kind had been concluded up to then since 1964, namely: 32 with (West) German, 16 with Austrian, 7 with French, 7 with British, 6 with Italian, 6 with Swiss, 5 with Swedish, and 5 with Dutch firms.

In the coming years, economic links between Hungary and West Germany will most probably increase at high speed. As was officially announced from Budapest on 7 September 1970, the volume of trade between the two countries was expected to be 30 per cent higher in that year than the year before, and this trend is to continue into the 1980s – unless Erich Honecker, the East German First Party Secretary, is both resentful and strong enough to check it. The basic characters of imports and exports between the two countries no longer differ so much as they did before the war: products of 'light industry' and of 'chemical industry and medicines' figure largely on both lists, though machine tools are conspicuous among goods coming in from Germany, while food and processed agricultural products remain prominent on the outgoing list from Hungary.

If Pankow or the diehards in Moscow might object to the fraternization with Bonn, they certainly have no such worries about improved relations with Falangist Spain. On 18 November 1970 at the Ministry of Foreign Trade in Budapest a five-year Hungarian–Spanish Trade Agreement was signed. It envisaged the growth of trade between the two countries to a value of approximately 20 million dollars in 1971. Up to the signing of this agreement Hungary had not been in diplomatic relations with the Franco government, and recognized the Spanish refugee government in Paris. This attitude has now been tacitly dropped.

Hungary, in a word, is allowed to trade with parliamentary countries and encouraged to do so with authoritarian ones, even right-wing authoritarians. But much more important is the role allotted to her *within* the Soviet Bloc – or its economic counterpart,

'Comecon' or 'Council for Mutual Economic Aid', whose members are the U.S.S.R., the German Democratic Republic, Poland, Czechoslovakia, Mongolia, Bulgaria, Romania (whose individualism in foreign relations has so far been tolerated by the Kremlin), and Hungary. The heads of government of these countries met in Warsaw on 12–13 May 1970, and decided to advance with increased impetus along their road of economic 'integration' under a succession of plans outlined for the coming twenty years. At the same time, they decided to found a common Investment Bank, and this scheme was within three weeks approved by all concerned–except Romania who dragged her feet and expressed some reservations. At the twenty-fifth session of Comecon, convoked on 26 July 1971 in Bucharest, with the clear intention of countering Romanian separatist endeavours, and with Fock and Vályi as leaders of the Hungarian delegation, the common will to 'integrate' was once again emphasized, but with less encroachment on the rights of the individual member states than had been expected (and feared).

So far so good: co-operation and economic integration, whether between communist or non-communist states, are desirable so long as they unite partners who consider one another as more or less equals. Between the Soviet Union and her client states, however, there can be no question of equality. This of course is partly due to their difference in size and power, but even more to the Soviet Union's claim, acknowledged by the client administrations, to decide when in a particular country 'socialism' is endangered. Consequently the smaller Comecon countries simply act as outposts of the Russian military empire.

Thus, approximately one-third of Hungary's foreign trade consists of imports from and exports to the U.S.S.R.; and, under three Soviet–Hungarian agreements signed on 15 September 1970, trade with the U.S.S.R. is expected to increase considerably faster than Hungary's other foreign trade activities. Until 1975, so it is reckoned, the volume of trade between the two countries must increase by at least 10 per cent a year, so as to reach 55 per cent by the end of the period; and the value of goods exchanged will amount to 9 milliard roubles (or, at the official rate, 10 milliard U.S. dollars in 1970). In particular Hungary will increase her export of light industry products (for example, textiles whose quality in Russia is notorious all over the world), and of canned or otherwise processed food, and medicine; while among Soviet deliveries to Hungary the most curious item consists of *Italian* motor-cars (manufactured under a special Fiat licence) and the essential items relate to fuel and power: blast-furnace coke, iron ore, crude oil, natural gas, and, perhaps most important, electricity. The Soviet contribution to the Hungarian economy is obviously a substantial one and serves for the U.S.S.R. as a link with other Danubian countries, both Comecon partners and non-aligned. 'Hungary', we read in an official Hungarian account,[1] 'imports electric power primarily from the Soviet Union . . . She is also linked in the same grid with Yugoslavia, Austria, Czechoslovakia'. Her crude-oil supplies from the U.S.S.R. come via Czechoslovakia through the 'Friendship' pipeline which also branches out to Austria. Hungary is in many respects, no doubt, the better for such deliveries and links; but it is equally obvious that she could do better still if not shackled politically. One of her important natural resources is the uranium-ore deposits in south-west Hungary (branching out to Yugoslavia). These are controlled in a way which makes them, to all intents, Soviet property. In the manifestos of the 1956 Revolution, clarification of this matter was repeatedly demanded, and it was not refused in principle by the U.S.S.R.; but once the Revolution had been defeated, no more was heard about it.

The number of foreign visitors to Hungary in the last decade has increased even more rapidly than foreign trade: it amounted to 244,000 (or, including transit visitors, 624,000) in 1960, and rose steadily to 2,419,000 (including those in transit, 4,335,000) in 1967. In 1967,[2] we learn,

> the breakdown of visitors according to their country of origin is as follows: most visitors came from Czechoslovakia (829,000), followed by Yugoslavia (689,000). There was not much difference between the German Democratic Republic (171,000) and Poland (156,000); and a small difference in the number of Soviet (118,000), Austrian (115,000), West-German (87,000) and Romanian (78,000) tourists. Many tourists also visit Hungary from other continents; in 1967, 29,000 visitors came from the United States of America.

To qualify these figures, it should be taken into account that many, and perhaps even most, of the tourists coming from neighbouring countries (and from the United States) are Hungarians by birth or mother-tongue; and of these the Romanian contingent would be much greater but for the illiberal attitude of the Romanian authorities to passport applications from their subjects, particularly the Magyars. Hungary was not the only country to increase her tourist traffic in these years – it was in the ascendant everywhere, particularly in countries previously less concerned with it, from Britain to Bulgaria. Yet, as far as the quality of Hungarian life is concerned, the influx of foreigners did much to make the atmosphere more cosmopolitan and even liberal, as the police did not noticeably interfere

[1] *Hungary 70*, p. 29.   [2] *Hungary 69*, p. 237.

with business or sporting, amorous, and social intercourse between the host nationals and their guests. Hard currency softened all barriers to communication.

Hungary is proud of her place at the forefront of bourgeois revivalism – but also worried lest the U.S.S.R. should resent it as she did with Dubček's Czechoslovakia. While making great sacrifices to *sell* her liberalization to the West, she deprecates a too lively Western appreciation of it, which might turn the Kremlin against her. Western bourgeois writers, a Hungarian communist complains in the official Party gazette,[1] absolutely misunderstand the progress of socialism in Hungary when they paint an 'idyllic picture of a capitalist restoration'; it is time for them to wake up, he urges, and to realize that fundamentally nothing has changed. Needless to say, such exhortations are addressed to Moscow rather than to the West. 'There is no separate road to socialism', Budapest Radio emphasizes,[2] correcting various Western papers which were tactless enough to draw attention to the national character of the great Hungarian experiment more enthusiastically than Budapest could have wished. Even the expression 'New Economic Mechanism', popularized at full blast on the eve of its go-ahead, was subsequently dropped on a wide scale lest the Kremlin might suspect a 'separate road to socialism' behind it; in publications such as *Hungary 69* and *Hungary 70*, 'the reform of economic management' of 1968 or some similar phrase is substituted for it. The Hungarian government must be equally careful both to promote and to moderate its popularity west of what is still, however frequently perforated, an iron curtain.

A Guess about the Future

Hungarians can be annoying with their passion for cracking jokes, particularly when the jokes are aimed at making them feel wittier and braver than they actually are. Yet it is true to say that for the last hundred years jokes have been their most authentic outlet for popular feeling, the best substitute for a free Press, free opinion polls, free elections in recording that feeling. One of the jokes most untiringly cracked, and one that is more significant than funny, goes like this:

'What is the difference between a wife and socialism?'
'?'
'Nothing. It's here and it has to be loved.'

'Ez van, ezt kell szeretni', runs the last sentence of this quip, and any Western visitor who masters some pigeon-Magyar can hear it

---

[1] József Horváth in *Népszabadság*, 26 July 1970.
[2] e.g. on 27 August 1970 – quoted by 'Free Europe', 18 September 1970.

cropping up as often as any Top-of-the-Pops phrase. 'Socialism' in this context, of course, means Soviet domination. 'Domination' is a horrible word, but there is domination *and* domination. Compared with what it was under Stalin it is quite tolerable. So long as people remember the early 1950s their grumbling will stop short of exasperation. Nor will they ever want to repeat the autumn of 1956, however proudly they cherish its memory. 'Let others shed their blood now, we've done more than our share', is their reaction if ever the spectre of organized resistance to the U.S.S.R. comes up in conversation. And sympathetic though they were towards Czechs and Slovaks at the time of the Soviet invasion (and ashamed of the Hungarian troops taking part), they could not extinguish a spark of *Schadenfreude* about their struggling neighbours who 'just sat by with their arms folded in 1956'. And they certainly do not feel kindlier towards the Romanians either.

In spite of so many military, political, and social upheavals, from the Napoleonic Wars down to recent years, the frigid relationship of the Hungarians with their neighbours has survived and is at the heart of their vital problems. They have undergone very similar trials and experiences; been liberated, oppressed, and set against one another by the same masters. Soviet power over them is very much like the Habsburg power used to be. The Habsburgs hammered their subjects into one and the same Imperial frame, but within that they ruled by dividing them; *viribus unitis* and *divide et impera* were equally appropriate for their dynastic motto. And to divide was always easier than to unite; chauvinism, nations fanned by interests vested in the local squirearchies, played into the hands of the oppressor. The subject nations felt, rightly or wrongly, that they were most threatened in their independence when their ruler wished them to make common cause—not with himself and his Court, whom most of them were prepared to accept as their superiors, but with other subject nations.

To do the Habsburgs justice one should recognize that since their collapse, both the fury of petty nationalisms and the use made of them by intruding imperial despots have become even more pernicious. The deepest depravity was of course reached under Hitler's rule; but to be liberated from it by Stalin (as a hundred Hungarian jokes, and really good ones, pointed out) was what the English call 'out of the frying-pan into the fire'. Yet, the fire was not so all-destroying as it seemed for a while. A tyrant's death and the complications of succession influence the development of an empire as powerfully today as they did two thousand years ago. Stalin's death gave a new turn to Russian, to Chinese, to Egyptian, and to Hungarian history.

It entailed, among other things, a more flexible attitude towards inter-state moves by the Soviet satellites. This change has been even

more marked in relations within the Socialist Camp than in those
with the world outside it. Stalin had always been more alarmed by
the possibilities of a palace conspiracy than by even obvious threats
of military attack from outside; and, correspondingly, the very idea of
a federation between his client states, however wedded to the cause
of 'socialism', angered him more than federalism between bourgeois
countries. His hostility to Tito and (though later hushed up) to
Dimitrov, the Bulgarian Party leader, had really started during the
war when the two aroused his suspicions by broaching the idea of a
Balkan Federation,[1] and his quislings in eastern Europe took this
lesson to heart: they knew that there was no safe route from Budapest
to Prague or from Bucharest to Sofia except through Moscow. On
Moscow's orders, they had to be jealous for their own 'sovereignties'
whether they liked it or not. Economically, what Stalin established
with his satellites was, in the words of a competent student of eastern
European economics,[2] 'a trading system of radial bilateralism, with
the Soviet Union symbolizing the hub, and the dependent countries
the spokes'; but 'Stalin's heirs recognized the immense waste inherent
in the Stalinist method of intra-bloc relations and were determined to
replace this economic insanity with a rational programme of co-
operation.' True though this is, de-Stalinization has neither in this
nor in other respects gone far enough to allow the subject nations to
create their own rational groupings in their respective geographical
regions before deciding to what extent and in what way they should
be linked to either the U.S.S.R. or to any of the Western Great
Powers and blocs. And should the Kremlin decide to rule them by
dividing, it could, like the Habsburgs–and for that matter, like
Hitler–count on misguided patriots; 'there is an ever-increasing
danger of a violent nationalism developing in the East-central
European area', a scholarly student of contemporary history writes,[3]
'one which would not only be directed against the common Soviet
oppressor but one which would line up, once again, one small nation
against the other'. This danger exists indeed. 1971 saw such miraculous combinations of separatist and internationalist passions as Croat
refugees steeped in a Ustasha-Fascist background, equally backed
by old-fashioned Catholic royalists and by orthodox Stalinists, called
into political activity by the Soviet directors of propaganda, in order
either to overthrow Tito or to deter him from continuing to adhere to
(what Hungarian newsmen acting under Kremlin guidance termed)
the 'Tirana–Belgrade–Bucharest Axis'. Such manipulations may be

---

[1] Cf. Milovan Djilas, *Conversations with Stalin*, London, 1962, p. 157.
[2] George Kemény, 'Economic Integration in the Soviet Bloc', *Problems of Communism*, Washington, September–October 1964.
[3] Ferenc A. Váli, 'The Regime and the Nation', *Ten Years After* (an anthology of essays), London, 1966, p. 151.

successful; but would a chaos of internecine nationalisms be very reassuring to a Soviet Union intent on consolidating her power and improving the standard of living of her population? Fortunately, a prospect of unbridled chauvinist furies threatens the Soviet structure of domination as much as it does the vital interests of the client countries. The question, in the long run, is not whether the Russian monolith will rest unmoved on a fermenting and explosive multitude of nations, but in what way it will be removed. To allow the subject nations to emancipate themselves in an atmosphere of co-operation may still be the best bargain; and one which could reconcile Soviet interests with those of the Western Powers.

All legitimate interests, in fact, converge on establishing a Danubian Federation. Those legitimate interests have little to do with the intellectual, artistic, and moral aspirations of the scholars, poets, and (mostly frustrated) statesmen who discovered their existence and legitimacy. But if progress exists in history it consists in the identifying of ordinary needs by noble minds and in the advent of extraordinary moments when, under the pressure of such needs, received ideas give way to commonsense. If Hungary, international power conditions permitting, is today ready for that leap into sound commonsense, she owes it to visionaries such as the maverick of Hungarian national radicalism, László Teleki; after 1849 to the refugee Louis Kossuth and the Habsburg loyalist József Eötvös; after the 1867 Compromise, once again to a maverick of the National Independence movement, Lajos Mocsáry; in the last decades of the Habsburg monarchy to the sociologist Oscar Jászi and the poet Endre Ady; in the inter-war period to another inspired poet, Attila József; and ever since, to the best and bravest intellects of the country. Neither Hungarian history nor speculation on what road Hungary and her neighbours will take can make sense without keeping in mind the heritage and examples left by such 'doctrinaires', and their opposite numbers across the national frontiers, to our contemporaries and the generations to come.

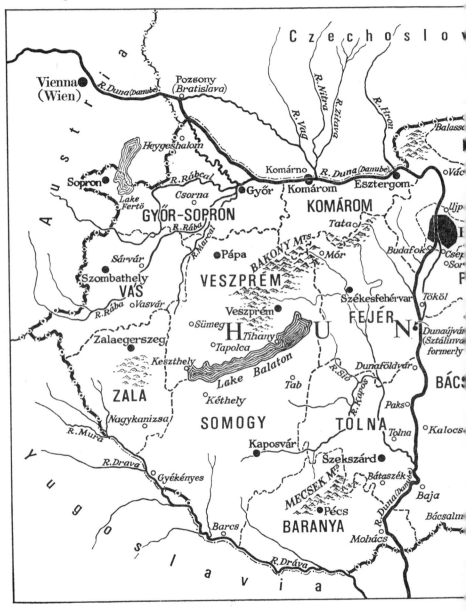

International boundaries

al map

On Hungarian Language and Poetry

IF HUNGARY HAD ANY SPECIAL part to play in European history, this was due to the peculiarities of the Hungarian language. How can one best give an idea of them to the non-Hungarian? The history of the language gives some clue, but a rather meagre one. Let us sum it up briefly. There had been an Ugrian language spoken by a tribe of fishermen and huntsmen, somewhere in or near the Urals, before the successive raids of Mongol and Turkish hordes into Europe began. At least twice, that Ugrian language came into close and lengthy contact with Turkish dialects. The first time was before the Hungarians conquered the mid-Danubian valley. According to one hypothesis, a Turkish warrior-group acquired leadership over the Ugrian masses while assimilating to them in language – rather as when, later, the Normans in the British Isles adopted the vernacular of the defeated Saxons. However it came about, an amalgam of these two branches of the Ural-Altaic family of languages resulted in which Ugrian (as in the case of Saxon) remained its basic element. The second long contact with the Turks came about a thousand years later, in the sixteenth century, when the Sultan's armies occupied most of historical Hungary. Uninspiring though this association was (there were Hungarians who relied on Turkish rather than Austrian power, but none who looked to Constantinople for cultural guidance), it naturally enhanced the Turkish characteristics of the language, especially in phonetics. The melody of Hungarian speech is more akin to Turkish than to anything Finno-Ugrian. (So, at any rate, it strikes my ear; an English friend, who knows both Turkish and Hungarian, thinks that 'Hungarian is a good deal harsher.')

Indo-European influences also began before the Hungarian onslaught on the Danubian peoples, with Persian and possibly Greek and Indian (or kindred) contacts. From the conquest of the Middle Danube (late ninth century A.D.) onward, the influx of words and speech habits from various European languages was incessant. There were practically all kinds of Slav. Serbo-Croat; Slovak, with a background of Czech and Moravian; Ukrainian, with a background of Russian proper; Slovene; Polish; etc. Many sorts of German, too:

besides the Austrian neighbours there were 'Swabian' (mainly Alsatian) and Saxon settlers, and also theologians and artisans coming from northern Germany, and the Yiddish spoken by Jews (which only made its mark later). Then there were the Romance languages, from the Italian and French imported by priests, knights, and traders down to their most plebeian offshoot (as the Hungarian gentlefolk saw it), the 'gypsy-like' Romanian. Above all there was Latin, even though a Latin that Cicero would hardly have recognized. All these contributed to making the Hungarian amalgam more and more complex; but the result was a true compound rather than just a mixture, for in the process each original element was entirely transformed.

In other words, Hungarian has absorbed, and reflects, a multitude of influences, but its own character transcends them all. Is this character, then, 'Ugrian'? I doubt it. Admittedly, even today an average Hungarian text contains some 90 per cent of words that are of Ugrian origin. This is due partly to the prevalence in most languages of auxiliary words: definite articles, for instance, are among the commonest words except in those languages which lack them altogether; Hungarian does have them, and they derive from the ancient Ugrian demonstrative pronoun. Another reason is the great variety of ways in which old words (particularly verbs) can be transformed in Hungarian by suffixes so as to create meanings quite different from those of their roots. Yet neither the rhythm of Hungarian nor its idiosyncracies are closely related to those of other Ugrian languages. The vagaries of this Asiatic language, Hungarian, really derive from European history. Some can be traced back to Slav, Romance, and Teutonic influences and some to, for instance, Slovak–though hardly any Hungarians have ever learned Slovak (at least between the foundation of the Hungarian Kingdom in 1000 and that of the Czechoslovak Republic in 1918) unless they happened to live in an overwhelmingly Slovak district.

Admittedly again, far more of the peculiarities of Hungarian can be classified as Ugrian, or generally Ural-Altaic, and even Turanian (though the latter is more of a mythological than a linguistic term) in so far as *analogies* with them can be found in those related languages. There are many such analogies with Vogul, less with Turkish and Mongolian, and a few with Japanese; but mostly, let me insist again on the word, they are *analogies* rather than likenesses. One may deduce from them certain tendencies that existed in their common ancestor language; but what each has evolved into since would seem as much a foreign language to their common ancestor as it does to the Englishman today. In other words, the character of Hungarian can no more be identified with its Asian ancestor than it can with modern European languages.

Just to illustrate what I mean by the distinction between 'like-nesses' and 'analogies' let me mention two examples. There was, apparently, a tendency among the ancestor tribes of the Finno-Ugrian nations to denote 'face' by a compound of its two conspicu-ous parts, such as 'nose-eye', or 'eye-mouth', or (as actually the Hungarian ancestor saw it) 'nose-mouth'. But the words standing for 'face' today show no likeness to one another; and hardly any with the compound in which they originated.

Another example is provided by that peculiarity of the Hungarian conjugation which may be called distinction between verb-endings according to the object. If, for instance, I want to say that 'I love' something, without pointing to one definite object, I say 'szeret*ek*'; when 'I love England', it should be 'szeret*em* Angliát'; and 'I love thee' is 'szeret*lek*', It is so very unlike anything in Indo-European grammar that one would suppose it had been in the language before the migration towards the Danube basin started. But this was not the case; the clear distinction between the meanings of such endings only developed when Hungarians had for centuries been settled on the banks of the Danube; yet, in other Finno-Ugrian languages, too, the tendency may be detectable to merge the object with the verb—which is at the bottom of the Hungarian peculiarity.

One way in which Hungarians and all their Ural-Altaic brethren from the Lapps and the Samoyeds to the Turks would seem to be more logical than the Indo-Europeans and Hamite-Semites is that they lack the very notion of a *gender*. The Indo-European universe, by the testimony of its nouns, pronouns, and adjectives, consists of beings that are masculine, feminine, and neuter, irrespective on the whole of their associations with either of the two sexes or with sexlessness. In German (more typical from this point of view than English or French, in which much of this pattern has been blurred or withered away) a table (*Tisch*) is masculine; a thing (*Sache*) is feminine; a house (*Haus*) is neuter—and so also is *Weib*, which means 'woman', to add to the piquancy of the system. There is nothing like this in Hungarian; not even a distinction between *he* and *she*: both are denoted by one and the same third person singular pronoun *ő*, pronounced like the French *eux*. It sounds a practical arrangement, but it is not always so. It is most inconvenient, for instance, for the translators of romantic fiction; there can be no 'he enfolded her hand between his', it must be something heavy like 'the man enfolded the woman's hand between the man's own', unless some ingenious way of getting round it can be devised. At the time of the Language Reform (turn of the eighteenth and nineteenth centuries) experi-ments were made to create a female pronoun but were killed by derision.

One could surmise on these grounds that Hungarians were humanitarians from the outset and therefore more concerned with someone's belonging to the human species, and less with his or her sex, than the Indo-Europeans; indeed there exists in Hungarian a noun, *ember* (pronounced a bit like 'amber'), standing for any human being, man and woman alike.

Yet the truth was far from this. A backward glance suffices to reveal that the ancient Hungarian was even less appreciative of his female partner's human qualities than the arch-Aryan. True enough, *ő* stood for woman as well as man, but it also stood for animals and soulless objects; 'he' and 'she' and 'it' were equally covered by that syllable. And on the other hand, *ember* used to stand only for 'man' – as it still does in country dialects. Gender-mindedness must not be equated with sex-mindedness. A language that outstrips even Hungarian in ignoring genders is the Japanese, in which 'Mr', 'Mrs', and 'Miss' are represented by one and the same syllable – the courtesy suffix *san*. Yet Japan is the classic country for inequality of the sexes and for feminine charm, as Britain is for inequality of accents and for parliamentarianism.

In Hungarian, as in Turkish or Finnish or Japanese, Mr John Smith would be 'Smith John mister'. Is this a meaningful difference? It is, perhaps, as it reveals a tendency to stress first things first. A *tendency*, I must underline, and not a hard and fast rule. The Hungarian sentence does often have its point at the end, but in general, the sentence starts with what is felt to be most important and then proceeds to its attributes. Correspondingly, the stress is on the first syllable in every word. A speaking style shared not only with kindred Finno-Ugrians but also with Czech and Slovak neighbours.

But here a word of warning about stress: in Hungarian it only means an emphasis on the syllable and not its domination over other syllables. To illustrate what I mean by this, let us take an English word: e.g. 'desert', as this happens to illustrate my point doubly. If used as a noun, its second *e* is practically swallowed and gets a colouring entirely different from the first one; if as a verb, it is for the first *e* to discolour itself. Such half-mute vowels (let alone near-mute ones such as the feminine *e* ending in French) do not exist in Hungarian; all syllables are supposed to be clearly and almost separately pronounced. This in itself produces vocal effects very different from those of English. A word associated in all languages with passionate rhetoric is, for example, 'intrepid'. In English, it is delivered like a single shot, banging down on the *e*. The Hungarian word for it is rettenthetetlen with five *e*'s given approximately equal strength and colouring: a volley rather than a shot.

Effects like this are mostly produced by suffixes. There are no

prepositions in Hungarian, and no case endings in the Latin or
Indo-European sense (although Hungarian grammarians, under
Latin influence, would refer to the 'Hungarian accusative', and
modern theoreticians of linguistics, disregarding etymology, would
argue that 'there are scores of Hungarian datives'); all this is
replaced by suffixes. It is a suffix-minded language, in the moulding
of its verbs as well as of its nouns and adjectives. Most of these suffixes, and presumably all, used to be separate words, post-positions,
or qualifying adverbs, before being, in the grammarians' term,
agglutinated.

Many a Hungarian word is a rattling conglomerate of such
suffixes or ex-words. Can this, the English or American reader may
ask, be pleasing to the ear? It can indeed. 'Use short Saxon words'
is the most common advice on good English style, and though
neither Shakespeare nor James Joyce seemed particularly mindful
of it, there is some sense in keeping it as a *desideratum*. But this does
not apply in the same way to other languages. Ancient mono-
syllables have a magic effect in all languages, I am sure, and
Hungarian is no exception; but the towering of suffixes, each adding
a new meaning to the one before, each making precision more complex and sensual, may be equally satisfying both to the ear and to the
intellect. Those Hungarian polysyllables have a strong beat and are—
or can be—more succinct than anything I have come across in other
languages. *Szerethettelek*—a word the very sight of which may appal
an English reader, but which is quite easily pronounceable to the
Hungarian—stands for 'I could have loved thee', a sentence that can
hardly be compressed into one word in other languages. One may
wonder whether it is worth doing so; but it is quite an achievement.

The two polysyllables I chose had only *e* vowels in them; and
indeed the frequency of the *e* is both a curse and a strength to the
Hungarian language. Allowing for differences between one *e* and the
other—differences more pronounced in one dialect than in another—
it may strike one's ears with such frequency like the rattling of the *a*
in 'rattling'. This is partly the result of the dominance over almost all
Ural-Altaic languages of the 'rule of vocal harmony'; all these
languages distinguish between 'high-pitched' and 'low-pitched'
vowels—although they pronounce and group them very differently—
and all tend to assimilate their suffixes to the vowels in the roots, so
that in one and the same word only high-pitched or only low-pitched
vowels will occur. In Hungarian, the *e* sound is (forgetting now about
exceptions) 'high-pitched'; the sound denoted by *a*, and pronounced
somewhat like the English *aw*, is 'low-pitched'. On the basis of such
harmonizing of suffixes, for instance, the verb *akarhattalak* means 'I
could have wanted thee'. *Akarhattalak, de nem szerethettelek*, pronounced

'awkawrrhawttawlawk, dae naem saerraett-haettaelaek'–'I could have wanted thee but could not have loved thee'–expresses not only a drama in four words but a contrast, high-and-low-pitched, in dazzling black-and-white flashes. This example may sound ludicrous; and so it is. I chose a contrived and extreme case to show the sort of effect made possible by the suffix-dominance and the phonetics of my language. To judge the potentialities of Hungarian poetry from such an example would be like guessing at English poetry through a clerihew. It would be absurd but not pointless; its very absurdity would demonstrate the rhythm which reflects the hidden shades of thoughts, feelings, landscapes, and social relations.

The music of Hungarian contrasts with that of European languages as percussion instruments do with strings. The drum-beat in particular is, I feel, very much akin to the throbbing of a Hungarian sentence. Its pounding, followed by a monotonous reverberation, evokes the mood of a man, musing over a vast plain. It is dryly articulated and its lyricism is muted–almost like a clearing of the throat when emotion threatens to overflow. The very dourness of the material makes its surrender to passion the more moving. Hungarians are not a particularly lyrically-minded people but the best thing they have ever created is their lyrical poetry.

In some respects, Hungarian is, as far as I can check, nearer to Latin than is any other living language. This may be partly due to social and political history; to the fact that Hungary, along with the equally squirearchic Poles, stuck to Latin as her official *lingua* longer than any other national community. There is a Hungarian Latinism clearly attributable to the centuries of dog-Latin class rule. There are, however, other affinities between Hungarian and Latin, particularly the classical Latin of Cicero and Tacitus, of Horace and Virgil, as distinct from that of the Hungarian Diets and court chambers. The syntax of classical Latin oratory can more faithfully be reflected in a Hungarian sentence, without violating its native characteristics, than in most living Indo-European languages; and the prosody of classical Latin poetry, when applied to Hungarian, can produce a rhythm more eloquent and natural than in any other living language I know of. This prosody, incidentally, has been taken over by the ancient Romans from the ancient Hellenes; but like the Japanese, whose fine art was sometimes more Chinese than the Chinese, it was the Latin poets of the Golden Age who produced, if not the most beautiful, yet in a way the most perfect, the most elaborate and dignified examples of classical versification. And the Hungarian language happened to be an admirable medium for reviving this craftsmanship many centuries later.

The reasons lie to a large extent in the Hungarian vocal system.

In Hungarian, as in Latin, there are clearly distinguishable long and short vowels, irrespective of whether they occur in a syllable stressed or unstressed in the sentence. Like in Latin (exceptions apart), every syllable becomes long 'by position' if its vowel is followed by more than one consonant; and when scanned, the duration of one long syllable may be equated with two short ones. As in antique Latin, the combination of this mathematical metric throb with emotional volleys enhances the meaning of a sentence with a kind of sonorous fireworks.

Since the end of the Middle Ages, experiments have been made in all European languages to adapt the classic Latin metres to living poetry; but they succeeded, at best, as nostalgic excursions into unearthly beauties, into the realm of gods, stars, and shepherds. They most signally failed in French, where not even a modernized version of Graeco-Latin metres could go down as more than a curiosity. In other languages, failure was less absolute; in Germany, Goethe and Schiller were among the champions of the hexameter applied to modern subjects; but fine though some of their pieces inspired by this venture were, their cadences fell far short of the Latin models. Graeco-Latin prosody entails the acceptance of a special music of the speech to which modern (post-medieval) European languages simply do not lend themselves. I, at any rate, was unable to find any exception to this rule other than the language classified, not without reason, as Asiatic: Hungarian.

By the beginning of the nineteenth century (peak moment of the struggle to polish and emancipate the national vernacular), Graeco-Latin verse forms had become the main vehicle for what the literate Hungarian audience felt was most important to be said.

Epics inspired by wishful thoughts of knightly Magyar ancestors flowed in smooth hexameters; epigrammatic wisdom clicked in distichons; even the most elaborate forms of Horatian poetry (Sapphic, Alcaic, Asclepiadic strophes) had their masters in Hungarian writers of odes and elegies. Of them all, the epic became to the highest degree dignified, artistic, and silly. The poet, playwright, critic, nobleman, and penniless tutor in stately homes, Mihály Vörösmarty (1800–55), himself a spokesman of Reform, was the undisputed master of this genre; the longest and most grandiose of his epics, *Zalán futása* (Zalán's Rout), published in 1825, visualized the tribes of demigods who had conquered the middle Danubian basin for the Hungarian nation, headed by Prince Árpád in his leopard-skin. An involved plot is, of course, developed round the historical event, one difficult to sum up without some yawns and titters, though generations of philologists have always produced scholars industrious and humourless enough to do so, even among

Oxford dons. Fortunately, however, the readability of a work does not entirely depend on its basic idea. Its details may be enthralling, whatever the concept they are supposed to illustrate. There is the young girl bathing at dusk while the wavelets of the brook curl round her hips in lulling hexameters; there are horses galloping in fierce hexameters; hills and valleys stretching in hexameters that sound like the breeze playing over them; even the hissing of arrows, however old-fashioned, makes one's heart beat faster with its hail of hexameters. Their vowel-contrasts of long and short, deep and high-pitched, with the interplay of metric and syntactic cadences, have not faded with the subject-matter.

Let me make clear that Graeco-Latin prosody is only one of the several systems to be met with in Hungarian verse, and by no means the most common or most typical one. The traditional Magyar verse, with its basic drum-beat, corresponds to quite a different auditive system; there are, besides, the modern neo-Western iambic lines (for instance in translations of Shakespeare) and the various stanzas modelled originally on German, Italian, and, less frequently, English and Russian examples (Byron, Pushkin); and experiments in free and near-free verse since the first decade of the twentieth century. Whichever may be the most 'modern', there is certainly an archaic flavour in the Graeco-Latin type of verse, and it has often been felt to be outdated, no longer good for anything but schoolroom send-ups. Yet it has been revitalized again and again, in slightly modified forms: young Babits, a most sophisticated virtuoso of poetry, displayed about 1910 a firework of 'New Leonines'; Attila József, the leading and symbolic poet of the inter-war period, wrote in hexameters his farewell letter before taking his own life; Miklós Radnóti, prisoner in a Nazi death camp, wrote in hexameters his last and perhaps most beautiful verses, hiding them in his overcoat, in the summer of 1944, shortly before his death; and even today, avant-garde poets will sometimes resort to Graeco-Latin metres, including Sándor Weöres, possibly the most important Hungarian poet of the last decades.

Hungarian poetry is essentially political. This is not to say that it concerns itself less than the poetry of other nations with 'love' and 'spring' and 'death'. But, ever since Zrínyi's appeals for national unity and European self-deliverance, the higher flights of Hungarian poetry have carried admonitions to the nation; and ever since the laments of fugitive Kuruc bards, if not before them, Magyar songs have expressed supremely a collective yearning that transcends the needs of the moment. A concrete, sensual imagery, inherited (one might imagine) from ancestral dwellers in the steppes and marshland, gave to our most fantastic epics and most lyrical effusions a sense, or illusion, of reality; while Latin influences in oratory, in the law, and, since the mid-eighteenth century, in prosody fostered abstract idealism, an enthusiasm for universal human values. It fell to the man of letters, and particularly to the poet, to say what the man of action was unable or reluctant to express. All that is articulate in Hungarian tends to be poetic.

Not that all is well with this intellectual climate. For one thing, it is steeped in national self-pity: the frustration and tragedy of being born Hungarian, which at the same time is prized as a glory and a privilege, have inspired innumerable poems in Hungary from the thirteenth century onwards, and especially in the dark years after the 1956 rising. In politics and philosophy self-pity, besides being repellent, may prove the worst possible counsellor; but can any poet be honest without giving expression to it? So far as I know, English – or at any rate the English of the British Isles – is the only language in which 'self-pity' rates as a vice. There is much to be said for this rating so far as behaviour is concerned; but anyone piercing the crust of behaviour will come upon deposits of self-pity among many other condemned emotions. Hungarians, making patriotic and social tragedy out of the story of their struggles, may be thought to have crassly deceived themselves – but their way of doing it enabled the best Hungarian thinkers to detect some aspects of truth ahead of even the Western world.

Bibliography

General reference books

Under the auspices of the Hungarian government, Pannonia Press, Budapest, publishes annually short handbooks in English entitled, in succession, *Hungary 69* and *Hungary 70* and so on; obviously serving propaganda purposes but factual, on the whole truthful, an neatly edited.

Information Hungary (Editor-in-Chief, Ferenc Erdei) was published by Pergamon Press, Oxford 1968, although it can to all intents and purposes be regarded as a Hungarian government publication. It is an imposing publication, 1,144 large pages lavishly illustrated and containing several valuable contributions, much interesting information on practically all subjects, and not a few outright lies, particularly concerning the communist takeover ('development of people's democracy') in the late 1940s and the 'counter-revolution' of 1956.

Facts about Hungary (edited by Imre Kovács) published by the *émigré* Hungarian Committee (and promoted by Free Europe) in New York, 1959, is a useful booklet but no less biassed than the Hungarian government publications in its conspicuous omissions.

In German, *Ungarn*, by D. Silagi (Verlag für Literatur und Zeitgeschehen, Hanover, 1964, 2nd ed. 1971) is a skilfully compiled handbook which I could recommend almost without reservations.

On the history and character of the Magyar language

In English: introductory essay 'On the Magyar Language' to *Poetry of the Magyars*, an anthology of Hungarian poems selected, translated, and edited by John Bowring, London, 1830.

In German: *Die ungarische Sprache*, by Sigismund Simonyi, Trübner Verlag, Strasbourg (then Germany), 1907.

In Magyar: *A magyar nyelv életrajza* ('Biography of the Hungarian Language'), by Géza Bárczi, Gondolat, Budapest, 1963.

History—general

History of Hungary by Denis Sinor, George Allen & Unwin, London, 1959. In Hungary, the two representative works of the last fifty years are:

Magyar Történet ('Hungarian History'), by Bálint Hóman and Gyula Szekfü, Magyar Szemle Társaság, Budapest (last volume published 1935).

Magyarország Története ('History of Hungary'), by a team of selected historians, ed. Erik Molnár, Gondolat, Budapest, 1964.

Pre-historical Hungarians and pre-Christian Hungary

A magyar nép őstörténete ('Ancestral History of the Hungarian People'), by Erik Molnár, Szikra, Budapest, 1954.

A IX.–X. századi magyar társadalom ('Hungarian Society of the ninth and tenth Centuries'), by Antal Bartha, Akadémiai kiadó, Budapest, 1968.

Preliminaries and protagonists of Liberal Hungary

Ez történt Mohács után (What Really Happened After Mohács), by István Nemeskürty, Budapest, 1968.

A magyar jobbágyság története (History of Serfdom in Hungary), by Ignác Acsády, Grill, Budapest, 1908.

A magyar világi nagybirtok története (History of Secular Latifundia in Hungary), by Péter Ágoston, Grill, Budapest, 1913.

A régi Magyarország (Old Hungary), *1711–1825*, by Béla Grünwald, Budapest, first ed. 1888–89.

Joseph II, by François Fejtő, Plon, Paris, 1953; F. K. Koehler, Stuttgart, 1956.

Ungarn und der geheime Mitarbeiterkreis Kaiser Leopolds II., by Denis Silagi, Südost-Institut, Munich, 1960.

Jakobiner in der Habsburger-Monarchie, by Denis Silagi, Verlag Herold, Vienna-Munich, 1962.

'Egy nagy magyar a XVIII. században' ('A great Hungarian in the eighteenth century'); essay on the liberal reformer Count Alajos Batthyány, by Géza K. Havas, *Szép Szó*, Budapest, March 1938.

Essay on the poet-botanist of the early nineteenth century Mihály Fazekas in *Magyarok*, by Gyula Illyés, Nyugat, Budapest, 1938.

Hungary in the Eighteenth Century, by Henri Marczali, Cambridge, 1910.

Csokonai (Vitéz Mihály) (outstanding poet of the late eighteenth century), by Ervin Sinkó, Novi Sad (Yugoslavia), 1965.

Berzeviczy Gergely (works and biography of G. Berzeviczy, economist, liberal reformer of the early nineteenth century), by Jenő Gaal, Budapest, 1902.

Stephen Széchenyi and the Awakening of Hungarian Nationalism, *1791–1841*, by George Barany, Princeton, 1968.

'From Feudalism to Capitalism: the Economic Background of [Count István] Széchenyi's Reform in Hungary', by B. G. Ivanyi, *Journal of Central European Affairs*, U.S.A., October 1960.

The British Travel-Diary of Sándor Bölöni Farkas, by István Gál, Hungarian Studies in English III, Debrecen, 1967.

Essay on the poet-scholar János Batsányi in *Örökség* ('Heritage'), by Dezső Keresztury, Magvető, Budapest, 1970.

'The Working Classes of Britain and the Eastern European Revolutions of 1848, with special reference to the Hungarian War for Independence', by B. G. Ivanyi, *Slavonic and East European Review*, London, 1947.

Memoirs in my Exile, by Louis Kossuth, Cassell & Co., London, 1880.

Kossuth, America and the Danubian Confederation, by István Gál, reprinted from the *Hungarian Quarterly*, Budapest, 1940.

Görgey, by Domokos Kosáry, Budapest, 1934.

Életem és Korom ('My Life and my Time'), memoirs by Ferenc Pulszky, published by Szépirodalmi, Budapest, 1958.

Petőfi, by Gyula Illyés, Gallimard, Paris, 1947.

Hallja kend, Táncsics (a biography of Mihály Táncsics), by György Bölöni, Budapest, 1946.

Teleki László, 1810–1861, by Zoltán Horváth, Akadémiai kiadó, Budapest, 1964.

Társadalmi és pártharcok a 48–49-es magyar forradalomban ('Social and Party Struggles in the Hungarian Revolution of 1848–49'), by Ervin Szabó, preface by Oscar Jászi, Bécsi Magyar Kiadó, Vienna, 1921.

A magyar forradalom 1848–49-ben (The Hungarian Revolution of 1848–49), by György Spira, Budapest, 1959.

S mi vagyok én . . . (on János Arany, I: 1817–1856), by Dezső Keresztury, Szépirodalmi, Budapest, 1967.

Forradalom és kiegyezés válaszutjám (At the Crossroads of Revolution and Compromise), 1860–61, by György Szabad, Budapest, 1967.

Under the Dual Monarchy and its dissolution

A dualizmus kora ('The Age of Dualism)', by Gustav Gratz, Magyar Szemle, Budapest, 1934.

Egy letünt nemzedék ('A Vanished Generation'), by Imre Halász, Budapest, 1911.

Bismarck és Andrássy ('B. and A.'), by Imre Halász, Budapest, 1913.

Két Andrássy és két Tisza ('Two Andrássys and Two Tiszas'), by Loránt Hegedüs, Athenaeum, Budapest, 1917.

Irodalmi ellenzéki mozgalmak a XIX. század második felében ('The literature of opposition in the second half of the nineteenth century'), by Aladár Komlós, Akadémiai kiadó, Budapest, 1956.

A magyar irodalom története a XX. században ('The History of Hungarian Literature in the twentieth century'), by Aladár Schöpflin, Nyugat, Budapest, 1937.

Ady, by Aladár Schöpflin, Budapest, 1934.

Az igazi Ady ('The Real Ady'), by György Bölöni, Paris, 1934.
Ady Endre, by Erzsébet Vezér, Gondolat, Budapest, 1969.

Gyulatól a marxista kritikáig ('From Pál Gyulai to Marxist Aesthetics —Seven Decades of Hungarian literary Criticism'), by Aladár Komlós, Akadémiai kiadó, Budapest, 1966.

Racial Problems in Hungary, by R. W. Seton-Watson (Scotus Viator), Constable, London, 1909.

Eötvös und die ungarische Nationalitätenfrage, by Johann Weber, R. Oldenburg, Munich, n.d.

A magyar nemzetiségi kérdés története, I: 1790–1918 ('History of the Hungarian Nationalities Question, I: 1790–1918'), by G. Gábor Kemény, Gergely, R., Budapest, 1947.

The Development of the Manufacturing Industry in Hungary (1900–1944), by I. T. Berend and György Ránki, Studia Historica, Academia Scientiarum Hungariae, Budapest, 1960.

The Rise of Nationalism and of the Nationality Problem in Hungary in the Last Decades of Dualism, by Zoltán Horváth, Acta Historica, Hungarian Academy of Sciences, Budapest, 1963.

The Habsburg Empire, 1790–1918, by C. A. Macartney, Weidenfeld and Nicolson, London, 1968.

Föderációs tervek Délkelet-Európában és a Habsburg monarchia (Federation Plans in South-East Europe, and the Habsburg Monarchy), *1840–1918*, by Gyula Mérei, Budapest, 1965.

Erzherzog Franz Ferdinand von Österreich-Este, by Rudolf Kiszling, Köln-Graz, 1953.

Kor-és jellemrajzok (Recollections), by Miksa (Max) Falk, Budapest, 1902–03.

Emlékezések (Recollections), by Dávid Angyal, Szepsi Csombor, London, 1971. (Memoirs of the outstanding conservative Liberal historian of the Hungary of the Dual Monarchy, posthumously published; ed. Lóránt Czigány; foreworded by László Péter.)

Die Jahrhundertwende in Ungarn Geschichte der zweiten Reformgeneration (*1896–1914*), by Zoltán Horváth, Corvin Verlag, Budapest, 1966.

'The Hungary of Michael Polanyi', essay by Paul Ignotus in *The Logic of Personal Knowledge*, Routledge and Kegan Paul, London, 1961.

La révolution littéraire en Hongrie au début du siècle, by Péter Nagy, Akadémiai kiadó, Budapest, 1970.

Ausztria és Magyarország nemzeti jövedelme (National Income of Austria and Hungary), by Frigyes V. Fellner, Budapest, 1916.

Magyarország Kálváriája (The Calvary of Hungary), by József Kristóffy, Budapest, 1927.

'A nemzetiségi kérdés a társadalmi és egyéni fejlődés szempontjából' (The Nationalities Question from the point of view of Social and Individual Progress), by Oscar Jászi, *Huszadik Század*, Budapest, 1918.

The Memoirs of Michael Károlyi, Jonathan Cape, London, 1956.

The Dissolution of the Habsburg Monarchy, by Oscar Jászi, University Press, Chicago, 1929.

Revolution and Counter-Revolution in Hungary, by Oscar Jászi, P. S. King, London, 1921.

White Hungary and her neighbours

Regent of Hungary, memoirs of Miklós Horthy, Hutchinson, London, 1956.

The White Terror in Hungary, report by the British Joint Labour Delegation (headed by J. C. Wedgwood, M.P.) in Hungary. London, May 1920.

The Murder of Somogyi and Bacsó on February 17th 1920, by Béla Menczer, reproduced from *Typography* (British Museum Reading Room), London, 1946.

The Confidential Papers of Admiral Horthy, Corvina Press, Budapest, 1965.

Csonka-Magyarország nemzeti jövedelme ('The National Income of Rump-Hungary'), by Frigyes V. Fellner, Hungarian Academy of Sciences, Budapest, 1930.

Hungary and Her Successors. The Treaty of Trianon and its Consequences, by C. A. Macartney, Royal Institute of International Affairs, London, 1937.

Czechs and Germans, by Elizabeth Wiskemann, Oxford, 1938.

Szabó Dezső, by Péter Nagy, Akadémiai kiadó, Budapest, 1967.

'Die intellektuelle Linke im Ungarn der "Horthy-Zeit",' by Paul Ignotus, offprint from *Südost-Forschungen*, Munich, 1968.

'Hungary', essay by J. Erős, in *European Fascism*, Weidenfeld and Nicolson, London, 1968.

'Storia dell' opposizione democratica' by János Eros, *Il Ponte*, 'Ungheria', Florence, April–May 1960.

Hungary, by C. A. Macartney, Ernest Benn, London, 1934.

October Fifteenth, A History of Modern Hungary 1929–1945, by C. A. Macartney, Edinburgh University Press, 1st ed. 1957, 2nd ed. 1961.

Emlékiratok és valóság—Magyarország második világháborus szerepéről ('Memoranda and Reality: about Hungary's Role in World War II'), by György Ránki, Kossuth könyvkiadó, Budapest, 1964.

Diplomacy in a Whirlpool, by Stephen (István) Kertész, U.S.A., 1953.

Hungarian Premier, Memoirs by Miklós Kállay, Cambridge University Press, New York, 1954.

Endkampf an der Donaum, 1944–45, by Peter Gosztony, Verlag Fritz Molden, Vienna-Munich-Zurich, 1969.

Der Kampf um Budapest 1944–45, by Peter Gosztony, Schnell und Steiner, Munich, 1964.

'Pages from a Diplomatic Diary, 1939–1946', by Borisz de Balla, *Studies in Modern History*, St John's University Press, New York, 1968.

Kilenc koffer ('Nine Suitcases'), recollections of Nazi deportation camps, etc., in Hungary, by Béla Zsolt, published in series in the weekly edited by Béla Zsolt, *Haladás* ('Progress'), Budapest, in 1945–47, but never published in a volume.

'Popular Front in the Balkans: Failure in Hungary and Rumania', by Béla Vágó, *Journal of Contemporary History*, London, 1970.

The People of the Puszta, by Gyula Illyés, Corvina, Budapest, 1969.

Irástudók felelőssége ('The Responsibility of Literati'), by György Lukács, Moscow, 1944; rearranged and reissued in the collection of essays *Magyar irodalom, magyar kultura* ('Hungarian Literature, Hungarian Culture'), Gondolat, Budapest, 1970.

Attila József, by Jean Rousselot, 'Les Nouveaux Cahiers de Jeunesse', Médianes, 1958.

József Attila és kora ('Attila József and his Time'), by Andor Németh, published in series in the periodical edited by Andor Németh, *Csillag* ('Star'), Budapest, in 1946–48, but never published in a volume.

History of the Czechs and Slovaks, by R. W. Seton-Watson, Hutchinson, London-New York-Melbourne, 1942.

'Czechs, Magyars, Slovaks', by Paul Ignotus, *The Political Quarterly*, London, April–June, 1969.

Hungary after the Second World War

i. *Documents and anthologies*

United Nations Report of the Special Committee on the Problem of Hungary, General Assembly Official Records, New York, 1957.

The Hungarian Revolution 'A White Book', ed. Melvin J. Lasky, Introduction by Hugh Seton-Watson, Epilogue by François Bondy, Secker and Warburg, London, 1957; 2nd ed. 1971.

On Communism, by Imre Nagy, Thames and Hudson, London, 1957. (*Un communisme qui n'oublie pas l'homme*, with a profile of 'Imre Nagy, the Communist who chose the People', by François Fejtő, Plon, Paris, 1957.)

A harmadik út ('The Third Road'), by István Bibó, *Magyar Könyves Céh*, ed. Zoltán Szabó, Hungarian Writers' Association Abroad, London, 1960.

Jeunesse d'Octobre, Témoins et combattants de la Révolution hongroise, ed. Nicolas Baudy, La Table Ronde, Paris, 1957.

The Truth about the Nagy Affair, Preface by Albert Camus, Secker and Warburg, London, 1959.

Hungary and the World, Meeting in commemoration of the Hungarian Revolution on its third anniversary, speeches by Christopher Chataway, Denis Healey, Hugh Seton-Watson, and P. M. T. Sheldon-Williams, published jointly by the Hungarian Writers' Association Abroad and the Hungarian Freedom Fighters' Federation, Central Executive Committee; London, 1969.

For Tibor Déry and the other 24 Hungarian intellectuals in prison, The Tibor Déry Committee, Paris and London, 1959.

Ten Years After, ed. Tamás Aczél, MacGibbon and Kee, London, 1966.

Ellenforradalom Magyarországon 1956 ('Counter-Revolution in Hungary, 1956'), Kossuth kiadó, Budapest, 1958.

. . . *The world's most orphaned nation*, Excerpts from Cardinal Joseph Mindszenty's speeches, letters, and private writings. The Book Mailer Inc., New York, 1962.

ii. Books, essays, articles by individual authors

The Revolt of the Mind, by Tamás Aczél and Tibor Méray, Thames and Hudson, London; Frederick A. Praeger, New York, 1959.

Októberi vihar ('October Storm'), novel by András Békesi, Zrínyi, Budapest, 1958.

What Really Happened in Hungary, by Basil Davidson, U.D.C. Publications, 1957.

Niki, the Story of a Dog, by Tibor Déry, Penguin, London, 1961.

La Tragédie Hongroise, ou une Révolution socialiste anti-sovietique (translated into English under the far less fitting title, *Behind the Rape of Hungary*), by François Fejtő, Preface by Jean-Paul Sartre, Pierre Horay, Paris, 1956; David McKay, New York, 1957.

The History of the People's Democracies, by François Fejtő, Pall Mall, London, and Praeger Publishers, New York, 1971.

The Hungarian Tragedy, by Peter Fryer, Dennis Dobson, London, 1956.

Essays and articles by Paul Ignotus: 'The Revolution of the Word', *Encounter*, London, April 1957; 'Hungary: Tanks *v.* Workers', *The Twentieth Century*, London, August 1957; 'Fading Fashions', *ibid.*, October 1960; 'Eastern Europe Today—The Hungarian Meritocracy', *The Guardian*, Manchester, 1 July 1965; 'Ruszkik, haza!', *ibid.*, 24 October 1966; 'L'unité nationale hongroise', *Preuves*, Paris, February 1957: 'La révolution hongroise', *Esprit*, Paris, March 1957; 'Ritorno a Budapest', *Tempo Presente*, Rome, November 1966.

Church and State in Eastern Europe, by B. G. Ivanyi, The London Institute of World Affairs, Stevens and Sons Ltd., 1952.

Uj történet kezdődött (A New Chapter Started), by Sándor Nógrádi, Kossuth, Budapest, 1966.

The Hungarian Revolution: The People's Demands, by William Juhasz, Free Europe Press, New York, 1957.

A magyarországi ellenforradalom a marxizmus-leninizmus fényében ('The Hungarian counter-revolution in the light of Marxism-Leninism'), by Gyula Kállai, Kossuth, Budapest, 1957.

The Unexpected Revolution, by Paul Kecskemeti, Stanford University Press, Stanford, California, 1961.

The Hungarian Revolution of 1956, by Béla Kiraly and A. F. Kovacs, Hungarian Freedom Fighters' Federation, Inc., New York, 1960.

'The Hungarian Novel in the Last Fifty Years', by Valérie Korek, *Fiction in Several Languages*, American Academy of Arts and Sciences, Boston, 1968.

Thirteen Days that Shook the Kremlin, by Tibor Meray, Thames and Hudson, London, 1959.

La rivolta degli intellettuali in Ungheria, by István Meszaros, Einaudi, Torino, 1958.

The Hungarian Revolution, by George Mikes, A. Deutsch, London, 1957.

Imre Nagy, Reformateur ou Révolutionnaire? by Miklós Molnar and László Nagy, Publications de Hautes Etudes Internationales, Geneva, 1959.

The Revolt that Rocked the Kremlin, by P. Nadanyi, Hungarian Reformed Federation of America, 1963.

The Struggle Behind the Iron Curtain, by Ferenc Nagy, Macmillan, New York, 1948.

The Hungarian Revolution, by David Pryce-Jones, Ernest Benn, London, 1969.

The East European Revolution, by Hugh Seton-Watson, Methuen, London, 1956.

Nationalism and Communism, by Hugh Seton-Watson, Methuen, London, 1964.

The Nineteen Days, by George Urban, Heinemann, London, 1957.

Rift and Revolt in Hungary, by Ferenc Vali, Harvard University Press, Cambridge, Mass., 1961.

Revolution in Hungary, by Paul E. Zinner, Columbia University Press, New York, 1962.

iii. Periodical publications in English

The New Hungarian Quarterly, ed. Iván Boldizsár, Corvina, Budapest, since September 1960.

The Hungarian Quarterly, ed. Imre Kovács, promoted by Free Europe, New York, 1962–65.

Index

Printed in Great Britain
by W & J Mackay Limited, Chatham

$12.50